Property and Equality

Property and Equality
Volume 1

Ritualisation, Sharing, Egalitarianism

Edited by
Thomas Widlok
and
Wolde Gossa Tadesse

Berghahn Books
New York • Oxford

First published in 2005 by
Berghahn Books
www.berghahnbooks.com

© 2005 Thomas Widlok and Wolde Gossa Tadesse
Reprinted in 2006
First paperback edition published in 2007

All rights reserved. Except for the quotation of short passages for the purposes of criticism and review, no part of this book may be reproduced in any form or by any means, electronic or mechanical, including photocopying, recording, or any information storage and retrieval system now known or to be invented, without written permission of Berghahn Books

Library of Congress Cataloging-in-Publication Data

Property and equality: ritualisation, sharing, egalitarianism / edited by Thomas Widlok and Wolde Gossa Tadesse.
    p. cm.
    Includes index.
    ISBN 1-57181-616-X (v. 1 : hbk.) -- ISBN 1-57181-617-8 (v. 2 : hbk.)
    ISBN 1-84545-213-5 (v. 1 : pbk.) -- ISBN 1-84545-214-3 (v. 2 : pbk.)
    1. Equality--Cross-cultural studies. 2. Property--Cross-cultural studies.
  I. Title: Ritualisation, sharing, egalitarianism. II. Widlok, Thomas. III. Tadesse, Wolde Gossa.

HM821.P67 2004
306.3'2--dc22
                                                       2004049096

British Library Cataloguing in Publication Data
A catalogue record for this book is available from the British Library.
Printed in the United States on acid-free paper

ISBN 1-57181-616-X (hardback)
ISBN 1-84545-213-5 (paperback)

Contents

List of Figures and Tables

Preface

Introduction   1
Thomas Widlok
Max Planck Institute for Psycholinguistics, Nijmegen,
and Institut für Ethnologie, Universität Heidelberg

1 **Egalitarian Societies Revisited**   18
   James Woodburn
   Department of Anthropology, London School of Economics and
   Political Science

2 **Individual Creativity and Property–Power Disjunction
   in an Australian Desert Society**   32
   Robert Tonkinson
   Department of Anthropology, University of Western Australia

3 **Knowledge about Plant Medicine and Practice
   among the Ituri Forest Foragers**   47
   Hideaki Terashima
   Kobe Gakuin University, Kyoto

4 **Space-Time, Ethnicity, and the Limits of Inuit
   and New Age Egalitarianism**   62
   David Riches
   Department of Anthropology, University of St. Andrews

5 **Sharing Costs: an Exploration of Personal and
   Individual Property, Equalities and Differentiation**   77
   Barbara Bodenhorn
   Pembroke College, University of Cambridge

6 **Possession, Equality and Gender Relations in |Gui Discourse**   105
   Kazuyoshi Sugawara
   Faculty of Integrated Human Studies, Kyoto University

7 Are Immediate-Return Strategies Adaptive? 130
  Robert Layton
  Department of Anthropology, University of Durham

8 **Food Sharing and Ownership among Central African Hunter-Gatherers: an Evolutionary Perspective** 151
  Mitsuo Ichikawa
  Graduate School of Asian and African Area Studies, Kyoto University

9 **Time, Memory and Property** 165
  Tim Ingold
  Department of Anthropology, University of Aberdeen

10 **To Share or not to Share: Notes about Authority and Anarchy among the Hamar of Southern Ethiopia** 175
  Ivo Strecker
  Institut für Ethnologie und Afrika-Studien, Universität Mainz

11 **'Their own oral histories': Items of Ju/'hoan Belief and Items of Ju/'hoan Property** 190
  Megan Biesele
  Kalahari Peoples Fund, Austin

12 **The Property of Sharing: Western Analytical Notions, Nayaka Contexts** 201
  Nurit Bird-David
  Department of Sociology and Anthropology, University of Haifa

Notes on Contributors 217

Index 221

List of Figures and Tables

Figures

7.1	Resource buffering	133
7.2	Marginal value	135
7.3	Delayed return as a composite category	140
9.1	(A) The descent-line, life-line and generation, according to the genealogical model of classical social anthropology; B) the mutually entangled life-lines of coeval person, according to the relational model.	168
9.2	(A) 'Getting water' versus (B) 'meeting the lake'	170

Tables

3.1	Similarity index of medicinal plants	57
7.1	Rainfall recorded at Curtin Springs homestead, 1960–77 (in millimetres)	132

Preface

Property relations have long been considered the key to our understanding of equality and inequality, not only through the work of thinkers such as Rousseau, Marx, Engels and others, but also through common everyday experience. Social anthropologists continue to collect data that are relevant to the fundamental issue of property and equality, but so far this work has rarely been a concerted effort. For this two-volume book we have brought together a wide range of well-known international specialists who have worked on issues of property and equality. They are the core group of more than fifty participants who came together at a conference held at Halle/Saale in June 2001. The conference, entitled 'Property and Equality', was the basis on which the present volumes have been compiled. Despite their different backgrounds the contributors share considerable common ground: all are anthropologists, all had read James Woodburn's seminal article on 'Egalitarian Societies' and have been inspired or challenged by his thoughts on the matter. Many of the participants had done field research with hunter-gatherers in the Arctic, in Africa, Australia or Asia. However, the present volumes do not deal exclusively with these groups. Some contributors have worked with pastoralists, with horticulturalists, agriculturalists, in industrial societies, and with nonhuman primates, comparing their results with the theoretical ideas that have been developed in hunter-gatherer studies.

The ethnography on egalitarian hunter-gatherer societies sent shock waves through anthropology in the 1960s' when ethnographers came forward and suggested that forager societies worked well without structures of dominance, without rigid hierarchies, without binding property relations, and without inherent inequality with regard to gender, age and status. This book brings together the current work of prominent members of this original group of researchers and the very recent ethnography of a new generation of researchers who are dealing with problems of property and equality. In preparing their contributions to the book the authors have revisited key debates of the field; they have taken stock, and have tackled issues that remained unresolved. They have reassessed how the existence of egalitarian societies still challenges established assumptions about the conditions of human political and economic life, how it continues to stand much of anthropological theory on its head and how it relates to research done in other fields. In the past the ethnography of egalitarian social systems was first met with sheer disbelief. Today it is still hotly debated in a number of ways but has gained sophistication as well as momentum. As the editors of this book, we have tried to account for this diversification by presenting two complementary volumes. Volume 1 focuses on the embeddedness of egalitarian property relations in dynamic processes of human sociality over time. Contributions highlight the role of ritual, of sharing in its various articulations, and of discourses of egalitarianism. Volume 2 focuses on the embeddedness of egalitarian property relations in the dynamics of larger social systems. It highlights the issues of encapsulation, commercialisation and discrimination. Despite their distinct foci there are many connecting lines between the two volumes, both in terms of the groups and regions that are being discussed and also with regard to systematic links that exist between the terms of the debates and the questions under consideration. Several contributions explicitly underline that 'internal' institutional dynamics and 'external' historical developments are really two sides of the same coin.

The Halle conference was fully funded by the then newly founded Max Planck Institute for Social Anthropology and, as conveners, we are indebted to the staff of the Institute who helped in organising the conference and who also assisted in preparing these two volumes. We are thankful to the Department of Anthropology at the University of Heidelberg for its institutional support in preparing the manuscript. We also gratefully acknowledge the intellectual input that we have received from Olga Artemova, the late Susan Kent, Nicolas Peterson, and Aiden Southall who do not appear in these volumes as authors but who have actively participated in our discussions at Halle and therefore shaped the course of the conversations. Thanks also go to Berghahn Books, who shared our conviction that, despite the size of the project, it was important not to let the contributions diffuse into isolated voices but to keep them together in these two volumes, reflecting the current state of anthropological research concerning the relation between 'property' and 'equality'.

Thomas Widlok	Wolde Gossa Tadesse
Heidelberg and Nijmegen	Palo Alto and Halle/Saale

Introduction

Thomas Widlok

Conversations about Social Inequality

Anthropological thought, like all social theory, progresses through debates and through conversations. Both forms have their rightful place in the scientific enterprise. Occasionally, however, it seems that debates are outweighing and silencing conversations, following a general tendency to make 'an easy living through setting up negativities, showing that this or that set of concepts does not apply to the ethnographic material' (Strathern 1988: 11). As a consequence, conversations are terminated rather than continued, often literally in the sense that the main proponents no longer speak to one another. This two-volume book on 'Property and Equality' tries to counter such silences and negativities by critically continuing a conversation that has a long history in the discipline and in the social sciences more generally. As events, debates usually involve more participants and views than conversations do (see Ingold 1996) but this is not necessarily so once we realise that conversations may continue productively across several generations (see Bird-David 1994). The conversation about property and equality is a case in point. As Dahrendorf reminds us, questions concerning the 'inequality among men' were historically 'the first questions asked by sociology' (1969: 17). And the first answers given historically by social theory referred to property as a key factor in the emergence of inequalities. When Jean-Jacques Rousseau sought to solve the question of the origins of inequality he found that property, especially private property, had to be the answer. He concluded that inequality was near to zero in the state of nature but had become legitimated through the establishment of property and the laws after 'the first man who, having enclosed a piece of land, thought of saying, 'This is mine', ... came across people simple enough to believe him' (Rousseau 1994: 54). Although Rousseau concedes that the idea of property is based on many other ideas and did not arise all at once, he maintains that competition, rivalry, opposition of interests and the hidden desire to make a profit on the cost of others are the first of a long list of ills brought about by property and inseparably linked to nascent inequality (see Rousseau 1994: 66). Inequality of wealth may have been the last kind of inequality to emerge but all others can be reduced to wealth in the end, he argued, because it can 'readily be used to buy all the rest' (Rousseau 1994: 80).

Rousseau was only one – if prominent – voice that connected conversations of property with conversations of (in-)equality and vice versa. This connection then became firmly entrenched, but the evolving strand in social thought has been conducted in various formats and with the help of various approaches and terminologies, covering a wide spectrum between Rousseauesque essays and computer simulations (see the 'Sugarscape' database at www.brook.edu/dybdocroot/sugarscape and Epstein and Axtell 1996). However, it is not only the format of the conversation that has changed over time. Considerable progress has been made in our understanding of the relation between property and equality. Rousseau took a presocial original state of complete equality for granted and he did not explain how property itself came into being. Since subsequent political movements succeeded to reduce private property considerably but could not abolish social stratification it is no longer convincing to present property as the sole cause for inequality. At the close of the nineteenth century further causes of inequality were identified, in particular the division of labour. This is true for the work of Marx, who – however – also continued to point at property, in particular at the ownership of the means of production (Marx 1962). It is also true for Durkheim and his theory of the division of labour (1960) who, at the same time, considered property – in the form of inheritance – as the main cause for morally objectionable inequalities (Durkheim 1979: 213). In the course of further research it became clear that the division of labour was equally unsatisfactory as a sole cause for inequality because for professional differentiation to turn into social distinction an element of evaluation has to come in that cannot be derived from the division of labour itself. The same holds for other single-cause theories. Parsons and other American sociologists in the mid-twentieth century provided new theoretical input by no longer considering inequality to be part of a transient phase in human history but a functional necessity of society that was to stay (see Parsons 1954). However, subsequent empirical work disproved their assumption that differentiated positions in a society can only be adequately filled through an unequal distribution of rewards (see Dahrendorf 1969: 29). From an anthropological perspective it is important to note that in the course of scholarly conversations the above-mentioned factors in the emergence of inequality did not disappear but were only reduced to a matter of probability instead of universal applicability. In other words, institutionalised property and the division of labour raise the likelihood that inequalities emerge; they seem to be sufficient but not necessary as factors in the emergence of inequality. Given that there seem to be a number of factors that can lead to inequality, it has been of prime anthropological concern to investigate under which conditions there *can* be equality, instead of reconfirming that there is a tendency or probability towards inequality in many cases. In this anthropological endeavour the study of hunter-gatherers and other nomadic peoples has taken centre stage, complemented by studies on subcultures in the West (see Prince and Riches 1999) and on other 'marginal people' (see Day et al. 1999). Anthropological studies of this kind therefore do not challenge the fact that there are hierarchical and nonegalitarian societies – nor are they challenged by these cases. Rather, they challenge political theories that claim to identify universal conditions that are sufficient as well as necessary for the emergence of inequality. Dahrendorf for one has claimed that 'the origin of inequality is … to be found in the existence in all human societies of norms of behavior to which sanctions are attached' (1969: 34) and that the anthropological insistence that there are tribes without rulers, self-regulating without positions of authority, are 'fantasies' (1969: 38). It would be facile to reduce this argument to a disagreement between neighbouring disciplines. Dahrendorf's argument that society by definition consists of norms that regulate conduct, which need authority positions to exert the threat of sanctions, is repeated within anthropology in particular with regard to hunter-gatherer studies. Brunton, in an exchange with Woodburn on the notion of immediate-return hunter-gatherers, argued that an inherent instability of these egalitarian societies is to be expected precisely because preventing mutual dependency and inequality is difficult – Dahrendorf would say 'impossible' – without the backup of institutionalised political power positions that affirm and transmit equality across generations (Brunton 1989: 674). As soon as these necessary institutions emerge, dependencies and inequalities are created. A number of responses have been put forward by anthropologists who have worked in immediate-return societies, that is, societies where there is little or no economic (or social) investment that has to be protected before a return is achieved after some delay. We may distinguish logical, conceptual and empirical solutions to the problem. It has been pointed out that it is possible to distinguish logically meta rules (shared by all) from object rules (on which people diverge) so that the obligation not to create any obligations or dependencies is conceived of on a higher logical level than, for instance, rules concerning the distribution of property (see Vogt 1992: 140). Alternatively, it has been argued that if society is defined as bundles of social relations organised on the premise that there are offices of power and authority, then it may be fair to say that many hunter-gatherers, according to this conceptual definition, do not live in societies (Ingold 1999). It has also been argued that there is indeed a tension in these societies between autonomy and equality which is, however, empirically resolved through a specific ideology, namely that of the holistic person as it is found in a diversity of cases (Riches 2000). In my own work I have tried to show that empirically the tension is not only resolved through ideological means but also through specific social practices, that is, by forms of social relations and cultural activities that do not rely on formal hierarchies or structures of authority. In a monograph concerned primarily with ≠Akhoe Hai//om in Namibia (who identify themselves as San hunter-gatherers and who are considered to be an immediate-return society) I have shown how cultural forms and patterns of social relatedness do emerge through a number of related practices rather than through a fixed set of sanctioned norms. These practices include participation in ritual events, constructing and using built space, narrating stories and developing a specific idiom of kinship and relatedness (see Widlok 1999: 264). These practices also include, very prominently, attempts to gain and maintain reliable access to economic assets, and this is where questions of property once again enter the conversation. At this point in the conversation, property is no longer a sole cause or independent variable that can be taken for granted and that can be simply correlated with states of equality or inequality. Rather, it is a field of social relations and practices through which we can analyse the emergence of society or, more precisely, the convergence of social relationships into structures that we have come to identify as society and its institutions. The contributions to this book aim to elucidate people's dealings with property and their attempts to achieve equality in the face of a tendency for inequality to emerge and to reconcile social equality with personal autonomy. While property may or may not be a decisive factor in the political theory of inequality, the contributions to this book suggest that – empirically – dealing with property relations is critical in the processes of achieving or maintaining equality in the social relations that the authors have observed.

Themes in Anthropological Research

The establishment of ethnography and comparative analysis as standard research tools in anthropology has provided a versatile means for empirically testing and for continually questioning the received views of what was considered to be 'property', what was considered to be 'equality' and what was thought to be the relation between the two concepts. The contributions to this book re-address the relation between these two key terms and thereby pursue a number of central themes in the conversation. James Woodburn's seminal Malinowski lecture on 'Egalitarian Societies' (Woodburn 1982) reemphasised the relevance of property with regard to equality not by contrasting a property-free state with societies based on property but by investigating the contrastive ways in which social systems deal with property. In immediate-return systems, he argued, direct and immediate access to food and other resources is enjoyed by all members of society (men, women and children). Access rights are taken for granted rather than formally allocated and with very few exceptions this regime applies to subsistence resources as well as to skills and intellectual property. This property regime goes together with a high degree of personal autonomy to associate with freely chosen partners. Access to resources is also paired with restrictions on accumulating these resources and with the obligation to share. Taken together, these elements, according to Woodburn, constitute integrated systems in which property rights exist but in which the potentiality to convert these rights into dependencies and inequalities is kept at bay (Woodburn 1982: 445; see also Barnard and Woodburn 1988). In his reassessment of the relation between property and equality Woodburn made use of the wealth of data that ethnographers had started to collect among hunter-gatherer societies during the second half of the twentieth century. At the same time, his synthesis of how the Hadza and other hunter-gatherers had developed strategies to 'disengage' people from property, encouraged numerous other researchers to empirically search for social strategies that inhibit dependency and foster the extension of equality 'to all mankind' (Woodburn 1982: 431). Property was no longer an either-or option, as Rousseau and other political philosophers had considered it to be, but the challenge now was to understand how some social systems were able to deal with property without giving up either on individual autonomy or on social equality. Twenty years later, Wolde Gossa Tadesse and I invited colleagues who had been working on these problems to participate in a conference (labelled 'Property and Equality' and held at the Max Planck Institute for Social Anthropology) to take stock, to revisit the relation between property relations and relations of equality, to continue the conversations that have evolved around these key concepts, and to develop the shared themes of this conversation further.

Engaging and Disengaging with Property Objects

At the conference, where most of these chapters began their life, we had grouped contributions according to types of property, namely material property, incorporeal property and knowledge as property. A number of case studies covered more than one type of property, and several contributions reemphasised that the object of property relations is a critical parameter that has to looked at carefully – it may at closer inspection turn out to consist of a number of elements that eclipse different and at times conflicting property relations. For example, in the case of the *!nara*, an endemic natural resource harvested by the Topnaar Nama of the Namib desert, the property object is subject to property relations in a number of different ways, namely in terms of land, water, plant and fruit (Widlok 2001: 252). These aspects of the property object, together with the spectrum of property relations, may be usefully analysed in terms of a developing institutional system that has repercussions on the relations of equality but also on the objects themselves (Widlok 2001: 266). Redirecting our attention to the diversity of property objects and to the implications of dealing with different property objects has therefore been an important incentive to rethink a number of related themes.

The nature of the property object may directly influence whether it is subject to sharing or not, as David Riches reminds us in his contribution. He discusses the fact that in a number of cases industrial objects, including money, are less extensively shared than local objects, above all 'country food'. The New Agers and the Inuit experience two arenas of sociality, one of 'high sociality, intensive and continuous in time' (New Agers/Inuit among themselves) and one of 'low intensity sociality', relatively discontinuous (New Agers/Inuit with the wider society). Since two distinct socialities are fixed in one and the same place, he suggests that industrial objects are excluded from the ethics of sharing in an attempt to manage these two distinct forms of sociality. This leads him to propose that groups with a sociality of sharing rely on a specific 'space-time'. The bifurcation into two distinct space-times can be considered to be yet another solution to the tension between autonomy and equality as pointed out above. It is a strategy that combines a conceptual and a practical move between two space-times.

Kazuyoshi Sugawara also considers the question of how the object of property influences property relations. He redraws the boundaries of what is usually considered to be property by including the everyday discourse of possession, especially that of 'having' another person. In the /Gui context possessing another person is to be engaged in a sexual, emotive relationship that may be trespassed by a third person at the equal peril of all parties involved. In these triadic relationships all ownership claims are negotiated and existing ones are not respected just because they have been legitimised in the past. The attitude that competing parties should share is not programmed once and for all but detailed discourse analysis can show how it is 'generated, negotiated, renewed and reconfirmed over the course of continuing face-to-face interaction'. In this egalitarian setting speech is not simply a form of sanction that ensures a sharing ethos but it is only through reiterated talking that eventually the threshold for acting according to consensus is crossed. In this case, it seems, property objects are defined and property relations are managed without the need to anchor sanctions in a wider, hierarchically structured 'society', maybe because the objects of property, as it were, can participate actively in the maintenance of the underlying social relations. This raises fundamental issues concerning the underlying assumptions about subject–object relations that form the background of many arguments in this book. As Ingold (2000) and Bird-David (1999) have pointed out elsewhere, these relations may be much more symmetrical in many instances, including instances of hunter-gatherer social organisation, than the idealised Western model may suggest. Woodburn's characterisation of forager social strategies as 'disengaging' people from property relies on a clear separation between subjects (persons) and objects (property objects). A number of chapters in this book explicitly question this separation and show that it is an intricate problem that deserves further attention.

Tim Ingold in his critique of the notion of disengagement directly refers to Sugawara's description of equality not as a state of affairs but as 'passionate performance' based on mutual engagement of a specific kind. He reintroduces a temporal dimension to the discussions about sharing. He notes that objects are often considered property because of past investments into these objects but that the same does not hold when we invest into relations with other humans. Hunter-gatherers in particular, he argues, engage with the nonhuman world in parallel to their engagement with other humans, i.e. in mutual engagement and coevalness without transforming or 'objectifying' the memory of engagement into a property claim. In societies with elaborate inheritance rules, by contrast, property is the link between successive generations. In societies with an emphasis on intertwined co-presence, as in many hunter-gatherer cases, humans share their lives *with* non-human entities rather than sharing land, plants and animals among themselves. This leads him to go beyond the division of common versus divided property by considering modes of interacting with the world that are not premised on the notion of property at all. Moreover, this suggest that the confines of what Dahrendorf and other political theorists define as 'the society' may be much too narrowly drawn.

Barbara Bodenhorn, in her contribution to this book, rephrases the definition of equal relations from 'disengaged from property' to 'differently engaged with property'. Her case study shows that sharing may not be an absolute obligation to give up everything but one that is largely left to the autonomous individual. In this context the category of property involves the circulation of many kinds of resources and it 'encompasses many sorts of relationships'. She distinguishes personal property relations, with claims made by (and on) social persons in particular positions, from individual property relations, with claims made by (and on) certain individuals with a unique set of relations. The complexity of social relations in which present-day Inupiat whaling captains accumulate as well as share assets is explained in terms of the interaction between these two kinds of property. It seems that here a bifurcation of another sort is cultivated, one that allows for disparities by placing them in two separate modes of engagement. This leads to another intricate problem, namely to what extend these different forms of engagement can be reconciled with existing distinctions, between private and public, personal and collective, individual and common or communal property.

Personal and Collective Property

Academics are writing primarily for an audience with a background that may be labelled 'bourgeois' in its widest sense rather than simply 'Western' (see Bird-David, this volume). The contributors to this volume have therefore been careful to elicit what 'bourgeois' assumptions there are, in particular with regard to our understanding of the implications of property for equality. One of these assumptions is that we take it for granted that property creates inequality. Another important assumption is that all people use property to create distinctions. This assumption has in turn been used by the social sciences to make distinctions between societies, social systems and the strategies of social groups within them according to the different ways in which they try to distinguish themselves through property in the widest sense (see Bourdieu 1979). People are known for what they own, in our society as well as in our social sciences. Maybe the most pervasive distinction made in this context has been the contrast between private and communal property systems. It has preoccupied many researchers throughout the twentieth century, especially during the Cold War, and it continues to haunt public debates. It seems that the obsession with the private/communal divide has even survived the breakdown of the state socialist systems insofar as it keeps numerous researchers and consultants, now engaged in 'postsocialist studies', preoccupied with analysing the ways in which the transition from communal to private property regimes proceeds (see Hann 2002; Mandel and Humphrey 2002).

Possibly, it was an uneasiness with the ambivalence of property relations in Europe which led colonisers to insist in the first place that the societies of the world needed to be classified into clear-cut types, namely of private and of communal property regimes. 'Private property' came to be identified both as the root cause of inequality in human society but inversely also, as the reference point of personal freedom, as the backbone of the equal rights of all citizens to live their individual lives unhampered by the state or other powers that redistribute wealth. Anthropologists have often sat uncomfortably between such conflicting bourgeois (or proletarian) assumptions that make specific links between property and equality and that search the ethnographic record for 'proofs' for particular positions in European politics. When investigated ethnographically, *all* property regimes seem to be more or less ordered conglomerates of both private rights and communal rights, including the dominant property regimes of Eastern and Western Europe, as well as property regimes in hunter-gatherer societies (see Schott 1956; Barnard and Woodburn 1988: 10–1). Consequently, several contributors to this book deal with the interplay between private and public rights.

Hideaki Terashima, in his case study from the Ituri forest, deals with two kinds of knowledge, namely secret and shared knowledge, and the social forms that are associated with them – hierarchy and equality. He points out that among foragers of the Ituri, knowledge about medicinal plants is public and shared, while among the neighbouring farmers it constitutes knowledge held by specialists. The foragers compensate for the low degree of specialised knowledge in medical care through communal healing practices. While personal treatment among farmers is usually directed at an individual patient and seeks to improve his or her condition, communal healing is aimed at 'recovering solidarity within the community'. It is the whole community that contributes to the treatment and that benefits from it. In other words, ritualisation seems to influence the interplay between 'private' and 'collective' in specific ways.

Nurit Bird-David's critique is directed against a preconceived image of a balanced interplay between 'personal' and 'collective'. She provides a case where there is sharing of property that is not derived from a group or collective. She emphasises that the equality she describes for the Nayaka is one of people in (kin-) relations to one another. Equality is not achieved by a standardisation of shares or of the position of recipients. Rather, as a liquid fills connected vessels of different shapes and sizes to the same level, so sharing amongst related people creates equality 'without an intentional intervening design'. In such a context sharing is not an instance of generosity or prescribed redistribution but one of 'relational levelling'. It would be misleading to consider Nayaka property of food and other resources to be an instance of 'collective' ownership because it is predicated on co-use between connected persons and not on the meta-entity of 'a group' or any other recognised collective entity. Once again we are given a case in which social levelling mechanisms occur without 'a society' enforcing them, and therefore without the underlying contradiction identified by political theory.

Case studies like these raise another thorny issue, namely how the anthropological contribution can go beyond the description of individual or regional property regimes without falling victim to unwarranted universalisations about property regimes. A case in point is the notion of 'primitive communism', which played an important role in Marxist theorising but which was subsequently used more widely, in particular with reference to hunter-gatherer societies. Consider the following two statements by I. Schapera, synthesising the material he had collected from the ethnography of Khoisan-speaking people in southern Africa:

> [A]lthough in effect it approaches a sort of communism, [the economic life a Bushman band] is really based on the notion of private property. (Schapera 1930: 147)

> [A]lthough an apparently pure communism is observable in the life of the Naman, actually this is not found. Everybody has his own property, which he seeks to increase and improve, and, preferably unobserved by others, to use for himself. (Schapera 1930: 319–20)

Like other anthropologists at the time Schapera is ambivalent in his analysis of 'a sort of communism' and 'an apparently pure communism'. It seems that he is not so much confused as to what was the case in Khoisan southern Africa as being cautious not to be aligned with particular ideological positions (see Barnard 1993: 38). He explicitly contrasts the existence of 'private property' among the Khoisan speakers of southern Africa with the European image of communism 'in the sense of all men having equal, free and unconditional access to all goods and privileges' (Schapera 1930: 319). Among the Nama of the Namib desert personal property rights exist with regard to huts, livestock, household utensils and the major endemic wild fruit, the !nara (Schapera 1930: 319, see Widlok 2001). The same holds for portable property among the so-called 'Bushmen', where 'the only thing owned in common is the land' (Schapera 1930: 147; see Widlok 1999). In both cases the emphasis on property is qualified through the strong social expectation of sharing freely and even of taking for use purposes without consulting the owner (Schapera 1930: 148, 320). Thus, both cases are characterised by what seems to be a fairly similar property regime, made up of individual property rights in combination with 'communal' obligations. This may not be surprising given that Nama and 'Bushmen' share many cultural features and a long history of living in the same region. However, a key difference between the two cases is a rather hierarchical social system with ranked clans and strong leadership positions in Nama groups and a rather egalitarian social system among 'Bushman' groups. Clearly, even within the context of such a controlled regional comparison there is no simple correlation between property rights and equality. It suggests that a simple correlation is even less likely in comparisons between more diverse cases. This is not to say that there are no demonstrable links between property and equality. In fact it has been a major point of debate to what extent the ownership of livestock, or the ownership of *!nara* in the case of Nama living in the Namib desert (mentioned above), is a major factor in the emergence of hierarchical relations among Khoisan-speaking people (see Kinahan 1991). What needs emphasising, however, is that ethnographic data and anthropological knowledge are likely to reveal a complex dynamic picture instead of stable correlations or fixed constellations between predefined types of property and types of (in)equality as we move from one case to the next.

Properties of Property and of Equality

Given the complexity of the connection between property and equality, as outlined above, the main contribution of this book is to go beyond that of reducing complexity by isolating two 'cultural variables' – namely the presence of equality and the presence of property – across cases and by testing correlations between the two on the basis of as many cases as possible. Rather, the task is that of elucidating the complexity by exploring the dynamic that connects property and equality and by trying to understand the properties of property (see Hunt 1998) and of equality. As the contributions in the present two volumes show, these properties vary not only across fields but also within regional ethnographic fields. For instance, it is useful to consider the material presented in this book that deals with 'Bushman' or 'San' not as a single unified case but as a number of cases that can be productively compared (see Biesele and Sugawara in this volume, Guenther, Hitchcock, and Lee in Volume 2). The potential of these comparisons is rather that of conceptual exploration than of observing the behaviour of predetermined variables across a regional sample of cases. Moreover, the critical themes of the conversations covered here frequently cross regional or ethnographic boundaries, which is why we have refrained from arranging contributions according to regions. Instead we have highlighted the properties of property that are at the centre of the conversations to which the contributors refer. Consequently, the chapters of this volume are more than simply case studies operating with two shared variables, comparing cases for the purpose of establishing correlations. Rather, each chapter is an exploration of whether our conceptual distinctions hold across cases. The contributors investigate a variety of ways in which 'property', 'equality' and the relation between the two terms can be conceived in order to understand the diverse cases at hand. The contributions have been arranged according to their focus along three key terms, namely ritualisation (Woodburn, Tonkinson, Terashima), sharing (Riches, Bodenhorn, Sugawara, Layton, Ichikawa, Ingold) and egalitarianism (Strecker, Biesele, Bird-David). However, the cross-references are manifold and new perspectives emerge in the interplay of individual contributions. The following remarks therefore make exemplary use of some of the contributions without claiming to be exhaustive. Taken together the contributions provide the basis for no more than a tentative systematisation of egalitarianism, ritualisation and sharing in the context of current research.

Egalitarianism in this context means the positive ideology of equal access to resources. Equality is more than the absence of hierarchy and many of the case studies show how egalitarianism aims at generating or maintaining equality. Moreover, egalitarianism is transmitted not only as a message (as contents) across situations and generations but also through the communicative forms themselves.

Ritualisation provides another set of shared cultural forms which in relation to discourses of egalitarianism are at the other end of the spectrum of strategies towards achieving equality, since it is predicated on form rather than on the specific contents of egalitarian ideologies. Property relations are subject not only to more or less formalised egalitarian rhetoric and discourse strategies but also to ritualised behaviour. In fact, rituals have been considered a means to reduce communication channels for the benefit of emerging hierarchies (see Bloch 1986) but they may also be considered to be tools to safeguard truth against potentially misleading rhetoric and ideology (see Rappaport 1999). In any case, it is clear that ritual is not simply another means of expression, readily instrumentalised to create hierarchies or to (re)establish equality, but that ritualisation deserves to be analysed in its own right along with the study of egalitarian rhetoric and ideology.

Sharing as a distinctive property of property relations receives by far the greatest attention in the contributions of this volume. It has become the central term of the discussion and it reappears in every single contribution. This may have to do with the fact that it is 'a total social fact' that involves a spectrum of forms of practice, the discourses about the practices, and the social relations created through these practices. Sharing relations are multifaceted, as the contributions to this volume show. Sharing is more than egalitarianism being 'acted out' and is not simply a form of standardised or 'ritualised' exchange. When searching for the dynamic that generates equal property relations, contributors to this book have identified practices of sharing as a central feature, even as *the* central feature. This indicates that the conversation about the relationship between property and equality, as it is reflected in the contributions to this volume, is initiating a major shift away from a paradigm that was predicated on an all-encompassing notion of reciprocity towards explanatory models that put the practice of sharing at the centre.

Ritualisation

Although ritual is a key field of anthropological enquiry, it has been markedly absent from discussions of issues connected with property and equality which are usually considered in the more narrow terms of 'socio-economic structures'. Several contributions in this volume counteract this tendency by including religious ritual, ritual power and healing practices. They underline that ritualisation is not an afterthought or a superstructure of a self-contained socioeconomic structure. In fact, rituals may mark important starting points for the political dynamics that connect property and equality. This is also reflected by the composition of this volume, which begins with contributions that deal primarily and explicitly with questions of ritualisation.

James Woodburn revisits his own distinction between immediate- and delayed-return systems. He emphasises that immediate-return systems have been transforming themselves in ways that are not sufficiently explained with reference to political and economic pressures from dominant neighbours. Comparing evidence from a number of groups in sub-Saharan Africa, Woodburn points at the sphere of ritual as a potential field where inequality and notions of property are tolerated in contrast to day-to-day secular life. He concludes that 'the religious route ... is likely to have been a major route, perhaps even the major route, in the repeated historical transitions from immediate to delayed return'. This is not necessarily contradicted by the observation that in today's contexts this transition towards a 'predatory and entrepreneurial' system with a weak egalitarian ideology and less effective sanctions to enforce sharing is likely to take 'a secular route'. There may be more continuities between religious ritual and secular ritual than initially meet the eye. As I have argued elsewhere (Widlok 2002) the nongovernmental sector, arguably one of the strongest transformative powers today, is characterised by rather formalised modes of corporateness through which social relations and property relations are organised. The procedures for establishing an accepted corporate body which can hold property rights is a secular affair but one in which social agents are connected through formal acts that they have not entirely encoded themselves – i.e., through ritual activity (see Rappaport 1999: 24).

Interrelations between ritualisation and political hierarchies have been well documented in anthropology. It is therefore not surprising to scholars that elaborated relations of dependency and inequality are also marked by ritual means (see Bloch 1986). The cases provided in this book focus on the emergence of these interrelations in contexts that have no sacred kingship or similarly formalised structures of inequality. Robert Tonkinson presents an illustration of this process from Aboriginal Australia, maybe the most distinctive case of interaction between ritual knowledge and political power in hunter-gatherer studies. He draws a distinction between the potential of individuals to convert their ritual creativity into forms of enduring power and the control of rituals through male collectives for the generation of political power. Although there is considerable exclusion from intellectual property or, to put it the other way round, privileged access for some individuals in this field, this ritual authority is not contested in Mardu society. Individual ritual innovators are 'deeply socialised into avoiding behaviours that might be construed as self-aggrandising' and they are considered to be only 'intermediaries' between Dreaming beings and the living, who are soon detached from control over the objects of creation, i.e., songs and dances. Men do not become powerful through being intermediaries but they become intermediaries because they already have senior status in the religious hierarchy led by male collectives.

How does ritualisation shape the 'properties of property'? It seems that the separation between a ritual and a nonritual sphere is a feature that allows the management of disparate tendencies in a society, including those of (in)equality in property and individual autonomy, as outlined by Woodburn. At the same time, the connections between ritualised and nonritualised life also have to be considered. Inequalities in the ritual sphere, for instance privileged access to 'sacred meat' may trigger inequalities at large. However, as Tonkinson shows, transformations can go both ways, the socialisation against self-aggrandising also works across the divide. This leads us to the most frequently described levelling mechanism in socialisation, namely sharing.

Sharing

Several contributions underline the fundamental nature of sharing in property relations. Since cooperation in consumption has also been observed among nonhumans, one of the underlying issues is what (if anything) marks off sharing and property among humans which also relates back to the question of subject–object relations discussed above.

Mitsuo Ichikawa rejects the treatment of human sharing as separate from sharing among nonhuman primates. He does not want to 'reduce human culture to primate behaviour' but aims to reestablish the continuity between human and nonhuman species. Sharing, possession and cooperation among nonhuman primates occur as separate events, they are not – as among humans – integrated into a system where shared effort is linked to shared benefits through a series of distributions over time and across different degrees of participation. For successful sharing to take place it seems to be 'more important that an owner exists than who the actual owner is'.

A preconceived divide between ecological needs for sharing and cultural rules about sharing is also rejected by Robert Layton. He argues against the claim that ecological factors can be disregarded when considering the issue of transformations between egalitarian and hierarchical systems and questions of access to property. In order to account for ecological factors he complements the notion of environmental adaptation with that of 'a system that possesses its own internal dynamic, realisable within the constraints imposed by ecology'. Sharing large game is ecologically adaptive but it is also driven by the internal dynamics of a system in which sharing involves not only a successful hunter who gives and someone else who receives but also numerous witnesses. Over a long period sharing also displays the intent to cooperate and provokes assistance from onlookers. Conversely, those who do not cooperate, whether Australian hunters or French farmers, are publicly denounced for their failure to cooperate.

Several contributors advocate an extension of the notion of sharing beyond that of a specialised form of reciprocity in which transfers eventually balance out. They reject the view that sharing is a form of reciprocity as inappropriate because it means that all acts of sharing that take place across an open history of interaction and engagement are collapsed into one equation at a single point in time. What emerges from these contributions is that there is more to sharing than a category denoting a distinct mode of transfer. It is inadequate to correlate a high rate of sharing with a particular 'type' of society, namely immediate-return hunter-gatherers, and leave it at that. Sharing also plays an important role in the creation of social relationships. In contradistinction to static social theories that presuppose the existence of 'a society' with its functional requirements, a focus on sharing allows us to analyse 'societies in the making'. In other words, we are led away from viewing society as a ready-made parcel of rights, obligations and requirements towards a more dynamic and realistic view of how society, and the tensions between property and equality within it, emerge. Sharing, in this view, is more than a mode of transaction selected and carried out after a property regime has been established. Central properties of property, for instance its continuity across individual events and across fixed dyadic relations, may be described as being conditioned by practices of sharing, as outlined by a number of contributions in this book. Moreover, sharing not only shapes the practice of property regimes; it is also central to the discourse about property regimes, especially in egalitarian systems.

Egalitarianism

It is useful to distinguish equality (of opportunity or of result) from egalitarianism (as the proactive pursuit of equality), and it is important to note that egalitarian discourse and equality do not necessarily go hand in hand. Contributions to this volume underline that there is more to egalitarianism than simply a discourse or an ethos of equality and that egalitarianism should not be confused with the ideational side of material equality. The case studies show that beyond the contents of discourses the modes of interaction and communication themselves structure social relations, including those concerning equality and property. A number of chapters focus on this impact of egalitarian modes of communication. It emerges that the strongest levelling mechanisms are those that are not based on intentional, designed rules but are directly built into everyday behaviour, including discursive action. With this insight the analysis of egalitarianism as a kind of formalised communicative pattern also reconnects to questions of ritualisation raised above.

Ivo Strecker reviews his notes on property relations among Hamar pastoralists in Ethiopia, a group characterised by both equality and hierarchy, constituting 'seemingly contradictory strains in Hamar culture.' These contradictions are reflected in rhetoric, more particularly in a 'rhetoric of property' in which patterns of sharing take a prominent position. The situation is more complicated than a mere opposition between the proclaimed ideals of sharing and actual behaviour. Tensions already saturate the level of conversation and of negotiating what is shared, or supposed to be shared, and what is not. At the same time the act of speaking (forcefully) is itself connected to differences of wealth, so that rhetoric and conversation are arenas in which tensions concerning property and those concerning equality meet and interact.

Another situation of emerging inequalities is investigated by Megan Biesele. The rules of storytelling in Ju/'hoan society are very lenient. Tolerance, inclusiveness, free access to information and allowing for temporary ambivalence are practised not only in storytelling but also in postforaging contexts of political debates and decision-making processes. Here, Biesele says, 'individualism can be celebrated without becoming divisive'. In this situation the community of San speakers sets limits to individual San to whom international organisations ascribe the new function of being a multiplicator and representative. The limits are inherent in an egalitarian mode of communication that sanctions one-sided communication as 'bragging' and encourages an interactive mode of storytelling. This reaffirms the link between egalitarian social relations, on the one hand, and the autonomy of individuals, on the other, as they participate in shared activities such as storytelling.

Property and Equality

Looking at the distribution of property as a tool for gauging equality and inequality has become entrenched in public as well as in scholarly discourse. The recent proposition that it is 'access' to resources that matters rather than possession of material assets (see Rifkin 2000) only underlines that it is ultimately property rights (of access) which matter most in the contemporary world. Companies and individuals may tend to accumulate fewer material possessions, in an attempt to reduce – through 'outsourcing' – the amount of tax they have to pay and to avoid their long-term commitments. This tendency notwithstanding, an increasing commercialisation of what used to be free access to services and resources creates new inequalities based on differential property rights of this sort. Not only has property been considered as a source of (in)equality, but, conversely, political inequality has been looked upon in terms of the ways in which it affects the distribution of property. Revolutions and rebellions against power holders and systems of inequality are commonly fuelled by the expectation that thereby the distribution of property can be changed, as well. A main justification for imposing and maintaining authoritarian rule is that it – supposedly – protects property rights. One of the purposes of the present book is to show that the relation between 'property' and 'equality' is not exhausted by the strategic use of these terms in political debates but that they also feature in critical conversations in anthropology that continue along a number of related strands or themes. The recurrent themes that emerged in the course of the discussions during the conference on which the present book is based do not form an exhaustive set and, as was to be expected, individual contributions touch upon several themes. They highlight the fact that property can take on new properties in the dynamic of social relations.

Ritualisation, sharing and egalitarianism will surface again in the companion volume to this volume of *Property and Equality*, and the contributions to the present volume should be read in the context of the themes of encapsulation, commercialisation and discrimination, which are elaborated in Volume 2. The key terms that we have selected as editors do not form two closed triads but rather outline an open field of enquiry. However, it is also important to note that discussions during conferences and cross-references between chapters of a book, just as conversations more generally, do not spread randomly but along the lines of shared theoretical interests and shared fields of expertise. Consequently the contributions in both these volumes do not cover each and every aspect to do with the conceptual pair of property and equality. They could not – given the complexity of the problems at hand. At the same time, they do share a number of related concerns and promising new perspectives. An important part of this shared general background is that all contributors are familiar with the anthropological conversations concerning 'egalitarian societies' and have sought to pursue these issues further. Many contributors have done field research with hunter-gatherers in Africa, the Arctic, Asia or Australia; others have worked with pastoralists, with horticulturalists, agriculturalists and in industrial societies. They have all related their work to themes that have evolved in the course of the conversations in hunter-gatherer studies. Across both volumes the contributions also constitute a dialogue between those who had been part of the first wave of intensive hunter-gatherer ethnography between the 1950s and the 1980s, and those who have begun their field research much later, within the last ten years. Thus, there is considerable shared ground but at the same time contributions are made from a range of specific backgrounds, geographically as well as in terms of the history of the discipline. In this way every single author in this collection not only brings his own unique voice to the conversation but also the voices of the people with whom she or he has worked in the field.

References

Barnard, A. 1993. 'Primitive Communism and Mutual Aid: Kropotkin visits the Bushmen'. In: C. Hann (ed.), *Socialism. Ideals, Ideologies, and Local Practice*. London: Routledge.
Barnard, A. and J. Woodburn 1988. 'Property, Power and Ideology in Hunting and Gathering Societies: an Introduction'. In: T. Ingold, D. Riches, and J. Woodburn (eds), *Hunters and Gatherers*. Vol. 2: *Property, Power and Ideology*, pp. 4–31. Oxford: Berg.
Bird-David, N. 1994. 'Sociality and Immediacy: or, Past and Present Conversations on Bands'. *Man* 29: 583–603.
―――― 1999. 'Animism' Revisited: Personhood, Environment, and Relational Epistemology'. *Current Anthropology*, 40 (Supplement): S67–91.
Bloch, M. 1986. *From Blessing to Violence: History and Ideology in the Circumcision Ritual of the Merina of Madagascar*. Cambridge: Cambridge University Press.
Bourdieu, P. 1979. *La distinction: critique sociale du jugement. Sens commun*. Paris: Éditions de Minuit.
Brunton, R. 1989. 'The Cultural Instability of Egalitarian Societies'. *Man* 24: 673–81.
Dahrendorf, R. 1969. 'On the Origins of Inequality Among Men'. In: A. Béteille (ed.), *Social Inequality. Selected Readings*, pp. 16–44. New York: Penguin.
Day, S., E. Papataxiarchis and M. Stewart (eds) 1999. *Lilies of the Field: Marginal People who Live for the Moment*. Boulder: Westview Press.
Durkheim, E. 1960. *De la divison du travail social*. Paris: Presses Universitaires de France.
―――― 1979. *Professional Ethics and Civic Morals*. London: Routledge.
Epstein, J. and R. Axtell 1996. *Growing Artificial Societies. Social Science from the bottom up*. Cambridge, MA: MIT Press.

Hann, C. 2002. *Postsocialism. Ideals, Ideologies and Practices in Eurasia.* Routledge: London.
Hunt, R. 1998. 'Properties of Property: Conceptual Issues'. In: R. Hunt and A. Gilman (eds), *Property in Economic Context.* pp. 7–27. Landham: University Press of America.
Ingold, T. (ed.). 1996. *Key Debates in Anthropology.* London: Routledge.
—— 1999. 'On the Social Relations of the Hunter-Gatherer Band'. In: R. Lee and R. Daly (eds), *The Cambridge Encyclopedia of Hunters and Gatherers.* pp. 399–410. Cambridge: Cambridge University Press.
—— 2000. *The Perception of the Environment. Essays in Livelihood, Dwelling and Skill.* London: Routledge.
Kinahan, J. 1991. *Pastoral Nomads of the Central Namib Desert: The People History Forgot.* Windhoek: New Namibia Books.
Mandel, R. and C. Humphrey (eds) 2002. *Markets and Moralities: Ethnographies of Postsocialism.* Oxford: Berg.
Marx, K. 1962. *Das Kapital. Kritik der politischen Ökonomie.* Berlin: Dietz.
Parsons, T. 1954. *Essays in Sociological Theory.* Glencoe: Free Press.
Prince, R. and D. Riches 1999. 'Back to the Future. The New Age Movement and Hunter-Gatherers'. *Anthropos* 94: 107–20.
Rappaport, R. 1999. *Ritual and Religion in the Making of Humanity.* Cambridge: Cambridge University Press.
Riches, D. 2000. 'The Holistic Person; or, the Ideology of Egalitarianism'. *Journal of the Royal Anthropological Institute,* 6: 669–85.
Rifkin, J. 2000. *The Age of Access. How the Shift from Ownership to Access is Transforming Capitalism.* London: Penguin.
Rousseau, J-J. 1994. *Discourse on Inequality.* Translated by F. Philip. Oxford: Oxford University Press.
Schapera, I. 1930. *The Khoisan Peoples of South Africa: Bushmen and Hottentots.* London: Routledge & Kegan Paul.
Schott, R. 1956. *Anfänge der Privat- und Planwirtschaft. Wirtschaftsordnung und Nahrungsverteilung bei Wildbeutervölkern.* Braunschweig: Limbach.
Strathern, M. 1988. *The Gender of the Gift. Problems with Women and Problems with Society in Melanesia.* Berkeley: University of California Press.
Vogt, C. 1992. *Das Savoir-vivre der Wildbeuter: Systemerhaltende Mechanismen bei egalitären Jägern und Sammlern im Lichte eines neuen Paradigmas.* Bonn: Mundus.
Widlok, T. 1999. *Living on Mangetti. 'Bushman' Autonomy and Namibian Independence.* Oxford: Oxford University Press.
—— 2001. 'Relational Properties: Understanding Ownership in the Namib Desert and Beyond'. *Zeitschrift für Ethnologie,*126: 237–68.
—— 2002. 'Corporatism and the Namibian San'. In: D. LeBeau and R. Gordon (eds), *Challenges for Anthropology in the 'African Renaissance': A Southern African Contribution,* pp. 206–16. Windhoek: University of Namibia Press.
Woodburn, J. 1982. 'Egalitarian Societies'. *Man,* 17: 431–51.

1
Egalitarian Societies Revisited

James Woodburn

My work over many years has been focused on the comparative analysis of the social systems of hunter-gatherer societies and societies which are locally acknowledged as having been hunter-gatherers in the recent past. I have given particular attention to hunter-gatherers with relatively simple forms of social organisation – with what I term immediate-return systems, which constitute the simplest known forms of human social system, true elementary forms more fundamental, I would argue, than the elementary forms discussed by Durkheim in *Les Formes Élémentaires de La Vie Religieuse* or by Lévi-Strauss in *Les Structures Élémentaires de La Parenté*, both of which gave too much attention to Australia and too little to Africa. My starting point has always been my experience of leading a nomadic life with the Hadza people of Tanzania, to whom I am enormously indebted for their wonderful conversations, their warmth and their companionship.

Property in the widest sense is central in my analysis. Without entering here into the complex issue of the definition of property and property rights, which I have discussed in some detail elsewhere (Barnard and Woodburn 1988), I would want to claim quite simply and directly that the social systems of hunter-gatherer societies, like those of other societies, are best understood when seen in relation to the way in which the rights of individuals and of groups over what we term property are held and transacted. Rights over land and resources, over tools and weapons and other moveable property, over game meat and harvested vegetable food, over knowledge and intellectual property and over certain capacities of people such as their hunting labour or their reproductive capacity – all these and other property rights are central in the operation of social relations and social groupings and in the way in which these social relations and social groupings change through history. Most important of all, I would claim that it is through rights to property, and the ideologies linked with such rights, that structures of equality and inequality among the kin and other close associates with whom hunter-gatherers live and work are established and maintained.

My intention in this paper is to examine some aspects of the evolutionary potential, the potential for change, in immediate-return systems. I shall argue that these systems have shown themselves to be remarkably stable and resistant to change in their mode of operation both in the past and in the present. But within every immediate-return system there are contexts in which the kinds of social relationship and social grouping characteristic of delayed return may develop. I shall focus on two of these contexts, one more relevant for the past, for understanding the history of immediate return, and the other more relevant for the present, for understanding possible ways in which immediate-return systems might transform themselves today.

But first of all I shall review and elaborate some of what I have said in previous papers. By far the most important and contentious issue is the status of immediate return. Is it to be explained as a response to political and economic pressures from politically and economically dominant neighbouring societies? Many people have argued directly or indirectly that immediate-return systems are part systems, not viable in their own right but explicable only as subordinated adjuncts of more powerful polities. In this approach the distinctive social relations of immediate return are treated either as broken-down social relations or as relations of solidarity generated by opposition to political domination, or as both. In spite of its attractions, I have rejected this approach for reasons which are set out at some length in my paper 'African Hunter-Gatherer Social Organization: Is it Best Understood as a Product of Encapsulation?' (1988). The core of my argument is set out in the following paragraphs:

> [A possible] explanation for immediate-return systems might be that they are a combined product of breakdown of delayed-return systems and of opposition to outsiders, in other words destroyed systems of delayed return that have developed a new form of organization to oppose outsiders. Are their sharing and their egalitarian levelling mechanisms oppositional, developed in opposition to domination by outsiders? Have we here a form of egalitarian oppositional solidarity of low-status groups, akin to the egalitarian solidarity manifest in some working-class or millenarian movements? Is it egalitarian solidarity born of a fear that any hunter-gatherer with more power, wealth or status than another might be tempted to increase it and to exploit his fellows by allying himself with outsiders, and that outsiders might be tempted to use such power-holders to impose some form of control, some form of indirect rule?

> Such an approach has obvious attractions. Oppositional solidarity may well have played some part in the perpetuation of immediate-return systems at particular points in their history when they were under great pressure. But I am sceptical about the idea that it constitutes an adequate general theory for their emergence or for their perpetuation through time when pressures from outsiders are not so severe. If delayed return is fundamental why does it not re-emerge when pressures ease? From the known history of immediate-return systems, I see little indication of such re-emergence. And, again, if immediate

return is a form of oppositional solidarity, why has it apparently not emerged in its characteristic form in Canada and Australia in response to the discriminatory and, at times, ruthless pressures on hunter-gatherers from outsiders in those countries?

The fundamental reason why I am sceptical about the idea of oppositional solidarity as a general explanation for the emergence and persistence of immediate-return systems is that a simpler theory, in which explanatory priority is given to people's day-to-day dealings with fellow-members of their own society, makes better sense to me than one which makes the structure of such dealings dependent on the less frequent and, for the people concerned, less important dealings with outsiders. Much of my own and other people's work in recent years in societies with immediate-return systems has demonstrated that their systems are internally coherent and viable, that they make sense politically and economically for their members and allow them to live reasonably rewarding and satisfying lives. These highly flexible systems, which lack the social groupings and binding social relationships familiar to earlier generations of anthropologists, can offer, as I have repeatedly witnessed, reasonable security, good health and nutrition and a greater amount of leisure than is available in most societies (Woodburn 1980: 106). It seems strange to suggest that people would wait to invent such systems until outsiders imposed pressures on them. I would expect that where economic circumstances are appropriate such systems would be repeatedly invented and re-invented historically in autonomous and near-autonomous hunter-gatherer societies as well as in hunter-gatherer societies with extensive dealings with politically dominant outsiders. (1988: 62–63, footnotes omitted)

For me, then, immediate-return systems are to be understood not as part systems,[1] but as coherent systems capable of functioning in a largely self-dependent manner, viable and enduring in their own right and with a momentum that is primarily internally derived. Quite simply they, with hunter-gatherer delayed-return systems in all their many varieties, constitute the two alternative viable forms of hunter-gatherer organisation. Both are likely to be ancient as well as modern. In the pre-agricultural period both are likely to have existed, though the frequency of occurrence of each type may well have been different then. For sub-Saharan Africa I think it would be reasonable to claim that in a world consisting exclusively of hunter-gatherers a higher proportion may have had delayed-return systems (Woodburn 1980: 112; 1988: 61). Immediate-return systems, though not simple in form, are intrinsically simpler than delayed-return systems and it seems plausible to argue that there will have been a time at which all societies had immediate-return systems.

The present-day form of immediate-return systems is not the only possible form. In the usual and widespread contemporary form a number of distinctive characteristics are interdependent, indeed are tightly interlocked: a system of material production for immediate use without significant storage or investment; an egalitarian ideology and an egalitarian practice in which even intergenerational relationships are near-equal; a system of social relations and social groupings minimising dependence and stressing direct, individual access to material resources, to knowledge and to skills with these resources, this knowledge and these skills not controlled or allocated by people of senior generation; an emphasis on individual freedom to select on a day-to-day basis one's residential and other associates; a system of transactions focused on entitlement to share other people's recognised property, the recognised yield of other people's labour. I shall be discussing these various characteristics later in this paper but I raise them now simply in order to argue that it is not difficult to imagine other, different types of immediate-return system. One might, for example, imagine a more predatory and more entrepreneurial system in which the egalitarian ideology and the system of social sanctions enforcing sharing were less elaborated and less effective, in which successful hunters were able to retain and make use of more of the meat of their kills so that they could eat well, trade well and marry well while other less successful hunters went hungry and found it difficult to trade or even to marry. However, I do have doubts about whether such a system would be viable and capable of self-replication over the generations for relatively autonomous groupings of hunter-gatherers who hunt large game animals. If large animals are killed, there are likely to be only two ways in which the meat can be used in an orderly way. It can either be distributed using the institutional apparatus of delayed return – intergenerational authority, committed kinship ties, corporate households with household heads, lineages and clans or other extra-household kinship groupings – or else it can be distributed through the obligatory sharing mechanisms characteristic of immediate-return systems like those of the Hadza, the Mbuti or the !Kung, in which an egalitarian ideology is combined with a strongly expressed entitlement to share beyond the boundary of the household. If there was a time before the development of delayed return when all societies had immediate-return systems, the most plausible hypothesis is that most such systems were not radically dissimilar to those of today. So I am making here – perhaps unwisely – a very sweeping claim. Such immediate-return systems constitute a stable and enduring social form, internally coherent and meaningful to participants in them, not just capable of self-replication but tending always to self-replication.

The Nature of Immediate-Return Systems

I now move to a closer examination of the nature of immediate return. In a series of papers (Woodburn 1979, 1980, 1982, 1988, 1998; Barnard and Woodburn 1988) which have been published over many years and in a number of others which have not yet been published, I have tried to explain why certain contemporary hunter-gatherer societies,[2] which I term societies with immediate-return systems, are, or until recently were, societies of equals – equals in wealth, equals in power and equals in status. My argument is that they are societies of equals because in these societies equality is actively promoted and inequality is actively resisted through a set of coherent interlocked and mutually reinforcing institutional procedures.

These institutional procedures together constitute one particular resolution – an extreme one – of the coexisting pressures for equality and for inequality which are present in the desires of every one of us as an individual and in the operation of the political systems, and indeed of the kinship systems and the religious systems, of every human society. The vast majority of the world's social systems provide people both with contexts in which they interact with others of their own ethnic group as equals and also with contexts in which they interact with others of their own ethnic group as unequals. Hunter-gatherer societies with immediate-return systems are unique in the degree to which almost all of the social contexts within these societies maximise equality although, of course, members of most of these societies today have much experience of inequality – usually profound inequality – in their dealings with members of other ethnic groups because, as people identified as hunter-gatherers, they are so politically weak and so subject to discrimination (Woodburn 1997).

Members of societies with immediate-return systems are, I have argued, ideologically egalitarian, active promoters of equality and active resisters of inequality in all its dimensions within their own communities. Equality is perceived as meritorious, as worthy, as honourable, and inequality as unacceptable, as disreputable and even as evil and dangerous.

The equality that is sought is to a considerable degree actually achieved. Those people in these societies who go against public opinion by seeking to assert authority over others, by seeking to obtain and to retain more assets than others, or by claiming higher status than others, live lives which seem often to be full of anger and anguish. Because their approach to life has no legitimacy in the eyes of the other members of their communities, sooner or later they are likely to have to face a degree of ostracism, conflict and rejection. It is striking to me that the Hadza, who are today under great stress from land loss and other pressures, seem to reserve their most trenchant criticisms and passionate denunciations for those fellow Hadza who offend against the ethic of equality.

In my various papers and especially in 'Egalitarian Societies' (1982) and in 'Sharing is not a Form of Exchange' (1998), I argue that certain key mechanisms are at work in these societies which together have the effect of creating a degree of human equality greater than that achieved in any other human societies. Three mechanisms are particularly significant:

1. *Provision of direct access to material resources, knowledge and skills*
   Unlike almost all other human societies, people – men, women and older children alike – are entitled to direct and immediate access to the ungarnered food and other resources of their country. These rights of access are not formally allocated to them and cannot be withdrawn from them. Neither parents nor other kin provide, control or direct access. Nor do political authorities (apart nowadays, in some cases, from alien political authorities outside their own ethnic group). These open rights of access to material resources are matched by open access to secular

knowledge and skills, and especially to those connected with subsistence. Apart from some limited restrictions linked to the division of labour by sex, there is almost no secular specialisation of knowledge and skills and certainly no legitimacy for any notion that areas of secular knowledge and skill could properly be reserved for or held exclusively by particular individuals or groups. The principle of open and uncontrolled access by members of one's own community applies equally, then, to both material resources and to secular intellectual resources.

2. *Autonomy: freedom to move around and to live and work with freely chosen associates*
It is not just that this right exists. What matters is that it is constantly exercised, limiting enduring bonds and subverting any development of authority and dependency within one's own ethnic community.

3. *Obligation to share*
While all individuals have an automatic right of access to ungarnered resources, they are elaborately constrained about how they can use them. Garnered resources have to be shared and used immediately. They cannot be accumulated for later use. Nor can they be given to other people in order to accumulate in another way, that is in terms of claims for future reciprocation. In many of these societies the model for sharing lies in the distribution of the meat of large game animals among all the people of a nomadic camp. Typically other things are less elaborately and less widely shared, but always the emphasis is on the immorality of accumulation, on the obligation to give away whatever one is not using at that moment and on entitlement to benefit immediately from any perceived accumulation by one's associates. Even accumulation of products for trading purposes can be very difficult, especially if these are valued consumable items such as meat or honey.

I argue that generally in immediate-return systems these processes (and some other less crucial processes) 'disengage people from property, from the potentiality in property rights for creating dependency' (1982: 445). Of course, in the various immediate-return systems in different parts of the world the processes of disengagement are not identical, but the outcome is remarkably similar. Property rights of course exist, as we shall see, but are minimised in secular contexts. For members of these societies one might almost say that the notion of property as theft is not a novel revolutionary ideology but an implicit everyday view of the world.

Such property disengagement is associated with disengagement from binding commitments or dependencies in close social relationships, including close kinship and affinal relationships. A father cannot control his son's labour or the yield of his labour. A husband cannot control his wife's labour or the yield of her labour. Most important of all, a father cannot control his daughter's destination in marriage nor can a brother control his sister's destination. People interact closely and warmly with their kin and other associates all the time both in subsistence and non-subsistence activities, but they are not controlled by or dependent on them. Clans, lineages and other similar kinship groupings are either absent or else exist only in nominal shadowy form, apparently borrowed from outsiders and used for little more than to establish a measure of respectability in dealings with outsiders.

What we have in societies with immediate-return systems is a set of distinctive ways of handling property, or more specifically of disengaging from property, of limiting committed linkages between people and things, and a distinctive pattern of social relations which, taken together, form a surprisingly closely integrated whole. We can tell that they are closely integrated, closely bound together, both because they occur together in many different parts of the world and because of their extraordinary persistence and resilience in changing ecological, economic and political circumstances even when they appear to be disadvantageous to the people involved. The evidence suggests that people find it exceptionally difficult, even intolerable, to give up or to limit their entitlement to share and equally difficult to accept the wealth or the authority or the superior status of any of their kin, their friends or other members of their own community. I think that it would be very hard to find well-documented instances of communities in societies with an immediate-return system that have in recent years changed their system of property relations and their system of social relations into ones in which a measure of wealth accumulation and kinship or household control over daily labour have become both generally accepted and effectively implemented.

The commonplace day-to-day planned saving and investment of African peasant farmer households – by systematically growing crops which are then sold, for example, to build a better house, to pay school fees or to buy a bicycle – is not something which people with an immediate-return background find it easy to adopt. It seems obvious to attribute the difficulty to lack of opportunity – to the fact that former hunter-gatherers are so often excluded from good land or good opportunities to market their crops. But although the discrimination is real, it is not a sufficient explanation. In many Pygmy communities in Central and West Africa there is no shortage of good land and yet we still commonly find that Pygmy farmers are far less systematic in their agriculture and have markedly lower crop yields than their agricultural neighbours. If the difference does not derive from exclusion, does it then derive from 'culture', from the fact that Pygmies, even long sedentarised Pygmies, commonly identify with hunting and the forest and are, for this reason, less committed to agriculture? Again, the explanation, though relevant, is insufficient. The fundamental reason, the general explanation which underlies the very many African and other cases, lies, I believe, at the sociopolitical level – the integrated nature of the egalitarian systems which I describe as immediate return. It is not easy for individuals, for households and for communities to break out of such systems, and it is unlikely ever to have been easy (Woodburn 2000).

In considering those factors which maintain immediate return and those which have the potential to change it, religion and ritual deserve particular attention. The notion that religion and ritual are secondary, are less important in understanding social continuity and social change than political and economic factors, still dominates a surprisingly wide range of approaches to the study of hunter-gatherer societies and should, I believe, be constantly challenged. Religion and ritual are not symbolic by-products of the real and the material but are active contexts for the maintenance and development of ideas and values, including those which relate to equality and inequality in social life. It seems strange to be still stressing this today, a century on from the work of Weber and Durkheim, but in the context of research on African hunter-gatherers this fundamental issue does still need emphasis.

In my paper 'Sharing is not a Form of Exchange' (1998: 56–57), I commented on the !Kung stress on sharing in their most important religious activity, the trance dance:

> Men who go into trance expel illness, actual and potential, from the men, women and children of the community. A man pays no fees to the healers who teach him to become a healer, and when he is qualified he shares the yield of his ability to heal with everyone in his community without fee or expectation of reciprocation. His ability to heal is believed to derive from *n/um*, a personally owned substance or force within him which is said to be warmed up and made available for curing with the help of other dancers and singers. He shares *n/um*, or the yield of *n/um*, in a way that is directly analogous to the sharing of a personally owned carcase of a game animal he has killed. (Barnard and Woodburn 1988: 20; Lee 1984: 109–13)

But I should go further than this. Sharing in this context is not merely analogous to the secular sharing of meat. It is consecrated sharing produced in the context of the joint participation of the entire community, a potent dramatisation of the production of the egalitarian community that has manifest appeal both to the reason and to the emotions of the participants. Its potency derives in part from its oppositional character: the shared unity of the participants in their joint opposition to the undifferentiated spirits of the dead, the bringers of illness and death. Sharing, equality and solidarity are commonly reinforced by opposition.

Let us return briefly to the issue of whether or not immediate return is essentially a product of domination, exploitation and discrimination. If this were so, one would expect the opposition expressed in ritual to be directed, at least some of the time in at least some of these societies, against those responsible for the domination, exploitation and discrimination. Yet, very surprisingly, this does not seem to be the case. As I mentioned in my paper on discrimination against hunter-gatherers and former hunter-gatherers in sub-Saharan Africa:

> ... there is little evidence of protest religion, of religion focused on dramatic repudiation of their menial status. We do not usually find millenarian movements or cargo cults, ecstatic possession cults, revitalisation movements. We do not, in general, find a proliferation of new religious forms like those of American or South African Blacks which are so widely interpreted as religious responses to the discrimination which they suffer. (1997: 358)[3]

I invited readers of my paper to draw my attention to exceptions to what I had to say but, so far, and disappointingly, I do not think that I have had any responses to this. I would actually have expected protest religion to have emerged and constantly re-emerged in the context of the suffering that members of so many of these societies have experienced, and the fact that it apparently is so rare must, it seems to me, be treated as evidence for the fact that the focus for the egalitarianism of these societies is still primarily internally generated.

So far, so good. But a problem, or at least a paradox, now arises. !Kung religion is indeed egalitarian, but Hadza religion and the religions of many of the Pygmy groups in the Congo Democratic Republic, in the Congo and in Cameroun are markedly less so. In these societies there are male cults and attempts to build a simple gender hierarchy of ritual privileges. In some cases there are female cults as well as male cults, though male cults always seem to be more powerful and more elaborated. In these societies gender distinctions and age distinctions (or rather distinctions based on whether or not one has been initiated into the gender cult group) are much more marked than in day-to-day secular life. Correspondingly notions of property, held exclusively by initiated persons of the relevant gendered group, are stressed in diametric contrast to the minimisation of exclusive property rights in day-to-day secular life. The property which is held takes many forms, ranging from the ritual trumpets of the Mbuti, which the men keep concealed in local rivers between rituals, to the sacred *epeme* meat eaten jointly in secret by Hadza initiated men, or the secret intellectual property of the Mbendjele in the form of key areas of knowledge which cannot be disclosed to anyone who has not been initiated into the relevant male or female cult. Usually the focus is on both material and intellectual property. These various forms of property are typically protected by secrecy, by deception and often by the threat of violence.

Within these gendered groups access to the property held exclusively by the group, whether it be material property or intellectual property or both, is usually freely available and equally available to all members but zealously guarded against access by non-members. Opposition to non-members fosters sharing and equality within. Among the Hadza, the sacred *epeme* meat – certain rigidly prescribed and highly valued joints of the meat of most large game animals – has to be eaten communally in secret by all of the co-resident initiated men together until it is finished. Hunters have no control of the *epeme* meat of any animal they kill. It is sacred meat belonging jointly to all the initiated men including the hunter, but only if he has already been initiated. Both in 'Egalitarian Societies' (1982) and in 'Sharing is not a Form of Exchange' (1998), I argue that the rigid allocation of this special meat to the initiated men provides a kind of precedent and a framework for the alienation of the rest of the meat of each large game animal from the hunter and its allocation as people's meat to all who are in the camp – men, women and children alike. Control is wrested from the hunter by the men's group acting, as they would see it, on behalf of the whole community and it is this forcible seizure which, in a sense, licenses the sharing of the remainder of the carcass by all in the community. The skilled labour of the successful hunter is acknowledged. He is recognised as the individual owner of the animal that he has killed, but his use rights and disposal rights over the carcase are greatly constrained by the always successful assertion of the collective rights of the initiated men to the sacred meat and the collective rights of the camp community as a whole to the residue of the meat.

This is not the only context in which male hierarchy and its privileges are mobilised in ways that are notionally beneficial for all. The central rituals both of the Hadza (in the *epeme* dance) and of these various Pygmy groups typically involve active and cooperative participation by all members of the community, men, women and children alike, but with much clearer gender and age demarcation than in secular life. Moreover, the rituals are believed to be essential for the well-being of the community as a whole and not just for, or even primarily for, the initiated ritual property holders. Opposition is expressed between men-as-a-group and women-as-a-group. But it is out of this opposition, which is viewed positively as fruitfully competitive, that community well-being is believed to arise.

Of course, hierarchical systems typically present themselves as being essential for community well-being, for the welfare of all and not just of the privileged section of the community. This kind of ideology is part of the process by which privilege is reproduced through time. I think that where equality is so stressed in secular life, we should anticipate that breaches of equality in the religious domain will be particularly well defended both in the ideology and in other ways or these breaches would not endure. Among the Hadza male ritual privilege is defended by the threat of force and, on occasion, by the use of force. Indeed in Hadza society this is perhaps the most conspicuous context for the threat of force.

In the case of the Hadza male privilege in ritual does seem highly discordant in a society in which men have so little authority over women in day-to-day life; in which women control the product of their own labour even more than men do since the obligation to share roots and berries is far less rigorous than the obligation to share meat; in which women have an immediate right at any time to divorce without having to provide an explanation; in which a man is not able to take his children away from his wife after divorce; in which in general a man is not able to command his wife; in which a man is not able to control the destination of his daughters in marriage.

So how are we to interpret the dissonance, the fact that gender and age inequality are more marked in ritual than in secular contexts? It is characteristic of ritual that social distinctions are more formalised, that boundaries between social categories are more sharply drawn than they are in day-to-day secular life. Is the dissonance no more than this? I think the evidence suggests that it is much more and that we should see male ritual privilege as a weak point in the operation of immediate-return systems and a possible opening for one of the potential routes to delayed return, a potential structure for domination by male elders though not yet a structure of domination. But it certainly is no more than a possible opening. If male ritual privilege led easily to delayed return, then systems like the Hadza one in which secular equality and male ritual privilege have, they say, coexisted throughout their known history, would long ago have been transformed into delayed return. However, I do think one could argue that an elaborated male cult creates an ideological rupture between men and women, a basis which, if further elaborated, could give rise to the devaluation of women's labour and of women's reproduction. Such ideas are likely to be an important component in the development of simple delayed-return systems with relatively autonomous property-holding households in which women's and children's labour is organised by the (usually male) household head.

This is where Australian data become relevant. Australians have an elaborate male cult, an emphasis on the importance of sacred property, especially intellectual property, and authoritarian male elders:

> ...ideological domination [is] well developed but with economic and political control restricted to a few limited contexts (Hiatt 1971, 1986; Bern 1979; Tonkinson, this volume). Interestingly, and perhaps surprisingly, there are consistent indications that men may more readily be able to control women's destination in marriage than to control the yields of women's productive labour.

> To open this possible route to delayed return, we would expect an onslaught on the considerable autonomy which women and young men enjoy in immediate-return systems. The process involves increasing incorporation of women and young men into committed kinship and affinal relationships, and into structured kinship groups in which ideological control is vested predominantly in older men. This development allows increasing control by the older men of their junior female kin, who are then bestowed in marriage on other men. Sons-in-law or prospective sons-in-law provide labour for their fathers-in-law. Ideologies of domination are developed, especially in ritual contexts, in which the substantial real control which, in immediate-return systems, women enjoy over their own sexual and reproductive capacities and their own labour is increasingly denied. The end of this process, which is not realised in some of the simpler delayed-return systems such as those of the Australian Aborigines, comes when women and young men are fully and effectively incorporated into household units with household heads who exercise control over the yield or a significant part of the yield of women's and young men's labour.

> Not enough attention has been paid to the way in which binding relationships are developed between close kin and affines. Without committed relationships there can be no real control. Committed relationships seem often to be developed through two related forms of ideological elaboration which deny the autonomy of participants. The first of these is the notion that people are mystically embodied in things, and things in people. Such a notion is fundamental to many systems of property rights and is particularly clear in the case of Australian Aboriginal land rights. The effect of such mystical involvement is not merely to tie people to things, but to tie people to other people through things. Mauss's work on the gift (Mauss 1954) and Parry's recent development of Mauss's ideas (Parry 1986) explore some of the ramifications of these notions.

> The second form of ideological elaboration denies the autonomy of the participants more directly. In this form people are believed to be involved mystically in other people and such involvement, intentional or unintentional, affects their health or welfare. The power to bless or to curse someone, the power to bewitch them, and the power to contaminate them through pollution are all examples of such elaboration. The particular forms in which such beliefs are expressed vary widely from society to society, but what seems to be constant is that increasing commitment to other people in binding relationships is commonly linked to ideologies of mystical dependence. Kratz's paper in this volume gives some particularly clear cases. In immediate-return systems, such ideologies may already be present in simple forms in those relationships in which some commitment does exist. Here the Hadza data are relevant: a man is mystically involved in his wife's reproduction while she is mystically involved in his hunting. (Barnard and Woodburn 1988: 28–30)

My opinion now is that the religious route, prolonged and tortuous though it is, is likely to have been a major route, perhaps even the major route, in the repeated historical transitions from immediate to delayed return.

However, I do not think that the religious route is likely to be operative as a significant route from immediate return to delayed return in the contemporary world. Although hunter-gatherer religions have proved to be resilient in some parts of the world, especially in Africa, they are not often able to command people's loyalties to the extent that they did in the known past when people were living more fully by hunting and gathering.

A secular route is, I believe, likely to be more operative today, at least in Africa. I described earlier in the present paper the possibility of a predatory and entrepreneurial form of immediate-return system in which the egalitarian ideology and system of social sanctions enforcing sharing are less elaborated and less effective, in which successful hunters are able to retain and make use of more of their kills (and more of the yield of the rest of their labour) so that they can eat well, trade well and marry well, while other less successful hunters go hungry and find it difficult to trade or even to marry. I argued there that I was doubtful whether such a system would be viable and capable of self-replication over the generations. But even if such a system is not viable in the long run, even if the pressures to restore sharing and equality are likely to cause reversion to the more familiar egalitarian form of immediate return, this more predatory form could constitute a possible bridgehead for some entrepreneurial families to move into delayed return, particularly in, for African hunter-gatherers, those rare cases in which individuals have succeeded in gaining access to education and to stable, paid employment. Are there many cases of African hunter-gatherer families with an immediate-return background who have not emigrated away from their fellows but who have differentiated themselves by saving, investing and refusing to share? I think that among people from an immediate-return background, few will attempt to differentiate themselves in these ways and even fewer will be able to maintain their refusal to share for long if they remain co-resident with other people from the same background. Among the Hadza there are people who nowadays do make the attempt but they find it exceptionally difficult, even impossible, to cope with the hostility that is directed towards them by other Hadza.

There is a tragic element in all this. If hunter-gatherers and recognised former hunter-gatherers in Africa are to have any hope of retaining even the very limited amounts of land they still possess today, they must somehow provide leaders who are able and willing both to identify closely with other members of their own communities and to lobby energetically on their behalf without coercing, intimidating or exploiting their fellow members. They can only act effectively if the community recognises them and supports them and allows them some leeway to differentiate themselves. Sadly the overwhelming weight of evidence suggests that members of these communities find it very difficult to accept leadership, particularly if these leaders seek to differentiate themselves.

There are, I believe, possibilities for devising new human rights strategies for countering the appalling discrimination and dispossession from which so many groups of African hunter-gatherers and former hunter-gatherers suffer today (Woodburn 1997, 2001). But we do need to recognise that for these communities conventional development strategies and conventional political action are most unlikely to be successful and that new thinking based on a much clearer knowledge and understanding of the values and the sociopolitical realities of their lives is urgently needed.

Notes

1. But of course they, just like delayed-return systems, can function as part systems.
2. For present purposes I define hunter-gatherer societies as those societies whose members perceive themselves (and are usually perceived by others) as being in essence hunter-gatherers, even if today they are living as landless labourers or in other ways with which they do not identify themselves.
3. I discussed one important exception, the incipient revitalisation movement of the Nharo described by Guenther (1986: 288–89).

References

Barnard, A. and J. Woodburn 1988. 'Property, Power and Ideology in Hunting and Gathering Societies: An Introduction'. In: T. Ingold, D. Riches and J. Woodburn, (eds), *Hunters and Gatherers, Vol. II: Property, Power and Ideology*. Oxford: Berg Publishers.

Bern, J. 1979. 'Ideology and Domination: Toward a Reconstruction of Australian Aboriginal Social Formation', *Oceania* 50, 2: 118–32.

Guenther, M. 1986. *The Nharo Bushmen of Botswana: Tradition and Change*, (Quellen zur Khoisan-Forschung, Vol.3). Hamburg: Helmet Buske.

Hiatt, L.R. 1971. 'Secret Pseudo-Procreation Rites among the Australian Aborigines'. In: L.R. Hiatt and C. Jayawardena, (eds), *Anthropology in Oceania*. Sydney: Angus and Robertson.

—— 1986. *Aboriginal Political Life*. The Wentworth Lecture 1984. Canberra: Australian Institute of Aboriginal Studies.

Lee, R.B. 1984. *The Dobe !Kung*. New York: Holt, Rinehart and Winston.

Mauss, M. 1954. *The Gift*. London: Cohen and West.

Parry, J. 1986. '*The Gift*, The Indian Gift and the "Indian Gift"', *Man* (n.s.), 21, 3: 453–73.

Tonkinson, R. 1988. '"Ideology and Domination" in Aboriginal Australia: a Western Desert Test Case'. In: T. Ingold, D. Riches and J. Woodburn, (eds), *Hunters and Gatherers, Vol. II: Property, Power and Ideology*. Oxford: Berg Publishers.

Woodburn, J. 1979. 'Minimal Politics: The Political Organization of the Hadza of Tanzania'. In: P. Cohen and W. Shack, (eds), *Politics in Leadership: A Comparative Perspective*. Oxford: Clarendon Press.

—— 1980. 'Hunters and Gatherers Today and Reconstruction of the Past'. In: E. Gellner, (ed.), *Soviet and Western Anthropology*. London: Gerald Duckworth.

—— 1982. 'Egalitarian Societies', *Man, the Journal of the Royal Anthropological Institute*, 17, 3: 431–51. (Malinowski Memorial Lecture delivered at the London School of Economics, 5 May 1981).

—— 1988. 'African Hunter-Gatherer Social Organization: Is it Best Understood as a Product of Encapsulation?' In: T. Ingold, D. Riches and J. Woodburn, (eds), *Hunters and Gatherers I: History, Evolution and Social Change*. Oxford: Berg Publishers.

—— 1997. 'Indigenous Discrimination: the Ideological Basis for Local Discrimination against Hunter-Gatherer Minorities in Sub-Saharan Africa', *Ethnic and Racial Studies*, 20, 2: 345–61.

—— 1998. '"Sharing is not a Form of Exchange": An Analysis of Property Sharing in Immediate-Return Hunter-Gatherer Societies.' In: C.M. Hann, (ed.), *Property Relations: Renewing the Anthropological Tradition*. Cambridge: Cambridge University Press.

—— 2000. 'Elusive Pygmies. A review of *Challenging Elusiveness: Central African Hunter-Gatherers in a Multidisciplinary Perspective* edited by K. Biesbrouck, S. Elders and G. Rossel. Research School for Asian, African and American Studies, University of Leiden, 1999', *Indigenous Affairs*, 2: 78–83.

—— 2001. 'The Political Status of Hunter-Gatherers in Present-Day and Future Africa.' In: A. Barnard and J. Kenrick, (eds), *Africa's Indigenous Peoples: 'First Peoples' or 'Marginalised Minorities'?* Centre of African Studies, University of Edinburgh.

2

Individual Creativity and Property–Power Disjunction in an Australian Desert Society

Robert Tonkinson

Introduction

At first glance, it would seem an unrewarding task to examine the place of property in societies whose nomadism discourages its accumulation and thereby seemingly consigns it to a marginal cultural status. However, when the object of enquiry is to describe and analyse the *processes* through which a given form of property generates, or is converted into, relations of either equality or inequality in hunter-gatherer societies, the prospects for fruitful investigation are considerably enhanced. My focus in this paper is on a particular kind of intellectual property – a genre of ritual that lends itself well to a consideration of factors that either facilitate or impede the generation and maintenance of inequalities – and the cultural context is an Aboriginal society whose dominant ethos is egalitarian, despite the undeniable presence of significant status inequalities.

Among the Mardu Aborigines, with whom I have worked since the early 1960s, dominance and the monopolisation of the means of production by individuals or localised groups are inhibited by a combination of ecological, social and religious factors that make for interdependence at all levels of Mardu society (Tonkinson 1988a: 150). My objective here is to describe one major category of Mardu ritual, then identify the mechanisms that prevent the conversion of this form of intellectual property, produced from what to an outside observer would be unambiguously designated as human creativity, into the exercise of individual power over either people or material resources. Elsewhere, I have argued that Western Desert society is more aptly characterised, in Woodburn's parlance, as an 'immediate-return' than a 'delayed-return' society, for a number of compelling reasons (Woodburn 1980, 1982; Tonkinson 1988b). One of these strong reasons is a notable stress in Mardu society on what has been described as the critical element of egalitarianism, individual autonomy (cf. Gardner 1991; Kelly 1995) – enacted, however, within the strong constraints of the kinship system and its concomitant obligations and responsibilities. Another is what is exemplified by the category of ritual considered here, which disengages persons from property in a manner that Woodburn would associate with immediate-return societies.

Although an anthropologist could readily predict a processual flow from control over intellectual property to its self-interested exploitation by individual agents engaged in political action, among the Mardu there is a barrier interposed between the two major phases of this process. This disjunction between creativity and the potential rewards it can bestow on the creative agent operates to minimise the generation of inequalities out of individual difference. In principle and practice, the insulation of creativity from its exploitation by individuals has clear parallels with other important characteristics of hunter-gatherer societies. Two good examples would be: first, the heavy obligation felt by the successful hunter to share large game (see, for example, Endicott 1988: 117 on the Batek of Malaysia, who speaks of this as a 'strict' and 'absolute' obligation). This obligation has the effect of removing from a highly skilled minority the opportunity to enhance personal power by converting recipients into dependents or followers (Barnard and Woodburn 1988: 21). Secondly, the Dobe Ju/'hoansi healer (Lee 1993: 109–24), whose status and role have a great deal in common with those of the Aboriginal diviner-curer. This practitioner has powers that are personally owned, but as Barnard and Woodburn (1988: 20) note, these 'are shared with the community without fee or expectation of reciprocity in a way that is directly analogous to the personal ownership of a game animal's carcass and its sharing with the community' (cf. Elkin 1977; Tonkinson 1991: 128–32).

For Aboriginal Australia, it is possible to distinguish between two major categories of knowledge, though all knowledge and power were traditionally attributable ultimately to the spiritual realm of the cosmic order. Unrestricted knowledge, in the form of technical and other mundane skills, is very widely shared in any given group; it is taken for granted and readily alienable. The second category is restricted religious knowledge, which, as Bern (1979) has pointed out, was the major foundation for the control exerted by mature men over the rest of society. While it is true that, in some areas, women possessed secret-sacred knowledge and rituals, nowhere was this corpus considered more important for social reproduction than that held by mature men, who claimed they exercised their responsibilities for the society as a whole (cf. Meggitt 1962). Keen (1988: 277) notes that the foundation of the authority of older men and women alike was an economy of religious knowledge in which ritual holdings are a kind of 'currency', and would therefore tend to be located at the inalienable end of a possible continuum of property rights.

For Barnard and Woodburn (1988: 11), the important question when considering the political relevance of property rights is not the distinction between rights held individually or by groups but 'the more fundamental question of the scale of equality and inequality in access by men, women and children to the range of material things that are desired and valued in hunting and gathering societies'. In societies where gender and age were major criteria in knowledge distribution and therefore closely related to issues of control and power relations, this question of differential access was certainly fundamental to an understanding of the Aboriginal social formation. In the case of intellectual property among the Mardu, however, I wish to demonstrate that there is an important distinction between the potential for *individuals* to convert new knowledge into forms of enduring power and that of *male collectivities* to generate political power from their control of the rituals that ultimately derive from such individual creativity. Within the realm of women's secret-sacred activity, however, I cannot comment on the relationship between these two loci of possibility for the exercise of power, but there are some clear hints in the available literature (see Munn 1973 and Dussart 2000 on Warlpiri women's creativity and ritual politics; see also, Berndt 1950, 1965 and Moyle 1979, 1997: 25–27 on women's religious creativity).

Barnard and Woodburn (1988: 13–14) have suggested that 'because property rights imply some restriction or exclusion of the rights of others, they are in a sense controversial and liable to challenge by those who are restricted or excluded'. In the Western Desert case, though, rights over intellectual property such as songlines, secret-sacred lore, ritual designs, and so on, exercised predominantly by mature initiated males, were generally not contested. These rights and entitlements were very firmly embedded as holy writ, which linked them and their possessors both to an indeterminately located but contemporaneous spiritual realm and back in time to the creative epoch wherein all things were instituted as immutable (Stanner 1966).

It is not my intention here to discuss Aboriginal property concepts generally, since Keen (1988) has provided an excellent overview of their application to Aboriginal social life and its gift-exchange economy. He concludes from his north-east Arnhem Land data that elements of use, possession, exclusion and disposal all imply the notion of 'control' (p. 272). In a later, fine-grained, ethnographically based work, Keen (1994) explores the nexus between religious knowledge, relations of power, and secrecy, and makes the important point that knowledge implies a *right*: 'a person who could not in the circumstances legitimately claim to be old enough or of the right group or gender to say or do something, such as recount a certain myth, would deny knowledge, at least in contexts where his or her actions were monitored' (1994: 2). In north-east Arnhem Land, as elsewhere in Aboriginal Australia, action was located within a complex web of sociopolitical relations and was organised 'on the basis of focused networks, gender and age categories, and patrifilial identity, rather than classes, communities, or corporate groups' (p. 19). While Keen (1994) also illuminates the controversial matter of what constitutes 'politics' in Aboriginal Australia, especially the nature of hierarchy and leadership, we are particularly indebted to Hiatt (1986) for his succinct overview of major scholarly debates and the salient issues surrounding this topic. Of the various possibilities he canvassed that relate religious leadership to the exercise of power more generally, the Mardu case as I have argued it (Tonkinson 1991: 138–42) reflects the highly situational nature of leadership, the pervasive centrality of kinship behaviours, and the absence of 'spill-over' of individual exercise of power from the religious into everyday life – much like what Meggitt (1962) has described for the Warlpiri. In other words, a variety of cultural mechanisms exist that inhibit the accretion of personal power.

Also of relevance here is the seminal work of Stanner (1966) on Aboriginal religion and worldview, particularly his point (p. 165) that the trajectory of these religious systems impelled them towards a degree of unity, integration and closure that was in reality rarely attained, or sustained, for very long. A major theme of Keen's (1994) study, for example, is the ubiquity of heterogeneity in Yolngu culture and practice, such that no degree of agreement over the meaning of any cultural element can be taken for granted by the anthropologist. Much scholarly writing on Aboriginal religion suggests the coexistence of a dominant ideology of nonchange and immutability *and* a high level of flexibility and negotiation, which would ensure that new knowledge could and did penetrate and affect the system. For Stanner, however, there was a proviso: change was welcomed, but only 'insofar as it would fit the forms of permanence' (1966: 168); that is, was congruent with the spiritual givens of life. As a rule, in this oral culture, much such lore slipped smoothly through time and space from the palpably here and now to be seamlessly absorbed into 'the Dreaming', a body of religious knowledge held to have existed since time immemorial, thus acquiring the status of timeless, immutable truths (cf. Stanner 1958, 1965; Tonkinson 1991).

The Mardu Aborigines and the Nature of Power

First, a brief description of the ethnographic setting is warranted. The Mardu Aborigines, who number about a thousand, live in several settlements and towns on the western side of the Gibson Desert in the huge state of Western Australia. Culturally, they are part of what is widely known to anthropologists as the Western Desert bloc, covering about one-sixth of the continent, and are among the most 'tradition-oriented' of Australia's indigenous minorities.[1] Many of the elderly Mardu still alive grew up in a 'pre-contact' environment, experiencing no direct interaction with the small scattering of Whites who settled along the margins of the desert. A prominent feature of Mardu coping strategies since making the huge transition from a nomadic lifestyle to a much more sedentary adaptation has been their strong determination to insulate the core of their religious life from what they regarded as threatening incursions by alien influences, such as Christianity. Elsewhere, I have described how the Mardu reacted by strongly affirming a conceptual separation of the domains of European and Aboriginal space, the former exemplified in the word *maya* 'house' and the latter in *ngurra* 'camp' (Tonkinson 1982; cf. Trigger 1992). The Whites engineered and maintained physical separation between the two areas, thus imposing a boundary that metaphorically framed the social and ideological separation of these domains. Despite a quarter-century of strong missionary presence and concerted attempts to subvert their culture, the Mardu held their ground very successfully (Tonkinson 1974). The highly paternalistic mission era was succeeded in the early 1970s by community incorporation and elected all-Aboriginal councils, part of a huge change in government policy to one of self-management. New challenges arose from external attempts to pressure the Mardu into exercising greater control over their dealings with government bureaucracies and with the society at large. Their reactive strategy was to consign their newly bestowed powers to a category they termed 'whitefella business', which they assiduously kept separated from what was for them the culturally very much more important domain of 'Dreaming Law', particularly the realm of religious affairs (Tonkinson 1982).

Today, the Mardu live in communities with electricity, television, telephones, faxes, supermarkets, vehicle workshops, and so on. As I have recently typified them, these remote settlements are structured along Western-oriented administrative lines, controlled by elected Aboriginal councils increasingly preoccupied with bureaucratic dealings with the outside world, and assisted by non-Aboriginal staff in positions such as project officer, adviser, mechanic, or book-keeper, and with government agents such as nurses and schoolteachers, who also live in the community (Tonkinson 1999). Among the Indigenous inhabitants, however, kinship continues to function as the central organising principle for social behaviour; and there is still unquestioning acceptance of the truth and reality of the body of knowledge, activities and prescriptions known as the Dreaming, or 'the Law'. In Meggitt's (1962: 251) words: 'As the law originated in the dreamtime, it is beyond critical questioning and conscious change.' The Law continues to underpin adult Aboriginal worldviews in the desert; and the religious life, with its strong focus on male initiation, as manifest particularly in the large regional gatherings or 'big meetings' that are held annually, is still accorded cultural priority over mundane concerns such as settlement economics and politics.

A Mardu Ritual Dichotomy

While they would readily concede that the power inherent in all rituals derives ultimately from the creative epoch of the Dreaming, the Mardu Aborigines nevertheless make a distinction between *mangunyjanu* ('from the creative period') rituals, said to be derived from the Dreaming, a time beyond human memory, and *partunjarrijanu* ('from the dream-spirit') rituals, created by human action in contemporary society. Dream-spirit rituals are said to emanate from communication between the spiritual and human realms of the cosmic order. *Jijikarrkaly*, the spirit-beings that act as intermediaries, are sent from the spiritual realm of the Dreaming by the creative beings, which have retreated from the human realm but are said to remain vitally interested in human affairs.[2]

Mardu do not rank these two kinds of ritual in any way, but to an observer the former would appear to be culturally more prominent, widespread, long-lasting and significant. Most of the large corpus of Mardu rituals belong to the *mangunyjanu* category, and all the major rituals contain elements that are secret-sacred to fully initiated men. A number of these rituals, including those associated with male initiation, have diffused to every part of the Western Desert cultural bloc (though we can only speculate about the process by which this occurred); and most of them commemorate the travels and adventures of certain ancestral beings over much of the region. Such rituals are not 'owned' by a single group, but every group through whose territory the *yiwarra* 'tracks' of these creative beings passed is recognised by all as owning or 'looking after' their particular section of the path – its sites, songlines, mythology, associated rituals and paraphernalia. At every periodic aggregation (*japalpa*, 'big meeting'), where the business of the society at large is conducted, including initiations, some of these rituals will be performed by the collectivity. These meetings are held in emulation of the creative beings who, during their travels in the Dreaming epoch, instituted and exchanged rituals and objects on the many occasions that their paths crossed.

The second kind of ritual, arising from dream-spirit revelations, begins locally and is much smaller in scale than those said to derive from the Dreaming. Every few years, one or more mature men would report being *yungu* 'given' or *nintijurnu* 'shown' elements of a new ritual during dreams (note the choice of verbs locating agency in the actions of the spiritual being rather than the human recipient).[3] This process of innovation, described in detail in Tonkinson (1970), occurs when their *partunjarri* 'dream-spirit' is travelling and encounters spirit-beings who, as intermediaries between the withdrawn creative beings and the living, reveal new knowledge to the dreamer: a tune, song, dance, body design, or sacred object that is potential raw material for the creation of a new ritual.

Berndt (1974: 24) describes these spirit-children as 'the intermediaries who bring life from out of the Dreaming, conferring this precious substance on man as on all natural species'. Similarly, ethnomusicologist Stephen Wild (1987: 109), writing of the creative process among the desert Warlpiri, speaks of these 'spirit agents' as occupying 'the interstice between contemporary reality and the *jukurrpa* [the Dreaming]', and notes that the songs, designs and dances that are revealed to humans by these 'spirit agents' are not necessarily the property of the dreamer.

The Mardu attach much significance to some of their dreams, so a man who claims to have had one or a number of thematically similar revelatory dreams will normally share his experience with others, seeking interpretations or perhaps also confirmation that others may have had similar dream encounters recently. (According to Munn 1973: 98, those Warlpiri women who sleep in the same camping area as the dreamer are supposed to have been in the dream, which strongly suggests shared knowledge of at least some of what transpired in it.) Perhaps excited and rendered hyper-suggestive by what they have been told, other mature men may soon dream about similar happenings or themes and wake up remembering songs or dances that they, too, have been given during their dream-spirit travels. Women, too, are sometimes participants in the collective creative process when they are given songs, which they then report to their husbands for possible inclusion in the emerging ritual.[4]

Through this collective collaboration, new knowledge is manipulated and integrated in such a way that the eternal truths and powers of the Dreaming are vivified and materialised by human agents in the here and now, via a process that both validates and reinforces the reality and relevance of the past for the present and future.[5] The basic structure of the dream-spirit ritual is the same: the bulk of each performance entails singing by men, women and perhaps children, and dancing that is witnessed by all present; then, as the ritual draws to a close, the advent of a brief men-only, secret-sacred segment is signalled when one of the dancers throws a firestick into the air from behind their brush 'hide', and women and children are then ordered to face away from the ground and to remain hidden under blankets, policed by a number of older men. During the dance or dances that follow, spectacular thread-crosses (large decorated objects, akin to 'gods-eyes', that in Western Desert societies are secret-sacred to initiated men) are carried. Each new ritual has a distinctive tune, body decorations, sequence of dances, and thread-crosses; and its songline may comprise a hundred or more verses. Women and children learn the songlines by listening to the men, and these attain a status akin to pop-tunes, being sung anywhere day or night, regardless of whether the ritual is performed or not.

The great appeal of these rituals is that they require minimal preparation and no special grounds, and relatively small groups can stage them effectively. They invigorate community life because of the great enjoyment derived from them by people of all ages. Although individual dream-spirit rituals wax and wane in popularity, and today they appear to be rare in the desert region, their existence suggests a profound truth to the Mardu: the great creative powers of the Dreaming are still 'out there' in the spiritual realm and remain vitally concerned about, and interested in, human affairs. More important still, they demonstrate their presence and reward the Mardu for conformity to their Law by regularly revealing to them new and powerful knowledge.

Intellectual Property and the Denial of Creativity

Initially, the dream-spirit ritual remains under the control of the individual or individuals on whom the new knowledge was bestowed by the spirit-being intermediaries who brought it from the spiritual realm, the source of all power. In a gift-exchange economy that is materially poor but rich in intellectual property, a new ritual is a valuable asset that generates interest and anticipation among neighbouring groups once they learn of its existence. The ritual offers those who control it the opportunity to assume the advantageous role of host by staging performances in their home territory and inviting visitors from other areas to participate. There is both prestige and dominance in playing the host role, and novices endure various restrictions on their movements and behaviour during their initial exposure to a new ritual. News of the new ritual's existence quickly spreads, and groups from surrounding areas will be anxious to be inducted, as a mandatory first step on the path to their eventual acquisition of significant property rights over it. In the Western Desert, the dominant political strategy is to restrict performances of a new ritual to its home locality until neighbouring groups have learnt it via repeated attendance at performances. What happens, however, is that these groups begin to pressure the owning group to grant rights of performance and transmission. As a valued form of property in some respects akin to 'currency', the ritual may be exchanged for a like ritual, or for goods (such as red ochre, secret-sacred objects or bundles of weapons). An essential element in the exchange is the gift by the hosts of secret-sacred objects intrinsic to the ritual; these symbolise, among other things, the entitlement of the receiving group to perform and then eventually pass it on.

Among the group that originates it, a dream-spirit ritual is in any case relatively short-lived in terms of full performances because, in just a few years, it will be supplanted by another newly 'found' or acquired dream-spirit ritual. Once the host group accedes to pressures from neighbouring groups for its release into circulation, the dream-spirit ritual begins its travels. Significantly, once it has entered the regional circuit, its status is transformed over time and as it is transmitted through space, from a contemporary *partunjarrijanu* ritual to an age-old, eternal *mangunyjanu* ritual. In other words, by the time it has reached groups many hundreds of kilometres away on the opposite side of the desert, it will be received and categorised as 'from the Dreaming', a now timeless, powerful ritual that has shed all information regarding the circumstances of its relatively recent creation and of the humans associated with its origin and composition. This process is almost certainly how most of the huge corpus of Aboriginal rituals originally came into being. Stemming initially from altered states of individual consciousness, then 'collectivised' as its elements are integrated into a ritual whole, the locus of the ritual as property moves to a local group of men – whose control over it, however, is necessarily impermanent. Inexorably, both their exclusive ownership and the localisation of the ritual are ceded; it is carried steadily away as highly valued exchange item in regional affairs, simultaneously political and religious, inevitably to falter at some time in the future as the competition for a place in a finite corpus of circulating Western Desert rituals becomes too great.

In an oral culture, the depersonalisation and decontextualisation of intellectual property of the kind I have just discussed are not difficult to achieve. These processes are aided by Aboriginal cultural values stressing the hegemony of a spiritual control of power, which inevitably demands that persons be disconnected from the nonmaterial products of their intellect.[6] Traditionally, there was an overwhelming stress on the primacy of spiritual causation and agency, strongly exemplified in the Western Desert case, for example, in the denial of major elements of both physiological paternity *and* maternity (Mountford 1981; Tonkinson 1984). Given this stress, little wonder that the human intermediary is relegated by the dominant ideology to the status of conduit or vehicle rather than creator (see Berndt 1974: 24 regarding notions of the body as a 'physical receptacle').[7] Individual Mardu are thus denied an innovatory function in ritual creativity, but the spiritual imperative underlying and directing all Aboriginal religions accords humans a central role in the reproduction of nature and society, wherein ritual can be seen as the dominant mode of production. In the case of dream-spirit rituals, mature men have the essential task of translating piecemeal information into highly structured and integrated ritual wholes. The bones of 'divinely' inspired but initially quite disconnected elements are fleshed out into the ritual body only through the cooperative endeavours of human actors.

All knowledge in Aboriginal society can be construed as in essence 'religious' since it derives ultimately from the actions of the Dreaming beings that created the pervasive Law. Yet it is clear to an outsider that certain kinds of knowledge, possessing elements of both power and danger and pertaining more directly to objects, sites, myths, songs, activities and beliefs, are more overtly 'religious' and highly valued than other kinds. The dominant worldview firmly locates spiritual control, human origins and the instituting of society and its rules in the creative epoch of the Dreaming as an essentially egalitarian domain. Given the ideological preeminence of the Dreaming, then, it is not surprising that the role of the individual as innovator should be minimised or denied. This cultural convention effectively removes a rich and potent source of status differentiation among men, and in the Mardu case their strident claims to be just as good and worthy as other men reflect a strongly egalitarian ethos among adults of the same sex. Because the Mardu believe that enabling powers are monopolised by the creative powers of the spiritual realm, the grand life design embodied in the Dreaming concept is effectively insulated from the egotistical and potentially subversive impulses of individual humans. As the Mardu aptly put it, 'Everyone is under the Dreaming', or, in the words of an Arnhem Land man, 'We are always running to catch up with what has been done before' (Morphy 1988: 249; cf. Maddock 1972: 129). These are surely emic counterparts to Stanner's conception of Aboriginal worldview as centred on an attitude of assent to pregiven, immutable terms of life, laid down in the Dreaming.

Although Mardu individuals who assert their role as conduits of new knowledge cannot convert that for which they are both medium and message into political capital, the foregoing discussion should have clearly established that dream-spirit rituals possess undoubted exchange-value at the level of *intergroup* sociopolitical relationships among mature males. They are part of the intellectual property that allows groups to assume the role of host, and ritual is the magnet that pulls in visitors for the periodic 'big meetings' that constitute the high points of the desert social calendar. In terms of 'segmentary divisions', Bern (1979) sees competitive relationships among structurally similar groups as having the potential to generate inequalities. The Western Desert case, however, provides corroboration for Stanner's (1966: 169) view that such divisions were Dreaming-ordained and validated and therefore mutually supportive rather than competitive. There, major ecological constraints combine with social factors to inhibit local groups from enhancing their political power at the expense of their neighbours (for example, by repeated assumption of the host role and consequent accumulation of resources at one node in the regional system of gift-exchange). Favoured big-meeting sites are scattered throughout the Western Desert, and the venue changes from one meeting to the next; in fact, an important order of business at any meeting is discussion to reach a decision on the location and timing of the next such meeting. What obtains, then, is the realisation of a degree of dominance, but it is essentially temporary and situational, and it neither endures nor accretes into structural inequalities. This fleeting realisation accords closely with other major elements of Mardu society: hierarchy emerges strongly in gender relations both during domestic conflict, which is essentially short-lived, and in the organisation and performance of the religious life, especially during the big meetings, which are also temporary aggregations.

Predictably, the discovery of sacred objects by individual Mardu men is not considered an individual accomplishment, since it too is revealed or hinted at through signs (which are myriad in the Aboriginal cosmic order) that prompt reaction. It may be that similar discoveries are made by women, but, if so, their repercussions are not part of the shared, public domain (in contrast to the situation among Warlpiri women; cf. Munn 1973; Dussart 2000). Men speak of having encountered spirit-beings during dreams, which tell them to go and look in some spot where they will find something important left behind by creative beings during the Dreaming. As in the case of dream-spirit rituals, the finder will disclose his discovery to others, telling them where and under what circumstances he found the object. This disclosure initiates the transfer of the matter to a collective level. An informal meeting of initiated men will be called, to discuss the facts of the case and arrive at the 'true' religious meaning of the find. The meeting will be guided by the men's knowledge of the paths and activities of the creative beings in the vicinity of the find, and by the shape, size and colour of the object. For example, any natural or incised concentric circle motif would establish its connection with Dingarri beings (cf. Berndt 1970). Some objects are so distinctive that their ancestral provenance is unmistakable, so their discovery at a certain location establishes new knowledge of the movement of the ancestor(s) concerned, and no doubt leads the Mardu to anticipate some later revelation of further corroborative proofs. This kind of incorporation has considerable practical and political implications for groups seeking to increase their identification with a given ancestral path and set of creative beings (see Tonkinson 1991: 136 for a Mardu example). The found object, as a sign from the Dreaming, is the property of the collectivity; so, as in the case of the elements of the dream-spirit ritual that are revealed to individuals, the finder is an intermediary and not the owner – though he may expect to be consulted about any planned disposition of the object.[8]

Conclusion

Consideration of one notable form of individual creativity in the service of religious knowledge and ritual power among the Mardu Aborigines has prompted conclusions that offer little support for explanations that focus heavily on processual dimensions. The barrier between what to the observer is individual creativity and control by the creator over the products of that creativity is less obviously processual than structural. By this I mean that it is underwritten and maintained by a worldview that stresses spiritual control over power, and positions the individual passively as a vehicle for its transfer into the human realm on behalf of collectivities. The ritual innovator, like the diviner-curer, channels power into society but has been deeply socialised into avoiding behaviours that might be construed as self-aggrandising. The essence of the Mardu definition of humanity is to be possessed of, and to know, shame. Thus to be *kurntaparni* 'without shame' is to be not human, and people go to great lengths to avoid any appearance of putting themselves above their fellows. Self-regulation, the key to social control in most hunter-gatherer societies, is more a matter of being than doing, or of personhood rather than process. Aboriginal socialisation inculcated what Stanner (1965: 213) describes as an 'assent to life's terms', and, as he notes, religious practice 'included a discipline to subdue egotistical man to a sacred, continuing purpose'.

Turner (1967, 1969), a major contributor to the study of the transformational dimensions of ritual process, focused on two levels or loci of transformation: the individual participant or observer, whose behaviour, identity and experience may undergo change 'both within the performative organization of the rituals themselves and in the contexts of meaning and action which extend around them' (Kapferer 1979: 3); and the broader social and political order in which the ritual is embedded. What benefits are derived by those Mardu who dream of receiving new knowledge yet are denied individual control over the power thus channelled through them? Though the Mardu appear not to talk much about such matters, it is difficult to believe that dreamers could remain unaffected by the momentousness of their encounters with the emissaries of the omnipotent ancestral creators, or that personal satisfaction would not result from being 'selected' as a conduit for introducing new knowledge into society. Change as experienced at this individual level is least amenable to anthropological investigation and analysis, especially in cultures where people are not given to elaboration and exegesis. From an outsider's perspective, however, it is significant that those who have the dreams which contribute to ritual innovation are mature adults, already senior in status in the religious hierarchy, and very much part of the segment of society that controls and guards the Law. In other words, those members of society who are 'chosen' as intermediaries are among the already powerful. While it is always safe to assume that some measure of prestige accrues to creative individuals in Mardu society, they are soon detached from control over their objects of creation. Their status as creators dissolves into the group's achievement, which in turn dissipates once it has released the ritual into the circuit of 'travelling rituals' and is eventually transformed into the other category of ritual, from the Dreaming (see Widlok 1997 on the transformatory potential of such rituals). It is at this broader processual level that the impacts of religious knowledge as both power and property are most readily observable and most amenable to analysis. In the Western Desert, among the world's most marginal of environments for human survival, an unimpeded flow of religious knowledge maximised both the limits of society as imagined by the several thousand Aboriginal inhabitants who owned and occupied an area covering one-sixth of the continent, and the sense of equality and cultural interdependence that characterised intergroup relations.

Finally, a sort of parallel can be discerned between Stanner's depiction of the fleeting attainment of closure in Aboriginal religious systems and the mobilisation of hierarchy in Western Desert societies. This hierarchy was manifest both in gender relations favouring male dominance and in same-sex ritual hierarchies and the division of labour. Both male and female ritual status hierarchies in Mardu society are religiously validated and contribute vitally to the successful prosecution of the complex of religious events that dominate big meetings. However, they do not override kinship, they do not spill over into other arenas of life, and their processual activation is temporary, though structurally, of course, they endure. The gap between the conditions for domination and its sociopolitical realisation on the ground was at times leapt, but never bridged.

Acknowledgements

For their helpful comments on an earlier draft of this manuscript, I thank Myrna Tonkinson and Laurent Dousset.

Notes

1. The term 'tradition-oriented' is an imperfect attempt to typify peoples for whom continuities with the pre-European past still play a more powerful role than Western elements in framing Aboriginal worldview, dominant values, and social structures; cf. Berndt and Berndt 1988: 515–32; Morphy 1998: 7.
2. Ethnomusicologist Richard Moyle (1979, 1997) reports a similar dichotomy elsewhere in the Western Desert, among the Pintipu on the eastern side and the people of Balgo to the north, both of whose musical lives share much in common with that of the Mardu.
3. With reference to the Western Desert Pitjantjatjara, Ellis (1984: 151) notes that 'a person ... dreams that he or she is rising to dance and sing. The dreamer must "catch" (learn) the song and dance and, once awake, can teach it to everyone.'

4. Catherine Berndt (1950: 27) reports one Northern Australian case that is the gendered reverse of this: a male diviner-curer had a dream concerning a women's ritual, which 'he passed on to the women as being their rightful property'.
5. Writing of Warlpiri iconography, Munn (1973: 113) describes the notion that ancestral designs originate in dream experiences as fundamental to Warlpiri thought, and suggests that such dreams entail the 'rerunning' of daily experience under the guise of ancestral experience. The imperative that such dream experiences be reproduced in the waking world and observed by others suggests to Munn (1973: 226) the importance of binding 'the inner self to the external social order'. From the accounts of both men and women, Munn (1973: 114, fn) gained the strong impression that 'the dreamer felt himself to be both a kind of observer of the events of the dream and at the same time an actor in the dream, identified with the ancestors'. This kind of identification accords strongly with the situation of the Mardu dancer while within the performance frame.
6. Speaking of this denial of their own cultural achievements as a kind of false consciousness, Maddock (1972: 129) describes Aborigines as being 'passive recipients of unmotivated gifts' from the spiritual realm, and concludes that 'As men deny the creativity which is truly theirs, they can account for their culture only by positing that to create is to be other than human. To be human is to reproduce forms.' In a similar vein, Clunies Ross (1987: 5) remarks that 'in keeping with their belief that creativity resides in the Dreamtime powers, Aborigines ascribe the creation of song and other artistic forms to ancestral beings rather than to men and women of the present age'.
7. The extent to which individual song 'composers' are able to retain control over their compositions and use them in ways that benefit them personally, tangibly or intangibly, would, of course, vary in Aboriginal Australia. Compared with data on corporate ownership of songs and other ritual 'property', and on interdependence as the structural basis of Aboriginal religious life, very little has been written on notions of individual ownership.
8. One scholar who has focused specifically on the creativity–power nexus in Aboriginal Australian song is von Sturmer (1987); he rightly notes that the literature is weak on processes linking the acquisition of power to access to songs and other ritual items. Having posed the question: is it the singer or the song? (p. 65), he then addresses it using ethnographic data from the western Cape York Peninsula in north Queensland. Predictably, the complex interplay of ecological, social and political factors militates against any firm answer, and while many songs refer to places, 'there is no clear evidence that they thereby come under the control or ownership of those people who control those sites' (p. 68). His suggestion is that, in those parts of the region where political structures transcend considerations of clan or estate identity, song and dance specialisation will reflect these structures; put differently, 'a performance virtuosity in ritual contexts will reflect and legitimate supremacy in the political arena' (p. 73).

References

Barnard, A. and J. Woodburn 1988. 'Introduction'. In: *Hunters and Gatherers, Vol.1: Property, Power and Ideology*, eds T. Ingold, D. Riches and J. Woodburn. Oxford, pp. 4–31.

Bern, J. 1979. 'Ideology and Domination: Toward a Reconstruction of Australian Aboriginal Social Formation', *Oceania*, 50: 118–32.

Berndt, C.H. 1950. *Women's Changing Ceremonies in Northern Australia*. Paris.

—— 1965. 'Women and the "secret life"'. In: *Aboriginal Man in Australia*, eds R.M. and C.H. Berndt. Sydney, pp. 238–82.

Berndt, R.M. 1970. 'Traditional Morality as Expressed Through the Medium of an Australian Aboriginal Religion'. In: *Australian Aboriginal Anthropology*, ed. R.M. Berndt, Perth, pp. 216–47.

—— 1974. *Australian Aboriginal Religion*, 4 fascicles, Leiden.

Berndt, R.M and C.H. 1988. *The World of the First Australians*. Canberra.

Clunies Ross, M. 1987. 'Research into Aboriginal Songs: the State of the Art'. In: Songs of Aboriginal Australia (*Oceania Monograph* 32), eds M. Clunies Ross, T. Donaldson and S.A. Wild. Sydney, pp. 1–13.

Dussart, F. 2000. *The Politics of Ritual in an Aboriginal Settlement: Kinship, Gender, and the Currency of Knowledge*. Washington.
Elkin, A.P. 1977. *Aboriginal Men of High Degree*. St Lucia.
Ellis, C.J. 1984. 'Time Consciousness of Aboriginal Performers'. In: *Problems and Solutions: Occasional Essays in Musicology presented to Alice M. Moyle*, eds J.C. Kassler and J. Stubington. Sydney, pp. 149–85.
Endicott, K. 1988. 'Property, Power and Conflict among the Batek of Malaysia'. In: *Hunters and Gatherers, Vol. 1: Property, Power and Ideology*, eds T. Ingold, D. Riches and J. Woodburn. Oxford, pp. 110–27.
Gardner, P. 1991. 'Foragers' Pursuit of Individual Autonomy', *Current Anthropology*, 32: 543–72.
Hiatt, L.R. 1986. *Aboriginal Political Life*. Canberra.
Kapferer, B. 1979. 'Introduction: Ritual Process and the Transformation of Context', *Social Analysis*, 1: 3–19 (Special Issue: The Power of Ritual: Transition, Transformation and Transcendence in Ritual Practice, ed. B. Kapferer).
Keen, I. 1988. 'Yolngu Religious Property'. In: *Hunters and Gatherers, Vol. 1: Property, Power and Ideology*, eds T. Ingold, D. Riches and J. Woodburn. Oxford, pp. 272–91.
—— 1994. *Knowledge and Secrecy in an Aboriginal Religion*. Oxford.
Kelly, R.L. 1995. *The Foraging Spectrum: Diversity in Hunter-Gatherer Lifeways*. Washington.
Lee, R. 1993. *The Dobe Ju/'hoansi*, 2nd edn. Fort Worth.
Maddock, K. 1972. *The Australian Aborigines: A Portrait of their Society*. London.
Meggitt, M.J. 1962. *Desert People*. Sydney.
Morphy, H. 1988. 'The Resurrection of the Hydra: Twenty Five Years of Research on Aboriginal Religion'. In: *Social Anthropology and Australian Aboriginal Studies*, eds R.M. Berndt and R. Tonkinson. Canberra, pp. 241–66.
—— 1998. *Aboriginal Art*. London.
Mountford, C.P. 1981. *Aboriginal Conception Beliefs*. Melbourne.
Moyle, R. 1979. *Songs of the Pintupi: Musical Life of a Central Australian Society*. Canberra.
1997. *Balgo: The Musical Life of a Desert Community*. Nedlands.
Munn, N.D. 1973. *Walbiri Iconography: Graphic Representation and Cultural Symbolism in a Central Australian Society*. Ithaca.
Stanner, W.E.H. 1958. 'The Dreaming'. In: *Reader in Comparative Religion*, eds W.A. Lessa and E.Z. Vogt. New York, pp. 513–25.
—— 1965 'Religion, Totemism and Symbolism'. In: *Aboriginal Man in Australia*, eds R.M. and C.H. Berndt. Sydney, pp. 207–37.
—— 1966. 'On Aboriginal Religion', *Oceania Monograph,* 11, Sydney. (Reprinted as *Oceania Monograph* 36 (1989), with Appreciation and Introduction.)
von Sturmer, J. 1987. 'Aboriginal Singing and Notions of Power'. In: Songs of Aboriginal Australia (*Oceania Monograph* 32), eds M. Clunies Ross, T. Donaldson and S.A. Wild. Sydney, pp. 63–76.
Tonkinson, R. 1970. 'Aboriginal Dream-Spirit Beliefs in a Contact Situation'. In: *Australian Aboriginal Anthropology*, ed. R.M. Berndt. Perth, pp. 277–91.
—— 1974. *The Jigalong Mob: Aboriginal Victors of the Desert Crusade*. Menlo Park.
—— 1982. 'Outside the Power of the Dreaming: Paternalism and Permissiveness in an Aboriginal Settlement'. In: *Aboriginal Power in Australian Society*, ed. M.C. Howard. St Lucia, pp. 115–30.
—— 1984 'Semen Versus Spirit-Child in a Western Desert Culture'. In: *Australian Aboriginal Concepts*, ed. L.R. Hiatt. Canberra, pp. 81–92.
—— 1988a. 'Ideology and Domination' in Aboriginal Australia: a Western Desert Test Case'. In: *Hunters and Gatherers, Vol. 1: Property, Power and Ideology*, eds T. Ingold, D. Riches and J. Woodburn. Oxford, pp. 170–84.
—— 1988b 'Egalitarianism and Inequality in a Western Desert Culture', *Anthropological Forum*, 5, 4: 545–58.
—— 1988c 'One Community, Two Laws: Aspects of Conflict and Convergence in a Western Australian Aboriginal Settlement'. In: *Indigenous Law and the State*, eds B. Morse and G. Woodman. Dordrecht, pp. 395–411.

—— 1991. *The Mardu Aborigines: Living the Dream in Australia's Desert*, 2nd edn. Fort Worth.
—— 1993 'Understanding "Tradition" – Ten Years On', *Anthropological Forum* 6, 4: 597–606.
—— 1996 'The Dynamics of Aboriginal Identity in Remote Australia'. *Anthropological Notebooks,* 11, 1: 27–42. (Special Issue: Multiple Identities, ed. B. Telban).
—— 1999 'The Pragmatics and Politics of Aboriginal Tradition and Identity in Australia', *Journal de la Société des Océanistes,* 109, 2: 133–47. (Special Issue: Les Politiques de la tradition: identités nationales et identités culturelles dans le Pacifique, ed. A. Babadzan).
Trigger, D.S. 1992. *Whitefella Comin': Aboriginal Responses to Colonialism in Northern Australia.* Cambridge.
Turner, V. 1967. *The Forest of Symbols.* Ithaca.
—— 1969. *The Ritual Process.* Chicago.
Widlok, T. 1997. 'Traditions of Transformation: Travelling Rituals in Australia'. In: *Cultural Dynamics of Religious Change in Oceania,* eds T. Otto and A. Borsboom. Leiden, pp. 11–22.
Wild, S.A. 1987. 'Recreating the *Jukurrpa*: Adaptation and Innovation of Songs and Ceremonies in Warlpiri Society. In: Songs of Aboriginal Australia (*Oceania Monograph* 32), eds M. Clunies Ross, T. Donaldson and S.A. Wild. Sydney, pp. 97–120.
Woodburn, J. 1980. 'Hunters and Gatherers Today and Reconstruction of the Past'. In: *Soviet and Western Anthropology,* ed. E. Gellner. London, pp. 795–815.
—— 1982. 'Egalitarian Societies', Man, 17: 431–51.

3

Knowledge about Plant Medicine and Practice among the Ituri Forest Foragers

Hideaki Terashima

Introduction

Roughly speaking, knowledge is classified into two categories. One is the knowledge characterised by its secrecy. Such knowledge is often concealed, mystified or combined with supernatural sanction and thus gives power to those who have access to it. For example, political leaders often claim for themselves sacred knowledge that connects them to the supreme beings, and utilise it to reinforce their power. Human relationships and social systems based on such secret knowledge cannot avoid inequality, since there is a large imbalance of power between those who have access to the secret knowledge and those who do not.

On the other hand, there is a type of knowledge that is open to the public and shared by the people. In the progress of modern sciences, such knowledge has played a very important role. This type of knowledge can be passed from one person to another, diffused, examined, affirmed or revised and accumulated as the common heritage of the whole society. Knowledge open to the public is important not only in natural sciences but also in social relationships. In modern democracies, the disclosure of information is one of the most important procedures. By getting accurate information, people can properly participate in the decision-making process and play their part in the political field. Where a country is ruled by a dictator, not only is the disclosure of information very limited, but false information is often given to the public.

The foragers living in the Ituri forest of the Democratic Republic of Congo (formerly Zaire) are in general called Pygmies. They are divided into two groups. One group is called *Mbuti* and lives in the southern part of the forest with the Bira farmers, speaking Bira as their mother tongue. The other group, called *Efe*, lives in the northern and eastern part of the forest with the Lese farmers, speaking Lese as their mother tongue. Both groups have a very similar lifestyle apart from the language and certain methods of hunting. They are known to be great naturalists, having an extensive knowledge of the surrounding environment. In this paper I would like to look into the ethnobotanical knowledge of Ituri foragers and show how their knowledge about the plant world, especially plant medicine and treatment, is related to their egalitarian social relationships.

Property and Knowledge among the Ituri Forest Foragers

Property Owned by the Ituri Foragers

The Ituri foragers have an immediate-return social system and, consequently, fairly egalitarian social relationships. Like other immediate-return societies, Ituri forest foragers have only limited personal property. They cannot own personal property beyond their immediate necessities; not because of poverty, but because there are mechanisms which prevent people from accumulating an excess of property.

As movable property, they have clothes, cooking utensils, tools for subsistence activities such as spears, bows and arrows, hunting nets, axes, knives and machetes. They do not own more of these things than they need. If someone possesses those things beyond what he/she needs (such a situation is not so common) they have to give them to others. If he/she does not do so, it will without fail bring reproach from others. Moreover, the borrowing and lending of things such as clothes, cooking utensils, knives and axes is quite common behaviour.

Each residential group of Ituri foragers, generally called a *band*, has a patch of the forest as their own territory. It usually extends along a path in the forest with the width of a few kilometres on both sides. Within this territory, the band migrates freely and forages throughout the year. The boundary of the territory is not very rigid. A band can move into another band's territory and dwell there for a while with the other's approval.

Resources in the forest are not appropriated by anybody until they are actually hunted or gathered. The only exception is the case of honey. When someone finds a hive of honeybees in a tree, he/she folds down a thin tree nearby as a sign of ownership of the honey in the hive. Nobody can collect this without the permission of the owner.

Food brought back to the camp has to be distributed among the camp members. Precious food especially, such as meat and honey, should be carefully distributed in order not to make anybody in the camp feel disappointed.

Meat sharing is one of the strongest social norms of the Ituri foragers and its violation may lead to serious conflict among the band members.

Various Kinds of Knowledge Shared by the Ituri Foragers

As intangible property of the Ituri foragers we can mention various kinds of knowledge related to subsistence activities and the natural world, including the plants and animals, medicines, rituals, symbols, dances and songs and so on. Here I offer a quick look at some of these kinds of knowledge.

Knowledge about Subsistence Activities

All Ituri foragers have sufficient knowledge and skills in subsistence activities. There are no specialists for ordinary activities. Although there are differences in the results of their activities among individuals, this is never actually mentioned and it makes no difference in everyday life.

Elephant hunting is an exceptional activity conducted only by specialists. Spearing an elephant is not an easy matter. It is quite dangerous but the reward is enormous. Although almost all Pygmy men are good hunters in bow-and-arrow or net hunting, only a few persons in each band can spear an elephant. Success in elephant hunting depends on a good combination of knowledge, hunting skill, courage and good luck. Elephant hunting demands knowledge of the behaviour and ecology of the elephant, but it is a matter of experience and not esoteric knowledge. Magic medicine for elephant hunting is used sometimes, but is actually not so important.

Specialists in elephant hunting are sometimes called *tuma* and their ability is recognised in the local community, including the neighbouring farmers. But this does not mean the elephant hunters acquire any special status or authority in everyday life. The elephant hunters never boast about their ability or courage. They always stay modest while the others around them show great excitement and joy. It is quite dangerous for hunters to gain in social status. People will certainly deny such authority to hunters.

Knowledge about subsistence activities is shared by all members of the society. There is no profit in keeping such knowledge secret since there is an obligation to share meat among all the band members. It makes no sense to hunt or collect more than the others using secret knowledge, if indeed such knowledge exists.

Knowledge about Religion, Supernatural Beings and Songs

Although there are some supernatural beings such as *tore* or *baketi*, no systematic religious concepts or rites have developed among the Ituri foragers. There is no sacred knowledge about supernatural beings, and there are no specialists who monopolise such knowledge. Of course, older men and women know better than the young people, but that does not lead them to enhance their social status.

Songs and dances are important amusements and social performances among the Ituri foragers. They have many songs and dances that they perform whenever they want. Some songs are for good hunting, collecting honey or other subsistence activities. Others are love songs, lamentations for dead persons or songs for initiation ceremonies. One important point of their songs and dances is that most of them have derived from someone's dreams in recent decades (Sawada 2001). They explain that dead people teach songs and dances in the dreams. Those songs and dances taught by dead people through dreams are performed with little delay before a general audience and shared by all.

Knowledge about Food Restrictions
Although symbolic objects are very few in the everyday life of the Ituri foragers, some animals are associated with symbolic meanings. Restrictions on certain animals as food are one of the most important concerns among all the Ituri foragers (Ichikawa 1987; Terashima 2001). Many of the important food animals such as mammals and birds are especially associated with various kinds of consumption taboo. Some meat is prohibited to certain people on certain occasions. If someone eats prohibited meat, it may bring diseases. The meat restrictions depend on the person's social affiliation, social status, physical condition and so on. Some restrictions are unchangeable for life, and some change through the life stages of the people. Some meat is feared because it brings a severe disease, called *eke* among the Efe and *kuweri* among the Mbuti, to the children of parents who eat it. The children may suffer from high fever, convulsions and so on, and if they are unlucky they will die. Thus people always have to be careful as to their personal attributes and social status before killing animals and eating any meat. The knowledge about food restrictions is shared by all the members of the society, although the degree of observation of the restrictions may vary from person to person.

Special Knowledge and Roles Attributed to the Foragers by the Farmers
Farmers who live together with the foragers in the Ituri forest believe that the foragers have special knowledge and skills about the forest. Knowledge of medicinal plants is one of the specialities of the foragers and they are sometimes asked by the farmers to treat diseases. Farmers also ask the foragers to gather medicinal plants from the forest.

There is a magical medicine called *ndibo,* which is used for finding a sorcerer or thief. The medicine is said to make the nose of man as keen as that of the dog. The Efe are believed to be good at handling this *ndibo.* On occasion, they are asked by farmers to smell out sorcerers from the village. However, such a role for the Efe is only occasional and it is hard to say that they specialise in it. They often say that they only perform the role expected of them by the farmers, but do not believe in it much themselves.

The farmers fear encountering bad things such as ghosts and sorcerers in the forest. The foragers are also believed to know much about those things and have skills to drive away such things. So farmers often ask their Mbuti or Efe friends to accompany them when they have to go deep into the forest for trap hunting, fishing or travelling.

Certainly, the knowledge and special skills that the farmers recognise among the foragers help to increase their social status in the eyes of the farmers. The foragers, however, do not have much interest in assuming themselves to be specialists of the forest. And among their group, no Mbuti or Efe can acquire any profit or authority by pretending to such special skills and knowledge.

Knowledge and Practice of the Plant World

Here I will analyse some ethnobotanical data on plant use by the Ituri foragers. Plants play a very important role in all aspects of everyday life, such as food, material culture, medicine, ritual/magical rites and so on. Ethnobotanical surveys have been conducted among the four local groups of the Ituri forest foragers since the 1970s (Tanno 1981; Terashima et al. 1988; Terashima and Ichikawa 2003). More than 1,100 specimens were collected from over 750 species. These plants are used for material goods (372 species), ritual and magical purposes (235 species), medicine (205 species), food (123 species), poison (103 species) and so on. Some general characteristics of plant use among the Ituri foragers have already been discussed (Ichikawa and Terashima 1996). Turnbull (1965) declares that the Mbuti have no magic of witchcraft or sorcery other than very simple ones. Therefore in this paper I will focus my attention on the ritual/magical and the medicinal use of plants.

Plants Used for Ritual and Magical Purposes

As mentioned above, 235 plant species are used for ritual and magical purposes. These plants are grouped into the following six categories from (a) to (f) (the numbers in brackets denote the number of plant species used for each purpose, and some plants are grouped into more than one category):

(a) *Plants used for good luck in subsistence activities* [102 species]: for hunting and fishing [64]; for palm-wine harvest [13]; for enhancing a dog's hunting ability [11]; for honey collection [7]; for crop harvest [6]; and for wild plant harvest [1].

Quite a few plants are used for good luck in hunting and fishing. This seems to indicate not only the importance of hunting activity but also its difficulty and unpredictability. There are various ways to use plants to ensure good results in hunting or fishing. Some plants are tied on the nets for net hunting and others are put into a fire and hunters expose themselves to the smoke or put the ashes to their face. The plants used for a good palm-wine harvest and for a crop harvest seem to have originated from the farmers.

(b) *Plants used for protecting the human body and for maintaining health* [76 species]: for protecting children against the disease from food taboo (*eke/kuweri*) [21]; for their healthy growth [19]; for protecting the body against sorcery [12]; for protecting people against wild animals [9]; for treating illnesses in magical ways [11]; and for an easy birth [4].

Although the Ituri foragers do not distinguish magical treatment from the truly medical treatment of diseases, I distinguished between them for the purpose of analysis. Here I take it as a medical treatment only when some kind of direct treatment is applied to the body. For example, it is a medical treatment when a medicine is given to a child as a drink, and it is a magical treatment when only a charm is hung from the waist. Many plants are used for children. This seems to indicate the anxiety parents have for their children. Plants used for protection from sorcery number only 5 percent of the total species used for ritual and magical use.

(c) *Plants used for various types of magic* [52 species]: for seducing women [21]; for preventing theft in the fields [14]; for stopping rain [10]; for preventing misfortune such as a slip of the tongue [4]; and for increasing physical ability such as walking and fighting [3].

(d) *Plants related to sorcery* [18 species]: among the plants used for sorcery, many are used for making a cursing pipe called *singbe* among the Efe. This knowledge may have been derived from the farmers. Knowledge about sorcery is likely to be concealed and it is difficult to collect accurate information. Judging from other evidence it seems clear that the Ituri foragers have rather little interest in sorcery. They often mention that sorcery is the work of the farmers and not of themselves.

(e) *Plants used for initiation ceremonies* [14 species]: the initiation ceremony for boys is called *kumbi* and that for girls is called *ima*. Usually Ituri foragers hold those ceremonies with the farmers whom they associate with.

(f) *Taboo plants* [12 species]: some plants are believed to do harm to man and animals when they are damaged. Among those plants is the *akobishi* (*Uvariopsis congolana* (De Wild.) R. E. Fr.), a small tree of the Annonaceae family. Throughout the Ituri forest, a very strong taboo is attached to this tree.

In summary, in the category of ritual and magical use, it is clear that a considerable number of plants are used positively for a better livelihood, and rather few plants are used for negative purposes such as cursing and sorcery. Although it is too early to arrive at any definite conclusion, at least we can see the positive and practical attitude of the Ituri foragers to the life here. The immediate-return production system and their optimistic view of life may have something to do with this. Egalitarian social relationships surely support such an attitude.

Plants Used as Medicine

In this section I describe the medical treatment of the Ituri foragers and the characteristics of the knowledge about plant medicine and treatment among them.

Number of Treatments

I employ the concept of 'treatment' to analyse the characteristics of medical practice among the Ituri foragers. Here I define treatment as composed of the combination of the following six factors: (a) the species of medicinal plant, (b) the part of plant used as medicine (i.e. leaf, root, bark), (c) the form of medicine (i.e. decoction, powder, paste), (d) the method of administering the medicine (i.e. drink, eat, spread), (e) the kind of disease and (f) the local groups. Any treatment different in at least one of these factors from another treatment is considered a different treatment. In total 205 plants are used for 370 treatments.

Diseases Treated with Plant Medicine

The diseases treated with plant medicine are grouped into the following twelve categories. Diseases which have many treatments in each category are mentioned with the number of treatments in brackets.

(a) *gastrointestinal diseases* [67 treatments in total] : stomach and intestinal disorders [20], stomach-ache [19], diarrhoea [18];
(b) *pains* [46 treatments]: headache [14], chest pain [9], toothache [6];
(c) *skin diseases* [43 treatments]: ulcers [30], eczema/scabies [13];
(d) *wounds* [37 treatments]: general cuts [16], cuts by animals [10], cuts by circumcision [9];
(e) *tonic and health promotion* [31 treatments]: tonic for sexual ability [9], tonic for general purposes [8], health promotion for children [8];
(f) *eke/kuweri* [26 treatments in total]: *eke* [15], *kuweri* [11];
(g) *respiratory diseases* [25 treatments]: sore throat and coughs [22];
(h) *anal and venereal diseases* [21 treatments]: haemorrhoids [11], venereal diseases [10];
(i) *childbirth and nursing* [20 treatments]: delivery [9], abortion [6];
(j) *fever* [16 treatments]: various kinds of fever;
(k) *head disorder* [15 treatments]: dizziness [4], mental disorder [2];
(l) *others* [23 treatments]: heart disease, hernia, leprosy, and so on.

The number of treatments seems to indicate the prevalence of that disease and the degree of interest shown by Ituri foragers in it. Most of the diseases with many treatments mentioned above are quite common in everyday life. The symptoms are usually apparent and are easily recognisable. For the first step of the treatment, usually only the symptoms are taken into consideration and no further pursuit of the nature of the disease is carried out. Although *eke/kuweri* is a culture-bound disease and may seem to be difficult to understand in the context of modern medicine, it is not uncommon. The symptoms, such as high fever and convulsion, sometimes happen among children. People suspect *kuweri* first when children show such symptoms.

Plant Parts Used as Medicine
The parts of the plants used as medicine are grouped into seven categories: (a) leaves and soft stems [126]; (b) bark [87]; (c) root [64]; (d) fruits and flowers [28]; (e) sap and resin [26]; (f) vine-stems and wood [13]; and (g) seeds [11].
  The three most frequent, leaves, bark and root, cover nearly 80 percent of total treatments. The concentration of medicinal use of plants into those three parts may be ascribed to the pattern of distribution of medicinal substance in the plants.

Forms of Medicine
The forms of medicine are grouped into seven categories: (a) decoction and infusion [104]; (b) usage without processing [79]; (c) charcoal and ash powder [62]; (d) sap [43]; (e) dried bark and root powder [41]; (f) paste [17]; and (g) smoke [5].
  Nearly half of the medicines are given in the form of liquid such as a decoction an infusion or as sap. Decoction/infusion is the most common way to administer plant medicine in most medical care systems such as Chinese medicine and Western herbal medicine. It is noteworthy that in nearly a quarter of treatments the plants are used as medicine without processing. Raw leaves are applied to injured parts, sap is drunk directly and roots are chewed raw. These simple ways of medicine use are useful when there is no means to process the medicine, particularly in a case of emergency in the forest. Smoke is a unique form of medicine. The patient is exposed to the smoke of burnt medicinal plants. Sometimes the vapour of boiled water containing medical plants is used as well, but such treatments are not very common.

Methods of Administrating Medicine
The methods of administrating medicine are grouped into ten categories: (a) drinking [74]; (b) smearing [53]; (c) *chanja* [52]; (d) dropping into eyes, nose or ears [39]; (e) bathing/washing [35]; (f) covering/rubbing with [30]; (g) licking/swallowing [23]; (h) eating/chewing [20]; (i) enema [14]; and (j) suppository [9].
  Chanja is a Swahili word meaning 'to cut' or 'to divide.' This is a quite popular method for administering medicine in Central Africa. Small cuts are made around the affected area with a knife or razor blade, then medicine is rubbed into the cuts. *Chanja* is a common method for various pains. It may look strange at first, but even in modern medicine we usually smear a painkilling ointment over the aching parts. Eye, nose and ear drops are used, especially for *eke/kuweri*, and to children who have fallen into coma. Bloodletting is a fairly common treatment among many African societies, but it is rarely practised among the Ituri foragers. Drinking, smearing and *chanja* compose more than half of all treatments.

The basic idea of administering medicine among the Ituri foragers is to apply it directly to the affected areas. For example, there are three methods which are used for different types of pains. For stomach-ache, decoction or infusion of medicinal plants is usual. For chest pains medicine is rubbed into incisions at the chest. Eye drops are commonly used for headaches, but rarely for other pains.

Popular Patterns of Treatments with Plant Medicine
The parts of plants, the form of medicine and the method of administration are interrelated and make up patterns of treatments for various illnesses. Some popular patterns of treatments for each disease category are described below. Most of these treatments seem fairly appropriate even in the framework of modern medicine. For some diseases, however, there is a variety of treatments and no conspicuous patterns.

(a) *gastrointestinal disorders* [67 treatments in total]: (i) a decoction/infusion of bark, leaves, or roots is taken or sap is drunk directly [41]; (ii) a decoction/infusion of bark, leaves or sap is administered by enema [12]; and (iii) seeds and resin are licked or swallowed [6];

(b) *pains* [46]: (i) powder of roasted roots, vine-stems or leaves is administered by *chanja* or a fruit paste or leaf is applied [17]; (ii) a decoction/infusion of root, a leaf squeeze or sap is dropped into the eyes for headache in particular [12]; (iii) crumpled or slightly heated leaves are put over aching areas [7]; and (iv) bark powder or leaf or fruit paste is smeared over aching areas [5];

(c) *skin diseases* [43]: (i) powder of bark or roots, or their ashes, fruit-paste or fruit-juice are spread over infected areas [17]; (ii) raw leaves are put over the infected area [9]; (iii) ashes of vine-stems or leaves are applied by *chanja* to the infected area [6]; and (iv) leaf decoction or infusion is given as a wash to the infected area or the patient is exposed to the smoke of burning vine-stems [6];

(d) *wounds* [37]: (i) bark or root-powder is spread over or leaf-paste or liquid is applied to the wounds [29]; and (ii) raw leaves are put over the wounds [4];

(e) *tonic and health promotion* [31]: (i) leaf or bark decoction/infusion, or liquid from a squeezed leaf is used as a wash to the body [10], (ii) root-powder is administered by *chanja* [5]; (iii) raw roots are chewed, or chipped roots or bark is mixed with food and eaten [5]; and (iv) bark decoction or sap is drunk [4];

(f) *eke/kuweri* [26]: (i) leaf-squeeze is dropped into the eyes or bark-powder is blown into the nose [9]; (ii) leaf decoction/infusion is used as a wash or the patient is exposed to the smoke of leaves [7]; and (iii) leaf-powder is given by *chanja* [4];

(g) *respiratory diseases* [25]: (i) powder of bark, roots, seeds or leaves is licked or seeds are swallowed [12]; (ii) bark decoction/infusion is drunk [7];

(h) *anal and venereal diseases* [21]: (i) bark or leaf decoction/infusion is drunk [6]; and (ii) powdered bark or root is put into the anus as a suppository [5];
(i) *childbirth, nursing and abortion* [20]: (i) bark or root decoction/infusion is drunk [7]; and (ii) leaf or root powder is applied by *chanja* [5];
(j) *fever* [16]: (i) leaf decoction is taken as a wash [3]; and (ii) fruit-juice is administered by *chanja* [3];
(k) *head disorders* [15]: (i) liquid from squeezed flowers or buds, bark decoction or sap is dropped into the eyes, nose, or ears [8]; and (ii) the aching parts are rubbed with raw leaves [4].

Summary and Discussion

Characteristics of Plant Medicine and Treatment among the Ituri Foragers

From the data mentioned above, the following characteristics of the medical treatments among the Ituri foragers can be noted:

- Many of the diseases treated with plant medicine are common in the everyday life of Ituri foragers. They have rather simple symptoms and these diseases are also familiar to us, except for a few diseases such as *eke/kuweri*.
- Symbolism concerning plant medicine is rather rare. People think the effectiveness of medicine derives almost entirely from the plants themselves and not from symbolic features such as the names, forms or legends connected with the plants.
- Many medicinal plants are used alone and the mixture of plants is not common.
- The basic idea of administering medicine is to apply it directly to the affected parts.
- Plants are processed into medicine by decocting, infusing, pounding, grinding, and so on. However, a fair number of plants are used without any processing.
- Most administration methods are found in modern medical practice, but there are some exceptions. *Chanja* may appear rather strange for us, but understandable nevertheless.
- There are popular patterns of treatment for various diseases, covering more than half of the total treatments. Those patterns are quite acceptable even in the context of modern medicine.
- There are multiple medicinal plants and treatments for most diseases. This helps people in finding appropriate medicinal treatment easily.

From the ideas and practices of the plant medicine and treatment depicted above, it seems clear that the Ituri foragers have fairly scientific and naturalistic attitudes towards diseases, plant medicine and treatment. Their treatment does not involve any esoteric knowledge, but is largely based on observation and practice.

Diversity of Plant Medicine and Treatment

It has already been pointed out that a large variation in plant use is found among the four local Ituri forager groups. For example, more than half the food plants collected in one group are not considered as food in another group (Ichikawa and Terashima 1996). That seems rather curious at first because we tend to think that whether something is edible or inedible is a very simple matter and the answer should be the same everywhere. Of course plants considered as major food are commonly recognised as food anywhere, but minor items are subject to rather different judgements about whether they are food or non food among each local group.

Here I compare the similarities and differences in medicinal plant use among the four local groups, of which two belong to the Mbuti and the other two belong to the Efe. Among the 205 plants recognised as medicine, 36 species are used in more than two groups. The remaining 169 species are used only in one group. Among the common 36 species, 4 species are used among all four groups, 7 species among three groups and 25 species among two groups. The commonality of plant use for medicine is apparently quite low. Moreover, even the commonly used plants are not necessarily used in the same way in different groups.

Table 3.1. Similarity index of medicinal plant use

Similarity index*	Same language group	Different language group
3	9 species	1 species
2	1 species	3 species
1	2 species	3 species
0	1 species	5 species

* 3: highly similar use, 2: fairly similar use, 1: slightly similar use, 0: completely different use

Table 3.1 shows the similarity of treatment concerning plants commonly used in two groups. The results are shown respectively for the cases when the two groups belong to the same language group and when they belong to a different language group. The similarity index '3' indicates that the common plant is used in almost the same way between the two groups. The similarity index '2' shows that there is a small difference in treatment, that is, except for a few points the plant is used in almost the same way. When the similarity index is '1', it means there is only a slight resemblance in treatment. When it is '0', it means that the common plant is used in a completely different way in the two groups.

It can be seen in Table 3.1 that many common plants are used in a similar way in the same language group. On the contrary, in the different language groups, even common plants are not likely to be used in a similar way.

However, even in the same language group, sometimes different treatments are practised, while even in a different language group some sort of similarity exists.

The quite low commonality of medicinal plant use and the diversity of treatment among the local groups illustrate the status of medical knowledge among the Ituri foragers. Some factors seem to be relevant here. First, there are no specialists or authorities that control the knowledge and practice of plant medicine among the Ituri foragers. From the diagnosis of the disease, selection of plants for medicine, preparation of the medicine and its administration are activities carried out by anyone who has even a little knowledge. So people have many opportunities to accumulate their own ideas on treatment. Moreover, the effectiveness of plant medicine is not always the same. It can vary depending on many natural factors such as the growth stage of the plant, soil fertility, sunshine, humidity and so on. The method of preparation influences the efficacy of the medicine. The status of the patient has also much to do with the matter. People often have to adjust the usual method and try different treatments to obtain desirable results. Treatment of the diseases is thus tried, tested, revised or newly invented continuously in the experience and practice of various people. So, variation of treatment together with the adaptive approach is common in this traditional medical care system.

Comparison of the Medical Care of the Ituri Foragers and the Tongwe Farmers

In the medical care system of the Ituri foragers, most treatments are based on a common knowledge of medicinal plants and on methods that are usually open to the public and shared by all group members. There are no specialists among the Ituri foragers today. Everyone has similar knowledge about the plant world, including medicinal plants. Of course some people know more than others, but that difference has few social consequences.

Among many other traditional African societies, however, medical care systems are usually more complicated. There exists a specialist called a shaman, medicine-man, herbalist or healer, who takes charge of medical treatment in the local community. The knowledge of specialists usually involves a lot of secrets and treatment is accompanied by many symbolic meanings. What is the cause of the difference between the Ituri foragers and these other societies? Here I would like to take the case of the Tongwe farmers who live in the woodland of west Tanzania in order to illustrate by comparison the characteristics of the medical system and social relationships of Ituri foragers.

According to Kakeya (1977), the Tongwe farmers live in a vast woodland with a very low population density, the size of a village ranging from five to forty persons at most. They change fields every year and move the village frequently. In addition to shifting cultivation, they conduct fishing, hunting and gathering. About 270 plants are considered as medicine and used for about a hundred diseases. Although medical specialists called *mufumo* know a lot about various medicines, ordinary people also know of many plant medicines that can be used to treat various symptoms. For explaining the characteristics of the Tongwe treatment, Kakeya picks five diseases: stomach-ache, headache, wound, eczema on the foot and venereal disease. In total, sixty-three medicinal plants are used for these five diseases. The methods of treatment can be grouped into the following nine kinds: (a) giving a decoction as an enema; (b) drinking a decoction; (c) chewing the raw medicinal plant; (d) washing the affected area with a decoction; (e) spreading a paste medicine; (f) rubbing powder into the affected part (*chanja*); (g) spreading charcoal powder on the affected part; (h) applying charcoal powder by *chanja*; and (i) covering the affected part with raw plant. Roots, bark and leaves are most frequently used as medicine. Fruit, seeds and wood are rarely used.

Popular treatments for the diseases mentioned are as follows: (a) for stomach-ache, a decoction is given as an enema in most treatments; (b) for headache, charcoal powder is applied by *chanja*; (c) for wounds, paste or powder of the plant medicine is applied; (d) for eczema on the foot, called *lutanga*, powdered charcoal is applied; and (e) for a venereal disease called *nsembe* an infusion of a medicinal plant is drunk.

The medicinal plants used among the Tongwe are not the same as those used in Ituri, but there are many similarities in the patterns of treatment, the forms of medicine, the methods of administration and also the parts of plants used as medicine. It is impossible to ascribe the similarity to a diffusion of knowledge between the two groups. At the same time it does not seem to be a mere coincidence. I think the similarity should be seen as a kind of natural convergence of two different medical systems.

Like the Ituri foragers, the Tongwe farmers are quite familiar with the plant world through various subsistence activities, and they have a broad knowledge about plants. Although there are medical care specialists in Tongwe society, people usually try to treat the illness by themselves since it is expensive to be treated by specialists. The diagnosis of the disease is at first via the symptoms and they treat the symptoms directly like the Ituri foragers. The methods of preparing and administering medicines are natural and simple. Given these conditions, it may not be so strange that similar treatment systems have developed in both groups, at least for primary care. This is the world of experience and practice where people share the same medicine plants and methods. Kakeya (1991) writes that Tongwe society shares many characteristics of the delayed-return system or even the immediate-return system of hunting and gathering societies. In their treatments the Tongwe may share many characteristics with the Ituri foragers.

There is, however, a sharp difference between the Ituri foragers and the Tongwe farmers after the stage of primary care. The Tongwe believe that all misfortunes have supernatural causes, such as the spirits of ancestors, wild animals and so on. Of course, all diseases are not considered to be related to supernatural causes. The Tongwe do not worry too much about common diseases such as stomach-ache or fever, only treating them with plants as described above. Special treatments, however, are considered necessary for serious diseases that linger and become worse. It is then that they draw on a *mufumo* (shaman).

The treatment by the *mufumo* consists of three types: (a) treatment of a bad agent, which hides itself in the patient's body and causes the disease; (b) treatment against the ultimate cause of the disease, that is, a supernatural agent; and (c) treatment of the symptoms of the disease. Those affecting agents must be detected by magical methods, after which treatments for them are conducted through ritual performances. During such performances, a lot of symbolic medicines, including *sikomelo*, which is made from animal or inorganic material, are used. Such symbolic medicines and their uses are usually kept secret by the *mufumo*. The last part of treatment is practical care to ease the actual ailment, just like primary care treatment (Kakeya 1977).

To seek a supernatural agent as an ultimate cause of the disease is a common attitude among African agricultural societies (Evans-Pritchard 1976). The relationship between a misfortune and its ultimate cause can be revealed only by magical means provided by the specialists who have the necessary secret knowledge. Among the Ituri foragers, their main concern is not about supernatural causes, but about medical treatment of symptoms.

The Ituri foragers' lack of interest in witchcraft or related areas apparently has to do with their immediate-return social system. Such a system undoubtedly decreases the possibility of inequality in property and status among people, things which could lead to envy, curses and sorcery. Also they have only very vague ideas about supernatural beings who could exert a strong influence on their lives. Their view of disease is simple and naturalistic. It is not surprising that they do not need an elaborate system of supernatural causation, which requires special treatments beyond the simple systems of medical treatment. Cavalli-Sforza (1986: 418) rightly comments that 'Pygmies are great observers of natural phenomena. Their ability as systematists of plants and animals matches that of trained specialists, and one can perhaps extend a similar confidence to their observations on diseases or causes of death.'

But the Ituri foragers sometimes also suffer from serious diseases. How do they cope in such cases? Here I would suggest just one thing, that is, communal treatment. The common style of treatment where a doctor diagnoses and treats the patient is, so to speak, a personal treatment. Self-diagnosis and self-treatment also belong to this type. In personal treatment, the patient faces up to the disease and fights it alone. In communal treatment, not only the patient, but also the family members, relatives, friends and neighbours attend the treatment. Healing dances performed by the San and Pygmy hunter-gatherers seem to be a typical feature of this treatment. Not only persons with special knowledge or experience attend the dance, but all the people participate as dancers, singers and audience. The whole community contributes to the treatment.

And this communal treatment seems to have a different and important purpose to that of personal treatment. In agricultural societies, the final causes that bring bad diseases usually derive from deterioration in human relationships and conflicts among relatives or community members. Such bad relationships lead to the anger of the ancestral spirits or supreme beings and bring misfortune to men. Many treatments with magical or symbolic procedures among the Tongwe farmers and other people work to repair those conflicts in human relationships. The healing dances of the hunter-gatherers play the same role, not in the context of magical procedures but in the context of communal treatment. It is not only the treatment of the patient, but also an occasion for reassuring good human relationships and for recovering solidarity within the community. It is the power of human relationships, so to speak, that heals the patients.

Acknowledgement

The ethnobotanical data on which this paper is based were collected with the collaboration of my colleagues. Here I would like to express my sincerest thanks to Dr T. Tanno (Hirosaki University), Dr M. Ichikawa (Kyoto Univerisity), and Dr M. Sawada (Kyoto Seika University) for their generosity in permitting me to use the data freely.

References

Cavalli-Sforza, L.L. 1986. 'African Pygmies: An Evaluation of the State of Research'. In: L.L. Cavalli-Sforza (ed.), *African Pygmies*, pp. 361–426. Academic Press.

Evans-Pritchard, E.E. 1976. *Witchcraft, Oracles, and Magic among the Azande*. Oxford: Oxford University Press.

Ichikawa, M. 1987. 'Food Restrictions of the Mbuti Pygmies, Eastern Zaire'. *African Study Monographs*, supplement. no. 6: 97–121.

Ichikawa, M. and H. Terashima 1996. 'Cultural Diversity in the Use of Plants by Mbuti Hunter-Gatherers in Northeastern Zaire: An Ethnobotanical Approach'. In S. Kent (ed.), *Cultural Diversity among Twentieth-Century Foragers*, pp. 276–93. Cambridge: Cambridge University Press.

Kakeya, M. 1977. 'The World of Witch-doctor among the Tongwe' (in Japanese). In J. Itani and R. Harako (eds), *Natural History of Mankind*, pp. 377–440. Tokyo: Yuzankaku.

—— 1991. 'Between Equality and Inequality: Mwami System among the Tongwe' (in Japanese). In J. Tanaka and M. Kakeya (eds), *Natural History of Man*, pp. 59–88. Tokyo: Heibonsha.

Sawada, M. 2001. 'Rethinking Methods and Concepts of Anthropological Studies on African Pygmies' World View: the Creator-God and the Dead'. *African Study Monographs*, supplement. no. 27: 29–42.

Tanno, T. 1981. 'Plant utilization of the Mbuti Pygmies: with Special Reference to Their Material Culture and Use of Wild Vegetable Foods'. *African Study Monographs*, 1: 1–53.

Terashima, H. 2001. 'The Relationships among Plants, Animals and Man in the African Tropical Rain Forest'. *African Study Monographs*, supplement. no. 27: 43–60.

Terashima, H. and M. Ichikawa 2003. 'A Comparative Ethnobotany of the Mbuti and Efe Hunter-Gatherers in the Ituri Forest, Democratic Republic of Congo'. *African Study Monographs*, 24, 1–2: 1–168.

Terashima, H., M. Ichikawa and M. Sawada 1988. 'Wild Plant Utilization of the Balese and the Efe of the Ituri Forest, the Republic of Zaire'. *African Study Monographs*, supplement. no. 8: 1–78.

Turnbull, C.M. 1965. *Wayward Servants*. New York: Natural History Press.

4

Space-Time, Ethnicity, and the Limits of Inuit and New Age Egalitarianism

David Riches

Introduction

Egalitarian societies, as described and analysed by James Woodburn (1982), are marked by a pervasive ethic of sharing. In these societies, we are told, the economically successful provide for all others in the group, without calculation of return. People in egalitarian communities fiercely resist anyone attempting to assume an elevated status on the strength of their superior economic or political prowess. The egalitarian societies that have been most subject to study are warm-latitude peoples practising hunting and gathering. Most discussion of these peoples refers to the sharing of meat and other locally collected food. But it is clear that, to quite a large degree, personally owned durable products, for example metal-headed arrows, knives, bead necklaces, and so on, are shared as well, such that a person, when asked, will surrender the use of a particular object without expecting any direct reciprocity (e.g. Woodburn 1998: 52). Thanks to sharing people who produce food and certain other objects can expect to make these freely available to others who had no part in their production.

This, at least, is the picture for traditional hunter-gatherers. In contemporary times, however, most egalitarian hunter-gatherers are at least partially interacting with a capitalist mode of production, by engaging in commodity production or wage labour. This comes from the fact that few, if any, such societies remain unaffected, in some way or another, by the industrial world (e.g. Wenzel et al. 2000). There are also, as we shall see, examples of egalitarian societies within the Western industrial scene, where the possibility of acquiring industrially manufactured objects and money abounds. This chapter considers some theoretical questions relating to how egalitarian societies in these latter sorts of circumstance engage with such manufactured objects and money.

By and large the literature shows that the sharing of industrial objects (including money) by such people is, with some exceptions, considerably less extensive than the sharing of country food, especially outside the household. In general discussion of egalitarian societies many anthropologists interpret the egalitarian ethic as fundamentally determinant of human behaviour within the total community, and insist that this ethic moreover structures the way the people concerned engage with and make sense of the encroaching wider world. The lesser willingness to share industrial objects seems to confound this. The theoretical discussion in this chapter proposes that something fundamental underlies this apparently paradoxical state of affairs, and this has to do with the symbolic significance of industrial objects, especially as this bears on the reproduction of the distinction between ethnic groups (i.e. members of the egalitarian society versus members of the wider society with whom the former come into contact).

All this said, there is a good deal of variation among egalitarian societies concerning the extent to which industrial objects are shared. This chapter focuses on two societies that are at an extreme in this sense, in that, outside the household, such objects are barely ever shared – the Inuit community in Port Burwell settlement in the Canadian Arctic (fieldwork 1970s) and the New Age community in Glastonbury, England (fieldwork 1990s). I have shown elsewhere (Riches 2000) that these two societies, while poles apart both historically and geographically, nonetheless share remarkably similar features of both social organisation and cosmology. In this chapter, I shall continue to work with the two societies together because of their similarity regarding the treatment of industrial objects. I might add that Port Burwell, though rather small-sized, is fairly typical of Inuit settlements in Arctic Canada, but, as I shall indicate, New Age communities in Britain vary a good deal. I shall make something of this latter fact when I offer some comparative observations at the end of the chapter.

The background to all these considerations lies in a concern to develop a way to understand the relationship between an egalitarian society and the surrounding Western world. I shall argue that encapsulation is an unsatisfactory concept to depict this relationship because encapsulation smacks of power inequality, restriction and control in favour of the encapsulating society. Taking the egalitarian society's standpoint I shall rather be considering the relationship with the surrounding society as a distinctive 'mode of sociality' with regard to space-time. I shall go on to say that this distinctive mode has to be integrated with other (space-time) modes of sociality that people in the egalitarian society are experiencing. Such integration, which effectively expresses the egalitarian society as a distinct ethnic group, is accomplished by ideological notions that bridge such discrepant modes. It will be seen that in Port Burwell and in Glastonbury rather particular spacetime circumstances obtain for Inuit and New Agers. In these circumstances, I shall argue, ideological attention focuses on the provenance of industrial objects, and this is what explains the nonsharing of these things. In a final section I push the discussion about ethnicity further, and indicate that in rather different space-time circumstances, among both hunter-gatherers and New Agers, somewhat different attitudes concerning transactions of industrial goods can be expected to occur.

Egalitarianism and Nonsharing among Inuit and New Agers: the Question of Encapsulation

Port Burwell Inuit and Glastonbury New Agers in many striking respects exemplify James Woodburn's notion of immediate-return society, especially with regard to matters of social organisation (Woodburn 1982; Riches 1995, 2000). In the case of the Inuit community in Port Burwell, whose hundred or so members are all related to one another through ties of kinship and marriage, egalitarianism of outcome (Fardon 1990) is definitely a clearly enunciated and strived-for social value. It is most strikingly evident in the still-vibrant hunting sector of the economy that mostly revolves around caribou and seal hunting. Men mostly hunt in tiny groups of twos and threes, so the food-sharing ethic means that in the case of a decent-sized catch their efforts will unquestionably benefit everyone in the community. As to the New Agers in Glastonbury – a 'counter-cultural' community of some 700 Westerners attracted to live in and around the town by its internationally famous 'energies' and its pre-Christian historical associations – these people likewise have egalitarianism as an explicit social goal. Members of this Alternative Community are enjoined, without calculation of reciprocity, to give care to one another, even as each individual is permitted the 'space' to pursue their life's strategy without interference from others. Most New Agers in the town conduct pretty independent lives, but 'giving care for one another' entails that individuals willingly provide services for others in need. Thus New Age spiritual healers are expected to exercise their skills for the benefit of everyone without payment, and are strongly criticised by fellow New Agers if they charge money. These healers' gifts, other New Agers say, were granted them by the cosmos; therefore they should be dispensed freely to all. (But some healers reply that they have to obtain money somehow, and anyway they learnt their skills in long and costly apprenticeships (Prince and Riches 2000: 152).)

Inuit in Port Burwell and New Agers in Glastonbury alike organise themselves into households which function as the everyday commensal unit. These households are best characterised as nuclear family households, though some are single-parent, others have the odd additional relative, and, among the Inuit, in quite a few all members, parents and 'children', are adults. This chapter is not concerned with the pooling (sharing) of industrial objects and money within such units, which, as may be expected, definitely occurs. It rather focuses on the fact that these sorts of things are not shared between the units; accordingly for the purposes of this paper 'sharing' refers to inter-household sharing.[1] In Port Burwell, Inuit obtain industrially manufactured objects and money through selling fish, animal skins and handicrafts in the market, engaging in wage labour, and receiving government transfer payments. The pattern is almost identical to what Hovelsrud-Broda describes for Isertoq, East Greenland (2000). For example, Inuit in Port Burwell do not share processed food purchased from the settlement shop, and money never passes between households, except in gambling, which hardly proceeds according to the ethic of sharing (Riches 1975). In Glastonbury, New Agers mostly live urban lives, running their own New Age enterprises such as retail shops, or making forays into the mainstream scene to secure social security payments or casual employment. Unlike the Inuit, few New Agers are engaged in primary food production, so their nonsharing of manufactured goods and money cannot even be contrasted with their treatment of the spoils of hunting, fishing and farming.

The literature on hunter-gatherers clearly describes some sharing of industrial objects among many such peoples. Therefore Port Burwell Inuit should not be regarded as typical among egalitarian societies in their treatment of industrial objects. For example, among Australian Aborigines, Altman (1987: 160–3) describes the sharing of both cash and market goods in multi-household 'outstation communities' in rurally-remote Arnhem Land, and MacDonald (2000) speaks of the demand sharing[2] of money in urban Koori communities sited on the edges of towns and cities in New South Wales. Similarly, among the Enxet of Paraguay, on reservations purchased for them by government and missionaries, people routinely demand-share both money and durable property (Kidd 1999). Again, Axel Köhler (volume 2 of this book), discussing the Baka (Pygmies) in the Republic of Congo, indicates that in both their roadside settlements and their forest camps, whilst money is not shared, the things it buys (on the market) generally are. One gets the impression from this literature that the sharing of industrial objects and money is generally more problematic than the sharing of country food. But, given the run of egalitarian hunter-gatherers, the relative absence of it among Port Burwell Inuit would be fairly extreme.

Analytical considerations bear on the assertion that the 'sharing of industrial objects and money is generally problematic' among present-day hunter-gatherers. These have to do with the fact that these days most hunter-gatherers engage in transactions other than sharing. In the case of manufactured objects and money we must be careful not to misconstrue such transactions as sharing. For example, present-day Alaskan Inupiat whaling is a highly complex and expensive enterprise, such that to put a whale boat in the water requires input, including monetary input, from a very large range of people other than those who will captain and crew. Bodenhorn, who describes this, is careful to report that when such people are provided with a portion of whale meat *in return*, this is not 'sharing' in the usual sense; sharing is correspondingly not occurring when the money is initially provided to help the captain purchase the necessary equipment (Bodenhorn 2000). Also sharing is not taking place when, as occurs among many contemporary hunter-gatherers, people loan out manufactured items or money. 'Loans' imply a definite expectation of return, and frequently the borrower will 'gift back' a portion of any goods produced, which offsets wear and tear. Sometimes custom will declare that a loan, when requested, may not be refused but, as with any type of transaction, the obligation so to transact does not alter the transaction's quality - the transaction remains a loan. Again, among yet other hunter-gatherers people may team up to go hunting, one person providing part of the necessary equipment and another person, or persons, the remainder. This in fact commonly occurs in Port Burwell in the case of transportation technology because canoes, outboard motors and snowmobiles are so expensive. Men tend to afford either a canoe or an outboard, and so to go hunting in summer a person needs to find someone else whose equipment complements theirs. But the partners are not thereby 'sharing' hunting technology, since each is providing one piece of equipment *in return for* the benefit from another. There is a final point. Household structure is increasingly difficult to unravel among hunter-gatherers in the modern world. For example one can be less sure of an equivalence between the physical house and the social household. Thus money or manufactured equipment may pass from house to house, yet the transaction remains within the single commensal unit (household). For example in one unusual household in Port Burwell, the elderly parents live in one government-supplied house, and their wage-earning adult daughter (and her child) live in another. The sharing transactions between these houses would not be a matter for this chapter, whose focus is inter-household sharing.

Two suggestions might be put forward to understand the varying hunter-gatherer attitudes to industrial objects. The first is that these attitudes are culturally programmed on the basis of the 'traditional past' (e.g. Wenzel 2000: 77). Hunter-gatherers treated locally fabricated, durable objects differently from locally produced foodstuffs even before historical contact with capitalist economy, and attitudes to industrial objects have been mapped on to such traditional practice. For example, Woodburn notes, of the Hadza, that whilst many locally produced objects are shared, certain items, notably the bow, the bird-arrow and the leather hunting bag, are not. The convincing suggestion is that to share these particular things would be detrimental because they are the essential tools that every individual (household) needs both to obtain food and to secure defence (Woodburn 1998: 53). Correspondingly, among the Inuit in traditional times the range of tools with these essential functions was very extensive, and so when a hunter obtained the animal products (skins and bones) requisite to fabricate them, these were likewise not subject to sharing strictures. For Port Burwell Inuit such cultural determinist logic would certainly explain why in this particular settlement people never share snowmobiles, outboard motors or canoes, and by extension why they also do not share manufactured objects or money obtained when, as nowadays importantly occurs, the animal skins and bones (sealskin, walrus ivory) are traded in the market place. But the Port Burwell situation can also be explained by the second possible argument that can be put to account for hunter-gatherer attitudes to the industrial product. This argument is opposite to cultural determinist reasoning, for it refers to Western practices regarding durable wealth and money. It can be put briefly. Westerners do not share industrial products outside the household, and so Port Burwell Inuit behaviour relating to these things can be seen as stemming from this. Inuit attitudes to industrial products seem to be much the same as Western attitudes because Western hegemony in relation to the Inuit has entailed that the Inuit come to follow Western values.

I find neither of these perspectives convincing. In the first the burden of explanation is put on the historical (i.e. precontact) hunter-gatherer culture, as if contact with the capitalist economy had no transformative effect. The problem with the second perspective is the reverse. Like in dependency theory, Western structures and values are held responsible for present-day hunter-gatherer practices, and indigenous cultural values are written out of the equation. Also neither perspective is satisfactory from an ethnographic point of view, in particular for the purpose of grasping the variety of hunter-gatherer attitudes to industrial products and money that are reported in the literature. The theoretical perspective in this chapter will accordingly focus on the *facts of interaction between peoples with quite different backgrounds*. The perspective will be deployed in relation to Port Burwell Inuit and New Ager attitudes to industrial products, which, as noted, are quite extreme among egalitarian societies. 'Facts of interaction' are variables. It will be shown, having tallied the Port Burwell and Glastonbury instances with a particular variation with regard to such facts, that other variations dispose rather different attitudes.

The concept of encapsulation is commonly used by anthropologists to theorise interaction between people with quite different backgrounds. It is found in hunter-gatherer studies and is implicit in New Age studies, and I believe it is unsatisfactory. Encapsulation connotes 'one people surrounding another' (e.g. the industrial Canadian world surrounding the Inuit). The image invoked is that the surrounding people amount to a more powerful society, such that this society effectively directs or controls the 'surrounded' society's social organisation and culture. But this is quite unsatisfactory, and the circumstances of the New Age movement in the West are useful to indicate why. In Europe and America New Agers group into an enormous variety of social organisations. Glastonbury, the focus of this chapter, has been mentioned. But another instance is Findhorn near Inverness in Scotland where, far from living interspersed among mainstreamers, New Agers have developed a commune which is geographically separate from neighbouring mainstream villages and towns (Riches, in press). Yet another instance is the Rainbow People in the United States, who uphold the New Age lifestyle in large 'gatherings' in remote forests through a few weeks of summer, before returning to more mainstream existences for the rest of the year (Niman

1997). Encapsulation (by the Western mainstream) is occurring in all three instances. Yet of itself it plainly cannot explicate the quite distinctive circumstances of each one. My position runs parallel with what James Woodburn stated on the controversial matter of the relation between present-day African hunter-gatherers and their nonhunting neighbours: encapsulation by surrounding nonhunting peoples may be a necessary cause of the hunter-gatherer social organisation, but it cannot be a sufficient cause (Woodburn 1988: 35). The task, then, is to tease out the sufficient causes, and in my view these causes should correspond with something in the experience of the 'surrounded people' whose organisation we are trying to elucidate. With regard to Port Burwell Inuit and Glastonbury New Agers I shall go on in this chapter to argue that a crucial part of this experience is the quality of sociality occurring between these people and members of the wider society, and how such sociality integrates with the peoples' sociality relating to dealings among themselves.

In brief I am going to argue that Inuit and New Age nonsharing relating to industrial products and money is reproduced in relation to very particular exigencies of Inuit and New Age social organisation in Port Burwell and Glastonbury in present-day times. These exigencies are to do with the nature of the close proximity of the Inuit and the New Agers with members of the mainstream Western society. Thus the settlements in which Inuit in Arctic Canada live today are government-erected permanent edifices of decent prefabricated housing, and the Inuit reside there, continuously, year-round, their houses dispersed among a substantial minority of also permanently resident European Canadians. These latter are present for a variety of reasons, above all to administer the infrastructure of the settlement and its Inuit inhabitants. The Inuit, for their part, as well as continuing with hunting, travelling out and back from the settlement on fairly brief trips, mostly participate in a quite significant wage-labour sector relating to these European-Canadians who are their employers. But it should be noted that Inuit and Europeans live entirely separate lives from one another outside work hours. Not dissimilarly, New Agers in Glastonbury are completely interspersed with the majority mainstream population in and around the town (the town numbers around 7,000 people, all told); for example, many of them rent accommodation from mainstreamers. It has already been mentioned that they interact with mainstreamers on a regular basis, from collecting social security payments to taking occasional employment from mainstream organisations. But again, it should be noted that New Agers and mainstreamers have little if anything to do with one another outside of these circumstances. I want to examine the sociality experiences of Inuit and New Agers in such contexts in terms of 'space-time'.

Modes of Space-Time Sociality

The notion of space-time sociality is inspired by my recent book, jointly authored with Ruth Prince, which examines the variety of social organisations among the 'new religious movements' in the West, i.e. taking in, as well as the New Age movement, such cults as the Hare Krishnas, the Rajneeshees and the Moonies (Prince and Riches 2000). We suggest that the anthropological approach most productive in understanding such organisations is not a focus on matters of doctrine, but rather the identification of a religious movement as a creative experiment in space-time. Thus the various religious movements may be understood as types of local social aggregation differing from one another in terms of modes of space-time. By 'aggregation' we have in mind that among those involved in such local groups (at Glastonbury, in Findhorn, etc.) there obtains a sociality, and from now on in this chapter we shall accordingly be talking about 'modes of sociality in space-time'. Thus when we come to consider variation in modes of sociality with respect to Inuit in Port Burwell and New Agers in Glastonbury we shall concentrate both on the manifestation of such sociality in respect of different qualities in space and time; and also variation in degrees of sociality. Discussions of space-time will, for example, consider a particular social aggregate according to whether it is fixed in relation to place or mobile in relation to place, continuous in relation to time or discontinuous in relation to time, and so on. Thus Glastonbury New Agers are 'fixed in relation to place' (for them the point of existence is living within the town's sacred boundaries) and, over an annual period, are relatively 'continuous' in that place (at most they make short visits to other New Age sacred sites during summer); but their level of sociality is quite low since they conduct their lives rather independently from one another. Meanwhile Findhorners in their closed commune are similar to Glastonbury New Agers in respect of space and time, but with close cooperation in their daily life (in farming and in presenting the commune as a tourism venue) theirs is a high-intensity sociality. As to the Rainbow People, these people experience a high-intensity sociality, fixed in place (the forest location) but discontinuous in time – after a few weeks the Gathering dissolves and the participants return to their homes in the Boston middle-class suburbs or else go back to treading the 'hobo' road.

The New Religious Movements study suggests to me that sociality in space-time is a fundamental human experience, and that a particular human 'lifeway' therefore comprises a particular combination of more than one, and probably several, space-time socialities. 'Lifeway' connotes a holistic sense of an interpenetration of different space-time socialities. A particular lifeway thus consists of a relatedness among such space-time socialities, even as, to make the lifeway distinct, these socialities must, in terms of experience, be kept separate. Later in this chapter, when I return to the question of the non-sharing of money and manufactured objects by Inuit in Port Burwell, I shall give an account of ideology as a body of collective representations that function to both link and keep separate the constituting space-time socialities of any given lifeway. I shall argue that such nonsharing is precisely an example of such ideology appropriate for the very distinctive space-time circumstances for Inuit in the Port Burwell settlement.

The theoretical advantage of addressing social organisation in terms of modes of space-time sociality is, for me, manifest. Anthropologists' descriptions of social organisation are normally trapped in concepts that predetermine the direction of analysis. Thus, 'power', or 'inequality' might be invoked to describe the relation between European Canadians and Inuit in Port Burwell, but this forecloses on Inuit agency and sees Inuit, improperly in my view, as the European Canadians' pawns (Riches 1985). Alternatively 'ethnicity' might frame the description of important social relations in Port Burwell. But this forecloses on what underlies the constitution of ethnicity. One could also talk of the kinship culture of the Inuit, or the sharing ethic, or one could talk about the Inuit economy (sharing hunted food, not sharing manufactured objects) in terms of 'spheres of economic exchange'. But for me all these notions are constituted in the flow of everyday life, and we should not want, by mobilising them as 'givens' to describe social life in such and such a place, to foreclose on the social processes that sustain them in being (e.g. Riches 1981). In my view, 'modes of space-time sociality' is an ideal tool comparatively to address the processes of human social life. It corresponds with fundamental human experiences, and, thanks to the possibility of variation in space-time aggregation, is highly suggestive with regard to how specific institutions and cultural concepts in specific societies are reproduced in being.

Let us therefore grasp the nature of New Ager and Inuit socialities in space-time in Glastonbury and Port Burwell. I suggest that both these peoples experience a double mode of space-time sociality. We shall take the Inuit as the example, since from now on the chapter will concentrate on them, in contrast with other hunter-gatherers. The first mode refers to high-intensity sociality, fixed in place and continuous in time. One does not wish to pre-empt analysis by talking in terms of ethnicity, but the Inuit community unto itself is clearly in mind here – this is the community where people spend the majority of time in one another's company, including continuous periods of twenty-four hours or more when engaged in hunting expeditions. The second space-time mode of sociality relevant to Inuit experience in Port Burwell is a fixed-in-place, relatively discontinuous and low-intensity sociality. Again it preempts matters to talk in terms of ethnic relations, but in mind now are Inuit–Canadian relations in the settlement. Discontinuity in relation to time refers to the fact that the sociality here is abruptly very substantially reduced in intensity when, as commonly happens among contemporary hunter-gatherers, a person disengages from wage labour and for a period devotes most of the time to hunting (Bird-David 1992). And when engaged in wage labour the intensity of sociality remains relatively low, not least because many wage labour jobs around the settlement, such as driving vehicles bringing fuel supplies to the houses, do not require much by way of supervision.

The fact that in human social life people generally experience more than one mode of sociality suggests another matter that turns out to be highly important when interpreting Inuit 'nonsharing' of industrial objects as ideology. This is the relative physical positioning of the modes of sociality at hand. I will illustrate this with three examples, which indicate some extremes in this respect: the first from the historical Australian Aborigines, the second from both contemporary and historical Pygmies, the third from present-day Inuit in Port Burwell. In giving these illustrations, especially those that refer to the Australians and the Pygmies, I want to emphasise that I am citing them merely to instance certain scenarios of space-time solidarity; these particular peoples of course experience still other types of sociality, both during the particular historical period being focused on and in other (later) periods.

First, with reference to historical Australian Aborigines, there is the scenario of marked physical separation with regard to space-time socialities. Here a first mode of sociality relates to large assemblies of people gathering together for initiation ceremonies, whilst a second mode relates to small groups of people engaging economically on the nomadic round. The first mode can be described as fixed-in-place but discontinuous in time – such ceremonies, though culturally absolutely crucial are, in space-time terms, relatively brief, intermittent occurrences. The second mode is relatively continuous in time but not fixed in place – the bulk of historical Aborigines' time is spent in such economic aggregations. The key point is that the ceremonies (first mode of sociality) are normally sited in an entirely different physical location from where people conduct the nomadic round (second mode). What occurs is that the same ceremony is attended by large numbers of economic groups from a wide regional area, many people travelling tens of miles to make the journey (for an analysis see Riches 1995).

The second scenario refers to the Pygmies and probably holds good for both historical and contemporary times; Turnbull's classic descriptions of the Mbuti in the 1950s would provide an example (Turnbull 1965), and the same pattern is described very recently for the Aka by Kitanishi (2000). I want to deal just with the part of the Pygmy annual cycle where people assemble in villages close to neighbouring Bantu agriculturalists, and leave aside Pygmy circumstances in the remaining several months of the year when they are in small camps distant in the forest. Thus a first mode of sociality refers to Pygmy villagers within their own villages. This is a fixed-in-place (i.e. village) sociality of very high intensity, but it is discontinuous in time precisely because of the Pygmies' annual dispersal to the forest. Meanwhile a second mode of sociality pertaining to village life refers to relations with Bantu neighbours, for example concerning Pygmy labour on Bantu farms; this is fixed in place and discontinuous in time, and the sociality is low intensive. Concerning the physical positioning of modes of sociality, the Pygmy scenario shows two modes of space-time sociality basically abutting one another. In contrast to the Australian Aborigines, these two modes of sociality are, so to say, 'right next door'.

The Port Burwell Inuit case (which would include Glastonbury New Agers) provides a third scenario, which is at the other extreme from the Australian Aborigines. In terms of the physical location the Inuit's two modes of sociality are experienced in one and the same physical place – the Port Burwell settlement. Again, we should remind ourselves that the Australian and Pygmy scenarios refer merely to a *part* of people's total space-time experiences – for example, Pygmy space-time sociality within the forests was not included in the illustration. But with the Port Burwell Inuit the two space-time modes that I have described are the *only* modes of sociality that they experience. As regards explaining Inuit ideology relating to not sharing industrial objects, I believe this double combination of circumstances is crucial, namely that all (i.e. both) Inuit space-time modes are located in the selfsame place.

As mentioned, an holistic view suggests that the various space-time socialities that people experience must be considered as parts of a total lifeway. As time passes individuals may objectively move from one space-time mode to another, but at the level of understanding each space-time modality remains continually of moment. The question of how individuals conceptualise the relation between the various space-time modes therefore becomes relevant. With regard to human understanding, for a lifeway to be distinctive requires that the component modes of space-time sociality should each hold their distinctive shapes, but for the lifeway to be holistic requires a relating of these various component modes; in short the component modes, even as they are experienced as separate, must be bridged. Ideological notions, I submit, accomplish this task, and I suggest that the ideological notions that are appropriate in any one instance will depend on both the nature of component space-time modes at issue and also their respective physical siting.

One can return to the Australian Aborigines to exemplify the point. In terms of the scenarios given above, one can cite two ideological notions, the first functioning to render the two space-time modes separate in the Australian lifeway, and the second to integrate them holistically. Australian conceptions of movement across the landscape are the first ideological notion. These reflect the fact that the principal factor in terms of which the two Australian space-time modes are experienced as separate is, unsurprisingly, their emplacement in quite separate physical locations. In Australian culture movements across the landscape are precisely conceptualised as sacred movements. But secondly there is the matter of integrating the two modes, given firstly that they are so qualitatively different and secondly that their positioning is grounded in physically entirely separate places. How do Australians in their everyday nomadic economic groups sustain in mind the qualitatively entirely different space-time experience of the initiation ceremony? This, it goes without saying, is a far more difficult question to answer. But elsewhere, in an analysis of historical Australian social organisation, I have made an argument that seems to have a bearing on this question, namely that Australian ideas and practices relating to totemism have as their rationale the providing of the ideological bridge between the great ceremonials and the mundane everyday

(Riches 1995). Something like such an argument could be directly adapted for the purposes of the present discussion.

The contrast between the Port Burwell Inuit and Australian scenarios is stark. For the Inuit, as has been noted, the high-intensity, continuous mode of sociality (Inuit among themselves) and the low-intensity, discontinuous mode of sociality (Inuit with Canadians) both occur in Port Burwell settlement. So, unlike the Australians, matters to do with distinct and distant physical locales cannot be mobilised as a symbolic idiom for them to be experienced as separate. On the other hand, the fact that both Inuit modes are sited in the same place entails that there are potentially plentiful means ideologically to integrate the two modes into one holistic lifeway. I argue that the nature of industrial objects and money is ideal for fulfilling the double symbolic task – of serving both to render separate and also to integrate the two Inuit modes of sociality in Port Burwell. The point about the industrial object is that *in terms of its practical meanings* it is experienced as having value in relation to both space-time modes of sociality. For example, for Inuit to deny the practical worth of industrial objects with regard to relations among themselves would be pointless and self-defeating not least because hunting with industrial equipment is crucially important from the point of view of subsistence. But on the other hand the industrial object can harmonise with a variety of *moral meanings*, and it is in relation to this, I suggest, that such property provides the perfect meaning ideologically to render the two Inuit space-time modes separate. The point here is that the industrial object is the rationale for one of the space-time modes existing. This is the low-intensity, discontinuous mode. Such a mode exists because economic exchange relating to industrial commodities occurs. Thus the industrial object is experienced as having a positive moral association with that particular mode. But if industrial objects are also to function ideologically to keep the two modes separate, this in turn means that such objects should be experienced negatively in relation to the *ethics* of the other mode – the high-intensity, continuous mode. It follows that the ethics of sharing should be denied to industrially manufactured objects and money.

Discussion

I believe that space-time experiences, together with their relationship with relative intensities of sociality, are fundamental human experiences that underpin the concepts and idioms that both natives and anthropologists use to describe the world. From the point of view of clarity, however, it has been difficult not to talk about different modes of space-time as if they 'belonged to', say, the Inuit, or to Inuit–Canadian relations. Therefore I should conclude with some remarks to indicate what I consider is actually the case, namely that such experiences underpin such social concepts and institutions. I shall concentrate on ethnicity.

This chapter has examined human experience where individuals participate in more than one mode of sociality, and has attended to the ideological resources that bridge such modes. In the Australian example, totemic notions and the idea of sacredness relating to movement function as ideological resources in this regard. Meanwhile the industrial object functions in this way in the Inuit example. I propose that ethnic identities arise, or do not arise, *out of* such processes. Specifically, concepts of ethnic identity arise when such ideological resources connote the notion of 'other'. And what determines this is the provenance of the ideological resource at issue. The key variable here is whether or not those who consume the resource – for whom the resource symbolically integrates relevant modes of sociality – also enjoy access to its mode of production. When such access is not enjoyed this signals an ideological division relating to consumers and producers such that the former experience the latter as culturally 'apart'.

Thus on the Port Burwell scene individuals who have lived in the Arctic all their lives find themselves in touch with similarly placed individuals and interact with them intensively; they are also in touch with more recent arrivals in the Arctic whom they know much less well and with whom their interaction is not intensive at all. But this is not parallel to the typical British village where 'locals' distinguish themselves from 'incomers' (McFarlane 1981). The life-long Arctic-dwellers in Port Burwell contrast themselves with the recent arrivals in the fact that they have little or no knowledge of or involvement in industrial production. For them this is pertinent because the industrial object functions to integrate the intensive and the nonintensive socialities relevant to their lifeway – from the recent arrivals the industrial good is obtained, with fellow long-term dwellers the industrial good is used. Thus 'Inuit' and 'Europeans' are delineated. Meanwhile, in historical Australia, whilst people participated in two modes of sociality this did not stimulate ethnic division, not least because the two modes were anchored to two quite different physical locations. I suggested that totemic knowledge functioned in historical Australia as the ideological resource integrating ceremonial sociality and economic sociality. Such knowledge was upheld by the elders. But the elders were local leaders who participated fully and prominently in both ceremonial life and the nomadic round; moreover eldership was available to all initiated men and did not connote an exclusive social group. There was therefore no sense of the integrating ideological resource being hidden or unavailable in terms of the nature of its production. This, in short, allowed no scope for the delineation of 'the other'.

This approach returns us to the central issue of this chapter, namely the treatment of industrial objects and money in egalitarian society. First I want to dispense with the obvious question relating to Port Burwell and Glastonbury. If ethnic demarcation is the issue would not this have been established through Inuit/New Agers *sharing* industrial objects – thus *distinguishing themselves* from Europeans/mainstreamers, who don't share? But such an argument would have been to treat the existence of the respective ethnic groups as givens. I have, to the contrary, addressed the *constituting* of ethnic groups – as occurring in a symbolic strategy relating to the experience of multiple modes of sociality. In Port Burwell and Glastonbury industrial objects (including money) and country food evidently have complementary functions in the constituting of ethnicity. The industrial object, integrating two modes of sociality, symbolically signals the notion of the 'other in contrast to self' (e.g. European as opposed to Inuit), whilst country food, associated solely with intensive sociality, symbolically anchors the notion of self (Inuit). So as not to confound these two, crucially different processes, different moralities – respectively nonsharing and sharing – attach to them.

In some egalitarian societies, in contrast to Port Burwell and Glastonbury, industrial objects and money are subject to sharing, to some degree. To the instances of hunter-gatherers reported earlier, we can add the New Age cases of the Findhorn commune and the Rainbow Gathering where durable property and money are, respectively, held communally and shared freely (Niman 1997; Riches, in press). For me, looking back at the descriptions of these various societies provided earlier in this chapter, the significant thing about all these cases is that, in each one, the mode of sociality relating to 'self' (e.g. Kooris, Findhorners) is physically sited at a geographical remove from the mode of sociality relating to 'other' (Europeans, mainstreamers). In such circumstances the specific function of the industrial object, as occurs in Port Burwell and Glastonbury, and which in these places disposes its complete removal from the domain of inter-household sharing, does not obtain. We may expect, where these two modes of sociality are geographically separated, that their integration may be accomplished, at least in part, by means other than through the symbolism of the industrial object. In these instances, then, the possibility of sharing industrial objects and money will be more open.

Notes

1. This is a purely heuristic definition. Indeed I recognise that when Price first formulated the notion of sharing he had particularly in mind transactions within the household (Price 1975).
2. 'Demand sharing' is a variant of sharing where the initiative for the transaction lies with the recipient. But the egalitarian ethic remains. Specifically, people subject to demand sharing have 'a generalised moral obligation to respond to demand' without expectation of return. The egalitarian ethic here is underscored by the fact that 'the obligation [to share] pre-dates the asking' (MacDonald 2000: 191). Elsewhere (Riches 2000) I have queried the idea of demand sharing for it seems to be compounded of two rather different and not ontologically compatible social processes – a notion (the obligation) and an action (the asking). However, I do not pursue this here.

References

Altman, J. 1987. *Hunter-Gatherers Today: an Aboriginal Economy in North Australia.* Australian Institute of Aboriginal Studies.
Bird-David, N. 1992. 'Beyond the 'Hunting and Gathering Mode of Subsistence': Observations on the Nayaka and Other Modern Hunter-Gatherers', *Man,* 27: 19–44.
Bodenhorn, B. 2000. 'It's Good to Know who Your Relatives Are but We Were Taught to Share with Everybody'. In: *The Social Economy of Sharing: Resource Allocation and Modern Hunter-Gatherers* (Senri Ethnological Series 53), ed. G. Wenzel et al. Osaka, pp.27–60.

Fardon, R. 1990. 'Malinowski's Precedent: the Imagination of Equality', *Man*, 25: 569–87.
Hovelsrud-Broda, G. 2000. 'Sharing, Transfers, Transactions and the Concept of Generalised Reciprocity'. In: *The Social Economy of Sharing: Resource Allocation and Modern Hunter-Gatherers* (Senri Ethnological Series 53), ed. G. Wenzel et al. Osaka, pp.193–214.
Kidd, S. 1999. 'Love and Hate among the People Without Things: the Social and Economic Relations of the Enxet people of Paraguay', Ph.D. thesis, University of St Andrews.
Kitanishi, K. 2000. 'The Aka and the Baka: Food Sharing among Two Central Africa Hunter-Gatherer Groups'. In: *The Social Economy of Sharing: Resource Allocation and Modern Hunter-Gatherers* (Senri Ethnological Series 53), ed. G. Wenzel et al. Osaka, pp.149–70.
MacDonald, G. 2000. 'Economies and Personhood; Demand Sharing among the Wiradjuri of New South Wales'. In: *The Social Economy of Sharing: Resource Allocation and Modern Hunter-Gatherers* (Senri Ethnological Series 53), ed. G. Wenzel et al. Osaka, pp.87–111.
McFarlane, G. 1981. 'Shetlanders and Incomers'. In: *The Structure of Folk Models*, ed. L. Holy and M.Stuchlik. London, pp. 119–36.
Niman, M. 1997. *People of the Rainbow: a Nomadic Utopia*. Knoxville.
Price, J. 1975. 'Sharing: the Integration of Intimate Economies', *Anthropologica*, 17: 3–27.
Prince, R. and D. Riches 2000. *The New Age in Glastonbury: the Construction of Religious Movements*. Oxford.
Riches, D. 1975. 'Cash, Credit and Gambling in a Modern Eskimo Economy', *Man*, 10: 21–36.
—— 1981. 'The Obligation to Give: an Interactionist Sketch'. In: *The Structure of Folk Models*, ed. L. Holy and M. Stuchlik. London, pp. 209–32.
—— 1985. 'Power as a Representational Model'. In: *Power and Knowledge*, ed. R. Fardon. Washington, pp. 71–90.
—— 1995. 'Hunter-gatherer Structural Transformations', *Journal of the Royal Anthropological Institute*, 1: 679–701.
—— 2000. 'The Holistic Person, or, the Ideology of Egalitarianism', *Journal of the Royal Anthropological Institute*, 6: 669-85.
—— in press. 'The Scottish Commune'. In: *Compendium of Scottish Ethnology*, ed. S. Storrier. Edinburgh.
Turnbull, C.1965. *Wayward Servants: the Two Worlds of the African Pygmies*, London.
Woodburn, J. 1982. 'Egalitarian Societies', *Man*, 17: 431–51.
—— 1988. 'African Hunter-Gather Social Organisation: is it Best Understood as a Product of Encapsulation'. In: *Hunters and Gatherers I: History, Evolution and Social Change*, eds T. Ingold et al. London, pp.31–64.
—— 1998. 'Sharing Is Not a Form of Exchange: an Analysis of Property-sharing in Immediate-return Hunter-gatherer Societies'. In: *Property Relations*, ed. C. Hann. Cambridge, pp.48–63.
Wenzel, G. 2000. 'Sharing, Money, and Modern Inuit Subsistence: Obligation and Reciprocity at Clyde River, Nunavut'. In: *The Social Economy of Sharing: Resource Allocation and Modern Hunter-Gatherers* (Senri Ethnological Series 53), ed. G. Wenzel et al. Osaka, pp.61–86.
Wenzel, G., G. Hovelsrud-Broda and N. Kishigami (eds) 2000. *The Social Economy of Sharing: Resource Allocation and Modern Hunter-Gatherers* (Senri Ethnological Series 53). Osaka.

5

Sharing Costs: an Exploration of Personal and Individual Property, Equalities and Differentiation

Barbara Bodenhorn

Woodburn's argument that (some) hunter/gatherers are assertively egalitarian is a satisfying antidote to those ecological determinists who assume hunters simply lack the means to develop hierarchy.[1] With reference to this model, Iñupiaq (north Alaskan) social organisation today includes virtually all of the characteristics Woodburn labels as 'immediate return' as well as most of the characteristics he labels 'delayed return'. The result is a system that protects individual autonomy to a very high degree – no one can tell anyone else what to do without potentially causing serious insult – whilst institutionalising and valorising cooperation and interdependence rather than individual independence.[2]

At the same time, pathways for the differential accumulation of durable wealth have long existed, historically particularly through trade. In the current chapter I want to look at this 'other side' of things. Concentrating primarily on the joint position of whaling captain couple (the *umialik* and his wife), I examine the organisation of social relations involving differential access to resources. Let me elaborate briefly. Today, anyone – man, woman or child; Iñupiaq or non-Iñupiaq – who contributes material or nonmaterial resources to the hunting effort generates a non-negotiable claim to a share (a *ningik*) of the successful harvest. This claim is not based on a hierarchy of 'goods': stories, good marksmanship, and the provision of a sturdy sled all potentially generate an equal claim at the end of a day's hunt. Thus people who start out with better equipment – or who are especially experienced, knowledgeable and skilful – do not necessarily end up with a greater share of the result. In contrast to a number of hunter/gatherer systems, this is not about entitlement to a common resource. If you choose to go to the office, stay home to watch television, play cards, 'party' or otherwise amuse yourself, that is up to you. But you will not earn a share unless you have already helped to provision the hunting effort. 'Help' is recognised in so many ways that virtually anyone who wishes to, is able to do so. Still, the bottom line is that the right to a share is based on having made a contribution.[3] This is, however, by no means the end of the story. The person who does the actual killing may claim the durable wealth-producing part of the animal: the polar bear pelt or the walrus ivory, for instance.[4] In the case of whaling, the whaling captain couple (the boat owners), the harpooner and the owner of the harpoon(s), all lay claim to named shares of the whale – meat, *maktak* and baleen – that are significantly larger than those distributed to the rest of the crew. The extent to which this differential access to resources either reflects or creates unequal social relations – and if so, what sorts of inequalities we mean – is a question addressed in the discussion.[5]

We begin with a brief examination of the bases of egalitarian relations on the Slope: rules of access and of distribution as they impinge on anyone taking part in the hunting process. We then turn to the special case of whaling captains and ask what sorts of property relations are involved in attaining and maintaining the position.[6] Now, as for a century ago, for a couple to start a crew, they must have the resources to provide the necessary equipment and they must be recognised as adept hunters and skilful social managers in order to attract a crew. An aspiring *umialik* must thus control material and nonmaterial resources in order to lay claim to the position. The rights and responsibilities making up the property are likewise material and nonmaterial. To paraphrase Sahlins, if being a whaling captain brings recognition, you need recognition to become a whaling captain. The public stature of whaling captains may include Very Big Men – and Women – for whom recognition is transformed into status (George Ahmaogak, current mayor of the North Slope Borough, for instance, married to Maggie Ahmaogak, Executive Director of the Alaska Eskimo Whaling Commission). Others, however, avoid the public sphere altogether. We need to ask what 'the payoff' is, if anything, and what the implications are for social relations in general.

What emerges is that although a whaling captain today must have considerable resources before becoming an *umialik*, achieving the position is not a stepping-stone to further material wealth. Now as perhaps never before, whaling captain couples must be willing to support the considerable costs of whaling with resources gained elsewhere in order to be able to give the result away. Nor can we assume that there is an easy substitution of material wealth for, let us say, political position, tempting as it might be. Some whaling captains come to wield significant power, but that is by no means automatic. It cannot be assumed that these practices of differentiation determine particular sorts of inequalities. Although whaling has long been at the centre of coastal Iñupiaq spiritual and social life, it has never been the sole source of subsistence. It is pertinent that any number of factors prevent whaling captains from taking up gatekeeping positions that might control the decisions others can make about their own livelihood. That 'property' as a category encompasses many sorts of relationships, may organise the circulation of many kinds of resources and often includes 'obligations' as well as 'rights' is not new.[7] What is striking here is the degree to which in Barrow, 'responsibility' is today perhaps the dominant value attached to the role of whaling captain couple, a value that has important implications for the social relations in which whaling captains and their wives find themselves in on a daily basis.[8]

This material leads me to suggest that for systems in which moral individuals may make property claims qua individuals (thus existing structurally in a relationship of equality), it may be useful to draw a distinction between individual and what I shall call for the moment *personal* property. A great deal of recent work by anthropologists working with hunter/gatherers has asserted the importance of recognising the extent to which individual as well as common property are present in most, if not all, hunter-gatherer systems.[9] As Nurit Bird-David has recently suggested, the category 'individual' needs to be interrogated as carefully amongst those who use it to talk about hunters as it does elsewhere.[10] On the North Slope where, as I have just said, individuals generate non-negotiable claims regardless of age, gender, marital status, kinship relationships or occupational position, the case for assuming the presence of moral individuals is strong. This contributes to a system of individual autonomy in which, to echo Woodburn, no one is dependent on specific others for the means of their survival. However, we need also to consider what I have just called personal property: claims that can be made by and to specific social persons in the Maussian sense of persona – that is, that the claims inhere in the role and not in the individual who occupies it.[11] Although it is not a distinction I have seen – indeed I would say that they are often conflated – it is certainly implicit in much anthropology. Durkheim, for instance, noted in *The Division of Labour* that the egalitarian meritocracy he envisioned under organic solidarity would not develop as long as wealth could be controlled through inheritance rules. The extent to which kinship or gender can be seen to control the economic organisation of inequality is, of course, at least in part a function of claims that may be made by social persons occupying particular positions. In many cases, however, discussions about these Maussian persons – including those put forward by Mauss himself – often suggest that these are powerful categories in the absence of moral individuals. Persons, in the Maussian sense, are assumed to diminish in importance in systems in which individuals occupy pride of place. Here I am suggesting that it is precisely in systems where individuals are moral persons, that other kinds of personal claims need to be explicitly examined as well. Although the importance of these sorts of claims stand out with Iñupiaq material because the positions of whaling captain couples carry so much extraordinary social weight, it is equally pertinent to modelling economic life in Cambridge, England.

This is quite different from what is generally meant in English by the term 'personal property' and invites a further distinction, not new by any means, but important to underline nonetheless. Very briefly, this is the distinction between the grounds on which one may establish claims to resources and the constraints that define what one can do with the resource once it is 'yours', that is, what ownership means.[12] Whaling captain couples and harpooners can both lay claim to large shares of whales they have helped to catch. For harpooners, this is a personal right to put forward a claim. What the claim is *to* is also personal – in the conventional usage of the term. Their shares become personal (private) property (the person in question being the moral individual) – to do with as they please. For the most part, what it does not become is personal property in the sense being examined by Humphrey (2002), that is, so attached to oneself that it becomes part of one's identity.[13] Whaling captain couples, on the other hand, are more constrained; they *must* provide the bulk of the resources needed for the whaling effort and *must* share out a considerable portion of their catch with the community. Their persona – their social position – thus defines not only what they have access to, but also what they can get up to once they have it. To understand how relations of equality and inequality play out in particular circumstances, it seems to me crucial not only that we examine these distinctions analytically, but also that we ask how they interact.

Context – a Skeletal History

Arctic conditions have never fostered the sort of 'lo-tech', non-labour intensive lifestyle imagined by Sahlins (1972) in 'The Original Affluent Society'. As Burch (1975: 9) notes for the nineteenth century, the Western Arctic was resource rich, albeit demanding that people needed to be in the right place at the right time. Iñupiat have long depended on specialised technologies, developed for survival under a wide variety of conditions: food, preservation techniques, clothing, housing and hunting equipment, for instance, as well as detailed knowledge of the weather, the ice, ocean currents, the tundra and animals. Survival demanded and continues to demand steady cooperative work, defined largely, although by no means only, as a marital division of labour. In contrast to the nomadic social organisation of the Central Canadian Inuit, permanent Iñupiaq communities have sprung up in the path of the bowhead whale migration for at least the last thousand years. These are places where food can be stored in permafrost-cooled meat cellars for a year or more, where *qargit* (ceremonial houses) customarily formed the focus of extra-household community life and where social organisation includes the enduring institution of whaling crews headed by an *umialik*, or whaling captain, and his wife – the whaling captain couple.[14] From the earliest available accounts, it is clear that the position of whaling captain couple included (and continues to include) ritual as well as practical responsibilities.[15] Whales, like all the other animals, offer themselves up to be killed to generous hunters. This is a gift, again as with all other animals, that is contingent upon proper human behaviour. Patrick Attungana, addressing the Alaska Eskimo Whaling Commission in 1986, drew on an *unipkaaq* to make the point that the gift is quite explicitly given through the whaling captain couple to the community and that it is up to the couple to make it feel welcome:

> When the whale is caught, ... the whole whale gives itself to all the people... the whale being or spirit never dies. ... The dead whale's being or spirit return to the live whales. The returning whales begin to listen to the whale that had been like camping. He tells them that his hosts were good, the married couple were good to it ... The whale that had good hosts starts wishing and telling others that it will camp again ... . (Attungana 1986: 16ff)

Unipkaat are legends, stories handed down over generations, and so give us an indication of how rules might have been expressed in earlier times. Today they often convey messages that remain a lively part of the Iñupiaq moral world. Harry Brower, Sr. was unequivocal about his experiences in that world: 'It's hard to explain what it's like when the whale gives itself up to you unless you see it', he affirmed, 'The whale is given to you out of nowhere... When this happens, no matter what you do, it's yours... You could shout at it, try to chase it away, but it will stay there' (1981: 3). Mary Aveoganna was equally unequivocal about the moral nature of that gift for whaling captains: 'Always be ready with hospitality,' she exhorted in 1991, 'so the whale will see an inviting place.'[16]

Given that whales are thought to give themselves up to the entire community through the whaling captain and his wife, it is not surprising that over time whaling captains developed certain responsibilities for ensuring the proper behaviour that would attract the whales back in the future. Barrow people who are today in their early fifties and sixties recall that collectivities of whaling captains have played an institutionalised role in community life for some time. Customarily, the *umialigiich* (whaling captains, plural) would meet, in Maggie Ahmaogak's words, 'to decide what kind of policies and rules they had... the way they would share with the community – the way they would give to the poor'. In Raymond Neakok, Sr.'s words, 'those people will determine exactly how we should treat a person that is breaking the structure of society's running'.[17] The very continuity of whaling depended on whaling captains being willing and able to gather together the necessary resources; collectivities of *umialiit* clearly wielded political influence. On the other hand, they needed labour. The ability of crew members to move between crews indicates that, in the early decades of the twentieth century at least, leadership and followership were interdependent to a significant degree.

The State of Alaska was formed in 1959; oil was discovered in Prudhoe Bay in 1969; the North Slope Borough was established in 1970; the Alaska Native Claims Settlement Act was passed in 1971, followed by the Marine Mammal Protection Act in 1972. Despite increasing levels of government oversight, the 1960s and 1970s were relatively good ones for Barrow Iñupiat. Both land and marine mammals were plentiful, as were jobs. Although whaling had never stopped, it now experienced a resurgence and new crews were established, particularly by younger men who were able to transform their monetary resources into whaling ones. In 1977 the International Whaling

Commission called for a moratorium on all Iñupiaq subsistence whaling. In response, the Alaska Eskimo Whaling Commission and the Inuit Circumpolar Conference – both of which are active advocates for Inuit sovereignty – were established in 1978 under the tenure of Eben Hopson, Sr., the first Mayor of the North Slope Borough.

Today the North Slope is a home-rule borough that spans some 88,000 square miles and includes eight Iñupiaq communities. The Borough – which encompasses the most oil-rich areas in the state of Alaska – was established in the face of active opposition on the part of oil companies and many Alaskan politicians. Its main sources of revenue are property taxes collected from those same oil companies. The considerable political power of the North Slope Borough; the extent to which it has effectively transformed oil revenues into far-reaching service delivery; and the successful economic strategies of the Arctic Slope Regional Corporation (ASRC, established under land claims), among other factors, has meant that North Slope Borough residents are for the most part significantly better off than Alaska Natives living in most other rural Alaskan communities. It should not come as a surprise, however, that recent developments have intensified existing disparities between those who have and those who have less – and between those who feel engaged in the system and those who feel marginalised by it.

Here as elsewhere, the costs of living have risen with the introduction of money in the form of wages – to be met easily by some and with increasing difficulty by others. 'I was glad when money came,' said one elder in 1985, 'it meant we didn't starve if the caribou didn't come.' 'NARL came, people started working and things got better,' Ruth Ipalook said simply. But equally, according to Mae Panigeo, a whaling captain's wife, 'prices started to go up and we had to work all the time… Now you have to work to go hunting.'[18]

By the beginning of the twenty-first century, then, Iñupiat have been engaging with global markets (for whale products, fox pelts, reindeer meat and petroleum among other things) for 150 years and with agencies of state (schools, churches, courts, branches of the federal government and NGOs) for just over a century. Engagement with these institutions has been both positive and negative and their representatives have been experienced as more and less dominating. Tools and rules that seemed to enhance Iñupiaq efficacy in an ambiguous world were welcomed; rules that constrained have been resisted. The fact that many people today feel under siege by powers that seem bent on regulating everything of meaning to them does not obviate the strength of several David and Goliath stories recounting successful Iñupiaq resistance to others' intrusions. The fact that sharing continues to underpin social life is a social fact of enormous significance.

Some Basic Rules of Access to Resources in Barrow Today

The resource base (land, rivers, sea) is common; as Ernest Kignak said, 'anyone who can get out there can go hunting'.[19] The arctic environment requires many resources if it is to be exploited for subsistence. Boats, snow machines, rifles, sleds, clothing, equipment, food, fuel, as well as detailed knowledge of the terrain, the weather and so forth, are all crucial to a hunter's survival. To be fully prepared, one must call upon friends and family for help. As I have said elsewhere (Bodenhorn 2000b), man-the-hunter is something of a consortium before setting out. Consequently, it should not be surprising to learn that, in contrast to Hadza custom, although the animal has given itself up through the hunter, the hunter does not own the carcass. Instead, it gets divided into shares – or *ningik* (the same term used by Iñupiat when talking about shares in a company) amongst all those who have helped the process.

The classification of bowhead whales as prey is accompanied by more complex organisation than any other hunting activity. Whalers form crews that endure over time and include the specialised positions of harpooner, captain, his wife, and the whaling captain couple as a collective entity. Although access to the whale is presented as a function of collective responsibility, entitlement to shares is dependent on crew membership. As with hunting partnerships, membership in these crews is largely a matter of choice and is extremely fluid. Sons of whaling captains generally whale with their father's crew, but they are not constrained to do so. A young man may whale with various crews over the course of several years to learn hunting skills from different people. Skilled whalers may be actively recruited by a whaling captain; conversely, a whaler may solicit a captain for permission to join his crew. In some families, sons might each whale with a different crew and a daughter join another. This explicit strategy maximises a household's access to shares in the whale meat when it is perceived to be in short supply.[20] Today, this is a response to the International Whaling Commission (IWC) quotas. A few people simultaneously whale with two crews, also in response to IWC restrictions.

Within crews, the captain, the harpooner and the owner of the harpoon (which might be a woman) all get specific shares. For the captain, this includes a portion that is physically set aside for communal feasts, as described below. All other shares within the crew are equal. Those who took part from the beginning of the whaling season to the end receive the same size share as those who may have participated for a day or two. The captain is then responsible for using part of his share to distribute further shares to any people who may have supported the crew indirectly. Many employed men and women contribute money for gas, or provide food and coffee, for instance, thus entitling themselves to a share.

In Barrow, the most important responsibilities of the whaling captain and his wife involve not only the distribution of shares, but also the provision of communal hospitality that make them 'good hosts' to the whale at several points during the year. As the whale is being butchered, women crew members prepare pots of fresh, boiled *maktak* (*uunaaliit*, literally 'hot things') and serve them with hot coffee to people helping on the ice. Simultaneously sled-loads of meat are taken to town so that other women can start preparing a meal at the captain's house, boiling huge portions of every part of the whale:

meat, *maktak*, heart, lungs, tongue, kidney, etc. When it is ready, the crew's flag goes up over the house and the entire community is invited in for a meal. The end of the whaling season is marked by *Apugauti,* a mini-feast. When the *umiaq* (skin-covered whaling boat) is brought to shore for the last time, the crew once again serves Iñupiaq food on the beach to all comers. The provision of hospitality is not about the distribution of 'shares' to people who have a right to claim them, but about sharing the catch literally as 'good hosts.'

Approximately the back third of the whale (the *uati*); the tail flippers (*aqikkaak*) and the organs (heart, intestine, kidney and half of the tongue) are designated as the community share and are distributed during three community feasts: *Nalukataq*, Thanksgiving, and Christmas (Ahmaogak, nd). Here everyone receives shares, regardless of their participation in the whaling itself. *Nalukataq* is celebrated approximately six weeks after the whaling season ends and is hosted by successful crews at a traditional site on the beach. If more than one crew has caught a whale during a season, they may hold separate feasts, or they may join forces. The captain, his wife and the crew spend weeks preparing for the feast. *Mikigaq* (whalemeat and *maktak* fermented in whale blood) must be prepared; ducks and geese hunted for soup. Hundreds of people will be fed. On the day, villagers and visitors assemble slowly, sitting with family in a large semi-circle inside the wind-break set up that morning. Crew members (male/female pairs) serve prepared food, which is eaten on the spot, and distribute shares of whale meat, *maktak*, and *quaq* (frozen meat, often caribou or fish). If meat is plentiful, shares are dispersed per household member; if it is scarce, each household receives the same amount.[21] At the end, the captain shouts *iglaat!* (visitors) and people from other communities are invited forward to help themselves to the portion of the tail that is reserved for them, much as the women were invited to help themselves at the end of the butchering.

Thanksgiving and Christmas feasts are not hosted in quite the same way by individual crews, but are community efforts that take place in the context of a church service. Whale meat, *maktak* and *quaq* are contributed by all of the whaling captains (not just those who were successful this season), while the community as a whole furnishes the prepared food: soup, tea, cakes and so forth. The distribution of shares is conducted by people chosen by the church deacons; the rules for distribution to each household, however, remain the same.

During the year, captains are expected to provide for those who are without through sharing. To ensure a successful whaling season, an *umialik* must have redistributed his previous year's entire share before setting out for the ice in the spring.

In sum, customary rules encourage maximum distribution of the whale over the course of a year; several pathways ensure access to shares in the whale, from the flexibility of crew membership, to the multiple rules for distribution which recognise any kind of contribution of effort as earning one a share. At the feasts, all comers have a right to take shares away; the shares are distributed from a common resource that literally includes anyone who is present. But unlike the distribution of other animals categorised as common property, such as polar bear or beluga, the distribution of the whale is not complete without commensality, that is, without transforming at least some of the shares into shared substance.

In a modification of Woodburn, shares serve to disengage participants, not from property – for it seems to me that this is clearly about property – but from the power of any individual to proffer or deny access to another through claims to 'ownership' of the animal that has been hunted. Man-the-hunter, I suggested, is something of a consortium in that the person who goes out 'looking around' for animals so rarely is self-sufficient. If the hunter is successful, the animal is neither his individual property, nor is it common property. Instead, it must be divided among those who helped hunt and butcher it. In significant ways, the division of shares is not based on comparable contribution. An able hunter who is a good shot may partner himself with another who 'has good stories'; the catch will be evenly divided at the end of the day even if all were killed by the former. The whaler who goes out with his crew after an eight-hour day at the office earns the same size share as the whaler who is on the ice from start to finish of the whaling season. Access to the means of subsistence then is virtually guaranteed along the lines of Woodburn's immediate return model (although not at all in the way Hadza share out game as a communal resource). Again in a modification of Woodburn, it seems that this system of earning shares spreads access to subsistence needs very broadly indeed in a way that not only works against the development of individual dependency on specific others, but also actively fosters a system that depends on cooperation among equals.

Woodburn, though, was not speaking of shares – a division of things – but of sharing – an enactment of sociality. In one of his recent articles (1998) he argued that sharing is not about reciprocity among Hadza. More recently still, I have argued (2000b) that although Iñupiaq categories of division which result in shares correspond almost exactly to Woodburn's model of the non-negotiable, nonreciprocal circulation of resources, much of what Iñupiat describe in English as sharing is enacted within relationships that are talked about in terms of morally obligated reciprocity. To sum up that argument very briefly here, once a *ningik* has entered a household, what happens to it is up to the share-owner (or, often, the married couple) to decide. Raymond Neakok, Sr., for instance, said that he likes to give away half of what he brings into the household. An analysis of what I have called 'sharing networks' reveals that households of kin of roughly equal productive activity share often and share many sorts of resources: hunted food, childcare, the use of equipment, space, meals, laughter and good company.[22] Close kin who live in different communities swap local delicacies: berries, duck eggs and smoked salmon may travel in one direction, for instance, to be reciprocated by seal oil and dried whitefish. People travel between villages, secure in the knowledge they can stay with relatives, taking advantage of the different ecozones to harvest food unavailable at home. The core of sharing is *niqipiaq*, 'real' (hunted) food. The reciprocity, I have suggested, is kept deliberately incommenserate: a zip-lock bag of cooked *maktak* is not the equivalent of a particular kind or a particular amount of frozen fish, or *quaq* – nor can it be calculated in terms of a particular kind of childcare. But it must be ongoing. People who are perceived to be only on the receiving end often become the object of complaint and may eventually find themselves 'out of the loop'.

There is, however, another very important aspect to sharing, namely that which is explicitly done without expectation of return – or *piatchiaq*-. Elders and single mothers often identify 'the people' as frequently as 'relatives' as crucial sources of Iñupiaq food.[23] When Neakok 'gives away half' of his shares, a lot of food travels along the sharing networks described above, but a considerable amount also goes to 'people in need'. This sharing is part of the social contract animals have with humans. They give themselves up in an understanding that people will be generous; the animals' return depends upon it. 'The animals come to me,' Harry Brower, Sr. said years ago, 'they know I share.' By giving without expectation of (a human) return, hunters are reciprocating the animals for their generosity. This is most elaborated in terms of whale/human relations, but the principle applies to all of the animal resources on which Iñupiaq lives depend. Crucially, the moral value attached to the injunction to share is generally experienced positively – as one of the profoundly satisfying aspects of social life.[24] Peterson (1993) has demonstrated that this is clearly not the case amongst hunter-gatherers in many parts of the world, an issue to which I return in the discussion. Sharing, then, seems frequently to be 'about' equality. The most intensive sharing networks take place between households in which it is not difficult to maintain a regular circulation of shared resources. By the same token, however, the most morally weighted form of sharing flows nonreciprocally from households with more to those who have less.

Staying with Woodburn's categories, we see that if shares foster cooperation in a quit-claim immediate return fashion, the morally obligated reciprocity of sharing as it is practised on the North Slope seems to support the egalitarian immediate return avoidance of debt and dependency but in a delayed return sort of way. Here again it seems to me that the centrality of incommensurability is crucial in understanding how long-term reciprocal sharing can take place without building up a sense of indebtedness that fosters inequality. And it is crucial that the most lopsided sharing of all – *piatchiaq* – is so clearly constructed as human reciprocity for animals' generosity in giving themselves up. The debt is thus the responsibility of the hunter and not that of the human recipient of nonreciprocated sharing.

Becoming a Whaling Captain in the Late Twentieth Century

We have seen something of the responsibilities whaling captain couples bear under the injunction to act as good hosts to the whales they have caught. To think about this as part of a complex of rights and responsibilities that makes up the property umialiit may be thought to have in whales, we need to ask what is involved in attaining the position as well as maintaining it.

Umialik literally means owner of the *umiaq*, or whaling boat. Owning a boat is a necessary, but not sufficient, condition for being able to take on the position of whaling captain couple. They must also provide the necessary equipment; to attract a crew they must be recognised for their hunting knowledge, and be respected as potential leaders. In the early 1980s, Worl and Smythe (1986) estimated that it would cost $10,000 for a new whaling captain to outfit his crew for the first time. 'Start-up costs' in fact were doubled in that a whaling captain was expected to give away his entire gear after his first whale. He would have to repeat the procedure if he wished to continue in the position.[25] The need for accumulated resources historically was often reflected in the relatively mature age most men reached before taking on the role. As with so many other aspects of Iñupiaq social life, however, the pathways to the position are varied. On being asked how they came to become captains in the early 1980s, responses across the Slope included: 'inherited', 'decided myself', 'elder chose me', 'crew chose me' and 'friends chose me'. In Barrow, slightly over one-third of the existing whaling captains had inherited their positions; an equivalent number had themselves decided to start a crew and approximately one-fifth had been chosen by an elder (Alaska Consultants 1984: 100–1).[26] Many younger men were able to use financial resources gained through increased wage-earning possibilities to start crews of their own during the 1960s and 1970s. The number of crews rose significantly and the mean age of *umialiit* dropped.[27]

If mounting a crew is expensive, so is maintaining one over time and here the emphasis on responsibilities becomes inescapable. Appendices A, B, C and D set out the degree to which resources must be marshalled and remarshalled on an ongoing basis at the beginning of the twenty-first century. They illustrate as well how many sorts of activities must be followed through by the whaling captain couple, from the particulars of organising the construction of the ice road in the spring to the generalities of 'ensuring the safety of the crew' and looking out for 'the people'.

Although I know of no whaling captains who currently sustain more than one boat, the costs of putting together a year's venture are considerable. As of February 2001, a sample of the prices for individual pieces of necessary supplies and equipment that were on sale in Barrow included the following:

	$
Shoulder gun	1,950.00
Darting gun	775.00
Gas bombs	96.55
Darting gun bomb	66.65
12-foot sled	400.00
1 quart injection oil	12.00

To understand the scale of these costs, it is important to realise that for whaling captain couples, whaling is a year-round activity. Bearded seal need to be caught in July for skin boat covers; walrus, hunted in summer, is considered particularly warming whaling food. Caribou hunted in the autumn provide the best sinew to make braided thread; the winter is taken up with boat construction, with more caribou hunting (for meat and for mattresses), with repairing gear and sewing clothing. The hunts that take place for around a month in the spring and again in the autumn are thus only punctuation marks in a constant set of activities (see Appendix A). The different seasons and the different eco-zones require significantly different equipment, clothing and knowledge. Skin boats are used for spring whaling, for example, whereas the much rougher autumn seas are met with motorised aluminium boats. Inland hunting in the spring – when rivers remain frozen -demands snow-machines and sleds whereas boats that can navigate shallow rivers are required for summer and autumn hunting (see Appendix B). The replacement costs of supplies and equipment vary widely – from the daily provision of food and ammunition, to longer-term costs of maintaining or replacing snow-machines, sleds, boats and the like which fluctuate from year to year (see Appendix C). The annual cycle of feasts already mentioned that celebrate community through whaling generates the expenses of large-scale hospitality several times of year (Appendix D).

Although 'costs' have been set out in terms of things that need purchasing, the other cost that needs to be included, of course, is time. By this I mean not only the time needed to prepare, conduct and celebrate the whale hunt, and time to attend to the needs of local people throughout the year, but also the very considerable time needed to deal with the agencies of state: time to provide statistics for the local Fish and Wildlife Department, for the International Whaling Commission, for NOAA (National Oceanic and Atmospheric Administration) and for the Internal Revenue Service to name a few. Time is needed to attend local whaling captains' association meetings, Alaska Eskimo Whaling Commission Meetings, 'one-off' meetings with visiting officials (and occasionally researchers) and so forth. And, of course, time is needed to earn the money necessary for providing the goods and services involved. Time on the North Slope, as elsewhere, has become one of the scarcest resources of all.

One major shift between the beginning of the twentieth century and the beginning of the twenty-first rests on the sources of money available to whaling captain couples to support these expenses; another reflects the radically different political position in which Iñupiat find themselves today. Although to my knowledge whale meat has never been acceptable as anything other than shared substance, baleen was the major source of revenue at the turn of the century. If an *umialik* were lucky enough to catch more than one whale in a season, his cash return could be quite significant and provided the means by which subsequent whaling efforts would be funded. Whaling never ceased, but it decreased in importance during the midtwentieth century. With the influx of oil-related revenue, it intensified in the 1960s. However, this time whaling itself became politicised almost immediately, taking place under intense public scrutiny. The Marine Mammal Protection Act of 1972, coupled with the whaling ban imposed by the International Whaling Commission (IWC) in 1978, has determined that the costs of whaling in the late twentieth century are as much political as economic. Not only has the technology become more expensive, expensive in a way that must be met with nonwhaling resources, but the right to whale itself is under constant question. Regulations currently exist for virtually all of the resources on which Iñupiat depend, but the question of whaling is the most morally loaded, for Iñupiat and for those who would oppose indigenous whaling altogether.[28] The collective decision-making bodies – *umialingat* – influencing midtwentieth-century community life are currently reflected in today's local whaling captains' associations. They have been supplemented by the Alaska Eskimo Whaling Commission (AEWC). This regional association of whaling captains lobbies the United States Government concerning its position vis-à-vis the International Whaling Commission, particularly with reference to the ever-changing quota allotted to Iñupiaq whalers. It negotiates with NOAA over the conduct of whale counts, it engages in negotiations with the IWC concerning the development of 'humane weapons' technology and administers the inter-village distribution of strikes.[29] Whereas once *angatkut* had to travel between Iñupiaq and non-Iñupiaq worlds in order to negotiate for whales, now it is AEWC members who must cross into other worlds in order to ensure that Iñupiaq whaling can continue. It is a responsibility they have fulfilled with determination and skill.

Discussion and Conclusion

The provisioning of whaling crews demands constant purchases – from boats to paper plates. In many and important ways, whaling crews are as much of a consortium as any other hunting effort. There is no way whaling captains could provide everything needed for a single season. Captains are expected to provide the material goods; crew join them in the necessary labour. Help with the material necessities is provided on a community basis whenever possible. During the build-up to whaling, for instance, public meetings of all sorts offer door prizes such as 50 gallons of fuel oil, a darting gun, whale bombs and the like – each contribution worth hundreds of dollars. The Utqiagvik Agviqsiuqtit Agnangiich (Barrow Whaling Wives' Auxiliary) sell 'pull-tabs' year round, raising thousands of dollars which get converted into whaling supplies that can be distributed to the captains during the whaling season. According to Maggie Ahmaogak (personal communication) the Alaska Eskimo Whaling Commission has mounted a successful campaign for the US Internal Revenue Service to allow each registered whaling captain a $10,000 'charitable deduction' for annual expenses incurred to maintain an existing crew for a single whaling season. Still, captains must be willing to carry the brunt of these costs if the community is to be able to continue whaling. They continue to provide not only the purchased supplies, but also the shared food that sustains the feasts so central to community life. And to them falls the major share of the responsibility for mounting formal political defences of their right to continue whaling.

In some ways this resonates with long-standing discussions of hunter/gatherer property relations that invert definitions of property which focus on 'having'.[30] Generally, when individuals earn shares on the North Slope, a *ningik* becomes a form of private property. You may do with it as you wish: consume it, share it, trade it or – in the case of things like fish or seal oil – sell it. This principle holds for harpooners. It does not hold true for whaling captains, for their 'rights' in the whale are, with the important exception of baleen, largely about the obligation to share it. Within the ideology of whaling, this generosity, which does not generate debt among humans, reciprocates the whale for its gift of itself. The potential for transforming a position of leadership into one of gatekeeping power to administer this most valuable of resources is diminished. Historically, the exception was the wealth-producing claims to baleen that did indeed fit the definition of private property and was indeed an avenue to uneven generation of wealth. Both the right to the captain's share of meat and *maktak* (as well as the obligation to give it away) and the right to the captain's share of baleen, which could be converted into wealth, are forms of personal property which distinguished this position from all others in the community. The former sustained an egalitarian system in which captains could not control access to food through a system of patronage; the latter equally sustained a system in which some people could clearly accumulate more than others. Today the former principle is the only one to remain. The extent to which authority for Iñupiat is seemingly never a given and the institution of effort as the source of non-negotiable individual claims have, I suspect, played a major role in shaping the relatively egalitarian nature of contemporary Iñupiaq society – both despite and because of its engagement with global markets.

Let us return briefly to our opening discussion of property. Following many recent discussions, I defined property as the claims people can legitimately make vis-à-vis each other with reference to recognised resources. The resources may be material or nonmaterial and the claims may be about responsibilities as well as privileges. In the late nineteenth century, according to Spencer (1959), people opted not to become whaling captains at the height of the commercial period because of the responsibilities involved. With the increasing politicalisation of Iñupiaq whaling, the responsibilities of the position are, I suspect, becoming more and more all-consuming.

This leads us to the question of why the position continues to be so important.[31] If being a whaling captain is no longer a pathway to becoming a 'rich man' and instead, an *umialik* and his wife can be sure that the responsibilities attached to this position will make constant demands on their material resources as well as their time, why are there thirty-three registered whaling captains in Barrow alone? One tempting answer, to borrow from Bourdieu, might be to think in terms of 'cultural capital'. Whaling is absolutely about twenty-first-century economic relations, but it is a profoundly Iñupiaq pursuit. In many ways it has become the marker of Iñupiaq ethnicity in their struggles to maintain a real degree of autonomy over their lives. Becoming a whaling captain may be one way of gaining recognition in a 'coin' that bypasses the Euro-American scale of valuation – you do not need a high-status job or educational degrees to 'count'. Another possibility, of course, is that the stakes lie in the realm of social capital, to continue in Bourdieu's terms. There is certainly an element of that. It is much easier to become elected Mayor of the North Slope Borough if one is a whaling captain to start with. But, as I said at the outset of this paper, there are many whaling captains who do not convert the status of their position into political power – many more, in fact, than those who do.[32]

It is important that we do not attempt a simple one-for-one substitution: material property for nonmaterial property. The commitment whaling captains as well as others show to the ongoing pursuit of whaling needs to be understood as economic; it is a commitment to the pursuit and distribution of valued resources – tons and tons of food. But it must also be clear by now how important whaling is in social/cosmological terms. And here we should perhaps heed Nurit Bird-David's warning against framing these discussions purely in individual terms. Whilst never denying that some whaling captains clearly revel in the potential glory of the position, it would be unwise to forget the extent to which taking it on is at least as much a willingness to assume responsibilities for a collective as it is to achieve respected status as an individual. The annual cycle of ceremonial feasts provides a forceful illustration of the extent to which shares and sharing – to echo Leach – both 'say' and 'do' things about the social relationship between whales and humans-as-a-collective. To characterise the motives of Iñupiaq whalers in whatever position simply in terms of maximising self-interest is, I think, profoundly to miss the boat. And so we return to personal property once again, in its most Maussian sense. In many ways, the person of the whaling captain couple is a conduit between the whale and the community. For many captain couples, *tutqiksi* – or contentment – is achieved precisely by acting as good hosts. This is a critical point. I have argued elsewhere that Iñupiaq (and, I think, many other) social lives include both indvidual and dividual aspects; individuals earn shares regardless of who they are; dividuals are 'called into being', so to speak, through multiple names and enact potentially infinitely transformative kinship relations (Bodenhorn 2000a). What we are talking about here is neither the bounded individual, nor performative fragmentary dividuals who sound so postmodern. Instead we are talking about being part of a whole that is neither indistinguishable nor separable from it. The cosmology of the whale/human relationship is profoundly unifying. That the whale gives itself to 'all the community' is as critical to understanding Iñupiaq social lives as is the concept that animals give themselves up to wives through their husbands. What I am emphatically not suggesting is a Dumontian holism in which individuals disappear. Each half of the whaling captain couple is an individual who, like any other individual, may earn shares in a multiplicity of hunting efforts; as relatives they are multiple; and as the whaling captain couple, they are both dual and part of a whole. A great deal of the strength of this system lies, I suspect, lies in the multifaceted way in which these seemingly contradictory principles coincide.

It is often when Iñupiat are unequal parties in negotiation processes with national and international agencies that the social capital recognised by Euro-American political agents – education, wealth, corporate experience – is transformed into the relative power to speak and be heard. These positions are often occupied by those (relatively few) whaling captains who not only are recognised locally for the skills which brought them to the position, but also possess the social capital acclaimed by outsiders. They are often put in positions where they are expected to defend incompatible value systems. This is in turn may create a kind of dependency on specific others that can intensify feelings of inequality vis-à-vis 'outsiders' felt by many Iñupiat not occupying these positions. It is here, it seems to me, that the greatest sorts of potential inequalities lie at the beginning of the twenty-first century. But even here, the lines are not drawn in 'the usual' way. Since the discovery of oil in the late 1960s, Iñupiat have fought hard to figure out how to be included without losing a sense of their own autonomous identity. Political lines do not fall between relatively uneducated elders who hunt and educated youngers who bring in 'change'. 'We need to figure out this money stuff better than you guys have,' Eileen Panigeo MacLean said to me some ten years ago. With luck, they may.

I have put forward several interrelated arguments. Although it is possible to distinguish between material and nonmaterial aspects of property, they are not necessarily distinguished on the North Slope in terms of the claims involved. If 'having good stories', being a good shot and owning a fast snow-machine can result in an even distribution of a day's hunting, this, I suspect, goes a long way in 'evening the playing field' when the material technologies needed for successful hunting can be very expensive. The multiple and individual opportunities to generate non-negotiable shares is a powerful protection of individual autonomy, acting as Woodburn noted long ago in a non-obligating, quit-claim way. In addition, sharing, gifting and commoditising are all built into the circulation of resources on the North Slope. Of these, the most morally loaded is sharing - not only among hunters. Sharing continues to be the language underpinning the moral relationship between human and nonhuman social beings. 'Sharing', as an economic category in this arctic context, however, is not homogenous. It can underpin both relations that are categorised as equal and it can facilitate the dispersal of resources from people who have a lot more to those who have a lot less. In the former, sharing is part of a system of morally obligated reciprocity that depends on the circulation of incommensurable resources and is explicitly held apart from gift. In the latter case, sharing is constructed as the human side of a gift relationship with animals who give themselves up, shifting the debt which generates obligatory reciprocity away from the human recipients.

The centrality of incommensurability marks both the avenues open to people for earning shares and the ways in which sharing is morally valued.

This incommensurability is a serious point of incompatibility when Iñupiat find themselves negotiating with national and international agencies.

This material stands in contrast to much of the other material in this volume, not because it is more complex (although it is certainly that) but because in curious ways it does not seem to reflect the tensions so clearly revealed in others' papers between the individual desire to have and the injunction to share 'with everybody'. In part, I suspect, this might be because Iñupiat to a significant degree do not have to give away everything. Like Neakok, they can decide how much and with whom they should share. As well, the deeply felt gratitude Iñupiat express toward the animals they depend on reflects, as far as I can tell, an absolutely genuine sense of satisfaction gained through sharing. It is a sense of satisfaction most clearly expressed in terms of participating in the whole with 'the mighty bowhead'.

The distinction between individual and personal property in general – as well as that between the relative emphasis of responsibilities and rights in the organisation of property – helps us to understand some of the ways in which structurally equal moral individuals may nonetheless find themselves in a system in which some persons (who may or may not be individuals) may make claims (and have claims made upon them) with reference to resources that are not open to others. It seems important to recognise that these relations are by no means disengaged from property, but differently engaged with property. Woodburn's insistence on recognising the importance of asking whether systems foster or avoid dependence on specific individuals seems key. To that point I would simply add, in quite a Durkheimian way, that the degree to which the division of labour fosters neither independence nor dependence but interdependence seems a crucial factor in allowing the pursuit of complex goals in the absence of complex hierarchy.

Acknowledgements

As always I wish to thank Raymond and Marie Neakok and Mattie Bodfish, who have provided me with friendship, 'family-ship' and guidance for twenty years. For the past several years, as I have worked with and for the Alaska Eskimo Whaling Commission, Maggie Ahmaogak has been a valued source of information, astute comment and direction. Ernest S. Burch, Jr., Julie Cruikshank and Marilyn Strathern, as so often, had things to say that made me think. For this set of arguments in particular, I would also like to express my thanks to Nurit Bird-David, Nick Peterson and Richard Lee, whose comments at the workshop out of which this volume developed were usefully thought-provoking.

Appendices

Appendix A: The Annual Cycle and the Gendered Division of Labour
This information, provided by Maggie Ahmaogak and her father, Arnold Brower, Sr., documents who needs to do what and when. It illustrates the

gendered nature of the division of a whaling captain couple's labour and identifies (at least some of) the purchases necessary to carry them out.

MEN
Winter

Under the direction of the whaling captain, the male members of the crew help with the tasks below. The captain purchases any necessary materials, equipment and/or provisions. [*Construct boat frame* – a long-term investment that should last for several years]. *Repair boat frame*. Purchase lumber, nails, etc. as well as coffee, tea and so forth. *Hunt caribou* – meat needed for whaling; skins needed as mattresses; responsibility of the captain. Purchase supplies needed for winter hunting.

Spring

Prepare *ugruk* skins for *umiaq* (thawing with natural gas; storing so they will stay pliable); purchase supplemental skins if not enough have been caught during the summer; rope for lashing; natural gas. This is the captain's responsibility.

Put on new boat cover. Men crew members bring the skins into the sheltered area where women will sew. Once the cover has been put together, the men take it to the boat frame and cover the frame.

The entire process for both women and men takes a full day.

WOMEN

The whaling captain wife must begin to *consider sewing needs*: fur parkas, fur socks, fur hats; *kammik*s (skin boots) if needed. Although other wives will help, it is the responsibility of the whaling captain wife to ensure that all crew members are adequately clothed for spring whaling conditions. Resources needed include furs, needles, thread. *Pull, scrape, dry caribou tendons* for sinew for skin boat cover. This is labour intensive, but should not require purchases unless sinew is not used for the thread.

Begin to prepare braided sinew; this is otherwise purchased. This may be a single or collective activity, but must be overseen by the whaling captain wife. According to M. Aiken, this is her single most important responsibility – namely the safety of the crew which would be jeopardised if anything happens to the skin boat while out on the water.

Prepare new boat cover (approximately every two years). Professional sewers, invited by the whaling captain wife, arrive to sew the *ugruk* skins. They will be paid, and often bring their own equipment (needles, thread, etc.); whaling captain wife responsible for ensuring proper supply is on hand. Coffee, tea, snacks also provided.

Once the cover is on, the sewers then check the cover for tears and repair them.

Clean ice cellar (captain and crew members)	Distribute meat/fish from ice cellar (captain wife and crew members)
Check and repair gear (camping gear, whaling equipment, communication technology, etc.); replace if needed. Whaling captain's responsibility, with crew's help	Check over camping clothing; make sure crew's gear is in good condition; sew *qatignisi*, snow shirts. Whaling captain wife responsibility. Purchase cloth, etc.
	Begin to stock 'grub box'; buy groceries, supply cooking utensils.
Make ice road (snow-machines, fuel, utensils). This is both labour intensive and potentially dangerous. Captain's oversight.	

I have omitted documenting activities involved in the spring whaling season itself as it is both familiar and well documented. Preparations for *Nalukataq* are detailed in Appendix D.

Summer

Ugruk hunting: skins, meat, oil will all be used for the following whaling season. Motorised boats will be used; must be maintained, repaired. Sealing equipment (guns, floats, harpoon, ammunition, etc) bought or repaired. Gunny sacks for seal skins; fuel, etc. purchased.	Groceries bought, food prepared for day and/or overnight trips. Purchases include materials needed for storage: ziplock bags, paper towels; coffee, tea, snacks for helpers and so forth.
Walrus hunting. Walrus meat is considered particularly warming whaling food. This hunt requires the same repair, purchase needs as above. Primary butchering usually done by the men on the ice floes.	Same responsibilities as for ugruk hunting.

Once meat is brought back to shore, both men and women finish butchering, preserving meat and oil, preparing flipper for fermentation and storing finished products. Depending on the community, walrus skins are prepared for use as boat covers.

Autumn
Caribou hunting: for dried meat, sinew and fresh meat. Often camping is undertaken by couples and/or families. Equipment for inland camping needed, including river-going boats. Butchering includes removal of sinew from legs and back for thread. Meat is dried on rack.

Fall whaling demands a sea-going vessel that can withstand potentially rough weather/seas. Basic gear is the same as in the spring. But because this is not ice-based whaling, separate expenses include: transportation of whaleboat to launch several miles out of town; equipment usage when whale is pulled up onto sand and then transported to butchering site on the tundra. Plastic sheeting is laid out on the ground before the whale is placed on the butchering site. Gendered responsibilities are generally the same.

Fishing takes place throughout the year and demands different equipment depending on the seasonal conditions. Dried fish is a staple food for both camping and whaling. Both men and women may be involved at all stages of fishing, preparing, storing.

Appendix B: The seasons and space
Seasonal variation as well as different eco-zones, documented below, demand different equipment, which must be available and in good repair. Whaling preparations depend on them all.

Hunting on the sea ice
- Spring whaling: skin boat, overnight camping equipment, winter clothing, sleds, snow-machines
- *Ugruk* and walrus hunting: motorised, sea-going boats

Spring inland travel
- Geese hunting: snow-machines, sleds, tents and related equipment

Summer and autumn inland travel
- Caribou hunting and fishing: boat appropriate for shallow water, camping equipment, fish/meat drying equipment

Autumn marine travel
- Autumn whaling: motorised (sea-going) boats.

Appendix C: Patterns of purchasing requirements.
The annual costs of whaling cannot be assumed to stay even approximately the same over the intermediate long-term experience of a whaling captain couple.

Examples of long-term purchases
- Autumn whaling boat (motor, etc.) – capable of navigating rough seas
- Navigational equipment (personal locator beacon, CB radio, etc.)
- Other equipment specific to whaling: darting guns, shoulder guns, lances, harpoons, winches, block and tackle, butchering utensils and so forth.

Examples of predictable expenditures that are incurred only with a successful hunt

- Food for everyone who comes to help butcher: coffee, tea, *uunaaliit* (hot boiled *maktak*); this is likely to be for well over 100 people.
- Food for the entire community. This happens on three different occasions, each of which varies slightly.

  1. *Immediately after the catch*, a hot meal is served at the house of the whaling captain couple for all who wish to attend. The *niqipiaq*, or real food, is whale – which demands considerable time to cut up and cook. As well, stewed fruit, eskimo doughnuts, sometimes cake, coffee, tea and cold drinks are prepared for as many as 2,000 people. Paper plates, cups, towels are supplied.
  2. *At appugauti* (when the whaling boat is brought up for the last time of the season), community members are invited to each on the beach. The captain and crew members have gone geese hunting in order to provide the basics for goose soup (demanding equipment needed for inland hunting); *mikigaq* (fermented whale meat and blood) has also been prepared, demanding special containers as well as close attention so that the fermentation process does not go wrong.
  3. *Nalukataq* is the most elaborate of all and will attract not only community members but visitors from elsewhere. All are welcomed. In Barrow the feast demands three separate servings, each of which involves different sorts of foods as well as different kinds of preparation: at noon, soup, coffee, tea; at 3 o'clock, *mikigak*, stewed fruit, coffee tea; at 6 o'clock, *quaq*, or frozen meat, multiple kinds of *maktak*, cakes, coffee and tea. The preparation is organised by the whaling captain wife, although the preparation itself is by no means carried out only by the women connected to the successful crew.

- Freight costs incurred shipping meat to other communities (sometimes, if as a gift from the whaling captain couple, at their expense; if as part of a share, at the expense of the receiving community)

Examples of purchases lasting more than one season, needing regular replacement

- Snow-machines
- Snow-machine parts
- Sleds
- Tents, tarpaulins for covering sleds etc.
- Skinboat frame
- Skinboat cover (see Appendix A)
- Braided sinew or other thread, either made or purchased
- Coleman stoves, lanterns, etc.
- Fur for clothing: parkas, socks, hats

- Storage containers for, eg, mikigaq (which is currently kept apart to lessen likelihood of botulism)
- Materials for setting up community-wide feasts: windbreak, tables

Examples of purchases requiring annual replacement
- *Qatignisi* – white snowshirts that are necessary for hunting on the ice, especially for whales – requires specific material.

Examples of ongoing expenses
- Ammunition: whale bombs, shells
- Food
- Clothing
- Fuel for snow-machines, coleman stoves, lanterns, trucks for transporting boats out to launching site, etc.

Appendix D: The Celebratory Cycle
The annual whaling cycle is punctuated by special costs of celebratory events. The cycle may never end, but the costs of things and demands on labour are unevenly spread throughout the year.

- *Fall whaling* (late September): community-wide hospitality is provided in the house of each captain couple who has successfully taken a whale.
- *Thanksgiving* (late November): a community-wide feast takes place in the village churches and is served by church deacons. The food is provided by whaling captain couples and their crew members.
- *Christmas* (December): This is celebrated in the same manner as Thanksgiving.
- *Spring whaling* (April/May): helpers are fed on the ice when a whale has been caught; hospitality is provided by the whaling captain couple from their home as soon as the whale meat and *maktak* has been brought ashore.
- *Apugauti* (May): food is provided for all comers when whale boat is brought back to shore for the last time in a season.
- *Nalukataq* (June): this feast marks the end of a successful whaling season; visitors often travel from as far as Anchorage, Kotzebue, sometimes Siberia, and beyond in order to attend. Whaling captains may – but do not have to – join forces in order to mount hospitality for over a thousand people. All are welcome and all are provided not only with shares, but also with a day-long meal of shared food. In Barrow and in Wainwright, *Nalukataq* takes place over the course of a day; in Point Hope, the celebration lasts for three days.

Although the cycle seen from this angle makes it clear how communal the period between September and June is, these events need to be seen as punctuation marks, as it were. As Maggie Ahmaogak's material shows very explicitly (Appendices A–C), activities connected directly to whaling take place throughout the entire year, sometimes as part of a communal effort and sometimes in much smaller groups.

Notes

1. See in particular Woodburn's (1980, 1982) arguments concerning the bases for egalitarianism among hunter/gatherers and Bodenhorn (1989, 1993, 1997, 2000a and 2000b) for specific attention to contemporary Iñupiaq material. Iñupiat is the collective name of the people who have inhabited the northern coast of what is now Alaska for millennia; Iñupiaq is the singular as well as the adjectival form.
2. E.S. Burch, Jr. argues that many of the egalitarian features of Iñupiaq social organisation developed during what he calls the 'transitional' period – between approximately 1850 and 1940 (1975: 205). The people talking to Burch as well as the people talking to me have insisted on the importance of recognising variation and warned consistently against overgeneralisation.
3. This was made crystal clear to me in a recent meeting of Iñupiaq translators which I had the good fortune to be invited to sit in on. An extended discussion about how to translate the phrase, 'you have the right to remain silent' into Iñupiaq ultimately came to agreement on a variant of 'expectation'. I asked James Nageak, my neighbour, if this would be the same as the expectation of a share as something that is non-negotiable. He looked at me in astonishment and said, 'but the right to a share depends on a responsibility!'
4. The Marine Mammal Protection Act prohibits the sale of these raw materials, but recognises the Iñupiaq right to continue their customary practices of transforming them into things that may be sold.
5. Practices vary significantly across the Arctic Slope region; ethnographic details refer to information given to me by Barrow and Wainwright people over the course of two decades. Today, Barrow is the regional capital with some 3,500 residents, 60 percent of whom are Iñupiaq; Wainwright, located approximately 70 miles to the west of Barrow, is a village of just over 400 inhabitants, approximately 90 percent of whom are Iñupiaq. This most recent research was conducted between 1997 and 2000 under the sponsorship of the Alaska Eskimo Whaling Commission and funded through the National Science Foundation.
6. For the purposes of this paper, I take property to mean the organisation of claims that can be made legitimately between people with reference to recognised resources. Claims may be about responsibilities as well as rights and they may refer to nonmaterial as well as material resources. Considerable debate has taken place around the question of whether 'rights' is too ethnocentric a term to use analytically across cultures. Iñupiat use the term when speaking English, although, as I have noted above, they distinguish the single English word with more than one Iñupiaq word when talking about different sorts of rights.
7. I am not going to undertake a review of this vast literature, but it is probably worth noting that within anthropology, Lévi-Strauss first discussed the balance between responsibilities and privileges for leadership in 1944; Firth included the notion of obligation in his definition of property as early as 1965. See Hann (1998) for a general overview; Barnard and Woodburn (1988) for a relatively recent review of work done among hunters and gatherers.
8. See Bodenhorn (in preparation) for an examination of the ways in which these relations have shifted historically.
9. There are many and varied sources re this, but see especially Ingold et al. (1988); Wilmsen (1988); Burch and Ellanna (1994).
10. Personal communication, Halle workshop.
11. See Carrithers et al. (1984). I am well aware how close this may sound to M. Strathern's discussions of the relational nature of transactions in Papua New Guinea (see especially 1988). A great deal of her argument rests on the distinction between property relations of dividual Mount Hageners and individual Europeans. My argument is very different. I am suggesting that in systems where individuals may be conceived as moral persons, they may also operate simultaneously within a system which recognises the claims of a smaller subset of persons (as they do in England). Their co-existence has implications for the possibilities of a property system that can unite and differentiate at the same time.

12. Tim Ingold discussed this notion of ownership quite explicitly with relation to hunter/gatherer social relations and the presence or absence of what he called 'social storage' (1983: 561).
13. This may well be a change. Both Burch (1988a) and Weyer (1967) suggest that historically some personal property would be buried with the person it belonged to. In addition, Burch mentions that some songs could be traded whereas others were so much part of the person that they could only be sung in secret (1988a: 101).
14. A whaling captain must be married, for it is the wife who, it is generally thought, attracts the whale (see Bodenhorn 1993). While reviewing 1991 Elders' Conference transcripts on whaling, I noticed that the *umialik* and his wife were often referred to as the 'whaling captain couple' – a convention I have adopted (see IHLC, in preparation).
15. These sources include the diaries of John Simpson (1875), ship's doctor, and Rochefort Maguire, first mate of the HMS *Plover* which wintered over in Barrow from 1851–53 (see Bockstoce 1988). Murdoch (1892) spent two years in Barrow thirty years; Charles D. Brower (nd) left a journal recounting his life in the Arctic from 1885 to 1933; Ernest S. Burch, Jr. continues his historical research on Northwestern Alaska which encompasses most of the nineteenth century (1970, 1975, 1988a, 1988b); the Iñupiat History, Language and Culture Commission (IHLC) has supported ongoing historical research and has organised annual Elders' Conferences since 1978, which are recorded on tape and, as time and resources allow, are transcribed into Iñupiaq and translated into English.
16. See the 1991 IHLC Elders' Conference on whaling; here Aveoganna was taking part in the women's session. See also Bodenhorn (2001) for a detailed consideration of the testimony produced during this three-day conference.
17. Ahmaogak, interview, 9/97; Neakok in Bodenhorn (1988a: 26); see also Marie Adams, in Bodenhorn (1988b).
18. See Bodenhorn (1988a). This was part of a project conducted for the IHLC, documenting those factors people felt strengthened and threatened their families. People not identified by name asked to remain anonymous.
19. Interview in Bodenhorn (1988: 57). This idea was stated in a number of ways. 'Land claims is open, free to everyone,' Gilbert Mongoyak asserted when asked about the idea of applying for an (individual) allotment (ibid: 81).
20. Participation in multiple crews increases the chances of being part of a 'first strike' crew, which receives the largest crew share.
21. Households in this case are defined by the commensal unit. Unmarried children who may sleep elsewhere but eat with parents, for instance, are counted.
22. See Bodenhorn (1988a, 1989, 1990, 2000b).
23. This is based on a survey of twenty-seven households conducted in 1985, supplemented by less systematic information from seventy-eight households. See Bodenhorn (2000b) for a more complete discussion.
24. And here it seems that households without active hunters potentially lose out. They can and do participate in share-earning activity – helping to butcher, gifting a rifle to a male relative, contributing cash to a hunting expedition – but their sharing networks will almost always be more restricted than those sustaining active hunting households.
25. Informal conversations over the past several years suggest that this custom continues to be followed to varying degrees and in different ways in different North Slope villages.
26. In my experience, these differences are not always clear cut. Recently, a whaling captain died who had several active whaling sons. His wife decided which son should take over based on her estimation of who possessed the multiple kinds of skills that were needed. 'Inherited position' in this case was achieved rather than ascribed through birth order.
27. See Burch (1975), Worl, Worl and Lonner (1981), Bockstoce (1986), Bodenhorn (1989).
28. See, e.g., Davies et al. (1991) for conservationist views; Einarsson (1994), Kalland (1994) and Wenzel (1991) for anthropological analyses.
29. See Jolles (1995), AEWC (1998), Bodenhorn (2001).
30. 'Ownership' of land meaning that one has the right to be asked before someone uses it, for instance, with the obligation to say 'yes'. See, for instance, Williams (1982).

31. I was intrigued to see that Lévi-Strauss asked precisely the same question about Nambikuara leaders. His answer, that 'there are in any human group men who, unlike most of their companions ... feel a strong appeal to responsibility...' (1967: 61), is perhaps not as satisfying as it might be.
32. During February 2001, I travelled to Wainwright and Kaktovik, villages to the west and east of Barrow, in order to meet with the local whaling captains' associations to discuss future directions of research. Of the twenty-odd captains we met with, one held a position in the local formal political system; others held jobs as mechanics or builders; still others were retired.

References

Ahmaogak, M. n.d. Draft of whaling activity costs submitted by M. Ahmaogak, Executive Director of the Alaska Eskimo Whaling Commission to the IRS.

Alaska Consultants. 1984. With Stephen Braund and Associates, *Subsistence Study of Alaskan Eskimo Whaling Villages*. Anchorage: US Department of Interior.

AEWC (Alaska Eskimo Whaling Commission). 1998. *AEWC: The Alaska Eskimo Whaling Commission*. Barrow, Alaska: AEWC.

Altman, J. and N. Peterson 1988. 'Rights to Game and Rights to Cash among Contemporary Australian Hunter-gatherers'. In T. Ingold, D. Riches and J. Woodburn (eds), *Hunters and Gatherers: Vol. 2, Property, Power and Ideology*. Oxford: Berg, pp. 75–94.

Appadurai, A. (ed.) 1986. 'Introduction: Commodities and the Politics of Value,' *The Social Life of Things: Commodities in Cultural Perspective*. Cambridge: Cambridge University Press, pp. 3–63.

Attungana, P. 1986. 'Address to the Alaska Eskimo Whaling Commission', *Uiñiq: The Open Lead*. April: 16ff., translation James Nageak.

Barnard, A. and J. Woodburn 1988. Introduction. In, T. Ingold, D. Riches and J. Woodburn (eds), *Hunters and Gatherers: Vol. 2, Property, Power and Ideology*. Oxford: Berg.

Bockstoce, J. 1986. *Whales, Ice and Men*. Seattle: University of Washington Press.

Bockstoce, J. (ed.) 1988. *The Journal of Rochefort Maguire, 1852–1854: Two Years at Point Barrow, Alaska, aboard H.M.S. 'Plover' in the Search for Sir John Franklin*. London: Hakluyt Society.

Bodenhorn, B. (ed.) 1988a. *Vol. I: Life Histories; Documenting Iñupiat Family Relationships in Changing Times*. Unpublished report prepared for the North Slope Borough Commission on Iñupiaq History, Language and Culture and the Alaska Humanities Forum, Barrow, Alaska.

Bodenhorn, B. 1988b. *Vol II: Family Stresses; Documenting Iñupiat Family Relationships in Changing Times*. Unpublished report prepared for the North Slope Borough Commission on Iñupiaq History, Language and Culture and the Alaska Humanities Forum, Barrow, Alaska.

—— 1989. '"The Animals Come to Me; They Know I Share": Iñupiaq Kinship, Changing Economic Relations and Enduring World Views on Alaska's North Slope'. Unpublished PhD dissertation, Cambridge University.

—— 1990. '"I'm not the great hunter; my wife is": Iñupiat and Anthropological Models of Gender', *Études/Inuit/Studies*, 14, 1–2: 55–74.

—— 1993. 'Public spaces; private places: public and private revisited on the North Slope of Alaska'. In B. Bender (ed.), *Landscape: Politics and Perspectives*. Oxford: Berg.

—— 1997. 'Person, Place and Parentage: Ecology, Identity and Social Relations on the North Slope of Alaska', in T. Mousalimas (ed.) *Arctic Ecology and Identity*. Los Angeles: International Society for Trans-Oceanic Research, pp. 103–32.

—— 2000a. '"He used to be my relative": exploring the bases of relatedness among Iñupiat of Alaska'. In J. Carsten (ed.) *Cultures of Relatedness*. Cambridge: Cambridge University Press, pp.128–48.

—— 2000b. '"It's good to know who your relatives are, but we were taught to share with everybody": Shares and Sharing among Iñupiaq Households'. In, G. Wenzel, G. Hovelsrud-Broda and N. Kishigami (eds), *The Social Economy of Sharing: Resource Allocation and Modern Hunter/Gatherers*. Osaka, Japan: Senri Ethnological Studies 53, pp. 27–60.

—— 2001. 'It's Traditional to Change: a Case Study of Strategic Decision-making', *Cambridge Anthropology* 22, 1: 24–51.
—— In preparation. The whaling captain couple, status, power and wealth: a historical re-examination of the sociodynamics of a shifting relationship.
Bourdieu, P. 1977. *Outline of a Theory of Practice*. Cambridge: Cambridge University Press.
Brower, C. n.d. *Barrow Journal, 1885–1933*. University of Alaska Archives, Fairbanks, Alaska.
Brower, H. 1981. Affidavit, Appendix G in ICAS v USII; brief filed before the 9th District Court.
Burch, E.S., Jr. 1970. 'The Eskimo trading partnership in Northwest Alaska: a study in "balanced reciprocity"', *Anthropological Papers of the University of Alaska* 15, 1: 49–80.
—— 1975. *Eskimo Kinsmen: Changing Family Relationships in Northwest Alaska*. NY: West Publishing Company.
—— 1980. 'Traditional Eskimo Society in Northwest Alaska'. In Y. Kotani and W.B. Workman (eds), *Alaskan Native Culture and History*. Osaka: Senri Ethnological Studies, 4.
—— 1988a. 'Modes of Exchange in North-west Alaska'. In T. Ingold, D. Riches and J. Woodburn (eds). *Hunters and Gatherers: Vol. 2, Property, Power and Ideology*. Oxford: Berg, pp. 95–109.
—— 1988b. 'War and trade'. In W. Fitzhugh and A. Crowell (eds), *Crossroads of Continents: cultures of Siberia and Alaska*. Washington D.C.: Smithsonian Insitution Press, pp. 227–40.
Burch, E.S., Jr. and T. Correll 1971. 'Alliance and Conflict: inter-regional relations in North Alaska'. In L. Guemple (ed.), *Alliance in Eskimo Society*. AES, Seattle: University of Washington Press.
Burch, E.S., Jr. and L. Ellanna (eds) 1994. Editorial, *Key Issues in Hunter-Gatherer Research*. Oxford: Berg Press, pp. 219–22.
Davies, N., A.M. Smith, S.R. Whyte and V. Williams (eds), 1991. *Why Whales?* Bath: The Whale and Dolphin Conservation Society.
Durkheim, E. 1972. [1893]. *The Division of Labour in Society* (De la division du travail social). In A. Giddens (ed.), *Emile Durkheim, Selected Writings*. Cambridge: Cambridge University Press.
Einarsson, N. 1993. All Animals are Created Equal, but Some are Cetaceans: Conservation and Culture Conflict. In K. Milton (ed.), *Environmentalism: the View from Anthropology*. London: Routledge.
Firth, R. 1965 (1939). *Primitive Polynesian Economy*. London: Routledge.
Freeman, M.R. and U.P. Kreuter (eds) 1994. *Elephants and Whales: Resources for whom?* Basel: Gordon and Breach.
Guemple, L. (ed.) 1971. *Alliance in Eskimo Society*. AES, Seattle: University of Washington Press.
Guemple, L. 1988. 'Teaching social relations to Inuit children'. In T. Ingold, D. Riches and J. Woodburn (eds) *Hunters and Gatherers (2): Property, Power and Ideology*. Oxford: Berg Press, pp.131–49.
Hann, C.M. 1998. *Property Relations: Renewing the Anthropological Tradition*. Cambridge: Cambridge University Press.
Hess, B. 1994. *A Photographic Celebration of Kivgiq, The Messenger Feast*. Barrow, Alaska: North Slope Borough.
Humphrey, C. 1998, 'The Domestic Mode of Production in Post-Soviet Russia', *Anthropology Today* 14, 3: 3–7.
—— 2002, Rituals of death and personal property in socialist Mongolia. *JRAI* 8, 1: 65–87.
Humphrey, C. and S. Hugh-Jones (eds) 1992. Introduction, *Barter, Exchange and Value: an Anthropological Approach*. Cambridge: Cambridge University Press.
Ingold, T. 1983. 'The Significance of Storage in Hunting Societies', *Man* (NS) 18: 553–71.
—— 1986. *The Appropriation of Nature*. Manchester: Manchester University Press.
Ingold, T., D. Riches and J. Woodburn (eds) 1988. *Hunters and Gatherers: Vol. 2, Property, Power and Ideology*. Oxford: Berg
(IHLC) Iñupiaq History, Language and Culture Commission 1981. *Puiguitkaat: the 1978 Elders' Conference*. Barrow, Alaska: North Slope Borough, transcribed and translated by Kisautaq/Leona Okakok.
—— 1993. *Uqaluktuat: 1980 Elders' Conference Women's Session*. Barrow, Alaska: North Slope Borough, transcribed and translated by Dorothy Panikpak Edwardsen.

—— In preparation. Transcribed and translated tapes to 1991 Elders' Conference on whaling; General Session, Women's Session and Men's Session, Barrow, Alaska, 10–12 July.

Jolles, C. (ed.) 1995. 'Speaking of Whaling: a Transcript of the Alaska Eskimo Whaling Commission Panel Presentation on Native Whaling'. In A. McCartney (ed.) *Hunting the Largest Animals: Native Whaling in the Western Arctic and Subarctic.* Studies in Whaling, 3, Occasional Publication no. 36. Edmonton: The Canadian Circumpolar Institute, University of Alberta.

Kalland, A. 1994. 'Whose whale is that? Diverting the Commodity Path'. In M. Freeman and V. Kreuter (eds), *Elephants and Whales: Resources for Whom?* Basel: Gordon and Breach, pp. 159–86.

Kruse, J. 1982. *Subsistence and the North Slope Iñupiat: An Analysis of the Effects of Energy Development.* Man in the Arctic Series, 56. Anchorage: University of Alaska Institute of Social and Economic Research.

Larson, M.A. 1995. 'And Then There were None: The "Disappearance" of the *Qargi* in Northern Alaska'. In A.P. McCartney (ed.), *Hunting the Largest Animals: Native Whaling in the Western Arctic and Subarctic.* Studies in Whaling, 3, Occasional Publication, 36. Edmonton: University of Alberta, pp. 207–20.

Leavitt, D. 1981. Affidavit/Appendix J, ICAS v. US II. Brief filed before the 9th District Court.

Lévi-Strauss, C. 1969. *The Elementary Structures of Kinship.* Boston: Beacon Press.

—— 1967 (1944). 'The Social and Psychological Aspects of Chieftenship in a Primitive Tribe: The Nambikuara of Northwest Mato Grosso'. In R. Cohen and J. Middleton (eds), *Comparative Political Systems: Studies in the Politics of Pre-industrial Societies.* Garden City, NY: The Natural History Press, pp. 45–62.

Lopez, B. 1986. *Arctic Dreams.* NY: Scribner and Sons.

Lowenstein, T. 1981. *Some Aspects of Sea Ice Subsistence Hunting in Point Hope.* Alaska, Barrow: North Slope Borough.

Luton, H. 1985. *Effects of Renewable Resource Harvest Disruptions on Socioeconomic and Sociocultural Systems: Wainwright.* Technical Report 91. Anchorage: Minerals Management Service.

Macpherson, C.B. 1978. *Property: Mainstream and Critical Positions.* Toronto: University of Toronto Press.

Mauss, M. 1984. 'The Category of the Person'. In M. Carrithers, S. Collins and S. Lukes (eds), *The Category of the Person: Anthropology, Philosophy, History.* Cambridge: Cambridge University Press.

Murdoch, J. 1892. *Ethnological Results of the Point Barrow Expedition.* Ninth Annual Report to the Bureau of Ethnology. Washington, D.C.: Government Printing Office.

Nelson, R. 1969. *Hunters of the Northern Ice.* Chicago: Chicago University Press.

—— 1981. *Harvest of the Sea: Coastal Subsistence in Modern Wainwright.* Barrow: North Slope Borough.

Peterson, N. 1993. 'Demand Sharing: Reciprocity and the Pressure for Generosity among Foragers'. *American Anthropologist* 95, 4: 860–74.

Pryor, F.L. 1977. *The Origins of the Economy: a Comparative Study of Distribution in Primitive and Peasant Economies.* NY: Academic Press.

Pulo, T. 1980. *Whaling: a Way of Life.* National Bilingual Materials Development Center, Rural Education, Anchorage: University of Alaska.

Rainey, F. 1947. *The Whale Men of Tigara.* Anthropological Papers of the Museum of Natural History 41, 2: 231–483.

Riches, D. 1975. 'Cash, Credit and Gambling in a Modern Eskimo Economy: Speculations on Origins of Spheres of Economic Exchange', *Man* (NS), 10: 21–33.

Sahlins, M. 1972. 'The Original Affluent Society', *Stone Age Economics.* Chicago: University of Chicago Press.

Simpson, J. 1875. 'Observations on the Western Eskimo and the Country they inhabit from Notes taken during two years at Point Barrow'. *Arctic Geography and Ethnology*, Royal Geographical Society, London: John Murray, Albemarle St.

Sonnenfeld, J. 1975. 'Changes in Subsistence among the Barrow Eskimo'. Unpublished doctoral dissertation, University of Pennsylvania.

Spencer, R.F. 1959. *The North Alaskan Eskimo: A Study in Ecology and Society*. Washington, D.C.: Smithsonian Institution Press.
—— 1971. 'The Social Composition of the North Alaskan Whaling Crew', in L. Guemple (ed.), *Alliance in Eskimo Society*. AES, Seattle: University of Washington Press.
Stackhouse, M. nd. 'Traditional Rules of Whaling'. Unpublished paper. Barrow, Alaska.
Stefansson, V. 1913. *My Life with the Eskimos*. NY: MacMillan and Company.
Strathern, M. 1988. *The Gender of the Gift*. Manchester: Manchester University Press.
Wenzel, G. 1991. *Animal Rights, Human Rights – Ecology, Economy and Ideology in the Canadian Arctic*. Toronto: University of Toronto Press.
Weyer, E.M. 1967. 'The Structure of Social Organisation among the Eskimo'. In R. Cohen and J. Middleton (eds), *Comparative Political Systems*. Garden City, NY: The Natural History Press, pp. 1–14.
Williams, N.M. 1982. 'A boundary is to cross' In N.H. Williams and E.S. Hunn (eds), *Resource Managers: North American and Australian Hunter/gatherers*. Canberra: Australian Institute of Aboriginal Studies.
Wilmsen, E.N. (ed.) 1988. *We are Here: Politics of Aboriginal Land Tenure*. Berkeley: University of California Press.
Woodburn, J. 1980. 'Hunters and Gatherers Today and the Reconstruction of the Past'. In E. Gellner (ed.), *Soviet and Western Anthropology*. London: Duckworth and Company, pp. 95–118.
—— 1982. 'Egalitarian Societies', *Man*, 17, 3: 431–51.
—— 1998. '"Sharing is not a Form of Exchange": An Analysis of Property-sharing in Immediate Return Hunter-Gatherer Societies.' In C. Hann (ed.), *Property Relations: Renewing the Anthropological Tradition*, Cambridge: Cambridge University Press, pp. 48–63.
Worl, R. 1980. 'North Slope Whaling Complex'. In Y. Kotani and W.B. Workman (eds), *Native Culture and History*. SENRI Series 4. Osaka: National Museum of Ethnology, pp. 305–20.
Worl, R. and C. Smythe 1986. *Barrow: a Decade of Modernization*. Technical Report 125. Anchorage, Alaska: Minerals Management Service.
Worl, R., R. Worl and T. Lonner 1981. *Beaufort Sea Sociocultural Systems Update Analysis*. Anchorage, Alaska: Bureau of Land Management.

6

Possession, Equality and Gender Relations in |Gui Discourse

Kazuyoshi Sugawara

Introduction

The fundamental question posed in this paper is quite simple: what does it mean to 'possess' another person? In everyday Japanese discourse, we hear phrases such as 'She is mine' or literally 'She is my *thing*' used in a male-centric context. Similarly, we might heave a sigh, saying, 'I have been thrown away by her (him)' or 'Our relationship has been broken.' These sentences sound so ordinary that it is difficult to recognise them as metaphorical. We are no more able to 'hold' another person in our hands than to 'break' a relationship, because interpersonal relationships are not tangible objects, but abstractions based on countless face-to-face interactions.

However, these metaphors concerning 'possession' in interpersonal relationships derive their life from our immediate experience, i.e. a mother can actually hold her baby in her arms. To develop this point more clearly, I would like to draw on an example from primatology, a neighbouring discipline to anthropology. I have chosen to examine the social organisation of the hamadryas baboons (*Papio hamadryas*) inhabiting the arid savannah of Ethiopia, not only because I studied their social behaviour during my early career as an anthropologist (Sugawara 1988), but also because their society provides valuable clues for understanding how one individual can 'possess' another.

The basic social unit of the hamadryas baboon is called a 'band', usually composed of forty to one hundred animals. Each band is segmented into a number of 'one-male units' or 'harems'. Hamadryas males are thought to be equipped with the genetically determined program of 'herding technique'. Whenever a female strays far away from the male leader, he attacks her, often biting her neck in an apparently ritualised way.

Another mechanism contributing to the cohesion of the one-male unit is the 'pair-gestalt inhibition'. During field experiments, H. Kummer and his students confirmed that a male who had observed a male-and-female pair in close contact, through either a glass window or a one-way mirror, would refrain from interacting with them, once introduced into the same room. This behaviour was consistent, whatever the dominance relationship between the two males. Kummer (1973) assumes that the hamadryas male is psychologically inhibited from intervening in the affinitive interactions of other animals. This inhibition is provoked by the visual perception of the pair's 'gestalt' or close physical proximity and contact. Furthermore, the male in contact with the female tends to groom her more eagerly when he can see his 'rival' through the glass than when his vision is obstructed.

In this example, we see the prototypical situation of the 'triangle of desire': the desire, while not directly oriented to the incentive per se, is mediated by the attention to the rival. Even though this interpretation sounds quite anthropomorphic, the following points are worth noticing, as they clarify the basic conditions under which the term 'possession of the other' is substantiated beyond metaphorical allusion:

- the subject maintains close contact or proximity with a particular individual;
- this contact/proximity can be observed by surrounding individuals;
- the potential rivals are inhibited from intervening in this specific interaction.

Turning to human society, we can easily find interpersonal relationships that are analogous to the above definition of 'possession', i.e., conjugal linkage. In order to balance the male-centric posture of hamadryas society, in which an aggressive male – his body weight is twice as much as the female's – will normally 'possess' several females, only slight modification of this definition of possession allows us to characterise the analogous voluntary, spontaneous and reciprocal interactions through which a wife and husband 'possess' each other. This analogy may seem rather predictable, because we tend to regard married couples as having an exclusive and universally respected bond.

However, serious difficulty arises when we attempt to identify hamadryas 'possession' with conjugal linkage in human foraging societies. The most distinctive adaptive value of conjugal pair formation is the division of labour. This precludes constant proximity and contact between bonded males and females, simply because they engage in different subsistence activities. In the Central Kalahari Desert, only men hunt, while gathering is primarily carried out by women. During the better part of the day, husband and wife cannot help becoming separated. It is unreasonable to expect potential rivals to be controlled by the pair-gestalt inhibition, when so many opportunities occur during which the gestalt is not apparent.

The remedy to this problem is quite simple and commonplace: laws, norms and sanctions. Ultimately, the 'language game' embedded in each society defines right and wrong, and thus endows certain forms of interpersonal relationship with legitimacy. Potential rivals are inhibited from trespassing the legitimate 'preserve'[1] of intimacy secured by a particular couple, not only through observation of the pair-gestalt, but also by the expectation that any breach will incur communal sanction. However, this concept of 'social contract' incurs another riddle, especially when we consider the nature of 'possession' in those foraging societies essentially characterised by 'egalitarianism'.

Generally speaking, any attempt to theorise the political process in 'egalitarian society' must tackle this riddle. How is it possible that members of egalitarian society are usually inhibited from wrongdoing, even in a society characterised by the virtual absence of laws and social hierarchy, or, more straightforwardly, by the lack of systematic devices for violent communal sanction? In his intriguing papers 'Minimum Politics' and 'Egalitarian Societies', J. Woodburn tackled this riddle. At least one of his inductions in the Hadza ethnography is quite striking; there undoubtedly exist implicit devices for violent sanction, i.e. 'the hazard of being shot when asleep in camp at night or being ambushed when out hunting alone in the bush' (Woodburn 1982: 436; see also 1979: 252). On the other hand, G. Silberbauer, in his effort to explicate the concept of 'coercion' among the G/wi (|Gui in my notation), proposed another answer. While the coercion implicit in communal consensus could not help being nullified 'when the other members exercised their freedom to move to another band[,] ... the band has the potential means of bringing a delinquent member ... to heel by withdrawing the normal social facilities of cooperation, protection and fellowship' (Silberbauer 1982: 33). Briefly, coercion in the |Gui political system derives from a dialectic between the threats by individual members to withdraw from the band, and the communal threat to 'withhold benefits of the band commonwealth from members' (ibid.).

My perception of the political process and sanction in egalitarian societies is different from those summarised above. Concentrating on sexual relationships among the |Gui, I will demonstrate that 'trespasses' of the conjugal bond actually occur quite frequently without incurring systematic sanction. This claim implies neither that the |Gui society is in constant turmoil, nor that they enjoy perpetual harmony. Rather, the involvement in extramarital relationships is definitely organised according to a 'shared schema of practice', which deeply motivates the |Gui's social attitudes and emotional life of the people. I will also argue that this schema of practice concerning extramarital relationships is closely associated with a |Gui 'sense of interaction' that is as strongly oriented towards equality among the participants, as towards individual autonomy.

Subject Group and Methodology

The |Gui and ||Gana

The |Gui and a closely related dialect group, the ||Gana, are hunter-gatherers who have adapted to the harsh dry environment of the Central Kalahari. Eco-anthropological studies have been carried out by G. Silberbauer (1981) and J. Tanaka (1980) on the people living in the Xade area, located in the mid-western part of the Central Kalahari Game Reserve (CKGR). In 1979, the Botswana government started to force the people from this area to settle around the !Koi!kom borehole (Tanaka 1987). From May to September of 1997, the government carried out its 'relocation programme' and all the residents of the Xade settlement, including |Gui, ||Gana, and Bakgalagadi agro-pastoralists, migrated to Kx'oensakene (New Xade), a new settlement outside the CKGR, about 70 km from Xade.

Methods and Theoretical Background

Since 1982, I have been studying face-to-face interaction and everyday conversation in several |Gui camps at the Xade Settlement (Sugawara 1990, 1996). From 1994 to the present, I have collected life-history narratives of thirteen senior men, all but one of whom are |Gui, and have interviewed a number of younger adult men on various topics. In this paper, both the analyses of conversations and of life-history narratives are collected under the term 'discourse analysis'.[2] Another source of data derives from an extensive investigation of personal names, which commemorate past events.

A number of recent works in cognitive anthropology have attempted to induce some 'cultural model' or 'shared schema' from the indigenous discourse (D'Andrade 1995). The guiding principle for this kind of analysis is delineated by Lakoff and Johnson, although their original subject is the Western philosophical canon:

> The kind of analysis we will be doing is not classical text interpretation. It is, instead, typical of the kinds of empirical analysis done in various cognitive sciences. It attempts to account in detail for regularities governing the unconscious inferential structure on which the comprehension of texts is based. ... And, as is common in cognitive science, it pays special attention to what is not overtly and consciously discussed in the text, but rather to what must be unconsciously taken for granted in order to make sense of the text. (Lakoff and Johnson 1999: 343)

If the term 'text' in the above citation is replaced by the term 'discourse', it becomes acceptable that discourse analysis has an affinity with what is 'common in cognitive science'.

The argument below holds true for both the |Gui and the ||Gana dialect groups. However, in this paper, the name of the entire 'ethnic group' which has previously been labelled 'Central [Kalahari] San (Bushmen)' is represented by the |Gui, partly because my discourse analysis concentrated mostly on the |Gui and partly to avoid the awkward repetition of 'the |Gui and the ||Gana'.

Basic Concepts Concerning Marital and Extra-Marital Relationships

J. Tanaka first pointed out that the prevalence of persistent extramarital relationships, called *zaaku*,[3] was the most peculiar aspect of the |Gui/||Gana sexuality (Tanaka 1989). He translated the term '*zaaku* relationship' as 'love-relationship'. Scrutinising many cases of marriage, divorce, remarriage and love-relationship, Tanaka argued that the significance of the *zaaku* relationship lay in the merging of two or more families through sexual relations. Emphasising that flexibility is the key to maintaining San society, Tanaka assumed that the same flexibility suffused the domain of sexual relationships.

Tanaka's view established the ground upon which further investigation of *zaaku* relationships were based. I also charted *zaaku* relationships in the sedentary community of Xade, in my summaries of conversation analysis (Sugawara 1991). The issues discussed there are reorganised in the following argument. In her paper analysing the curing rituals among the |Gui, K. Imamura proposed a unique view on *zaaku* relationships (Imamura 2001). The following explanation of marital and extramarital relationships is based primarily on these articles.

Firstly, certain elementary constituents of |Gui language must be mentioned. Numerous derivative morphemes play a variety of roles in |Gui semantics and syntax. For the purpose of this paper, three morphemes are of special significance; '*-ku*', '*-bi*' ('*-ma*' in the objective case) and '*-si*' ('*-sa*' in the objective case). The first morpheme, *-ku*, connected to the preceding verb, means 'each other'. 'To marry' is *sieku*, which means literally 'take each other'.[4] Similarly, *zaaku* means 'to have a mutual love relationship'. The morphemes *-bi* (*-ma*) and *-si* (*-sa*) function as suffixes, which indicate male singular and female singular. Thus, *zaabi* (or *zaama*) means 'male lover' while *zaasi* (or *zaasa*) means 'female lover'. 'Husband' and 'wife' are *kx'aoko-bi* and *||gaeko-si*, respectively. Here, *-ko* is another derivative morpheme, which means 'person'. It is worth noting that these terms, *kx'aoko* and *||gaeko*, generally mean 'man' and 'woman'. It is worth emphasising that there is no a priori reason for us to believe that these terms – *sieku*, *kx'aoko* and *||gaeko* – accurately correspond to our concepts of marriage, husband and wife. These English terms are merely interpretive, and are too often assumed to have universal meaning (Sperber 1996).

Secondly, we must offer a preliminary explanation of cultural representations and practices among the |Gui, which make the interpretive correlation between *sieku* and marriage plausible:

1. A small ceremony is held at the commencement of *sieku*. Several parts of the bodies of 'groom' and 'bride' are cut with a razor by an elder

kinswoman of the bride, and the subsequent blood is rubbed into each other's wounds. Thus, this ceremony is called 'mixing blood' (|ao-sa ||qx'ae||qx'are).
2. *Kx'aoko* and ||*gaeko* live in the same hut, usually share meals, and are cooperative in sustenance activities.
3. *Kx'aoko* and ||*gaeko* rear the children to whom the latter has given birth. The *kx'aoko* is usually the 'genitor' of the children.

Thirdly, and most problematic, |Gui language lacks the term 'genitor'. Instead, the verb *abaxo* is used to refer to the biological relation between the father and the baby. The transitive verb *aba* means 'bear' and *-xo* is the causative morpheme. Therefore, *abaxo* literally means, 'let [a woman] bear [a child]'. In so far as *zaaku* relationships frequently occur, the *kx'aoko* is often deceived in his supposition that he caused the ||*gaeko*'s pregnancy. For convenience, when people claim that a man X surely has let a woman have a baby, then X is designated the baby's 'genitor'. This supposition is usually based on the perceived similarity between the children in question and their assumed 'genitor' of the face, shape of the head, or even manner of walking. The insistence of the mother herself is also regarded as reliable evidence.

The term *zaaku* actually covers a wide semantic range. In social encounters, people often call another party 'my *zaabi* (*zaasi*)', as a joke. Close friendship between persons of the same sex is also called *zaaku*. This suggests that the *zaaku* relationship is primarily connected with positive feelings. The love between adolescent boys and girls is also called *zaaku*, and if this relationship leads to the *sieku* of the couple, there is no problem. However, this kind of happy-ending story is not typical of *zaaku*. More often, *zaaku* causes serious conflict between 'rivals' who 'are panicked by jealousy' (||*au-ma tsaa*). This phrase, ||*au-ma tsaa*, is most important to my argument.

Another important aspect of *zaaku* has yet to be noted – its association with illness. Since Imamura (2001) analysed this correlation, I will just summarise the principal points here. Sexual intercourse in a *zaaku* relationship is believed to have the potential to cause serious illness, especially in the man and/or the small children of those involved in this relationship. This illness is attributed to the 'dirt' (|qx'ori) latent in the female's body, which is contagious through intercourse, suckling and close physical contact. If both parties involved can agree, they hold a ritual to cure the disease. The leitmotif organising the ritual is the mixing of materials shed from the bodies of all the participants: urine, sweat and fingernails. The urine collected from both participants is mixed and boiled in a pot, around which they tent themselves using a large blanket, to bathe in the steam and to sweat. If fingernail clippings are used, they are crushed to powder, which the participants snuff to induce sneezing. Thus, this ritual is generally called 'sneeze-medicine' (*tseen-tsoo*). The symbolic logic of this ritual is plainly organised using the principles of metonymy (the material separated from the body 'means' the body) and metaphor (mixing of this material 'means' the oneness of the different bodies), and can be interpreted as a dialectic between the heterogeneity and homogeneity of the sexualised human body. Male and female bodies are heterogeneous, and therefore, potentially dangerous to each other. 'Mixing blood' is a straightforward symbolic device to attain homogeneity. When a man and a woman have not yet attained this homogeneity, they and their children become vulnerable to the 'dirt', i.e. the alien nature of the other sexualised body. They therefore participate in a symbolic process homologous to 'mixing blood'.[5]

In the following analysis, I focus my attention on the 'triangle of desire' in which *kx'aoko*, ||*gaeko* and either party's lover are involved. This relationship is designated as a 'triadic relationship'. The triadic relationship is clearly denoted by the term *!naaku*, which translates as 'share [a sexual partner] with'. This term also applies to polygamy. For example, if a man has two wives, the women are in a *!naaku* relationship with each other. Used as nouns, *!naabi* and *!naasi* mean 'male rival' (male Ego) and 'female rival' (female Ego), respectively. In order to lighten the cognitive load for the reader, I will use the interpretive terms husband (H) and wife (W) instead of the native terms *kx'aoko* and ||*gaeko*. *Zaabi* (male lover) and *zaasi* (female lover) are abbreviated as Zm and Zf, respectively.

Schema of Practice Inducted from Personal Names

In |Gui/G||ana society, newborn babies are usually named after some notable incident which occurred during pregnancy or infancy. Therefore, it is possible to reconstruct a past event by inquiring why a particular name had been given. More than 40 percent of 167 personal names analysed commemorate some type of conflict, the most frequent being conflict caused by a *zaaku* relationship, which accounted for 21.9 percent of all names; and 53.6 percent of names derived from conflict (Sugawara 2002a).

These anecdotes of conflict can be boiled down into simple scripts, e.g., 'H abused Zm', 'W blamed H', 'H beat W', and so on. According to J. Austin's speech act theory, saying something exerts an 'illocutionary force' (1962). From this point of view, both physical violence and negative speech such as abuse and blame are the same kind of social act, i.e. the exertion of 'force'. The person who had exerted 'force' is designated as 'the agent of force' (abbreviated as AgF). An analysis was done of who acted as AgF in triadic relationships, composed either of H, W and Zf, or H, W and Zm. The outcome of this analysis may be summarised as follows:

1. In most cases, those engaged in *sieku*, irrespective of gender, were AgF.
2. In the triad {H/W + Zm}, the force exerted by H usually targeted Zm, while the force exerted by W usually concentrated on H in {Zf + H/W}.[6]
3. H engaged in *zaaku* acted as AgF, while W engaged in *zaaku* never acted as AgF.

Points (2) and (3) above indicate asymmetry between male and female dispositions towards exerting force. Also, (2) implies that H often attempts to make Zm abandon the relationship by immediately threatening him, while W will tend to direct her blame at H, rather than Zf. Proposition (3) may more explicitly reflect human dimorphism. Speaking more simply, a wife who abuses her husband for his infidelity could become victim to his violence, while a husband would be unlikely to be confronted by his wife, if their positions were reversed.

It is worth remembering that the name of a newborn baby is usually given by the father. Thus, the 'memory' framed by the naming might be only a fragment of the entire incident, and thus suspect and, at worse, a distortion that favours the husband-father. Even so, this AgF distribution pattern in triadic relationships provides an invaluable element for understanding how *sieku* and *zaaku* are differentiated from each other in the |Gui social experience. Therefore, the notion that most AgF were engaged in *sieku* deserves special attention. From H's point of view, the possibility of acting as AgF is preferentially allocated to those engaged in *sieku*.

Let me paraphrase the above point in emotional terms. Generally, human social acts are explicable when the action's immediate motivation is specified. Emotion is often the focal point of the primary constituent of motivation. This is certainly true in |Gui society. Therefore, when I wanted to know the immediate reason for someone's violent act, I would ask questions such as:

Q: Why did he beat her?
A1: Because he got angry at her, for sleeping with another man.
or
A2: Because he was panicked by jealousy.

According to my experience in the field, an answer like A2 was usually given in a situation where a triadic relationship caused conflict. If we admit that the |Gui – or at least |Gui husbands-fathers – share a schema of practice in which those engaged in *sieku* preferentially exert their force in triadic relationships, then the subsequent anger and jealousy are also preferentially allocated to the *sieku*. In sum, the anger and jealousy felt by husband and wife would more likely be regarded as 'legitimate', than that felt by the lovers. In the following section, I examine this hypothesis by analysing variable patterns in the development of triadic relationships.

Variation in Triadic Relation Practices

All of the ethnographic descriptions below are short excerpts from longer discourses, which arose in both conversation and narrative. As a principle of editing, I emphasised the speech of participants, which the informant represented as direct narration (set in single quotations and numbered with angled parentheses as <n>), because I believe the words spoken at the critical phase in a series of incidents most vividly illuminate the essence of the speakers' relationship. Of course, one cannot assume that these direct narrations are always faithful to the actual discourse. However, it is quite likely that they reflect the core of reality, as perceived by the informant. 'Ground' speech sentences extracted from either conversation or narrative are set in double parentheses « ».

A Married Woman Seduces an Adolescent Man

It is not unusual for a married woman to seduce a younger man. In the following case, the woman is at least twenty years older than her lover.

1. <My heart isn't yet mature> [1983–85]
   KAA/Xao (middle-aged ||Gana) + CIR (Adolescent |Gui)[7]
   Xao seduced the younger CIR, who had occasionally helped KAA with his work. CIR rejected her advances at first, but she was so persistent that he eventually yielded to the seduction.
   <1> 'No, my heart isn't yet mature. I don't know how you [*mf. dl.*][8] can properly take each other. Don't speak of such things.'
   <2> 'No, you're so clever with everything. Yea, you can make fire, and you're so good at scraping steenbok skins.'
   <3>:'No, you might be tricking me, and I'll be disabled.'
   <4> 'No, I'll take you one way or another, so you can't refuse me! You're an adult, so you have nothing to fear.'
   Xao boasted so openly of her affair that KAA heard of it. But when I stayed at Xade in 1984, their relationship seemed quite peaceful. CIR often worked and stayed at KAA/Xao's hut. However, after I left, Xao began to boast that she would divorce KAA and remarry CIR. KAA took this case to the appointed ||Gana chief, and asked him to convene a court. KAA was permitted to whip CIR in public. CIR ended this *zaaku* relationship, and married a ||Gana girl three years later.

As far as I know, this is the only case in which public sanction was imposed on a *zaaku* relationship. The following case stands in marked contrast with the above.

2. <Let us make *zaaku*> [1982–87]
   XAR (adult)/Kha (young adult) + KER (adolescent): All are |Gui
   KER was XAR's classificatory cross-cousin and had lived in the same camp since childhood, separated from his father. His mother had died when he was an infant. When XAR was going horseback hunting, KER complained to Kha that XAR worked him too hard. Then, Kha seduced KER:
   <5> 'Let's make *zaaku*. Then, his heart will hurt, as yours hurts, although he won't be able to kill you.'
   Hearing this, XAR at once felt sad, became angry, but soon decided, <6> 'I'll leave them as they are.'
   Two years later, in 1984, XAR's senior kinsmen arranged a marriage between KER and an adolescent girl. The ceremony of 'mixing blood' was held. But Kha was 'panicked by jealousy', behaving so fiercely that the girl was frightened. She refused to sleep with KER, so that KER had to lie out-

doors, shivering with cold. During this period, he joined XAR in horseback hunting. XAR laughed at KER, saying:
<7> 'As you love the woman I took, you can't take [another] woman for yourself.'
Coming back from hunting, KER gifted a large bundle of dried meat to his 'bride', but she threw it away on the ground. Another girl picked it up, saying, <8> 'Well then, I'll take it.' Soon KER deserted his 'bride' and went back to XAR and Kha's camp. It was said that XAR and KER were in agreement with each other (≠gomku). During hunting trips, they always slept side by side. Once, when chasing a female giraffe, XAR shouted to KER:
<9> 'We're scrambling after the same female. You, go chase another female! Remember! You took my wife! So, go kill that other female over there!'
This triadic relation continued until KER married the girl who had picked up the bundle of meat three years earlier (see <8>). During the six years of the relationship, Kha gave birth to three children, one of whom died. It is believed that KER is the 'genitor' of all of them. In 1994, XAR was killed in a traffic accident. Weeping, KER buried him.

This case illuminates an important aspect of *zaaku* relationship. It seems that the husband was himself attracted by his younger rival. For four or five years, a kind of 'polyandry' situation existed. This situation was interpreted by the surrounding people as the peculiar consensus between the two men, in a *!naaku* (rival) relationship; this was condensed as the locution 'agreeing with each other' (≠gomku). This term (≠gom), as well as its antonym 'disagree' (≠nue), has an essential meaning, not only in triadic relationships, but also in the micro-political process in general, through which the |Gui negotiate and decide various social matters.

Husband's Initiative Ignites Relationship

Analysing the life-history narratives of senior |Gui men, I encountered a number of cases in which a married man developed a *zaaku* relationship with a married woman. Some of these cases resulted not in triadic, but 'quadruple' relationships.

3. <Saw them off gladly> [1970?]
   SIK/Nae + GYO/Kxo: All participants are |Gui, 30–40 years old
   GYO/Kxo were from Tsetseng (about 200 km south of Xade). SIK and GYO were close friends, and often went hunting together. They resolved to initiate a *zaaku* relationship. Coming home, SIK proposed this to Nae, but at first she refused. However, soon both Nae and Kxo accepted the idea. Their camps were located close to each other's (about a fifteen-minute walk). Each husband visited the other's camp and slept with his wife. When GYO/Kxo returned to Tsetseng, SIK felt fulfilled, and gladly saw them off.

This kind of 'mate-swapping' embodies a most important aspect of the *zaaku* relationship, which will be discussed in detail below.

4. <I don't care for such a thing> [1971?]
   TSM/Gae + Sus: All participants are |Gui, 25–37 years old
   Just after Gae had her third baby, TSM approached Sus, who was not yet married. TSM often visited her with a lot of meat. She was a classificatory younger sister of Gae. Gae got angry:
   <10> 'Why are you taking my sister? It is only we two, who're married.'
   <11> 'Because she is your sister, I'll put her together with you.'
   <12> '*Uuh-* I don't care for such a thing!'
   Consequently, a ||Gana man, NOS, the most notorious 'master' of *zaaku*, made advances to Sus and at last married her. «He was such a useless man that he could not even set a snare for steenbok, and he cheated women with mere flattery.»

It is worth noting that, so far as I know, TSM/Gae have maintained a most affectionate relationship until the present. Up until 1987, Gae had given birth to eleven children with TSM, two of whom had died in infancy, though it is believed that one of them was fathered by another man [see (7) below]. This case suggests that in |Gui society it is quite difficult to find a married couple who are able to avoid a *zaaku* relationship for their entire life together.

5. <We two shouldn't torment each other> [1950?]
   CIE/Kya + NUE/Cik: All participants are |Gui in their twenties
   CIE was of mixed |Gui and Bakgalagadi agro-pastoralist (≠*kebe*) blood. He had two wives who were sisters. Kya was the younger sister and the second wife. NUE loved Kya and gave her gifts of various prizes from the hunt, such as antelope meat, ostrich eggs and honey. They loved each other. At first, CIE got angry and argued with NUE:
   <13> 'I'm ≠*kebe* and you're *kua* (Bushman), but you persist in your *zaaku* with my wife. You are *kua*, but you're entering my hut.'
   <14> 'Because she loved me, I entered into *zaaku* with her. Why should not we [*mf. dl.*] enter into *zaaku*? She is ≠*kebe*, while I'm *kua*. You two are both ≠*kebe*. But, when she proposed *zaa* to me, I agreed.' «He was angry, very angry, but at last, left me alone.»
   <15> 'We two shouldn't torment each other. Such a situation is terrible, but I cannot kill you. Since we're ≠*gowao* (cross-cousins), I'll leave you alone. But, you must give me things, and help me.'
   They lived in the same camp. They entered each other's hut and slept with each other's wife. However, CIE was less willing, because he did not like *kua* woman very much. Soon Kya had a baby girl with NUE. All of them participated in the ritual of *tseen-tsoo* (sneeze-medicine). Commemorating this, CIE named this baby '*tseen-tsoo*'. As this baby was CIE's first child (i.e., CIE is the *pater* of this baby), he was called with the teknonymy, '*tseen-tsoo*'s father', for the rest of his life. He died in 1996.

|Gui people of mixed Bakgalagadi blood sometimes emphasise their background and differentiate themselves from other people, as is suggested by the case above. However, it is more striking that the former husband soon accepted the latter's challenge, resulting in this type of mate-swapping (3).

Zaaku Develops During the Absence of a Husband

According to the hamadryas model, pair-gestalt inhibition cannot be effective when male and female are spatially separated. In |Gui society, long absences of the husband also provide a good opportunity for rivals to initiate a *zaaku* relationship.

6. <From olden times, we men all have been ill-natured...> [middle of 1970s?]
SIK/Nae, KHO/Nap + XOU + KUK: All participants are |Gui in their late thirties or early forties.
SIK was half younger brother of KHO. They were arrested for poaching elands and were sentenced to prison for about half a year. Upon returning home, they found their wives involved in *zaaku* relationships with their kin, XOU and KUK. SIK and KHO got angry and abused them:
<16> 'What have you [*m. dl.*] done? We're kin, yet you two divided our [*m. dl. exc.*] wives between you. Don't carry on as if we were dead.'
KHO attacked KUK, but SIK did not:
<17> 'No, leave them [*m. dl.*] alone. From olden times, we men all have been ill-natured, so that if they were absent, we'd do the same thing. Maybe we would initiate *zaaku* with their wives.'

7. <Since then, she has never again entered into *zaaku*> [1975–76]
TSM (about 42 years old)/Gae + CIE (about 50 years old)/Kya. All participants are |Gui.
TSM was staying in a hospital in Gaborone for an operation. During his absence, CIE living in the same camp had a *zaaku* relationship with Gae. Upon returning home, TSM realised what had been going on, and got so angry that he almost choked. Next year Gae bore a male child. TSM named him *Kurya-|qx'onsi* (*Huupeera* in Setswana) which means 'get angry, and kill oneself' or, more figuratively, 'die of indignation'.
Transcription of an interview [1994]:
S: Has your wife had *zaaku*?
TSM: I don't know.
S: I heard it was so. CIE had *zaaku* with your wife, didn't he?
[long silence]
TSM: But I didn't know that...
S: I heard that when Huupeera was born you got very angry.
TSM: I got very angry. As you heard, I got angry because she had *zaaku*, and so she quit *zaaku*. Since then, she has never again entered into *zaaku*.
The following is CIE's narrative:
«I remained and stole his wife [Laugh]... and only slept with her. Then he came back. I kept silent, saying nothing, and hid. Then he asked his wife about it. She didn't answer either. This woman (Kya) said, 'That man stole your wife, and slept with her in your hut.' Ah! He got very, very, very, very, angry, and felt hurt ... Then Huupeera was born. 'Die of indignation'. Therefore, we call him Huupeera. *Eheh*. Kya got angry, and TSM got angry. Therefore, we both were ashamed and kept silent. One couple got angry, and the other kept silent.»

My questioning in case (7) above may appear intrusive. However, all the people were well acquainted with this incident, because they shouted the boy's name every day. To my surprise, in spite of its public nature, the experience of having one's wife 'stolen' remained traumatic in the husband's memory.

The above descriptions substantiate the fact that participants in triadic relationships are far from calm; they usually feel anger deeply enough to 'die of indignation'. So, why do the |Gui sustain such consuming relationships? Why haven't they developed some systematic device that effectively prohibits trespass on any legitimate *sieku* link? I will now try to answer these questions.

Ipso Facto Establishment of Paternity

When one criticises his or her opponent in some conflict, the term *kx'ooxa* is often used. It means literally 'having nature', but can more freely be translated as 'ill-natured' [see <17> in (6) above]. In the context of sexuality, the behaviour typified as *kx'ooxa* is having sexual relations with many partners. Among my close informants, there are several men who have maintained long-term *sieku* relationships with wives that are referred to as *kx'ooxa*.

8. <I felt hurt, but I didn't feel hurt>
   PIR (about 77 years old in 2000) is the eldest among my |Gui male informants. Although his life history is very complicated, I am going to focus on his wife's *zaaku* relationships. Before marrying an immature girl named Hoe, he had already married twice; he divorced one wife, and the other was dead. The former gave birth to a daughter who is now about 50 years old. Since PIR's late thirties, his wife Hoe has had *zaaku* relationships with at least four different men, and borne four children. In particular, her relationship with the third Zm, QMK, continued for at least five years (1975–80), and produced two daughters. It is said that PIR himself sired none of these children. In 1986, the notorious *zaaku* master, NOS [see (4) above], initiated a *zaaku* relationship with Hoe. This affair was the most frequent topic in everyday conversation when I stayed at PIR's camp during 1987. The co-residents vociferously criticised this relationship. Hoe's late father's younger brother (classificatory father) argued with NOS:
   <18> 'I have just one thing to say to you. Go fetch those two women's skulls and bring them for us to see. If you do that, he [PIR] will be very happy.'
   NOS had married and divorced many women, and before he initiated this relationship his |Gui wives had died of illness, one after another. The above 'two skulls' is bitter rhetoric evoking NOS's infamous career.
   PIR/Hoe's first son, CIR, criticised his mother to her face:
   <19> 'Mummy, you used to call NOS "father", but what are you doing now? ... Alas, what did you say, Mummy? [When NOS came with news that his wife had died,] You said, "He has come after dining on my mother." And you threw away the head of duiker you were eating.'
   NOS's last |Gui wife, who died in 1985, was Hoe's classificatory mother, so Hoe called her 'my mother' and correspondingly called NOS 'my father'. CIR criticises Hoe for her bad conduct, that is, for having sexual relations with her 'father'.

In 1988, when I was absent in the field, both PIR and QMK beat NOS. However, neither he nor Hoe quit their relationship, which continued until NOS's death by illness, in 1990. Two years later, Hoe also died of illness.

In 1996, I recorded PIR's life-history narrative. In the following transcription, 'A' is my research assistant:

A: As you provided food for their [Zms'] children, you didn't feel hurt?
P: I provided food only for their children. However, I haven't visited their wives. I only provided food for their children.
A: But, didn't you feel hurt?
P: <20> Well, I felt hurt, but I didn't feel hurt ... she was with me, and I owned her.

The discourse <20> illuminates the essential nature of possession in the interpersonal context among the |Gui. I will elaborate by citing another example.

9. <I looked at him, I loved him>
   SIK/Nae + NHO (||Gana)
   A ||Gana man, NHO, had been SIK's playmate from childhood. Since around 1968, NHO had developed a *zaaku* relationship with Nae. When SIK found NHO in his hut with his wife, he attacked NHO, driving him out. The couple's second son was soon born. Although it was believed that his genitor was SIK, he named the baby, !Kao≠qx'oaxo ('attack-drive out') commemorating the above incident. About ten years later, SIK travelled to the town of Ghanzi, and stayed there for many months. Returning home, he found his wife pregnant. SIK questioned her closely, and she soon admitted that her *zaaku* relationship with NHO had recommenced. SIK had believed that their relationship had ended a long time ago, but they had cheated him. SIK's third son was soon born. The baby was so like NHO that nobody doubted he was the genitor. Therefore, SIK named the baby Pakika ('cheat'; loan word from Setswana):
   <21> 'But she bore the little one, and when I looked at him, I loved him. He is my son. As my wife bore the boy, he is my son. I won't kill him. That's ugly. Thinking thusly, I leave him alone. He will work for me. Returning [home], he will work, and provide for me. Therefore, I will not kill him. But, I assaulted his father and drove him from my home.'
   <22> [SIK spoke to Pakika like this]: 'NHO came, and entered your mother's [hut] and begot you. But, you are my son, not NHO's son. His children are with his wives. He came to my place and begot you. You were born of my wife. Therefore, you are mine.'

One of the field experiences that impressed me most concerns this father-son relationship. In 1987, soon after I had begun analysing everyday conversation, I became interested in the *zaaku* relationship. One day, I was sitting with my cheerful research assistant CIR (PIR's eldest son), and SIK was lying on the sand nearby. Perceptively noticing my interest, CIR pointed to SIK and frankly said, 'Look! NHO caused his wife bear this son, and SIK named him Pakika.' SIK was only smiling wryly, and the son in question, about nine years old, was leaning quite intimately onto SIK's back.

After that, I noticed a number of cases in which the father was tender with his children, whose genitor was believed to be another man. I was struck by the information that PIR's two daughters' genitor was QMK, as I had been impressed by his affectionate attitude towards them, during my initial research five years before. Undoubtedly, the husband becomes angry and 'panicked by jealousy', when he is faced with the fact that his wife has been made pregnant by another. Furthermore, after the birth of the baby, he condenses his grudge into the baby's name, probably expecting that all the people around him and his wife will continue to cry this name aloud, the emblem of his grudge, all their life. If this baby is a first child for either *sieku* partner, the consequence is more drastic; they themselves will almost certainly be called the teknonymy into which this name is set, as in 'Tseentsoo's father' (5). In spite of all of this, the husband will eventually accept this child, and establish an affectionate bond with them. This is the most essential feature of |Gui paternity.

Possession and Reciprocity in Sexualised Relationships

The Exertion of Force is Inhibited

The ethnographic descriptions in the preceding section revealed the extent to which the schema abstracted from personal names deviates from the actual course of events in *zaaku* relationships. First, the hypothesis that the legitimacy for exerting force is preferentially allocated to conjugal pairs can be supported, as we have found no case in which Zm or Zf exerted their force on either H or W. However, in spite of the frequent encoding of aggression by the husband or wife in the children's names, serious violence is quite rare during a long *zaaku* relationship.

Although KAA whipped CIR in court, this sanction was only possible through an institution externally imposed by the government. I recorded another case in which public sanction was imposed on Zm in the early 1970s. However, in this case the party who demanded this sanction was a Bakgalagadi agro-pastoralist. In fact, PIR and QMK beat NOS when I was absent in the field. However, this minor violence was apparently ineffective as a means of forcing NOS to abandon his attempt to continue *zaaku*. On the contrary, after his beating, he maintained the relationship with Hoe for more two years until his death. Actually, a number of cases point to another schema in which the rivals are disposed to 'agree with each other' (≠*gom-ku*). This issue is elaborated in the following section.

Husband and Wife, Father and Child

It is necessary to examine the logic (or unconscious inferential structure, in Lakoff and Johnson's terms) which organises discourses such as <20>, <21> and <22>. Focusing on the problem of paternity, this logic can be summarised as a kind of syllogism:

- I > W: I own my wife;
- W » C: My wife is connected with the child by the fact that she bore him/her;
- therefore, I > C: I own the child.

Ultimately, what does it mean to 'own' somebody? In the |Gui language, there is a semantic distinction between the two transitive verbs, *!xoo* ('have [something] in hand' or 'grasp something') and *!oa*, which means the more abstract 'possession'. For example, if someone says 'I have many goats' or 'I have a hut', the latter term is used. The native term translated as 'own' in <20> is *!oa* (*!owaha* in complete form). Another examples were derived from an everyday conversation, as well as from a narrative.

> 10. <the person who owns her> (excerpt from a conversation)
> Gae's (TSM's W) younger sister had been CIE's third wife since 1981. In a conversation recorded in 1987, Gae was criticising a |Gui man, GIS, for his frequent visit to her sister, who was living apart from the husband at that time:
> <23> ' |Qaya≠qx'oaxo's father [teknonymy referring to GIS] will come often tomorrow and thereafter. Therefore, they contend that the person who owns Giu [sister's name] is saying, "Kx'ombee's mother [teknonymy referring to Gae herself] is breaking her contract [loan word from Setswana] by doing such a thing." '
> She also criticised her other sister, younger than CIE's W, who had received many gifts from GIS. The following is the direct narration of Gae's earlier speech to her sister:
> <24> 'When |Qaya≠qx'oaxo's father brought two bags of sugar with him, you consumed them, didn't you? … They will talk about it and say to me, "Kx'ombee's mother owns her [sister]." Saying so, they will summon me.'
>
> 11. < both of us owned you >[1989–94] TAB /Tei+Top(||Gana)
> In 1989 my informant TAB (NUE's second son; about 25 years old) got married with Tei (about 20 years old). Tei bore a baby boy in 1992, but died of illness in 1994. She had a close friendship with a middle-aged ||Gana woman Top, who had been widowed in 1990. After Tei's death, Top seduced TAB. The following is TAB's representation as direct narration of Top's earlier speech to him. In this discourse, close friendship between the two women is also called *zaaku*.
> <25> 'As I had been in *zaaku* with her (Tei), both of us [*f. dl.*] owned you.'

The above discourses <23> and <25> embraces the proposition that the husband (or the wife) owns the wife (or the husband), while in the discourse <24> people state that the elder sister owns the younger sister. The implications of these two propositions are slightly different from each other. The former implies that the husband (or the wife) has some specific authority over his wife (or her husband), while the latter implies that the elder sister is responsible for the demeanour of the younger sister.

The simplest definition of the term 'own' may be to have a right to deal with an owned subject or object at will. Of course, one cannot deal with another person as one deals with goats. However, in the |Gui inferential structure, similar to ours, it is presupposed that a father owns a child, a husband owns a wife (and vice versa), and an elder sibling owns the younger. Avoiding metaphor, the essential core of the statement 'P (a person) owns Q (another person)' can be formularised as follows:

- It is admitted or expected by most members of the community that;
- P will do a specific favour, tangible, psychological or both, for Q, and;
- consequently, benefit in the long-term from culturally encoded social interactions with Q.

Let us apply this formula to the ipso facto assignment of paternity. For example, N. Howell (1979) points out that among the !Kung (Ju|'hoansi), a man will bring up the children of his remarried wife, while there is no case in which a wife fosters the stepchildren, except in sororate marriage. Thus, it is very difficult for an infant deprived of its mother to survive. On the other hand, even if children were deprived of their father, their mother could easily remarry other men. If she didn't, the children would benefit from the influence of other male members of their camp. Thus, by extension, it emerges that children's survival depends upon mothers, and not upon fathers. Howell concludes that !Kung men practise 'true altruism' in the sociobiological sense. |Gui husbands who treat the children of Zm tenderly, establish another case of 'true altruism'. It may be tempting to explain this altruistic disposition in terms of an implicit strategy of inclusive fitness, as follows.

If the genitor (Zm) is pater (H)'s close kin, it is advantageous to rear the children. Moreover, having many children, irrespective of their genetic relationship to the pater, increases his social resources, from which not only he, but also other kin can benefit in the long term. At the very least, he can expect to be supported in his dotage by all of his children, whatever their relationship to him ('He will work for me' in <21>).

According to this explanation, the jealousy and anger experienced by the husband-father is ultimately pointless, and could be eliminated, were a better strategy developed. However, this is the paradox, in terms of evolutionary psychology, that sibling discipline of sociobiology which assumes that human emotion itself has been patterned, in order to foster inclusive fitness.

Why does the husband-father not direct his anger at the child? Remember the phrases in discourse <21>:«I won't kill him. That's ugly.» These phrases express the moral and creative impetus which inspires the attitude of |Gui men towards *zaaku* relationships. Also, remember PIR's discourse <20>: «Well, I felt hurt, but I didn't feel hurt... she was with me, and I owned her.» This statement, apparently violating the law of the excluded middle, illuminates the ambivalent relationship between *sieku* and *zaaku*. On the one hand, his wife's *zaaku* is traumatic for the husband [also see (7)], but on the other hand, *zaaku* provides an outstanding moment to substantiate the legitimacy of possession in *sieku*. Before examining the origin of this legitimacy, we need to analyse the dialectic between *sieku* and *zaaku* in |Gui emotional life, that is, between possession and its trespass. This dialectic produces a kind of synthesis, a mutualism between two conjugal pairs as preliminarily outlined in (3) and (5).

Orientation Towards the Reciprocal Mutualism

I have pointed out previously, that the term ≠*gomku* ('agree with each other') has an essential significance in the triadic relationship. If the two couples agree with each other, there arises a stable quadruple relationship called *zaaku-≠ero-e* (literally 'the *zaaku* itself', or more intuitively 'true *zaaku*').

> **12.** <All of the blood of our hearts has been mixed> [1987–98]
> KHO/Nap + HAB/Mur: All participants are |Gui in their fifties (W) or sixties (H).
> In 1987, Nap proposed *zaaku* between two couples. She hoped to sleep with HAB, and with persistence, persuaded KHO and Mur to have *zaaku*. Finally, all agreed, and HAB and Nap travelled to |Gae. Just after they left Xade, another couple came back from |Gae. Hearing the situation in |Gae, Mur spoke vociferously to the people of her decision:
> <26> 'I will carry out what my husband HAB has proposed, "Let us engage in *zaaku*." Even if KHO won't carry it out, I will. All of the blood of our [*mf. dl.*] hearts has been mixed.'
> Soon KHO and Mur left Xade, and the two couples stayed in |Gae for three months. However, news came that HAB/Mur's daughter was seriously ill at Xade. Although HAB began to prepare to go home, KHO and Mur were unwilling to leave. HAB became angry, and urged and threatened them by filing a knife on their heads. After coming back to Xade, they lived near each other in the same camp. This relationship continued for twelve years, until the end of their first year at the new settlement.
> <27> [KHO answering my questions] 'HAB was angry ... He was about to kill me ... because I dreaded him, I'm still alive ... at last he frustrated me. I thought, "Ah! You [KHO himself] always distress him. Because of his wife, you always distress him. For that, he will kill you. Therefore, I will separate from his wife." Thinking in this way, I took my leave of her.'

A puzzling question surfaces: if KHO was so afraid of HAB's anger, why had he started such a dangerous relationship in the first place? Moreover, if HAB has been so distressed, why on earth had he agreed with the proposition to initiate *zaaku*? The answer may be quite simple. All of them were pursuing their ideal, embracing one of their most profound communal values. Forming a quadruple relationship, they intended to help each other, to exchange food and gifts with each other. The following case corroborates this notion.

13. <I will visit your camp> [late 1960s?]
   GIS/Qai + TAK/Teh : All participants are |Gui in their late twenties or early thirties.
   GIS is another master of *zaaku*. He had married two women, and had *zaaku* relationships with at least five women. When he was living with the first wife, Qai, he loved a girl, Teh, who had not yet experienced menarche. He waited for her, and once she went through the eland dance ceremony, visited her frequently. However, this girl had a fiancé, TAK. He vociferously expressed his dissatisfaction with GIS's behaviour:
   <28> 'Hey! All you! Why is it that I always see GIS here? When this woman was not yet female, he was putting new footprints. He torments me. Just recently the women brought her out [from the eland dance ceremony], but the way he acts, is more appropriate towards an older woman.'
   Then the other men rebuked him:
   <29> 'Oh! You are liar. If he had no other woman, then it would be a problem. However, he is married to another. Therefore, as both of you are sitting, beg your food from each other. If another man had no woman, then he would bother you for yours. Only then, should you hate him. In fact, your [*m. dl.*] prospects are beautiful, as he is married to Qai. You will marry Teh, so your [*m. dl.*] affairs can proceed directly.'
   One day, TAK asked GIS to go hunting. GIS was afraid that he would be murdered in the bush. However, they caught many springhares cooperatively. Coming home, TAK did not get the springhares out of his hunting bag. Both of them slept together with Teh in the same hut. The next morning, TAK picked up the swelling hunting bag, and said to GIS;
   <30> 'I will visit your camp.' GIS replied, '*Aeh*, if you ever do ... but it sounds beautiful.'
   TAK visited GIS's camp, giving many springhares to Qai, and slept with her.

This discourse <29> quite plainly codifies the moral maxim of *zaaku*. The conflict is most apt to arise from a triadic relationship. Therefore, you should pursue quadruple relationships in which you and your rival 'beg each other' and, of course, swap mates with each other. In this sense, *zaaku* is the embodied and emotionally engaged aspect of the 'sharing system'. If we use the teleological term, the prevalent desire for *zaaku* is channelled by a kind of 'communal reason', which encourages people to augment the radical mutualism indispensable for their survival. Tanaka's view that the *zaaku* relationship serves to unite two or more married families through sexual relations hits the mark. In addition, this sociological function of *zaaku* is not contingent on the sexual relationship, but |Gui sexuality itself is embedded with a fundamental orientation towards mutualism.

However, this is paradoxical. If the 'communal reason' motivates intense sexual desire, necessitating satisfaction in extramarital relations, how can the anger and jealousy inevitably flowing from the dishonoured 'possessor', be sublimated into mutualism? Ultimately they cannot. Hence, the dialectic of agreeing (≠*gom*) and disagreeing (≠*nue*) never produces a true synthesis. This is the reason why KHO was so fearful of HAB's anger for the ten years of their relationship. This consideration leads to another question: why, then, should the *sieku* relationship be more legitimate than *zaaku*?

What Differentiates Sieku from Zaaku?

The following discourse provides a valuable clue to solve the above question.

> **14.** <If I could have two wives ... > [1999]
> KHO/Nap + Ugu (||Gana)
> At the Kx'oensakene, the village established by the relocation programme, KHO [see (12)] initiated a *zaaku* relationship with Ugu who came from Gyom, about 120 km northeast of Xade, and moved into her hut:
> <31> 'I thought, "*Eh!* New wife ... I wonder if I could find a woman with whom I can continue, or if I could have two wives." I said so in my heart. ...In the meanwhile, I loved this woman ... she also loved me. So, we agreed with each other.'
> <32> 'I have not yet met her parents, and say [in my heart], "Will you [*mf. pl.*; her parents and kin] agree about me? Will you like me? As she likes me, will you like me?" I don't know that. I think this. Soon, I will go to her parents' place. There I will tell them that I have stolen their daughter and am living with her. '
> <33> 'Hey, you [Nap] are panicked by jealousy and say that [you will] not let me take a new woman, [and you tell me] to take only you. However, I say no! Don't say such a thing, and let me admonish you both to embrace each other, as my wives. You are very old, and have become so disabled, that you can do nothing, not even collect firewood. So give me leave to take both of you my wives. Then, probably, while you are sitting declining, that new wife would get up to gather and bring you firewood, for you to set the fire.'
> [Answering my question: If Nap had *zaaku* with another man, would not you be panicked by jealousy?]
> <34> '[Laugh] I would be panicked by jealousy, of course. *Eh-*, he would destroy me. He won't treat my camp nicely. ... I won't let a man enter my camp, because he'll ruin it. Rather than only my 'order' (*raola*; loan word from Setswana) in the camp, there would be two 'orders.' It would come out that there were two "orders" '.

In discourse <31> KHO was very eager to emphasise that what he was initiating was not *zaaku* but *sieku*. Furthermore, he stated that he tried to sway his wife with the prospect that the new wife will take charge of the housework <33>. So, how can this relationship with a new woman be transformed into a more desirable *sieku* relationship? Nothing is required, other than getting the agreement of her parents who live at a distance (see <32>). This analysis leads us to a recurring issue. The exogamy and incest taboos are two sides of the same coin, the essential core being the communication between groups, through the medium of women as signs, etc. Only the *sieku* can unfold a new social space of 'affines' (|*ui*). In this space, not only 'two or more families', but larger kin groups can align with each other.

This argument surely sheds light on an important aspect of differentiation in |Gui social relationships. It has been argued, that |*ui* (affines) is a marked category, and this marked-ness is embodied in the peculiar organisation of conversational interaction, more specifically, of turn taking, which I labelled 'formalisation' (Sugawara 1996). However, discourse analysis should not be limited to the apparent message that the speaker intends to send out. It should pay special attention to the unconscious inferential structure and underlying motivation. Accordingly, KHO is deeply motivated to rationalise his attempt. Remember that KHO himself had been involved in a quadruple relationship for as long as twelve years. After such a long time, in his old age, he articulated his admiration for having two wives, that is, for polygyny. He is obliged to artificially separate *sieku* from *zaaku*, and to put special emphasis on *sieku*'s unique value, that is, legitimacy. In this sense, the legitimacy of *sieku* is ideological, which can be used strategically to manage sexually-emotionally engaged relationships.

Any attempt to rigorously analyse indigenous concepts is vulnerable to the temptation of artificially separating one concept from another. However, it should be remembered that in |Gui emotional life, *zaaku* and *sieku* are not at all independent of each other. Rather, they are two aspects of |Gui sexuality and procreation which are complementary. If this is true, it misses the mark to conclude that *zaaku* is an institution subordinate to *sieku*, because the former lacks the potential to unfold the social space of affines. Conversely, one can initiate a *zaaku* relationship with another, if, and only if, both parties spontaneously agree. The fact that Zm/Zf rarely acts as the agent of force implies that *zaaku* is essentially immune from any compulsion for legitimacy. If the |Gui always long for the 'freedom' of *zaaku*, then their *sieku* – which is always open to the possibility of *zaaku* – is not the same institution as our marriage, which remains steadfastly opposed to 'immorality' (*Furin*, in Japanese, exclusively denotes adultery in the modern sense).

Equality and on-and-on Continuation: Discussion and Conclusion

We have returned to the first question: 'What does it mean to possess another person?' In the ethnographic context of the |Gui, it means having sexually-emotionally engaged relationships with another, which are vulnerable to trespass. Essential to this definition is the concept of possession, characterised by an intrinsic contradiction that I have labelled the 'dialectic of emotional life'. My final position is that this dialectic provides the fundamental schema for |Gui social practice, and functions as the engine for the dynamics of everyday face-to-face interaction. This engine can be roughly designated as 'equality'.

The preceding discourse analyses reveal that the conspicuous feature of the *zaaku* relationship is active choice on the part of women, especially as illustrated in (1), (2), (8), (9) and (12). Taking into consideration cases in which the husband took the initiative, it can safely be concluded that women and men play virtually equal roles in developing *zaaku* relationships. Even if a largely polyandrous situation were somehow possible, it would be quite different from the institutionalised polyandry of certain South American Indians, in which the husbands are forced by primarily demographic factors to share their wives with other men (Clastre 1974). Nevertheless, it must be noted that |Gui men have developed various devices that emphasise male dominance. When describing their attempt to look for a *zaaku* partner, men sometimes say, 'I'm hunting (*!qae*) women'. Correspondingly, the husband is often designated as *gyiabi*, which means the 'owner'. This term is also used to refer to a hunter who has killed a game animal. In actuality, though, husbands seem to have mostly given up making any effort to control their wives' sexual activity.

This 'giving up' is condensed into the phrase 'I leave him/her alone' (*cire ama/esa xou*), which is heard repeatedly in the discourse on *zaaku* relationships (see <6><15><17> and <21>). Leaving somebody alone, giving up coercing somebody to do or not to do something, and leaving the initiative for interaction to the other's spontaneous will (Kitamura 1990), are all fundamental to the |Gui dialectic of emotional life. This attitude negates any a priori claim that ownership must be respected because it had once been legitimated. In other words, it is a unique way of counteracting the power imbalance implicit in the allocation of legitimacy to a specific type of relationship. Thus, in triadic relationships, those engaged in *sieku* do not have a priori precedence over his or her rival, but are involved in perpetual negotiation, where all parties play almost equal roles.

The final challenge is to unravel the convoluted interrelation between mutualist orientation, on the one hand, and the destructive effect of negative feelings such as anger and jealousy, on the other. In order to examine this topic, we should turn again to the discourse <34>. Briefly, KHO stated that were his wife to have *zaaku*, he would be panicked by jealousy because the order of his camp would be disturbed by another man, i.e. Zm. This is a curious sort of logic. Here, we come to doubt the adequacy of literal translation of ||*au-ma tsaa* as 'be panicked by jealousy'. According to our common experience, we are involuntarily assailed by emotional responses. Yet, KHO's discourse sounds as if he would intentionally act jealous, with the purpose of defending the 'order of the camp'. If we were faithful to KHO's logic, we would not regard ||*au* as an invisible psychological entity which inevitably drives somebody to act irrationally. Rather, it would signify a shared schema for the interpretation of visible acts and attitudes in the triadic relationship. In this context of action and attitude, discourse <20> 'Well, I felt hurt, but I didn't feel hurt', is no longer illogical. This is PIR's interpretation of his own consistent attitude over many years of triadic relationship.

This argument should not imply that the |Gui effortlessly control their emotions, guided by some 'communal reason'. For convenience, I have used problematic terms such as 'shared schema' and 'communal reason'. However, what do these terms actually mean? If these terms conveyed that |Gui's social practices are predetermined by some 'program' which had been embedded in some deep layer of this 'egalitarian society', then they would be quite misleading. The most crucial point is that one's social attitude or stance in triadic relationships is generated, negotiated, renewed and reconfirmed over the course of continuing face-to-face interaction.

Regarding continuity as an essential characteristic of the political process in egalitarian societies, we cannot help being sceptical about the dominant view encountered in hunter-gatherer studies, that the bitter criticism expressed during informal conversation functions as a communal sanction of those who deviate from communal norms. So, what are the |Gui actually doing in this continuity? Probably they are learning, again and again, their mode of life from the deep lessons of the dialectic of emotional life. These lessons are made possible by the fundamental maxim of communal reason: 'do not hide anything' (Sugawara 1991). One of the most deeply-seated |Gui social attitudes demands disclosure in conversation of sexually-emotionally-loaded experiences, and thereafter, discussing them repeatedly.

If we emphasise the critical effect of continuous interaction on decision making and consensus formation, it necessitates a critique of speech act theory, which is based on the Western-centric model of argument and discussion. It is also necessary to posit another theory, which elucidates the logic of indigenous speech acts in the micro-political context of egalitarian societies. In analyses of a number of cases of |Gui negotiation, in which at least one participant tried to achieve his or her transactional goal to gain something, I paid special attention to the cumulative effect caused by reiterating the same act. I argued that this cumulative effect had to be defined as independent from the propositional content of each speech act. This hypothesis is well represented by contrasting the 'balance model' of speech act with the 'billiard ball model'. According to the 'billiard ball model', the hearer's mind is 'moved' at a stroke when, and only when, 'hit' with a speaker's illocutionary act, which is sufficient to meet all the felicity conditions (Searle 1969). On the other hand, according to the 'balance model', the hearer's mind is not moved until the 'illocutionary forces' that have accumulated through iteration exceed some threshold (Sugawara 2002b).

Case (13) <I will visit your camp> exemplifies the validity of the balance model for the |Gui. The narrator, GIS, iterated quite minutely how he and TAK were cooperating with each other at killing springhares. With a long pole, GIS hooked a springhare lurking under the ground five times and then TAK pulled out and hit them, while TAK succeeded in hooking two, after which GIS hit them. A man can of course, succeed at springhare hunting by himself. '[It] cannot simply be pulled out, however; the hunter fastens the pole down at the entrance to the burrow and, after estimating the location of springhare, digs straight down a meter or so and grabs it' (Tanaka 1980: 35). Thus, it is easier and more dependable for one man to grasp the pole while another digs to pull out the springhare. GIS and TAK could not attain consensus for a quadruple relationship, until they were involved in a cooperative labour that anchored them in the iteration of particular bodily configurations. Actually, they never observed the communal reasoning, that encouraged 'sharing' sexual partners. It was not through the abstract direction of the will, but by the iteration and accumulation of the same acts, that their 'embodied thought' attained the consensus.

Involved in sexually-emotionally engaged relationships for many years, most |Gui have plenty of opportunities to endure the persistent conflict between acceptance and opposition. This domain of emotional experience is, of course, very different from that of economic transaction and negotiation. However, it is quite probable that partaking in the dialectics of emotional life forms the bedrock on which their social nature as hunter-gatherers is established.

Notes

1. E. Goffman's argument about the 'territory of the self' is revealing, particularly the claim for the 'preserve', whether physical or mental (Goffman 1971).
2. My discourse analysis was corroborated by three |Gui research assistants. As they were native |Gui speakers and understood neither English nor Setswana, a mediating language was not used.
3. In this paper I have modified Tanaka's original notation *zaku*, following the current orthography established by H. Nakagawa (1996). However, the notation in this paper is not strictly in accordance with this orthography. The symbol '≠' substitutes for the phonetic alphabet denoting the palatal click. Five kinds of tone symbols and pre-vowel glottal stops are omitted. The nasalisation of vowels is approximated by adding the consonant 'n'.
4. The verb *sie* also means 'to have sexual intercourse with'.
5. However, Imamura seems to be sceptical about the above interpretation, in terms of symbolic logic. She extends her interpretation of the |Gui curing ritual to their fundamental life view (Imamura 2001).
6. When citing cases of triadic relationships, the slash '/' indicates the conjugal linkage and the symbol '+' indicates someone's *zaaku* relation with one of the couple.
7. The notations are as follows: Case number <Title: segment of the discourse> [estimated period when the incident occurred]. H's name/W's name + Zf's or Zm's name. Three capitals designate a man's name, while a woman's name is designated by the head capital followed by two small letters.
8. |Gui personal pronouns are structured in an almost complete paradigm: *m., f, mf*: gender of pronoun or noun, male, female and common respectively; *pl., dl.*: form of pronoun or noun, plural and dual, respectively; *inc., exc.*: inclusive and exclusive form of the first-person pronouns, respectively.

References

Austin, J.L. 1962. *How to Do Things with Words*. London: Oxford University Press.
Clastres, P. 1974. *La société contre l'État. Recherches d'anthropologie politique*. Paris: Minuit.
D'Andrade, R. 1995. *The Development of Cognitive Anthropology*. Cambridge: Cambridge University Press.
Goffman, E. 1971. *Relations in Public*. New York: Harper & Row.
Howell, N. 1979. *Demography of the Dobe !Kung*. New York: Academic Press.
Imamura, K. 2001. 'Water in the Desert: Rituals and Vital Power among the Central Kalahari Hunter-gatherers', *African Study Monographs, Supplementary Issue* 27 : 125–63.
Kitamura, K. 1990. 'Interactional Synchrony: A Fundamental Condition for Communication'. In: *Culture Embodied* (Senri Ethnological Studies 27), ed. M. Moerman and M. Nomura. Osaka: National Museum of Ethnology, pp. 123–40.
Kummer, H. 1973. 'Dominance versus Possession: An Experiment on Hamadryas Baboons'. In: *Proceedings of 4th Congress on Primatology. Vol. 1: Precultural Primate Behavior*. Basel: Karger, pp. 226–31.

Lakoff, G. and M. Johnson 1999. *Philosophy in the Flesh: The Embodied Mind and Its Challenge to Western Thought*. New York: Basic Books.
Nakagawa, H. 1996. 'An Outline of |Gui Phonology', *African Study Monographs, Supplementary Issue* 22: 101–24.
Searle, J.R. 1969. *Speech Acts*. Cambridge: Cambridge University Press.
Silberbauer, G.B. 1981. *Hunter and Habitat in the Central Kalahari Desert*. Cambridge: Cambridge University Press.
—— 1982. 'Political Process in G/wi Band'. In: *Politics and History in Band Societies*, ed. E. Leacock and R. Lee. Cambridge: Cambridge University Press, pp. 23–35.
Sperber, D. 1996. *Explaining Culture: A Naturalistic Approach*. Cambridge: Cambirdge University Press.
Sugawara, K. 1988. 'Ethological Study of the Social Behavior of Hybrid Baboons between *Papio anubis* and *P. hamadryas* in Free-ranging Groups', *Primates* 29, 4: 429–48.
—— 1990. 'Interactional Aspects of the Body in Co-presence: Observations on the Central Kalahari San'. In: *Culture Embodied* (Senri Ethnological Studies 27), ed. M. Moerman and M. Nomura. Osaka: National Museum of Ethnology, pp. 79–122.
—— 1991. 'The Economics of Social Life among the Central Kalahari San (G/wikhwe and G//anakwe) in the Sedentary Community at !Koi!kom'. In: *Cash, Commoditisation and Changing Forgers* (Senri Ethnological Studies 30), ed. N. Peterson and T. Matsuyama. Osaka: National Museum of Ethnology, pp. 91–116.
—— 1996. 'Some Methodological Issues for the Analysis of Everyday Conversation among the |Gui', *African Study Monographs, Supplementary Issue* 22: 145–61.
—— 2002a. 'Optimistic Realism or Opportunistic Subordination?: The Interaction of the G/wi and G//ana with Outsiders'. In: *Ethnicity, Hunter-Gatherers, and the "Other": Association or Assimilation in Africa*, ed. S. Kent. Washington: Smithonian Institution Press, pp. 93–126.
—— 2002b. 'Speech Acts, Moves and Meta-communication in Negotiation: Three cases of everyday conversation observed in the |Gui society'. Paper presented at Ninth International Conference on Hunting and Gathering Societies, Edinburgh, 9–13 September 2002.
Tanaka, J. 1980. *The San, Hunter-Gatherers of the Kalahari: A Study in Ecological Anthropology*. Tokyo: University of Tokyo Press.
—— 1987. 'The Recent Changes in the Life and Society of the Central Kalahari San', *African Study Monographs* 7: 37–51.
—— 1989. 'Social Integration of the San Society from the Viewpoint of Sexual Relationships', *African Study Monographs* 9, 3: 55–64.
Woodburn, J. 1979. 'Minimal Politics: The Political Organization of the Hadza of North Tanzania'. In: *Politics in Leadership: A Comparative Perspective*, ed. W.A. Shack and P.S. Cohen. Oxford: Clarendon Press, pp. 244–66.
—— 1982 . 'Egalitarian Societies', *Man*, (N. S.) 17: 431–51.

7

Are Immediate-Return Strategies Adaptive?

Robert Layton

In this paper I look critically at James Woodburn's rejection of ecological explanations for the distribution of immediate-return systems among hunter-gatherers. I review the arguments to the contrary proposed by anthropologists working within a Darwinian paradigm. A number of statements in two of Woodburn's most influential papers are addressed under three linked propositions. I address three claims: there is no correlation between immediate return and ecology; the good hunter never gets back as much as he gives; and immediate-return systems can work effectively only among hunter-gatherers. Following the line of argument in earlier papers (Layton 1986 and 1989) I propose that 'delayed return' is a composite category whose elements need to be differentiated. When this is done, it becomes easier to detect correlations between mobility, sharing and ecology. Anthropologists have argued extensively over the possible adaptive significance of meat sharing. I summarise some of the arguments. I look at strategies in peasant communities that are in some ways similar to those in immediate-return hunter-gatherer communities, and suggest that the parallels may be more interesting than Woodburn allows. Finally, I ask whether the distrust of Darwinian explanations among some social anthropologists is justified, noting that adaptive explanations cannot provide the whole answer to the distribution of immediate- and delayed-return systems.

There is no Correlation between Immediate Return and Ecology

> We cannot attribute the distinction I am making [between immediate and delayed return] to simple environmental factors ... [No immediate-return societies] are excluded by the difficulties of their environment or by the limitations of their technology from having a system with the stress on delayed return. Although I can imagine ecological and other factors which might favour one approach rather than the other, I cannot imagine any environment in which either of the two strategies is impracticable (Woodburn 1980: 101).
>
> Nomadism is fundamental [to immediate return] ... individuals have full rights of access to camps in several of these areas .... People can and do move from one camp to another ... without economic penalty. (Woodburn 1982: 435)

Woodburn rightly regards the ability to change camps as a vital way of preventing the emergence of overbearing leaders, and therefore integral to the egalitarianism characteristic of immediate-return societies. The ability to move between bands is fundamental to human hunter-gatherer behaviour. Humans can move between bands within a regional community, whereas chimpanzees cannot easily move between troops. Hunter-gatherers differ from chimpanzees in belonging to a regional community larger than the band (see Layton and Barton 2001). Such communities range in size from around 300 to 1000 individuals. A male chimpanzee has to spend his entire life living in the troop into which he was born. Female chimpanzees can change troop, particularly at adolescence, but do not always do so (Goodall 1986: 223; Nishida et al. 1990: 66). In contrast, Lee wrote that the !Kung he studied in the Kalahari moved camp 'with distressing frequency' (Lee 1979: 42), meaning that it was hard for him, the anthropologist, to keep track of individual families. Turnbull wrote of the Mbuti, that 'individuals or whole families sometimes wander ... until they are several territories distant from their home territory' (Turnbull 1965: 96). Typically the regional community of hunter-gatherers corresponds to the speakers of a particular language or dialect. Is such mobility purely an expression of the political will to avoid domination, or does it have adaptive consequences?

The proper question to ask, I submit, is not 'can both immediate and delayed return be practised in any environment?' but 'which strategy will do best where both are attempted in a particular environment?' This can be illustrated through the case of territoriality. Freedom of movement between band territories is typical of low-latitude hunter-gatherers, but is also found among the Arctic Inuit. Claiming exclusive access over territories is most profitable where resources are densely and evenly distributed, but in sufficiently short supply to make it worth while competing for them (Dyson-Hudson and Smith 1978; Gould 1982). As resources become more scarce, an increasingly large territory would be needed to guarantee self-sufficiency. This constraint applies to both semi-arid and Arctic environments. As resources become more unpredictable, it becomes increasingly less certain that the individual or group will

Table 7.1 Rainfall recorded at Curtin Springs homestead, 1960–77 (in millimetres)

	1960	1961	1962	1963	1964	1965	1966	1967	1968	1969	1970	1971	1972	1973	1974	1975	1976	1977	Monthly average
January	23.6	6.3	50.0	–	9.3	–	3.6	27.9	56.6	26.1	–	5.3	2.8	60.4	258.9	13.2	24.6	–	31.6
February	6.2	–	–	–	–	–	5.1	84.8	8.1	153.8	–	–	–	21.6	134.5	21.8	36.0	93.1	31.4
March	–	–	4.3	2.8	–	5.3	0.3	141.1	26.1	53.5	2.8	34.0	81.2	3.8	3.3	4.1	–	54.0	22.9
April	27.7	37.5	–	3.5	38.8	–	12.2	–	40.6	1.3	10.4	–	–	3.8	145.4	1.5	–	–	17.9
May	21.0	–	10.3	27.8	7.3	1.0	9.4	11.4	69.0	4.8	16.8	–	–	10.9	33.0	–	–	8.6	12.9
June	–	–	4.0	19.5	1.3	1.5	48.2	–	96.2	14.7	–	10.9	–	42.6	–	–	–	–	13.3
July	3.8	–	7.0	3.0	–	1.5	–	–	45.4	3.0	–	–	1.0	74.1	7.1	14.7	–	–	8.9
August	–	3.5	10.8	–	–	18.0	10.7	–	21.8	–	–	18.0	14.5	28.9	30.5	65.0	–	3.3	12.5
September	–	–	–	–	20.8	7.5	–	–	5.6	8.1	19.3	14.5	15.7	9.1	43.9	66.2	1.3	3.8	12.0
October	26.7	–	48.8	–	22.3	2.3	10.9	–	6.6	36.8	0.8	–	–	9.9	108.6	43.1	57.9	34.1	22.7
November	–	1.3	–	–	7.8	12.8	27.4	14.0	20.8	4.1	29.7	88.3	9.4	3.6	38.3	62.7	0.6	48.0	20.5
December	3.8	–	1.3	10.0	2.8	4.8	67.0	–	7.9	67.3	7.9	8.9	–	5.3	17.3	48.7	1.7	10.6	14.8
Annual totals	113.7	48.6	136.5	66.6	110.43	54.7	195.0	279.3	400.2	373.3	87.7	179.9	124.6	273.5	820.8	341.0	122.0	255.4	221.3

Source: Figures kindly provided by Peter Severin of Curtin Springs Station and reproduced from Robert Layton (1986), *Uluru: an Aboriginal History of Ayers Rock*, with the permission of Aboriginal Studies Press, Canberra.

be repaid for defending the territory and defence eventually becomes uneconomic. The costs of patrolling its boundary would therefore increase until eventually they outweighed the benefits. Rather than generalising about related groups such as the Inuit and native North-west Coast Americans, we might note how some of the most interesting studies show how territoriality varies according to latitude and resource (Richardson 1982; Renouf 1991: 91–94; Andrews 1996). Cashdan was the first to point out that low-latitude hunter-gatherers generally adapt to this constraint by allowing the kind of inter-access described by Lee, Turnbull and others rather than abandoning territoriality altogether (Cashdan 1983). Peterson (1975) and Cashdan called this 'social boundary defence', that is, defending access to the social group that holds the territory. It is impossible to enter the boundary of a desert hunter-gatherer territory without leaving footprints that will be found sooner or later by the resident group, so it is better to ask permission to join the group than risk punishment. A common pattern is for groups from two or more territories to join forces to exploit a 'major' resource such as tsin beans or mongongo nuts (Lee 1979: 351). Lee was told, 'It's when they eat alone and you come along later and you find them there [in your n!ore], that's when the fight starts' (Lee 1979: 336; compare Turnbull 1965: 96). Smith argues that when all hunter-gatherer bands in a region suffer equally from uncertainty as to current resource distribution, and the risk of local resource failure is unsynchronised, permitting mutual access is a way of insuring against starvation. If one band's territory experiences better rainfall than that of its neighbours, it will benefit the band to allow other bands to share its windfall, providing those bands in turn allow their former hosts to camp with them when the unpredictable sequence of rainfall favours them (Smith 1988: 250). The rainfall chart from Curtin Springs homestead, 70 km east of Uluṟu, shows annual rainfall ranging from 50 to 820 mm. In some years, no rain fell for five or six months (see

Table 7.1). Silberbauer (1971) estimates that in a summer month (October–March) 58 mm of rain were required to produce plant growth in the Australian Western Desert, and 14.5 mm in a winter month (April–September). The figures from Curtin Springs imply this occurred, on average, in only two to three months of the year. Anangu in the region of Uluṟu, with whom I worked during the 1970s, recalled the traditional pattern of foraging movement. Distant rain clouds (*ngankali*) signal where fresh plants and feed for animals will spring up. The 'big green grass' time which follows rain was an opportunity to visit relatives in other bands: not only did the unpredictable distribution of food resources compel people to move from water hole to water hole; it was good to keep in touch with cousins in case one's own water failed (Layton 1995: 213).

Wiessner (1982) described the hxaro gift-exchange networks within and between bands among the !Kung as a means of reducing risk. Hxaro partners extend well beyond one's own band. The aim is to have partners in as many independent bands as possible, bands whose territories (n!ore) contain as great a variety of resources as possible. Where partners live far apart, a continual balanced flow of gifts is important, to let each partner know the relationship is intact. In this way, the risk of resources failing in one's own N!ore is offset by guaranteed access to other bands and their resources. There is also a connection with meat sharing (which I discuss in the next section). If someone has a hxaro partner in camp who is visiting from another band, they are likely to be in 'the first wave' of meat sharing by the owner of the kill. They will be included in all daily reciprocal exchanges in the camp.

Figure 7.1 Resource buffering

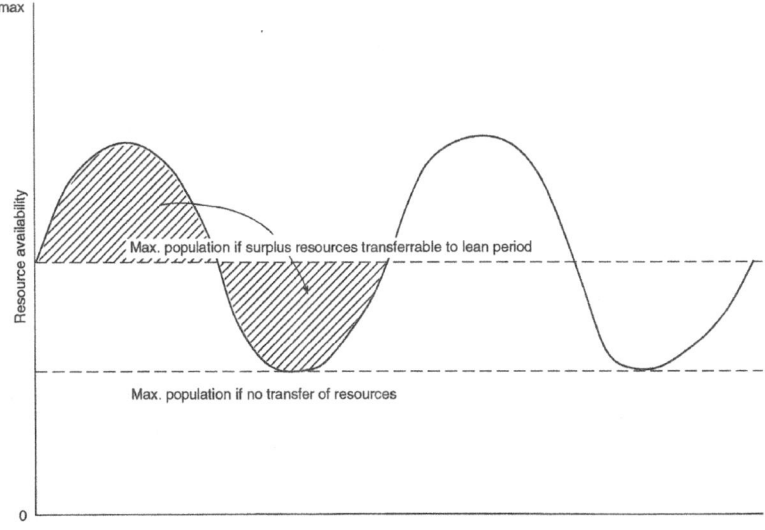

There are no direct parallels to hxaro in Australia, although there were long-distance exchange networks in ceremonial goods such as pearlshell and red ochre, as well as of exceptional raw materials such as obsidian (Thomson 1949; McBryde 1978). However, the same principle of spreading one's social links as widely as possible, as an insurance against local resource failure, can be seen in Western Desert marriage strategies. People never marry into their own clan, and very rarely into adjacent ones. Young men travel widely before initiation, in the company of older sponsors, to build up social contacts (Layton 1995).

Game theory predicts that cooperation or reciprocity will only succeed when the benefits to each participant are greater than if each individual acted selfishly, alone. If the rewards of foraging were limited and fixed, cooperation or reciprocity would tend to break down and be replaced by competition. The phenomenon of 'resource buffering' demonstrates the potential benefits of sharing. Imagine an environment in which there are sometimes plentiful resources, but at other times resources are scarce (see Figure 7.1). If there is no way of carrying over the abundant resources into the lean times, the number of people who can survive will be the number who can survive the times of *minimum* resources. If cooperation or reciprocity enables the surplus abundant resources to be 'carried over', then the number who can survive will be those who can subsist on the *average* resource availability. I return to this issue later.

The Good Hunter Never gets Back as Much as He Gives

> The theory that meat sharing is a way of cushioning variability is inadequate, because hunting success is very unequal; and sharing is not based on reciprocal exchange. (Woodburn 1982: 441)

> Successful individual hunters are specifically denied the opportunity to make effective use of their kills to build wealth and prestige or to attract dependants. (Woodburn 1982: 440)

Evolutionary anthropologists have devoted much research to investigating reasons why it might be adaptive for the hunter to share his prey. Winterhalder (1987) devised a model to predict the consequences of hunter-gatherer food sharing. If a set of individuals hunt and gather independently, pooling their catches will not reduce the average yield, but will compensate for variations in each actor's personal catch. This is an example of resource buffering on a daily time-scale, rather than the seasonal time-scale of mutual access between territories. If all foragers do equally well each time, there would be no benefit from sharing. If, on the other hand, hunting success is unpredictable, and if the hunter's catch (when he's successful) is more than he and his immediate family can consume, some would go to waste, and there is no benefit from keeping it all (see Figure 7.2, marginal value figure). Among the Ache, a family of four could only make use of 50–60 percent of the calories provided by a single peccary before it spoiled (Kaplan et al. 1990: 114).

Ethnographic studies show that a distinction is commonly made between plants and small game, which are not expected to be shared between households, and large game. The Hadza have obligatory meat-sharing rules for large game (Woodburn 1980: 103). Among the Nyae-Nyae !Kung, meat sharing is practised with big game weighing hundreds of pounds (Marshall 1976: 357). Among the Ache, a single peccary yields 50,000 to 60,000 calories; a wild bees' nest yields up to 100,000 calories, but an Ache adult consumes a maximum of 5,000 calories per day (Kaplan and Hill 1985); note, however, that smaller game are also shared among the Ache (Kaplan et al. 1990: 124). Gidjingali (Altman and Peterson 1988) call large game (kangaroo, emu etc.) maih nagimuk and distinguish it from small game (fish, lizard, bird) which they call maih yawut. People are expected to bring large game back to camp and distribute it among the resident households. 'The rules relating to sharing are not directed at the small game essential to provisioning the household

Figure 7.2 Marginal value

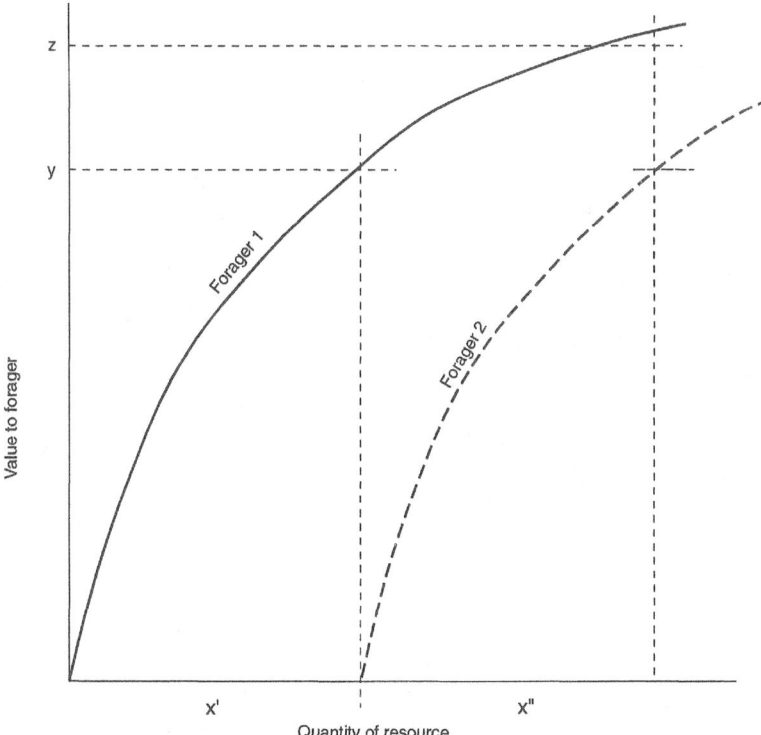

The first quantity x' eaten by the forager is worth a lot (y): the second quantity x" is worth less (z) because (s)he is less hungry BUT to <u>another forager</u> who has eaten nothing the second quantity is worth (y).

but to occasions when there is an immediate surplus to household needs' (Altman and Peterson 1988: 92). Altman and Peterson describe arguments that may develop over ambiguous cases, such as a large catch of small fish. The fisherman wants to class this as small game, others want to call it large game. Peterson later argued that Aboriginal game distribution depends on what he calls 'demand sharing', i.e. others must insist on their rights (Peterson 1993; cf. Erdal and Whiten 1994).

Providing hunters expect their mutual dependence to continue indefinitely into the future, and they can spot and punish people who cheat, it will benefit each hunter to share his catch when he is lucky, and to receive, through return giving, when other hunters are successful. Kaplan and Hill calculate that the sharing of honey alone increases the nutritional status of Ache by 20 percent, sharing of meat alone increases it by 40 percent, while all observed food sharing increases nutritional status by 80 percent (Kaplan and Hill 1985: 233). Kaplan et al. have since calculated that if there were no food sharing, Ache households would experience two weeks every two years in which they acquired less than 50 percent of the calories they need to survive (Kaplan et al. 1990: 114). It is true that at some point the advantage of pooling will be overcome by the increased size of the band over-hunting local prey. Winterhalder's model showed that six hunters sharing would reduce variation in meat supply by 60 percent under any circumstance (Winterhalder 1987: 383). This corresponds quite well with a typical band size of thirty to thirty-five individuals.

The risk-minimising explanation for meat sharing works best where all hunters are equally successful, and each gives away his excess catch. There are two reasons why the explanation must be incomplete, both of which were identified by Woodburn in the passages at the head of this section. First, an Ache hunter eats significantly less of his own kill than do others (Hawkes 1990: 149), or even none at all (Kaplan et al. 1990: 129). Rouja reports the same practice ('renunciation') among the Bardi of northwest Australia (Rouja 1998). Second, some hunters are always more successful than others. This has caused some anthropologists to argue that the successful hunter must benefit indirectly. Hawkes (1993) accepts Woodburn's argument that the effort and risk of hunting is greater than the material benefits of sharing among societies such as the !Kung, Hadza and Ache.

Kaplan et al. report that the best hunters among the Ache father more legitimate children and are reported to have more affairs (Kaplan et al. 1990: 116). This explanation is also insufficient. Kaplan and Hill note that single men are the biggest losers among the Ache, and that sharing is not carried out on a 'tit-for-tat' (strictly reciprocal) basis (Kaplan and Hill 1985: 233). Bliege-Bird and Bird make the same observation of turtle hunters in the Torres Straits (Bliege-Bird and Bird 1997: 66). Hawkes (1993), however, argues sharing can still be adaptive for the individual as a result of increased status (the right to make decisions on behalf of the group), support in disputes, and support when injured and unable to hunt. Kaplan and Hill similarly concluded 'even above-average foragers may be willing to give more than their share in order to avoid the risk of [injury leading to] long stretches without food' (Kaplan and Hill 1985: 237). This argument has since been supported by further work with the Hiwi. Gurven et al. (2000: 266) report that among the Hiwi of Venezuela adults were sick for roughly 6.5 percent of all days during a three-month period, and cite comparable figures for other hunter-gatherer communities. 'Even if these "down" periods are infrequent, getting food and proper care during them can be essential to prolonged survival and future reproductive success' (Gurven et al. 2000: 267).

High producers among the Ache can also expect to be well treated, to prevent them joining another band (Kaplan and Hill 1985: 237). Although good hunters are generally not expected to boast (Lee 1969; Woodburn 1982), they do tend to gain prestige (Altman 1987: 134). Bliege-Bird and Bird argue that young men increase their prospects of inheriting land by presenting meat to elders (1997: 65). Young men among at least some San and Australian Aboriginal societies hunt for their wives' parents to initiate or cement a marriage (Hart and Pilling 1960: 31–33; Lewis-Williams 1981: 69–70; Keen 1994: 188). Among the Tiwi of North Australia a young man, once promised a wife, is likely to join his prospective father-in-law's band to ensure the donor does not change his mind (Hart and Pilling 1960: 31). 'The meat, fish and game provided for the large household of an old man was provided by the young men ... . Typically [a son], when he returned at nightfall with a kangaroo ... would ignore the old man [with whom relations might be strained] and dump the carcass at the feet of his mother as if to say, "I brought this back for you, not that old so and so"' (1960: 34).

On balance, therefore, there appears to be sufficient evidence to conclude that meat sharing is indirectly in the good hunter's personal interests (for further discussion see Charlton 1997). If the hunter received no benefit whatsoever from sharing his catch, why wouldn't good hunters go and live on their own? According to Woodburn, some do: it is not rare, at least among the Hadza, to find individuals, usually males, living entirely on their own as hermits for long periods (1982: 438). However, according to Marshall (1976: 350, cited Woodburn 1980: 102) this does not apply to the !Kung. Turnbull describes an objectionable Mbuti man who was excluded from two bands as a punishment (Turnbull 1965: 101, 106, 154), although it might be argued that cooperative net hunting makes exclusion a more telling sanction among the Mbuti (cf. Woodburn 1980: 103). The only case I know of from Australia was Gudang, a legendary Alawa who refused to move to a cattle-station camp, and continued to live on his own in the bush until shortly before his death (Layton 1992: 110, 112). I am inclined to think the general lack of solitary hunters implies everyone gains more than they lose from living in a band. I also consider the argument for resource buffering through sharing should not yet be rejected, despite the fact some hunters contribute more than others. There will always be some variation. The question is, how much variation is needed to invalidate the argument for mutual benefit? The 'marginal value theorem' shows that there is little point in a hunter keeping meat to himself, once he has eaten enough to satisfy himself. In tropical climates, meat decays very quickly (see Kaplan et al. 1990: 114, cited above). The successful hunter would need only a very small benefit from sharing to make sharing a better option than allowing meat to decay.

Although Hadza have rules for sharing large game, Woodburn argues that in immediate-return systems there are no binding obligations of reciprocity between specific individuals. Rather than giving to specified others, in immediate-return systems there is 'generalized mutuality' (1980: 104) in camps whose membership is constantly changing. Hawkes has also argued that hunter-gatherer sharing is more generalised than the theory of reciprocal altruism predicts (Hawkes 1993). While this argument is a strong criticism of Trivers and Axelrod's theories for the evolution of reciprocal altruism (Trivers 1985; Axelrod 1990), more recent models can accommodate it. Nowak and Sigmund constructed a computer model of a situation in which individuals are willing to help others in a community even if they do not anticipate direct reciprocation in the future. The success of this strategy depends on what Nowak and Sigmund call the 'image score' of participants, a score that is increased when others witness, or learn about, the altruistic act. Others will be more likely to help altruists than selfish individuals. The increased probability that a third party will reward the giver offsets the cost of an altruistic act. Nowak and Sigmund argue that this kind of giving will be most sustainable if the number of interactions per generation of players is large and the community is small (Nowak and Sigmund 1998), as will be true in a hunter-gatherer society. Gurven et al.'s explanation for meat sharing among the Hiwi takes the same approach. Calling it *display sharing*, they write: 'If food is intentionally shared with the same groups of people over time, this could signal high productive ability and *intent to cooperate* with those people' (Gurven et al. 2000: 265, my italics).

While the alternative of storage becomes more feasible in high latitudes (Woodburn 1980: 112), the absence of a narrow correlation between meat sharing and a specific ecology is not proof that an adaptive explanation is invalid. A comparative study of Inuit communities suggests sharing is practised even where storage is possible, where hunters' success is unsynchronised (Kaplan and Hill 1985: 238). Sharing large game will, therefore, probably always be adaptive wherever hunter-gatherers pursue game weighing substantially more than the hunter and his immediate family can eat in a single day, and different hunters are successful on different occasions.

Are Immediate- and Delayed-Return Discrete Categories?

> I recognize not only that there is always some immediate-return activity in delayed return systems (most strikingly in the case of Australian Aboriginal societies) but also that there is some delayed-return activity in immediate-return systems. (Woodburn 1982: 449)

Woodburn classes !Kung, Mbuti and Hadza as egalitarian, immediate-return societies. Among inegalitarian, delayed-return societies he includes Australian Aborigines, Plains Indians, North-west Coast Indians and 'some' Inuit. Riches (1995) develops Woodburn's typology to distinguish three types of hunter-gatherer society:

(a) the simple, 'flexible' type (Hadza, San, Inuit, Mbuti);
(b) the 'stratified' type (North-west Coast of North America and Calusa of Florida);
(c) the 'sociocentric structure' type (Australian Aboriginal).

Riches treats the second and third as alternative 'transformations' of the first. Inuit and Australian Aborigines are, however, anomalous in both typologies. Woodburn includes 'some' Inuit in the category of 'delayed return'; Riches puts Inuit in 'simple', Australian Aborigines in 'complex'.

In my view, both Arctic Inuit and Australian Aborigines would better be characterised as part immediate, part delayed-return societies. This is because the category 'delayed return' conflates at least two axes of variation (Layton 1986). The Arctic Inuit have a complex technology and store food. The complexity of their technology is convincingly explained as a response to their high dependence on animal rather than plant foods, and the limited time periods when those prey species are available (Torrence 1983, 2001). Storage is both possible because of the cold climate and desirable because of the seasonal availability of food (Binford 1980). There is, on the other hand, often much flexibility of movement within the named Inuit community and no descent groups claim prerogatives over particular parts of the community's territory (Gubser 1965: 166; Smith 1991: 113). Arctic Inuit society was traditionally egalitarian (Smith 1991: 137). Mauss and Beuchat long ago reported that in summer, when individual families forage independently, there is no obligation to share meat beyond the family. Where hunters co-operate, the catch is divided between them (Balikci 1970: 134–8, Smith 1991: 165, 313ff.). In winter, however, food is shared throughout the co-resident extended family (Mauss and Beuchat 1979: 70–1). Smith concludes from detailed analysis of Inujjuamuit hunting strategies that the reduction in risk gained by pooling catches gives the best explanation for the greater size of Inujjuamuit winter villages (1991: 330). Leveling transactions exist throughout Greenland, Labrador and the central regions of the Canadian Arctic. Households which possess more than what is judged to be the normal level of material goods must distribute some to poorer individuals (Briggs 1970: 209–211; Mauss and Beuchat 1979: 73).

Woodburn classes Australian Aborigines as having delayed return primarily because they practise strategic marriage alliances linking clans (1982: 449, n3). The cultures found through northern and parts of central Australia also embody clan totemism, making them seem to resemble the totemic clans of the undoubtedly delayed-return societies of the North-west Coast of North America. Indeed, cross-cousin marriage will only generate regular alliances when it is practised between unilineal descent groups. On the other hand, Aboriginal technology is as simple as that of hunter-gatherers in other semi-arid environments, and inter-band movement is as flexible as among the San and Hadza. Inherited membership of a totemic clan does not confer exclusive rights to hunt and gather within the clan's territory, only exclusive rights to enter sacred sites, wear the clan's totemic paintings during restricted ceremonies and look after its sacred objects. Water is the most predictable, localised resource and the only one susceptible to boundary defence. Northern and central Australian cultures appear to have followed a historical trajectory towards the territorial aspects of delayed return, but only as far as the ecology permits (Layton 1997: 379–81, 384). Flexibility is greatest in the Western Desert, whose ecology is similar to the Kalahari (Layton 1986: 27–8, 1995: 223–4; Tonkinson 1991: 67–8). The unpredictability of rainfall and the distribution of food resources make it beneficial for clans to allow each other reciprocal access to their territories; social boundary defence is typical of both the Kalahari and Australia. Opportunities for the emergence of differences in power are confined to two spheres. The most common is to acquire more religious knowledge than others of one's generation within the region (Bern 1979). Some societies, including the Tiwi and Yolngu, give the opportunity to negotiate marriage exchanges that link clans in such a way that a successful man ends up with more wives than his brothers and hence develops a larger, more productive household. In practice, the latter opportunity is only available among a few communities in the extreme north of Australia (Hart and Pilling 1960: 15–18; Keen 1982).

The North-west Coast was, on the other hand, characterised by dense, predictable resources. Totemic clans defended their territories and killed

Figure 7.3 Delayed return as a composite category

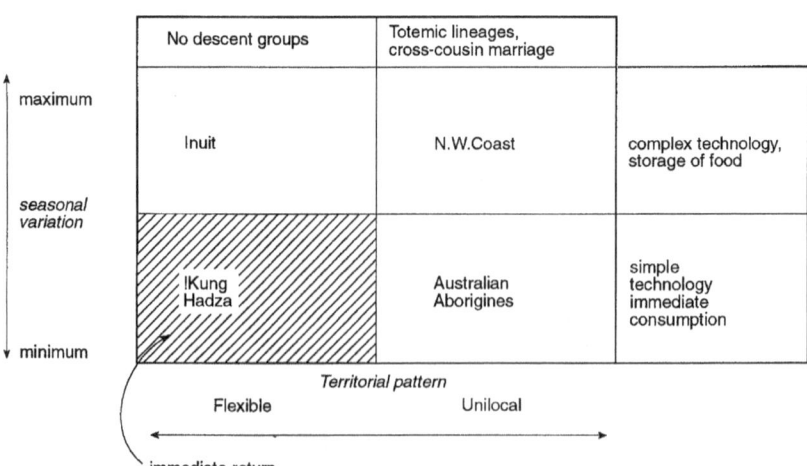

trespassers. Food was processed by smoking, drying or potting in fat, and stored for the winter. During the summer, clans accumulated surpluses of food which were then distributed through competitive inter-clan feasting in the potlatch. Some surplus food was invested in feeding specialist craftsmen, who produced carved and painted wooden artefacts – boxes, spoons, hats, masks – emblazoned with the group's totemic images displayed at potlatches; and objects such as woven blankets bearing designs that were not clan specific, for distribution during potlatches. The quantity of valuables each lineage could give away demonstrated its wealth, and hence its rank. Poor lineages were vulnerable to attack; their land could be taken by the attackers and the members of the group enslaved.

I therefore conclude that technological complexity and territoriality constitute different axes of variation (see Figure 7.3). Once they are distinguished, it is easier to demonstrate that immediate- and delayed-return strategies are adaptive in different circumstances. Woodburn's archetypal immediate-return societies (Hadza and to a slightly lesser degree, the !Kung) live in environments which render all the immediate-return options more adaptive, producing the overall effect of egalitarianism which Woodburn predicts. While the Hadza are dramatically free of binding relationships of mutual dependency, this is not true of the !Kung. As Woodburn admits (1982: 444), hxaro relationships are enduring and carefully sustained.

Immediate-Return Systems can only Work effectively among Hunter-Gatherers

Woodburn argues that it is not only in state systems that egalitarianism needs to be politically asserted; it is asserted (and not inevitable) even in very simply organised hunter-gatherer communities (Woodburn 1982: 432). Among horticulturalists, however, (as in Papua New Guinea) equality is maintained by strident competition (446): 'In principle all farming systems, unless based on wage or slave labour, must be delayed return ...They imply binding commitments and dependencies between people ... The farmer, for example, will almost invariably pool his labour with others ... and depends on others for the protection of his growing crops, of his use rights to land ...' (433).

The transition from hunting and gathering to farming undoubtedly transformed the adaptive niche of many human populations. While I agree with Woodburn on this point, I consider the parallels between the levelling mechanisms found among peasants and hunter-gatherers more profound and more interesting than Woodburn implies in his brief reference to competitive exchange in the New Guinea Highlands. A number of studies suggest that the regional community of interacting hunter-gatherer bands is of about the same size as peasant villages, that is, between 150 and 500 people (see data collated in Kelly 1995: 209–10, and compare Dunbar 1993: 865). All humans (including both hunter-gatherers and peasants) have the ability to keep track of whether partners in exchange are honouring reciprocal social obligations.

Trivers (1985) has argued this is a genetically determined skill that has helped humans adapt to uncertain environments (see also Charlton 1997). Peasant farmers, like hunter-gatherers, are subject to unpredictable or stochastic variability in environment that creates risk (Winterhalder 1990: 67). Like hunter-gatherers, peasants minimise risk both through their subsistence strategies and through social relationships between households.

However, while humans have a unique capacity to maintain social relationships, I agree with Woodburn that hunter-gatherers and peasants use this ability in different ways. Hunter-gatherers move between bands where they have friends and relatives to exploit temporary local abundances of food and to escape drought. In a peasant village, the entire community is living in a single place. Woodburn is undoubtedly correct to argue that this transforms the opportunities for and constraints on negotiating social relationships. Winterhalder (1990) compares the peasant strategy of dispersing fields and diversifying crops to the hunter-gatherer strategy of relying on more than one prey species in a patchy environment. Hunter-gatherers reduce risk by sharing the meat obtained from hunting large game animals and moving between bands. Winterhalder argues that farmers do not reduce risk by pooling their harvest because the scale of temporal variation is very different: a foraging trip occurs over hours or days, whereas the agricultural cycle lasts a whole year.

In writing a recent study of traditional farming communities in Europe (Layton 2000), I have been reminded of the parallels between behaviours experienced during fieldwork among Australian hunter-gatherers and farmers in eastern France. Networks of reciprocal, noncontractual assistance are integral to peasant life throughout the world (Erasmus 1956; Panter-Brick 1993). They constitute what Scott called 'the moral economy of the peasant' (Scott 1976). In general, mutual aid takes two forms: reciprocal exchanges between individual households, often linked by kinship, and occasions when the entire community comes together to help one person in need.

During the 1950s and 1960s, a school of thought represented by Banfield (1958) and Foster (1960, 1965) saw the levelling mechanisms found among peasant societies as the principal force impeding development and modernisation (Foster 1965: 305–6). Foster coined the term 'peasant pie' to express his interpretation of peasant mentality: a view that the world's resources were fixed, so anyone who did better than his neighbours must have grown wealthy at others' expense (1960: 177, 1965: 297). Selfish individuals were therefore ostracised or punished by the envious neighbours, rather than rewarded for their entrepreneurial spirit.

Foster misconstrued levelling transactions as an obstruction to cooperation and reciprocity. Reciprocal aid and community-wide pooling of labour to help individuals in need are in fact widespread in peasant societies. Every household needs to call on neighbours for help when a member falls ill, or crops fail through accident, but none can anticipate when it will need help in future (see Layton 2000, chapter 4, for a case study and Erasmus 1956 for a comparative survey). Each member participates regularly in the expectation that all will need to call to a larger extent on the community's labour pool sooner or later. This is not totally dissimilar to meat sharing among hunter-gatherers. We tolerate the fact that insurance companies make a profit as long as we know they will pay out when we suffer misfortune. Maybe this is why good hunters tolerate the camp's profit at their expense, as long as they can count on receiving meat when injured or unsuccessful in the hunt. Risk-reducing strategies must anticipate the worst case, not the average one (Rowley-Conwy and Zvelebil 1989).

Two inheritance systems coexist in Western Europe: unigeniture and partible inheritance. My study area in Franche-Comté is characterised by the partible inheritance. The French anthropologist Augustins argued that partible inheritance and unigeniture have fundamentally different goals (Augustins 1989: 59, cf. Barthelemy 1988: 199). The contrast can in some ways be compared to the contrasting outcomes of immediate- and delayed return. Unigeniture aims to perpetuate the *house* (*maison, casa* or *ostal*) associated with a family line at the expense of disinherited siblings, by passing the land and house to a single heir. His siblings must either leave to seek work elsewhere or remain as unpaid servants. Partible inheritance aims to perpetuate a wider kindred (*parentèle*) of equals by sharing portions of land between all children, even if it entails sacrificing the continuing association between a family line, its ancestral home and land. Sometimes the house itself is divided, or passes via a daughter to another family (Augustins 1990: 59; cf. Barthelemy 1988: 199). These offer an analogy to the distinction between immediate- and delayed return. Partibility, unlike unigeniture, acts as a levelling mechanism within and between households. Rosenberg regards its levelling effect as an integral part of the democratic society that existed in the French alpine village of Abriès before the 1789 Revolution. Both men and women inherited and bequeathed land, and widows managing property had the right to speak at the village assembly (Rosenberg 1988: 22–23, 27). In the Spanish village of Santa María del Monte, widows become household heads and can attend the village assembly (Behar 1986: 121). Partible inheritance in Törbel (Switzerland) ensured that differences of family wealth were negligible and restricted the capacity of particular families to dominate village government (Netting 1981: 198).

Partible inheritance is generally associated with a dense network of mutual aid sanctioned by the threat of ostracism. In both St Felix (northern Italy) and Ste Foy (southern France), on the other hand, unigeniture is associated with an ideal of household self-sufficiency, minimising inter-household networks of mutual aid (Cole and Wolf 1974: 168, 243; Rogers 1991: 101). Cole and Wolf were struck by the difference, in this regard, between the neighbouring north Italian villages of Tret and St Felix. In Tret, which practises partible inheritance, households frequently cooperated, often shared food and wine and, while ostracising households guilty of 'sharp practice', denied that a formal reckoning of debt and credit was necessary. Household heads in St Felix strove for complete self-sufficiency and, when help was needed from other households, kept a strict account of service rendered (Cole and Wolf 1974: 168–9, 243–4). Rogers was similarly impressed when she moved from Lorraine to the Aveyronnais village of Ste Foy, from a community with partible inheritance to one practising unigeniture. Instead of the reciprocal exchanges she had seen in the former village, there was little mutual aid and, where exchange between households occurred, labour flowed disproportionately from small to big holdings while equipment and money were loaned in the opposite direction, contributing to the general ethos of patronage (Rogers 1991: 106, 118).

Families in Törbel (a Swiss village) agree on the division of the family holding into equal portions when it is inherited by the children, before drawing lots to determine who will receive each part (Netting 1981: 193–4). Is there a distant parallel here with the Hadza practice of gambling with bark discs to even out the distribution of possessions (Woodburn 1982: 442–3)? Lotteries are used in Pellaport, the French village I studied, to allocate wood from the communal forest and, in the past, portions of common meadow. In every case, the opportunity for favouritism or appropriation by the powerful is eliminated. The inhabitants of both Kippel and Santa María (northern Spain) rely on the rigorous application of rotas so that each household can rest assured that every other one will make a fair contribution to work on behalf of the whole group (Friedl 1974: 55; Behar 1986: 203–5). As McCay and Acheson (1987), and Ostrom (1990) showed, such a system (like meat sharing) only works when 'free-riders' can be detected and punished. Many were reluctant to take on the role of village headman in Santa María, since the occupant had to enforce fines on fellow-villagers who failed to join collective work parties (Behar 1986: 149). People who grazed livestock in closed fields rather than making their grazing available to all would be publicly denounced by the hayward at meetings of the assembly (202). I don't think it is fanciful to see a parallel here with the way a good Hadza and !Kung hunter who might grow arrogant is ridiculed.

Is a Darwinian Approach Adequate?

When social behaviour is studied from an evolutionary or neo-Darwinian perspective, the question posed is: what is the relative advantage of alternative behaviours for the reproductive success of an individual within a given environment? Apart from those studying the Ache, researchers have generally used 'proxy measures' of fitness, such as nutritional status, to answer this question. I have argued that adaptive explanations can nonetheless be helpful.

Many social anthropologists, however, find a Darwinian approach problematic for two reasons:

1. *Darwinian theory is premised on the selfishness of the individual.* Even where social strategies consist of cooperation or reciprocity, they must benefit the individual. This is a peculiarly Western, market-oriented, vision. Recently, however, some evolutionary theorists accepted that indi-

viduals in other cultures may be more trusting than Western economists (e.g. Mace 2000). Nowak and Sigmund (1998) have shown that more generous strategies than Axelrod's tit-for-tat may succeed. Nonetheless, the theoretical premise remains, that strategies must benefit the organism that enacts them, at least for long enough for them to be transmitted to others.

2. *Darwinian theory appears to deny free will.* Giddens claims that conscious agency frees humans from the blind forces of social evolution (Giddens 1984: 237). Ingold similarly argues that social relations must be understood intersubjectively in terms of their meaning for participants, which (in his view) exempts social behaviour from adaptive pressures (Ingold 1986: 130). We are certainly free to choose between alternative courses of action. There is sufficient uncertainty in the world to prevent us from knowing in advance the outcomes of our choices. But I do not accept that this exempts the practical consequences of human behaviour from selective pressures.

Some authors (e.g. Trivers 1985; Cosmides et al. 1992) argue that social strategies are 'hard-wired' in the brain. We do not have to accept this argument. Learnt strategies can also have different consequences for people's reproductive success (only the capacity to learn them need be genetically determined). However, if we allow that social strategies may be learnt, and specific to particular cultural traditions, a Darwinian perspective still points to certain interesting research questions:

(a) It is not necessary to assume that everyone in a population behaves optimally (in fact, it would be more interesting if we could actually plot the outcome of alternative strategies). This would require very long-term participant observation, but some of the best hunter-gatherer research groups, such as those studying the Ache and Ju/'hoansi, may be able to explore the issue.
(b) The strategies which make the most effective contribution to the actors' reproductive success should, however, spread through the population at the expense of the alternatives (by copying, if not genetically transmitted). This does not mean less adaptive strategies will have been completely replaced in most cases. Alternative strategies may keep being 'invented' over and over again. The concept of an 'evolutionarily stable strategy' implies that several strategies may coexist. For example, there may always be some cheating in a system of reciprocal altruism (see Vickery et al. 1991; Winterhalder 1996). This also poses interesting, but answerable questions for field research.

While a neo-Darwinian approach highlights a range of interesting research questions, an adaptationist explanation is relatively ineffective at explaining long-term processes of social change. The focus on the individual encouraged by neo-Darwinian theory tends to discount the emergent ('self-organising') properties of social systems that Durkheim was so careful to point out (Durkheim 1938). Renfrew recognised the value of 'Catastrophe Theory' for archaeology more than twenty years ago (Renfrew 1978). Writers such as Maschner (1991), Erwin (1997), and McGlade (1997) have since applied complex systems theory in archaeology. In these applications, society is treated as if it were an ecological system. The complex interactions between sectors of society generate unpredictable historical trajectories, somewhat in the way that changes in the rate at which populations evolve may be explained in terms of their complex interaction with predator and prey species in an ecological system (Kauffman 1993; Conway Morris 1998). Ames and Maschner (1999) reconstruct the trajectory that led to the competitive, delayed-return societies of the North-west Coast of North America. Some years ago, Bender summarised the current state of archaeological knowledge concerning the development and subsequent collapse of delayed-return hunter-gatherer societies in the North American mid Continent (Bender 1985a and 1985b). I argued above that the archaeology of Australian societies suggests a trend toward delayed-return traits over the past 5,000 years. In other words, I prefer Woodburn's point that there is some delayed-return activity in immediate-return systems (Woodburn 1982: 449), to his attempt to devise exclusive types, immediate-return and delayed-return systems. If the former is more accurate, then ecology will determine which strategies are most likely to succeed when played against themselves or competing strategies (Maynard-Smith's concept of evolutionarily stable strategies, Maynard-Smith 1982). Archaeology suggests that the outcome of competing strategies within the dynamics of social interaction may only become apparent over a period of several thousand years.

There is no obvious ecological explanation for the distribution of partible inheritance and unigeniture in Europe; both occur in the Alps. Northern Germany is characterised by unigeniture but northern France by partible inheritance. Their distribution is better explained as the outcome of strong or weak feudal control: in other words, a dynamic process within the social system. On the other hand, local control of significant areas of common land is another determinant of village democracy in Europe, and common land has demonstrably survived best in mountainous areas where the land is simply too poor to be worth fencing and dividing. This phenomenon is well explained by Dyson-Hudson and Smith's model of territoriality, mentioned above. I argue that a theory of evolution which combines the concept of adaptation to an external environment with one of a system that possesses its own internal dynamic, realisable within the constraints imposed by ecology, can help us better to understand the history of hunter-gatherer societies, and thus the distribution of immediate- and delayed-return strategies in time and space.

References

Altman, J.C. 1987. *Hunter-gatherers Today. An Aboriginal Economy in North Australia.* Canberra: Aboriginal Studies Press.
Altman, J. and N. Peterson 1988. 'Rights to game and rights to cash among contemporary hunter-gatherers'. In: T. Ingold, D. Riches and J. Woodburn (eds) *Hunters and Gatherers: Property, Power and Ideology,* pp. 75–94. Oxford: Berg.
Ames, K. and H. Maschner 1999. *Peoples of the Northwest Coast: Their Archaeology and Prehistory.* London: Thames and Hudson.
Andrews, E. 1996 'Territoriality and land use among the Akulmiut of Western Alaska'. In: E. Burch and L. Ellanna (eds) *Key Issues in Hunter-gatherer Research,* pp. 65–93. Oxford: Berg.
Augustins, G. 1989. *Comment se perpétuer? Devenir des lignées et destins des patrimoines dans les paysanneries européennes.* Nanterre : Société d'Ethnologie.
Axelrod, R. 1990. *The Evolution of Co-operation.* Harmondsworth: Penguin. (First published 1984, New York: Basic Books).
Balikci, A. 1970. *The Netsilik Eskimo.* New York: Garden City.
Banfield, E. 1958. *The Moral Basis of a Backward Society.* New York: Free Press.
Barthelemy, T. 1988. 'Les modes de transmission du patrimoine: synthèse des travaux effectués depuis quinze ans par les ethnologues de la France'. *Études Rurales,* 110–12: 195–212.
Behar, R. 1986. *Santa María del Monte: the Presence of the Past in a Spanish Village.* Princeton: Princeton University Press.
Bender, B. 1985a. 'Emergent Tribal Formations in the American Midcontinent'. *American Antiquity,* 50: 52–62.
—— 1985b. 'Prehistoric Developments in the American Midcontinent and in Brittany, Northwest France'. In: T.D. Price and J.A. Brown (eds) *Prehistoric Hunter-gatherers. The Emergence of Cultural Complexity,* pp. 21–57. London: Academic.
Bern, J. 1979. 'Ideology and domination: toward a reconstruction of the Australian Aboriginal social formation'. *Oceania.* 50: 118–32.
Binford, L. 1980. 'Willow Smoke and Dogs' Tails: Hunter-gatherer Settlement Systems and Archaeological Site Formation'. *American Antiquity,* 45: 4–20.
Bliege-Bird, R.L. and Bird, D.W. 1997 'Delayed Reciprocity and Tolerated Theft: the Behavioural Ecology of Food-Sharing Strategies', *Current Anthropology,* 38: 49–78.
Briggs, J.L. 1970. *Never in Anger: Portrait of an Eskimo Family.* Cambridge, Mass.: Harvard University Press.
Cashdan, E. 1983. 'Territoriality among Human Foragers: Ecological Models and an Application to Four Bushman Groups'. *Current Anthropology,* 24: 47–66.
Charlton, B. 1997. 'Injustice, Inequality and Evolutionary Psychology', *Journal of Health Psychology,* 2: 413–25.
Cole, J.W. and E.R. Wolf 1974. *The Hidden Frontier: Ecology and Ethnicity in an Alpine Valley.* New York: Academic Press.
Conway Morris, S. 1998. *The Crucible of Creation. The Burgess Shale and the Rise of Animals.* Oxford: Oxford University Press.
Cosmides, L, J. Tooby and J.H. Barkow. 1992. 'Introduction: Evolutionary Psychology and Conceptual Integration'. In: J.H. Barkow, L. Cosmides and J. Tooby (eds) *The Adapted Mind : Evolutionary Psychology and the Generation of Culture,* pp. 4–136. Oxford: Oxford University Press.
Dunbar, R. 1993. 'Co-evolution of Neocortical Size, Group Size and Language in Humans'. *Behavioural and Brain Sciences Evolution* 16: 681–735.
Durkheim, E. 1938. *The Rules of Sociological Method,* trans. S.A. Solovay and J.H. Mueller. London: Macmillan (French edition 1901).
Dyson-Hudson, R. and E.A. Smith 1978. 'Human Territoriality: an Ecological Assessment'. *American Anthropologist,* 80: 21–41.
Erasmus, C.J. 1956. 'Culture Structure and Process: the Occurrence and Disappearance of Reciprocal Farm Labour'. *Southwestern Journal of Anthropology,* 12: 444–69.

Erdal, D. and A. Whiten. 1994. 'On Human Egalitarianism: An Evolutionary Product of Machiavellian Status Escalation?' *Current Anthropology*, 35: 175–8.

Erwin, H.R. 1997. 'The Dynamics of Peer Polities'. In: S. Van de Leeuw and J. McGlade (eds), *Time, Process and Structured Transformation in Archaeology*, pp. 57–96. London: Routledge.

Foster, G. 1960. 'Interpersonal Relations in Peasant Society'. *Human Organization*, 19: 174–8.

—— 1965. 'Peasant Society and the Image of the Limited Good'. *American Anthropologist*, 67: 293–315.

Friedl, J. 1974. *Kippel, a Changing Village in the Alps.* New York: Holt, Rinehart.

Giddens, A. 1984. *The Constitution of Society.* Cambridge: Polity Press.

Goodall, J. 1986. *The Chimpanzees of Gombe: Principles of Behaviour.* Cambridge, Mass.: Harvard/Bellknap.

Gould, R. 1982. 'To Have and Have not: the Ecology of Sharing among Hunter-gatherers'. In: N.M. Williams and E.S. Hunn (eds), *Resource Managers: North American and Australian Hunter-gatherers*, pp. 69–91. Canberra: Australian Institute of Aboriginal Studies.

Gubser, N.J. 1965. *The Nunamuit Eskimo, Hunters of Caribou.* New Haven: Yale University Press.

Gurven, M., K. Hill, H. Kaplan, M. Hurtado and R. Lyles 2000 'Food transfers among Hiwi foragers of Venezuela: tests of reciprocity'. *Human Ecology* 28, 2: 171–218.

Hart, C. and A. Pilling. 1960. *The Tiwi of North Australia* (1st edn). New York: Holt, Rinehart.

Hart, C., A. Pilling and J. Goodale. 1988. *The Tiwi of North Australia* (3rd edn). New York: Holt, Rinehart.

Hawkes, K. 1990. 'Why do Some Men Hunt? Benefits for Risky Choices'. In: E. Cashdan (ed.), *Risk and Uncertainty in Tribal and Peasant Economies*, pp. 145–66. Boulder, Col.: Westview.

—— 1993. 'Why Hunters Work: an Ancient Version of the Problem of Public Goods'. *Current Anthropology*, 34: 341–61.

Ingold, T. 1986. 'Territoriality and Tenure: the Appropriation of Space in Hunting and Gathering Societies'. In: T. Ingold, *The Appropriation of Nature: Essays on Human Ecology and Social Relations*, pp. 130–64. Manchester: University of Manchester Press.

Kaplan, H. and K. Hill 1985. 'Food Sharing among Ache Foragers: Tests of Explanatory Hypotheses'. *Current Anthropology*, 26: 223–46.

Kaplan, H., K. Hill and A.M. Hurtado. 1990. 'Risk, Foraging and Foodsharing among the Ache'. In: E. Cashdan (ed.), *Risk and Uncertainty in Tribal and Peasant Economies*, pp. 107–43. Boulder, Col.: Westview.

Kauffman, S. 1993. *The Origins of Order: Self-organisation and Selection in Evolution*, Oxford: Oxford University Press.

Keen, I. 1982. 'How some Murngin men marry ten wives'. *Man* (N.S.), 17: 620–42.

—— 1994. *Knowledge and secrecy in an Aboriginal religion.* Oxford: Oxford University Press.

Kelly, R. 1995. *The foraging spectrum: diversity in hunter-gatherer lifeways.* Washington: Smithsonian.

Layton, R. 1986. 'Political and territorial structures among hunter-gatherers'. *Man* (N.S.), 21: 18–33.

—— 1989. 'Are Social Anthropology and Sociobiology Compatible?' In: R. Foley and V. Standen (eds), *The Comparative Socio-ecology of Mammals and Man*, pp. 433–55. Oxford: Blackwell.

—— 1992. *Australian Rock Art: a New Synthesis.* Cambridge: Cambridge University Press.

—— 1995. 'Relating to the Country in the Western Desert', In: E. Hirsch and M. O'Hanlon (eds) *The Anthropology of Landscape: Perspectives on Place and Space*, pp. 210–31. Oxford: Clarendon.

—— 1997. 'Small Tools and Social Change'. In: P. McConvell and N. Evans (eds), *Archaeology and Linguistics: Aboriginal Australia in Global Perspective*, pp. 377–84. Melbourne: Oxford University Press.

—— 2000. *Anthropology and History in Franche-Comté; a Critique of Social Theory.* Oxford: Oxford University Press.

Layton, R. and R. Barton. 2001. 'Warfare and Human Social Evolution'. In K.J. Fewster and M. Zvelebil (eds), *Ethnoarchaeology of Hunter-gatherers: Pictures at an Exhibition.* BAR International Series 955, pp. 13-24. Oxford: Archaeopress.

Lee, R.B. 1969. 'Eating Christmas in the Kalahari'. In: J. Spradley and D. McCurdy (eds), *Conformity and Conflict* (7th edn), pp. 30–37. Glenville, Ill.: Scott, Foresman.

—— 1979. *The !Kung San: Men, Women and Work in a Foraging Society.* Cambridge: Cambridge University Press.
Lewis-Williams, D. 1981. *Believing and Seeing: Symbolic Meanings in Southern San Rock Paintings.* London: Academic Press.
Mace, R. 2000. 'Human Behaviour: Fair Game'. *Nature,* 406: 248–9.
Marshall, L. 1976. 'Sharing, Talking and Giving: Relief of Social Tensions among the !Kung'. In: R.B. Lee and I. deVore (eds), *Kalahari Hunter-gatherers: Studies of the !Kung San and their Neighbours,* pp. 350–71. Cambridge, Mass.: Harvard University Press.
Maschner, H. 1991. 'The Emergence of Cultural Complexity on the Northern Northwest Coast'. *Antiquity,* 65: 924–34.
Mauss, M. and H. Beuchat. 1979. *Seasonal Variations of the Eskimo: a Study in Social Morphology,* trans. J. Fox. London: Routledge (French edn. 1950).
Maynard Smith, J. 1982. *Evolution and the Theory of Games.* Cambridge: Cambridge University Press.
McBryde, I. 1978. 'Wil-im-ee Moor-ing: or Where do Axes Come From?' *Mankind,* 11: 354–28.
McCay, B. and J.M. Acheson 1987. *The Question of the Commons: the Culture and Ecology of Communal Resources.* Tucson: University of Arizona Press.
McGlade, J. 1997. 'The limits of social control: coherence and chaos in a prestige-goods economy' In: S. Van de Leeuw and J. McGlade (eds), *Time, Process and Structured Transformation in Archaeology,* pp. 298–330. London: Routledge.
Netting, R. McC. 1981. *Balancing on an Alp: Ecological Change and Continuity in a Swiss Mountain Community.* Cambridge: Cambridge University Press.
Nishida, T., H. Takasaki and Y. Takahata. 1990. 'Demography and Reproductive Profiles.' In: T. Nishida (ed.), *The Chimpanzees of the Mahale Mountains: Sexual and Life History Strategies,* pp. 64–97. Tokyo: University of Tokyo Press.
Nowak, M.A. and K. Sigmund. 1998. 'Evolution of Indirect Reciprocity by Image Scoring'. *Nature,* 393 (11.6.98): 573–7.
Ostrom. E. 1990. *Governing the Commons: the Evolution of Institutions for Collective Action.* Cambridge: University of Cambridge Press.
Panter-Brick, C. 1993. 'Seasonal Organisation of Work Patterns'. In: S.J. Ulijaszek and S.S. Strickland (eds), *Seasonality and Human Ecology,* pp. 220–34. Cambridge: Cambridge University Press.
Peterson, N. 1975. 'Hunter-gatherer Territoriality: the Perspective from Australia'. *American Anthropologist,* 77: 53–68.
—— 1993. 'Demand Sharing: Reciprocity and the Pressure for Generosity among Foragers'. *American Anthropologist,* 95: 860–74.
Renfrew, C. 1978. 'Trajectory Discontinuity and Morphogenesis: the Implications of Catastrophe Theory for Archaeology', *American Antiquity,* 43: 203–21.
Renouf, P. 1991. 'Sedentary Hunter-gatherers: a Case for the Northern Coasts'. In: S.A. Gregg (ed.), *Between Bands and States,* pp. 89–107. Carbondale: Southern Illinois University Center for Archaeological Investigations (Occasional Paper 9).
Richardson, A. 1982. 'The Control of Productive Resources on the North West Coast of North America'. In: N.M. Williams and E.S. Hunn (eds), *Resource Managers: North American and Australian Hunter-gatherers,* pp. 93–112. Canberra: Australian Institute of Aboriginal Studies.
Riches, D. 1995. 'Hunter-gatherer Structural Transformations'. *Journal of the Royal Anthropological Institute,* 1: 679–701.
Rogers, S.C. 1991. *Shaping Modern Times in Rural France: the Transformation and Reproduction of an Aveyronnais Community.* Princeton, N.J.: Princeton University Press.
Rosenberg, H.G. 1988. *A Negotiated World: Three Centuries of Change in a French Alpine Community.* Toronto: University of Toronto Press.
Rouja, P. 1998. 'Fishing For Culture: Toward an Aboriginal Theory of Marine Resource Use among the Bardi Aborigines of One Arm Point, Western Australia'. Ph.D. thesis, Anthropology Department, Durham University.

Rowley-Conwy, P. and M. Zvelebil. 1989. 'Saving It for Later: Storage by Prehistoric Hunter-gatherers in Europe'. In: P. Halstead and J. O'Shea (eds), *Bad Year Economics*, pp. 40–56. Cambridge: Cambridge University Press.
Scott, J. 1976. *The Moral Economy of the Peasant: Rebellion and Subsistence in Southeast Asia*. New Haven: Yale University Press.
Silberbauer, G. 1971. 'Ecology of the Ernabella Aboriginal Community'. *Anthropological Forum*, 3: 21–36.
Smith, E.A. 1988. 'Risk and Uncertainty in the 'original affluent society': Evolutionary Ecology of Resource-sharing and Land Tenure'. In T. Ingold, J. Woodburn and R. Riches (eds), *Hunters and Gatherers: History, Evolution and Social Change*, pp. 222–51. Oxford: Berg.
—— 1991. *Inujjuamiut Foraging Strategies: Evolutionary Ecology of an Arctic Hunting Economy*. New York: Aldine de Gruyter.
Thomson, D.F. 1949. *Economic Structure and the Ceremonial Exchange Cycle in Arnhem Land*. Melbourne: Macmillan.
Tonkinson, R. 1991. *The Mardu Aborigines: Living the Dream in Australia's Desert*. Fort Worth: Holt Rinehart.
Torrence, R. 1983. 'Time Budgeting and Hunter-gatherer Technology'. In G. Bailey (ed.), *Hunter-gatherer Economy in Prehistory*, pp. 11–22. Cambridge: Cambridge University Press.
—— 2001. 'Hunter-gatherer Technology: Macro- and Micro-scale Approaches'. In: C. Panter-Brick, R. Layton and P. Rowley-Conwy (eds), *Hunter-gatherers: an Interdisciplinary Perspective*, pp. 73–98. Cambridge: Cambridge University Press.
Trivers, R. 1985. *Social Evolution*. Menlo Park: Benjamin/Cummins.
Turnbull, C.M. 1965. *Wayward Servants: the Two Worlds of the African Pygmies*. Westport, Conn.: Greenwood.
Vickery, W.L., L-A Giraldeau, J. Templeton, D. Kramer and C. Chapman. 1991. 'Producers, Scroungers, and Group Foraging', *American Naturalist*, 137: 847–63.
Wiessner, P. 1982. 'Risk, Reciprocity and Social Influences on !Kung San Economics'. In: E. Leacock and R. Lee (eds), *Politics and History in Band Societies*, pp. 61–84. Cambridge: Cambridge University Press.
Winterhalder, B. 1987. 'Diet Choice, Risk and Food Sharing in a Stochastic Environment', *Journal of Anthropological Archaeology*, 5: 369–92.
Winterhalder, B. 1990. 'Open Field, Common Pot: Harvest Variability and Risk Avoidance in Agricultural and Foraging Societies'. In: E. Cashdan (ed.), *Risk and Uncertainty in Tribal and Peasant Economies*, pp. 67–87. Boulder, Col.: Westview.
—— 1996. 'Social Foraging and the Behavioural Ecology of Intragroup Resource Transfers'. *Evolutionary Anthropology*, 5: 46–57.
Woodburn, J. 1980. 'Hunters and Gatherers Today and Reconstruction of the Past'. In: E. Gellner (ed.), *Soviet and Western Anthropology*, pp. 95–117. London: Duckworth.
—— 1982. 'Egalitarian Societies'. *Man* (N.S.), 17, 431–51.

8

Food Sharing and Ownership among Central African Hunter-Gatherers: an Evolutionary Perspective

Mitsuo Ichikawa

Introduction

Recent advances in primatology require us to reconsider the uniqueness of human culture. In terms of subsistence-related activities, for example, it has long been thought that tool making and tool using, food sharing and cooperative hunting are unique to humans, and that higher cultural systems have developed through these behaviours. These behaviours are, however, also found in a rudimentary form among chimpanzees and other higher primate species. The chimpanzees of the Gombe Stream in Tanzania, for example, are well known for making a tool for termite fishing out of a small twig (Goodall 1986). Among the chimpanzees in Guinea, a combined use of two or more stones were reported for cracking a hard oil-palm nut; one stone is used as a hammer, another for placing a nut on, which is sometimes supported by a third small stone for stability (Matsuzawa 1991). Bonobos in Congo-Kinshasa share valued food with other individuals, sometimes following a sexual contact (Kuroda 1982). Other groups of chimpanzees in Côte d'Ivoire even cooperate in hunting; some individuals chase the target animal, while others wait for it, anticipating the direction of the chase. In this group of chimpanzees, meat sharing occurs when the prey is successfully killed (Boesch and Boesch 1989; Boesch 1994). These examples suggest a similarity of nonhuman primate behaviour to that of humans. The similarity seems to be much greater than it was assumed to be.

We are taught in introductory anthropology courses that human culture is of a different order (or dimension) from that of nonhuman animal species. However, this does not mean that there is no similarity at all. It is misleading to suppose human culture has no relationship with that of its nearest nonhuman relatives. It is not, however, fruitful to try to reduce human culture to primate behaviour. In the course of evolution, humans added some important inventions, through which they transformed existing behaviour into a cultural practice of a higher level. If we look at hunter-gatherer societies from the viewpoint of more complicated agricultural or industrial societies, they appear to be characterised by the lack, the denial, of regulatory institutions and structures (Ingold 1999). However, if we compare these societies with nonhuman primate societies, they exhibit a variety of unique institutional inventions. Or, it may even be said that hunter-gatherers seem to negate the development of institutions by using institutional means (of other kinds). It is, therefore, an important task in understanding the relationship between human and other primates properly, to delineate what humans took with them from their primate heritage and what they added to this heritage as their unique invention. It is an evolutionary enquiry and as such it will help us to restore the continuity between human and nonhuman species. It may also lead us to reconsideration of the modern view of human–nature relationship, which has long been dominated by discontinuity and opposition, and has produced a variety of problems in our age.

As stated above, chimpanzees are reported to make and use tools, cooperate in hunting and share the hunted meat with others. This behaviour, however, occurs as separate events, and is not integrated into a system, unlike those found among human hunter-gatherers. Hunter-gatherers, for example, distribute the meat according to the roles they have played in the hunt, as will be described later. Likewise, while both tool use and 'possession' do exist among chimpanzees and other nonhuman primates, they are not combined to establish a human form of 'ownership,' which involves indirect or 'remote control' of ownership through the tool used for procuring the food.

If we extend this discussion to other aspects of life, a variety of such examples can be found. For example, both long-term consort relationships (primate form of conjugal bond) and blood relationships (primate form of kin) are found in nonhuman primate societies (see for example Kawamura 1958; Kummer 1968). Humans are unique in that they have affines, or brothers-in-law in particular, who embody in themselves a combination of consanguineous and conjugal ties. Affinal relationship is important to the evolution of human societies, because it enables them to utilise a reproductive bond for making an alliance relationship with other groups. Another example is the formation of a household, which represents a combination of food sharing and sexual division of labour. Again, both food sharing and differentiation in subsistence-related activities by sex are found in primate societies, but they appear only as a separate form.

Thus, as Robin Fox (1972; 1980) pointed out thirty years ago, the elements (or materials) necessary for constructing human culture are found in the primate baseline, and humans are unique only in combining these elements to construct cultural systems of a higher level. Such a viewpoint is fruitful for comparing the primate behaviour with that of humans, as it provides us with empirical, observable criteria for comparison. In this paper, I will first discuss some of these human inventions, human forms of 'ownership' and food sharing in particular, and try to show how humans differ from other primates on an observable level. Then I will examine the ecological and evolutionary basis for human food sharing and analyse its social significances. I will finally discuss different forms of these developments among contemporary hunter-gatherers in central Africa.

Human Form of Possession: Remote Control of Ownership

Nonhuman primate societies are generally characterised by dominant–subordinate relationships. In such 'unequal' primate societies, there is certainly a form of 'possession'. This is obvious from the fact that even a higher-ranking individual cannot snatch away the food in the hand of a lower-ranking one. For the recognition of 'possession' by other primate individuals, it is necessary for an individual to hold an object in its hand, or keep it in its immediate proximity. The distance at which an individual can safely keep the object differs depending on the relationship between the 'possessor' and other individuals. We may even measure the effects of such 'possession' and of rank difference by the distance at which others stretch their arms to seize the object. Whether we call it 'possession' or 'proximity effect', it is confined to the object literally in its hands, or in its immediate proximity. Once shifted into another's hands, an object can no longer be regarded as the 'possession' of the previous holder in any sense.

The notion of 'possession' was first applied to primate societies by Hans Kummer (1968, 1971) in his study of the social life of hamadryas baboons. The society of hamadryas baboons is comprised of two types of groups; one is a one-male group consisting of one mature male, several females and their offspring; the other is a group of males, who are excluded from the one-male groups. According to Kummer, the males outside the one-male group seem to be 'inhibited' from seducing the females 'possessed' by the harem male; they do not usually approach close to the harem when the male is present. The male in a one-male group, on the other hand, makes enormous efforts to maintain his harem. When his group is moving, he must look back every few metres to see if his harem females are still following him. If he finds a female likely to leave the group, he rushes up to her and bites her on the neck (known as neck-bite behaviour). A hamadryas male cannot maintain his harem in any other way. We see in this example the limitation of a primate form of 'possession'.

Man as a tool user, however, established a new form of material possession: the indirect ownership established by the use of tools. A tool enables a man to exert control over an object that is not in his hand, nor in the immediate area. I call this 'remote control of ownership', which is based on the separation of an individual who owns an object from the one who actually uses or carries it about.

The primary function of a tool in subsistence activities was to extract natural resources more efficiently than with the bare hands. Tools are particularly effective in hunting. It was, of course, necessary for a hunter to have the skill to use a tool and the knowledge about the animals to be hunted. But without a tool humans, as weak, powerless predators, could not have killed animals larger than medium-sized mammals. Humans invented a number of hunting tools as they depended increasingly on hunting for subsistence. Contemporary hunter-gatherers also have a variety of hunting tools and use them depending on the environmental conditions and habits of target animals. The Mbuti hunters in the Ituri forest, for example, use nets, spears, bows and spring traps for hunting. They can obviously improve hunting efficiency by using these tools.

The point is, however, that tools are often used for social purposes. Simple hand-held tools such as those used by hunter-gatherers may be considered an extension of the body when they are used for manipulating the environment, as Leroi-Gourhan (1965) pointed out. Tools are, however, detachable from the body, and actually detached from an individual when exchanged with another individual. In this context, they are no longer just an extension of the body, but become socially manipulable objects.

The Mbuti hunters in the Ituri forest, for example, use hunting tools for generating and maintaining social relationships. The Mbuti youth, who have no nets of their own, often borrow nets from old men, who remain in the camp and make nets. In this way, a role differentiation and interdependence are maintained between the youth who actively hunt and the old who provide them with hunting tools. They also lend their nets to visitors as a sign of hospitality. Visitors are usually given food, but a more intimate welcome is to provide them with nets and a chance to hunt together. We were treated in this way while visiting their forest camps with a Mbuti man, who joined in the net hunting and received a share. Bows, arrows and spears are also lent and borrowed in a similar way, though less frequently, among the Mbuti.

Another important social aspect of tool use is ownership. Even among egalitarian hunter-gatherer societies in central Africa, the owner of the game is clearly defined,[1] although 'owner' in their language often conveys different but related meanings depending on the context, such as 'host', 'guardian', 'master', as well as 'owner' in the Western sense. In most cases, the owner of the animal is the owner of the hunting tool with which the animal is killed.[2] For an animal killed with a spear, the owner of the animal is the owner of the spear that gave the first fatal blow to the animal. For net hunting, it is the owner of the net in which the animal is entangled. For a trapped animal, the owner of the steel wire used for capturing the animal is its owner. Unlike hunted animals, a termite mound or the honey in a natural beehive is owned by the individual who first finds and puts a mark on it. In this way, an owner is clearly defined, at least in principle, when the resource is extracted from or located in the forest.

The actual situation is more complicated, however, since there is sometimes no fixed rule for determining the owner of a tool. Various people are often involved at different stages in the process of making a tool. For example, several steps are necessary for making a hunting net: collecting the bark of *kusa* (*Manniophyton fulvum*) in the forest; separating the inner bark (bast) from the outer bark and drying it; making it into a cord, which is then woven into a net. At each stage of this process, different people may be involved and it is usually difficult to know, by observation alone, who will be the ultimate owner of the net being made. However, a net, or a part of it, is always owned by a single person and this is enough to make clear the ownership of the animal captured with the net. When two or more nets owned by different persons are combined, they put a mark at the joint to show clearly in which part of the net the animal is entangled.

The important point about such a definition of ownership is that an owner is not necessarily the hunter who uses the tool and kills the animal; it may even be a person who does not participate in the actual hunt. In fact, Mbuti frequently lend and borrow tools for hunting, through which the distribution of the meat is facilitated, or even manipulated. Through such a manipulation, or 'remote control' of ownership, social relationships can also be manipulated to some extent.

Human Form of Food Sharing: Hunting–Sharing Complex as a Unique Human Invention

While food sharing is important to hunter-gatherer social life, food is not randomly distributed. Valued food like meat is always shared carefully. Even if the meat from hunting is eventually distributed quite extensively in a camp, not everyone in the camp has equal access to the meat brought by a particular person. While some people demand a share more easily, others find it difficult and may leave the place where meat is being shared out. However, they may also get a portion afterwards from those who have received a share. In many cases, sharing is closely linked with existing and/or potential social or interpersonal relationships.

Among the Mbuti hunter-gatherers in the Ituri forest, meat is first distributed to those who either directly or indirectly participate in the hunt. This is called 'first distribution', which is obligatory and clearly defined (Harako 1976; Tanno 1976; Ichikawa 1982). The meat is then distributed in an informal way to others from those who have received it in the first distribution (this we call 'second distribution', which is similar to 'sharing' discussed by Woodburn 1998). The meat thus distributed to individuals is concentrated to each household, where it is cooked by women; then, it is distributed again, with vegetable foods, to the members of their households and others ('third distribution'). The men gathering at the central place called *tele* share the meal brought from their households. In this way, they eventually distribute the meat extensively to other members of a camp, unless there is not enough to do so.

Particularly interesting in this chain of food distribution is the first distribution, in which certain parts of the meat are obligatorily distributed to others, depending on the roles they have performed in the hunt. In Mbuti net hunting, the first distribution is made in the following way: the hunter who actually uses another's net takes a hind leg (*kipe*); the one who helps the hunter kill the animal takes the chest (*esosi*), the woman who carries the carcass back to the camp takes a front leg (*mbombo*); the one who makes a hunting fire (*kungya*) in the morning before the hunt takes a lower part of the rib cage (three ribs from the lowest, called *seka*) of a medium-sized duiker or the head (*mo'o*) of a blue duiker.

Among the Aka in northern Congo-Brazzaville, such a distribution is called *mo.bando*, and is made in a following way: the head (*mo.soko*) is for the net user; the rump (*ngondo*) for the one who first seizes the animal in the net, the belly (*lombo*) for the one who assists in the seizure; the meat around the pelvis (*e.kango*) for the one called *mo.so* who leads the day's hunt; and front (*mo.pela*) or hind (*e.belo*) leg for the one who carries the carcass to the campsite (Takeuchi 1995). The basic roles in net hunting and the obligatory distribution of meat to each of the role players are recognised in a similar way among the Mbuti and the Aka, although the slaughtering of a carcass and the parts allocated to each individual differs from one society to the other.

The obligatory first distribution described above demonstrates that there is a system in which cooperation in hunting is closely linked with sharing of the game. In other words, they together form a hunting–sharing complex. An interesting point about this first distribution is that the owner of the animal is not necessarily the hunter who captures it, but the owner of the net in which it is entangled, as stated above. However, if we consider that a net owner also indirectly participates in the hunt, through making his net, in a preparatory stage of hunting, ownership in this case is also defined in relation to the hunt. Or it may be said that the 'owner' receives his share like other role players in the first distribution, although his portion is determined after other role players take their portions. Cooperation in hunting and in its preparatory activities thus determines the manner of distribution of the meat obtained from the hunt. To put it another way, cooperation in production on the one hand and cooperation in consumption on the other represent the two phases of a hunting–sharing complex.

Now we can understand the gap between human and nonhuman forms of cooperation and food sharing. As stated above, chimpanzees also cooperate in hunting and share the food they possess with others. The chimpanzees of the Tai National Park in the Côte d'Ivoire hunt in a fairly organised, cooperative manner; some chase the prey animal while others wait for it (Boesch and Boesch 1989; Boesch 1994). They also share the meat with other individuals, although rather reluctantly. The question is, however, whether chimpanzees combine these two behaviours. Cooperative hunting and meat sharing among chimpanzees seem to occur as separate and independent events. According to Boesch (1994), both the bystanders (those present for the hunt site but not participating in it) and latecomers (those absent from the hunt, but coming after the prey is killed) are granted access to the meat by the hunters (those actively participating in the cooperative hunt). Moreover, the hunters do not always eat significantly more meat than the bystanders, although they eat more than the latecomers.[3] We do not know in this chimpanzee case, if the participation in the hunt implies more than just being close to the killing site, which enables them to reach the sharing site quickly. The chimpanzees rather seem to share the meat with others regardless of participation in the preceding hunt. When other individuals hear the screams, which are often emitted on killing an animal, they rush to the site and beg the individuals possessing the meat for a share.

In human hunting, at least among the Mbuti, who are relatively modest in demanding meat from one another, it is rare for an individual who has not participated in the hunt in any sense to go to the butchering site and overtly demand a share, unless he/she has a special social relationship with the meat owner. There is an atmosphere that prevents nonrelevant individuals from approaching the butchering and sharing site. Those at the butchering site turn their eyes away from those who are not expected to participate in the distribution. This is expressed as 'they refuse by the eyes' ('*bakumi na eso*' in the Mbuti language, or '*wananyima na macho*' in KiNgwana, a Swahili dialect). Such a slight sign is enough to inform the intention of the owner, and no one in the Mbuti society wants to be blamed for shameless or covetous behaviour.[4]

In the chimpanzee case, all the individuals who even by chance witness the killing probably rush to the killing site, whether or not they have participated in the preceding hunt. This suggests that cooperation in hunting is not internally linked to the sharing which follows hunting. In other words, they do not establish a hunting–sharing complex, unlike human hunter-gatherers. While both food sharing and cooperative hunting are observed among nonhuman primates, it seems to be a unique human invention to integrate these two practices into a single system.

Ecological and Evolutionary Basis for Food Sharing

Food sharing among African hunter-gatherers is more than just a give-and-take exchange. It is also supported by the ethic that those who have food should give it to others. Such an extensive sharing practice may have derived from the human innate propensity for reciprocity. However, there may also have been some practical or ecological basis for the food-sharing practice to be firmly established and maintained for a long period of time. I will, in what follows, examine the ecological or evolutionary basis for extensive food- sharing practice among hunter-gatherers.

Chimpanzees also share the food among themselves, in particular meat and large-sized fruit, but the food thus shared comprises only a tiny proportion in their subsistence. While social significance is often emphasised for food sharing among chimpanzees, its ecological significance is thought to be minimal. In other words, non-human primate (adult) individuals normally practise a self-sustaining subsistence in that they acquire most of the food they need by themselves. Humans, by contrast, depend heavily and systematically on one another for their subsistence. In a quantitative analysis of food distribution among the Aka, Kitanishi (1998) revealed that 75 percent of the food consumed by a household came from other households, and 80 percent of the food produced by a household was distributed to other households. It seems ironical that, in these cases, ecological rather than social significance makes human food sharing unique and different from that of other primates.

Evolutionary ecologists point out that food sharing among hunter-gatherers serves as a buffer against instability in the food supply (there are a number of articles on this issue, but see, for example, Cashdan 1985). If a man with more food than he requires immediately shares it with others, he may be given food some day when he is short of it. Sharing in this case performs an insurance function; it reduces the fluctuation in an individual's food supply on the group level. Frequent exchange of hunting tools and resulting food distribution often has such a function, as will be pointed out later.

As the major targets of the Mbuti's net hunting are small to medium-sized duikers, the yield is more stable than that in other types of hunting which aim at larger game. There is still a considerable difference and fluctuation in the individual's catch. Of the ten net owners observed in a Mbuti camp, the most successful one caught 140 kg of prey during four weeks of hunting, whereas the least successful one had only 24 kg. Even a successful hunter had no luck for more than a week, whereas some had no animals for almost two weeks (Ichikawa 1983). They could hardly have survived, if they had not shared the meat with others, since they depended for their subsistence on the meat and the vegetable foods obtained in exchange for the meat during the survey period.

Among the Kalahari hunter-gatherers, daily fluctuation and individual difference in the catch are much more pronounced. During twenty-eight observation days, there were four days with more than 100 kg of meat, whereas no prey was caught for as many as sixteen days. Of the 412 kg of prey (206 kg of edible meat) hunted during this period, nearly three-quarters were supplied by a single hunter (Lee 1979). If there had been no sharing during this period, most of the San in the camp could not have eaten the meat, whereas a few would have had much more than they needed. These data show that there is certainly a considerable daily fluctuation and individual difference in the catch, and that sharing actually reduces the fluctuation and difference, among both the Mbuti and the San.

One of the reasons for such fluctuation in the catch derives from the characteristics of the animals hunted as human food. The major targets of San hunting are kudus, gemsboks, wildebeests and other larger mammals weighing 200 to 300 kg each, and warthogs, which are smaller, but still have a body weight of 80 kg. A large-sized antelope contains in its edible parts about 180,000 to 270,000 kcal, which is equivalent to the food energy required for 90 to 135 adult consumption days. Even a medium-sized duiker, one of the major targets of the Mbuti net hunting, weighs 20 kg (which contains the energy for nine adult days). While a successful hunt supplies such a huge amount of food, hunting more often fails without yielding any meat. Hunting is thus an activity aiming at a large package of food energy and as such it is essentially unstable.

The prey animals of other carnivores share the same characteristics. Larger-sized carnivores, therefore, cope with this problem by eating a large quantity of meat at a time. Lions in the wild, for example, eat 20 to 30 kg of meat – enough for five days of consumption – at a time and can remain without food for more than a week (Schaller 1972). The most striking example are hyenas. They can eat almost a quarter (15 to 20 kg) of their body weight at a time. One female hyena ate 14 to 15 kg of meat in 45 minutes and another consumed an infant Thompson's gazelle in only two minutes (Kruuk 1972). These examples clearly demonstrate that gluttony is the characteristic feeding habit of carnivores. Their basic feeding strategy (rhythm) is to eat as much as they can when there is food and live with hunger when there is no food. In addition, co-feeding is often found among carnivorous species, which also moderates the instability in the food supply.

Primates generally depend on vegetable food, which is abundant and obtained with less effort than animal food. But it contains less energy per unit weight. Primates therefore have a feeding rhythm like other herbivores; they feed frequently and over a long period of time. While humans are omnivorous and eat less frequently than other primate species, they also belong to the group of frequent eaters. This is clearly expressed in the frequency of meals or other food taken between meals. Humans, unlike carnivores, do not have the capacity for digesting a large quantity of food at a time. An ecological and evolutionary basis of food sharing may thus be found in the discrepancy between the need for stable food supply, which is based on the primate herbivorous heritage, and irregular supply of meat, which is the food of carnivores. As they depend more on hunting for their subsistence, interindividual dependence on food sharing increases accordingly.

While food sharing among contemporary hunter-gatherers is not always influenced by ecological factors (they share food even when ecologically unnecessary), there may once have been an ecological basis for it, otherwise it may not have been reinforced, nor established as a social norm and as a 'sharing way of life'. Social aspects of food sharing have also developed along with the development of its material aspects, since most human practices are polysemic (the same practice having multiple meanings).

There is another way to cope with such a fluctuation in the food supply: food preservation and storage. It is well known that most of the present-day hunter-gatherers know how to preserve meat and other food, although equatorial hunter-gatherers seldom do so for their own consumption. From an evolutionary perspective, this does not make much sense, however. Food sharing already existed in the primate baseline. While most higher primate species do share food, no primate species except humans has been reported to store food. It is therefore quite natural that, at least in the context of human evolution, early humans first utilised what was already there, i.e., what they had inherited from their primate ancestors, rather than inventing a totally new practice of food storing.

Different Effects of Remote Control of Ownership

The indirect, remote control of ownership works differently in different societies, or in different situations even in the same society. Among the !Kung San (Ju'/hoansi) in the Kalahari, the owner of the meat is defined as the owner of the arrows with which the animal is shot, as in the Mbuti case. However, they have an exchange relationship called *hxaro* (Wiessner 1981, 1982), in which arrows are frequently exchanged. According to Lee (1979), two out of four hunters surveyed had in their quivers eighteen and nineteen arrows respectively, all of which were obtained from several different men. A third hunter had thirteen arrows, of which only two were his own.

One reason for such a high rate of arrow sharing may be ecological; that is, low and unstable success rate in hunting with bows and arrows. Lee (1979) calculated the average success rate (days with a kill compared to the total hunting days) at 0.23, which means hunting is successful only in every four to five hunts on the average. When a hunter kills an animal he brings a large quantity of meat, but he more often returns empty-handed. The exchange of arrows with other hunters has thus the effect of increasing the chance of acquiring meat, since the meat always goes to the owners of the arrows. They may also change the arrows for hunting luck, particularly when they are not blessed with success for many days.

Another important reason is social; the exchange of arrows diffuses the ownership of the meat to others than a few skilful hunters. As Lee (1979) pointed out, meat distribution brings prestige to its owner; or, it may result in accusations by others if the distribution is not to everybody's liking, which is almost impossible. Through exchange of arrows, the San diffuse the responsibility for meat distribution, thereby relieving potential tension in their egalitarian society.

A similar practice is found among the Aka Pygmies in Congo-Brazzaville, who frequently exchange hunting nets among themselves. While hunting nets are owned by adult men, it is mainly the young men who actually use the nets in hunting. According to Takeuchi (1995), Aka men frequently lend their nets to other men, more often to those of other households. This practice is called '*njambi*'. Of a total of 178 net users recorded, as many as 113 (63 percent) belonged to a household other than that of the net owner (only 65 belonged to the same household as the owner). Moreover, Aka hunters often change the nets they use, even on the same day. Frequent exchange of hunting tools seems to be a common practice among African hunter-gatherers.

In these cases, the 'institution' that defines indirect, remote control of ownership contributes to maintaining their egalitarian social relationships. We should note, however, the same 'institution' is used for an opposite purpose, for accumulating wealth, in other societies, or in other situations. In the Ituri forest, the agricultural patrons of the Mbuti formerly owned hunting tools of their own, lent them to the Mbuti and Efe and claimed the ownership of the animals killed with them. This was a conventional way of acquiring the tusks of elephants, as large spearheads used for elephant hunting were one of the scarce items in the Ituri forest. It is still a common practice among the Efe, who need the neighbouring Lese villagers as mediators with the outside world. The Lese villagers know how to sell the tusks secretly to the merchants and control their circulation. In the mid-1970s, when I did my first research in the Ituri forest, there were some Bira villagers who had hunting nets of their own and lent them to the Mbuti in the hunting season.

While most of the Mbuti and Efe today have their own hunting tools, such as spears, bows and nets, firearms (shotguns) are owned exclusively by the villagers. In the northern part of Congo-Brazzaville, an animal killed with a gun belongs to the villager who owns the gun and the Aka are given only the head of the animal and a few tobacco sticks for each killed duiker. As the demand for bush meat increased, largely due to the logging industry operating in the area, some villagers entered into a new business of organising long-term hunting expeditions, manned mainly by Aka hunters, providing them with guns, cartridges and food during the expedition. The benefits in such a new business also derive from the same 'institution', remote control of ownership, which separates the owner from the hunter who actually kills an animal.[5] The potential of this 'institution' can easily be understood if we see its most developed form in the modern capitalist system, where wage labour is systematically separated from the capital and the means of production.

Why Owners Exist: Ownership and Social Order

Let us now return to the issue of ownership. As stated above, the owner cannot monopolise the food, nor distribute it only to his own household. The ownership of food among African hunter-gatherers is rather nominal; the food is extensively distributed through first, second and third distributions (mentioned above), and the owner is not necessarily the one who consumes the largest amount. According to Kitanishi (1998), 80 percent of the food was distributed to households other than that of the owner, with only 20 percent consumed by the owner's household. In the distribution of an elephant killed by a Mbuti hunter, the owner-hunter took 44 kg of meat, whereas others took as much as the owner, and some even took more than 50 kg (Ichikawa 1982). Althouge at least some share is usually reserved for the owner, he is not necessarily the person who consumes the largest portion. And although an owner may be thanked for his generosity to some extent, he is not better respected because of it. There is an egalitarian sentiment that prevents him from earning much prestige, as many anthropologists have pointed out.

The question arises, then, of why there is an owner for almost every kind of food, despite the fact that it is, after all, shared quite extensively with other members of a camp, without obvious benefit to the owner. The social factor seems to be more important than the ecological factor. Namely, ownership enables them to recognise, or even manipulate to some extent, inter-individual relationships, which would otherwise be obscured in a joint meal like that observed in the co-feeding of other carnivorous animals. In other words, the owner has a potential to use sharing for achieving other, often social, goals through a material transfer. Such a social function is well acknowledged by the hunter-gatherers themselves who share the meat through the frequent exchange of hunting tools.

However, the social implication of ownership in food distribution can be better understood by examining the situation in which there is no owner responsible for the distribution. Kitanishi's report (1998, 2001) on the Aka case eloquently demonstrates a chaotic situation on such an occasion.

Among the Aka, food is usually distributed by its owner, or by his wife. When they are absent from the camp, one of their close relatives acts in their place. While the first (obligatory) distribution may take place in the absence of the owner and his representative, the remaining portion is reserved for second distribution until the owner or his representative returns to the camp.

In the rather rare case where there is no owner nor a representative, the food is treated as if it had been found in the forest without a recognisable owner. Kitanishi (2001) gave two examples of such a case. The first example took place when a villager gave a large quantity of cooked food to the Aka men, who helped him carry a dugout canoe out of the forest. The villager, however, left the place without appointing a person to take responsibility for the distribution. When the villager left, they immediately rushed in to take as much food as they could and nothing was left for those who were left behind. Another example was the case in which Kitanishi was offered cooked yams by an Aka woman in a forest camp. He could not take the yams, as it was during a period of food shortage in the camp, and he had his own food but not enough to reciprocate the offer from the woman. The woman seemed embarrassed by his response, but children playing nearby immediately scrambled to take the yams. This is an unusual event, since we know that in Aka society, even a child of ten years of age will normally share with others the food he/she possesses. If one of the children had been given all the food, he/she would have taken the responsibility for distributing it to others.

The Aka and the Mbuti are usually modest in demanding food. They seldom demand in a loud voice, and even pretend to be uninterested in the distribution (see endnote 4). However, chaotic food consumption described above shows the importance of the owner to orderly distribution. In other words, an owner, as the one responsible for distribution, is indispensable to maintaining the order of Aka social life.[6] This seems to be obvious, but its significance is not always fully understood. In Aka society, it is sometimes more important that an owner exists than knowing who the actual owner is.

Notes

1. 'Owner' in English is roughly translated into '*kumisi*' (meaning a host) or '*apa-*' (a prefix deriving from 'father', but also meaning 'owner', equivalent to '*mwenye*' in KiNgwana, a Swahili dialect) in the Mbuti language, and '*konja*' in Aka (Kitanishi 1998). The actual meaning differs depending on the context, sometimes overlapping the concept of 'owner' in English, but conveying different but related meanings of 'host', 'master' or 'guardian' in other contexts. Barnard and Woodburn (1988) and Riches (1995) argue that the term 'ownership' should be used only in cases where people deny others the right to use particular resources. According to such a view, the '*apa-*' or '*konja*' may in most cases not be the 'owner' in the same sense as in English. However, we should also note that '*apa*' or '*konja*' may convey a meaning closer to a private owner, for example in a commercial context, in that they have the right to sell their meat to traders without sharing it with others. '*Kumisi*', '*apa-*' or '*konja*' may be better understood to mean more general association between a person and a thing, and private ownership in modern societies may be a specialised form of this association.
2. As will be disussed later, this ownership applies only to the part that remains after the first distribution.
3. Boesch (1994) emphasises that there is a difference between the hunters and bystanders in the amount of meat eaten and <u>shared</u>. This may not make much sense, however, because the first possessor of the prey, who has the largest amount to share, is most probably one of the hunters.
4. However, if they were overtly demanded a share, they would find difficulty in refusing it. Hence, they have a special 'medicine' of plant material, though seldom used, for preventing others from approaching them while eating valued food. Demanding loudly for a share is occasionally made from a distant quarter of a camp, without overtly specifying the person addressed, but in most cases it takes place when sharing is unlikely, for example, when there is little or nothing left to share. When there is an expectation and probability of an actual share, they usually sit and wait, casting glances now and then at the butchering and distribution site.
5. Indirect ownership might first have been established in the context of external relationships with other dominant groups, who tried to control or exploit neighbouring hunter-gatherers through controlling hunting tools. Hunter-gatherers themselves might then have adopted this ownership of external origin into their society. I was once inclined to think this way. But from an evolutionary perspective, it seems more attractive to suppose that such indirect ownership among hunter-gatherers, which had originally been meant for something else, for maintaining egalitarian relationships, provided other dominant groups with a chance to use them for the opposite purpose, i.e. to exploit the products of hunter-gatherers' labour.
6. There is little dissension about the owner of the animal among the Mbuti, as Marshall (1976) pointed out for the !Kung San. Even when a discussion takes place about the ownership, it may be better understood as a process of recalling the social relationship originated or maintained by the preceding exchange of hunting tools, since in most cases dissension arises from the ambiguity of the ownership of the hunting tools. In some cases, it is not clear even to themselves whether the tool is given, or simply lent.

References

Barnard, A. and J. Woodburn, 1988. 'Property, Power and Ideology in Hunting-gathering Societies: An Introduction'. In: *Hunters and Gatherers: Property, Power and Ideology*, ed. T. Ingold, D. Riches and J. Woodburn. Oxford: Berg, pp.4–31.
Boesch, C. 1994. 'Cooperative Hunting in Wild Chimpanzees', *Animal Behaviour*, 48: 227–54.
Boesch, C. and H. Boesch, 1989. 'Hunting Behaviour of Wild Chimpanzees in the Tai National Park', *American Journal of Physical Anthropology*, 78: 547–73.

Cashdan, E. 1985. 'Coping with Risk : Reciprocity among the Basarwa of Northern Botswana', *Man (N.S.)*, 20: 454–74.
Fox, R.1972. 'Primate Kin and Human Kinship'. In: *Biosocial Anthropology*, ed. R. Fox, New York: Academic Press, pp.9–35.
—— 1980. *The Red Lamp of Incest*. New York: Dutton.
Goodall, J. 1986. *The Chimpanzees of Gombe*. Cambridge, Mass: Harvard University Press.
Harako, R. 1986 'The Mbuti as Hunters', *Kyoto University African Studies*,10: 37–99.
Ichikawa, M. 1982. *Hunters of the Forest*. Kyoto: Jinbun-Shoin.
—— 1983. 'An Examination of the Hunting-dependent Life of the Mbuti Pygmies, Eastern Zaire', *African Study Monographs*, 4: 55–76.
Ingold, T. 1999. 'On the Social Relations of the Hunter-gatherer Band'. In: *The Cambridge Encyclopedia of Hunter-Gatherers*, ed. R.B. Lee and R.Daly. Cambridge: Cambridge University Press, pp.399–410.
Kawamura, S.1958. 'Matriarchal Social Ranks in the Minoo-BT: A Study of the Rank System of Japanese Monkeys', *Primates*, 1: 149–56.
Kitanishi, K. 1998. 'Food Sharing among the Aka Hunter-gatherers in Northeastern Congo', *African Study Monographs,* supplementary issue 25: 3–32.
—— 2001. 'The Owner as distributor: Food Sharing among the Aka'. In: *The Coexistence of Man and Forest in Africa*, ed. M. Ichikawa and H. Sato. Kyoto: Kyoto University Press, pp.61–91 (in Japanese).
Kuroda, S. 1982. *The Pygmy Chimpanzees*. Tokyo: Yomiuri-Shinbun (in Japanese).
Kruuk, H. 1972. *The Spotted Hyena*. Chicago: The University of Chicago Press.
Kummer, H. 1968. *Social Organization of Hamadryas Baboons*. Basel: Karger.
—— 1971. *Primate Societies*. New York: Aldine-Atherton.
Lee, R.B. 1979. *The Kung San: Men, Women and Work in a Foraging Society*. Cambridge: Cambridge University Press.
Leroi-Gourhan, A. 1965. *Le Geste et la Parol*. Paris: Albin Michel, Paris.
Marshall, L. 1976. *The !Kung of Nyae Nyae*. Cambridge, Mass: Harvard University Press.
Matsuzawa, T. 1991. 'Nesting Cups and Metatools in Chimpanzees', *Behavioural and Brain Sciences*, 14: 570–1.
Riches, D. 1995. 'Hunter-gatherer Structural Transformations', *Journal of Royal Anthropological Institute (N. S.)*, 1: 679–701.
Schaller, G. 1972. *The Serengeti Lion*. Chicago: The University of Chicago Press.
Takeuchi, K. 1995. 'Ritual Aspects and Pleasure in Hunting Activity: Cooperation and Distribution in the Net-hunting of the Aka Hunter-gatherers in Northeastern Congo', *Afrika-Kenkyu*, 46: 57–76 (in Japanese).
Tanno, T. 1976. 'The Mbuti Net-hunters in the Ituri forest, Eastern Zaire: Their Hunting Activities and Band Composition', *Kyoto University African Studies*, 10: 101–135.
Wiessner, P. 1981. 'Measuring the Impact of Social Ties on Nutritional Status among the !Kung San', *Social Science Information*, 20-4/5: 641–78.
—— 1982. 'Risk, Reciprocity and Social Influences on !Kung San Economics'. In: *Politics and History in Band Societies,* ed. R.B. Lee and E. Leacock. Cambridge: Cambridge University Press, pp.61–84.
Woodburn, J. 1982. 'Egalitarian Societies', *Man (N.S.)*, 17: 431–51.
—— 1998. 'Sharing Is Not a Form of Exchange: An Analysis of Property-sharing in Immediate-return Hunter-gatherer Societies'. In: *Property Relations*, ed. C. Hann, Cambridge: Cambridge University Press, pp.48–63.

9
Time, Memory and Property

Tim Ingold

It is not inherently in the nature of the world that it should consist of things that may or may not be appropriated by people. As Thomas Widlok reminded us, in his introduction to the conference that gave rise to this volume, the appearance of such things can only be the outcome of some kind of process. What, then, are the processes that give rise to actual or potential property? How can these processes be linked to the passage of time, to life histories, and to the succession of generations? And if we can identify certain processes that give rise to property, then can we identify others that do not? In the following remarks I want to suggest that the appearance of property is a consequence of a process that I shall call the *objectification of memory*. And I shall show that such objectification is systematically inhibited by a practice of remembering that remains embedded in the contexts of people's engagement with one another and with the nonhuman constituents of their environment. In the literature on hunting and gathering societies, this practice has been characteristically described under the rubric of *sharing*.

It has been argued, most notably by James Woodburn, that sharing has the effect of disengaging people from property (Woodburn 1982: 445). But this is to assume an a priori division between human persons and the things to which, were it not for the activities of sharing, they might become attached. These are things that have come into being, as such, in consequence of some human action: an animal hunted and killed, a basket of gathered fruits, a manufactured tool. Each one is supposed to embody, in its objective constitution, a memory of that action. Indeed it is precisely to such a memory, sedimented in the object, that we refer when we speak of it as the 'yield' of someone's labour. Rephrased in our terms, the import of Woodburn's argument might be that sharing disperses the memories embodied in objects, thereby preventing the build-up of lasting attachments between particular persons and particular things. But if the labour invested in nonhuman aspects of the environment converts them into *objects* of memory, what about the labour invested in the care of fellow human beings? Does this likewise turn them into objects? Surely not. For the work one does in caring or 'looking after' others, for example in the conduct of sharing, constitutes them not as objects of memory but as *subjects* and as co-participants in a process of remembering. Humans, it seems, are people you share with, they are not what is shared.

The people whom we call hunters and gatherers, however, do not generally distinguish human from nonhuman components of the environment as radically as we are inclined to do. For them what applies to humans applies also, and with equal force, to nonhumans. That is to say, people look after animals and plants in their activities of hunting and gathering, or look after the land by journeying from place to place, just as they look after other humans by sharing with them. These engagements – involving work, care and attention – do not convert nonhumans into detachable objects of memory, as the material residues of an already completed past. It is not by turning your back on others that you look after them, but rather by keeping them in mind, so that they are always 'with you' in your present thoughts and actions. Both humans and nonhumans, in short, figure as fellow-participants in an ongoing process of remembering. This process is tantamount to the process of social life itself. The 'hunter-gatherer society', then, is not exclusive to human beings, but also includes animals, plants, and all the other manifold inhabitants of the land. And to understand how people might come to possess, or to be possessed by, nonhuman beings, we need to understand the dynamics of the relations by which humans 'possess' one another.

Exactly fifty years ago, Claude Lévi-Strauss reminded the delegates at a conference of anthropologists and linguists that seated among them was an 'uninvited guest' who – unbeknown to them – had all along been quietly directing their deliberations. That guest was the *human mind* (Lévi-Strauss 1968: 71). I believe that the conference on which this volume is based was likewise honoured by the presence of a guest who, unacknowledged and uninvited, lent meaning and coherence to the proceedings. Now is perhaps the moment to reveal his identity. He is, of course, Old Man Time. Along with memory, time is key to understanding the relation between property and process. There was much discussion, during the conference, about the difference between those systems of production in which the 'return on labour' is immediate, and those in which it is delayed. But just as the objectification of memory is implicit in the notion of the return on labour, so also the distinction between immediacy and delay in such return hinges on time. There was talk at the conference of equality and inequality, but outside the passage of time the difference between them is meaningless. And there was a concern to give priority to process over structure, but how can there be process without time?

Above all, however, the challenge was to understand the nature of persons and relationships. And it is in precisely this connection that a focus on time and temporality is most revealing. It has often been noted that, at least among hunting and gathering people – but possibly, in practice, among people everywhere – the person is *relational.* That is to say, every person comes into being as a locus of perception, action and self-awareness through the experience of growing, and being grown, within a field of ongoing relationships. A person's identity, at any moment of his or her life, is the crystallisation of these relationships. Severally, therefore, persons continually bring each other into existence. As Alfred Schutz once put it, as consociates we 'grow older together' (Schutz 1962: 17). Through the entwining of their life histories persons enfold, into their patterns of awareness and response, the experience of their engagements with others. Thus consciousness and social existence, though they may appear at any particular moment to offer alternative perspectives on the person, respectively inward-looking and outward-looking, turn out in their temporal unfolding to be one and the same, like the single surface of a Möbius strip (Ingold 2001: 266).

The relational person, then, can only exist within the current of real time. It is inevitably and intrinsically temporal. How, then, can the existence of such persons be reconciled with the temporal *immediacy* of the so-called immediate-return systems in which they are characteristically found? It seems to me that once the hand of time, our uninvited guest, is revealed, we find that what we have been talking about under the guise of immediate returns is something else entirely: namely, a certain way of making the past present through acts of remembering. And this goes directly against the grain of the way in which the present is made past through an objectification of memory that reduces the outcomes of current engagements to a series of 'returns on labour'.

Introducing her conference paper on gender and equality among the agro-pastoral Hamar people of Ethiopia, Jean Lydall depicted the life histories of a man and a woman as parallel, vertical bands. It is instructive to compare this kind of depiction with the way in which lives are typically depicted in the kinship diagrams of classical social anthropology. Figure 9.1a shows a line of descent linking three successive generations (whether the line is traced patrilineally of matrilineally is immaterial for my argument). What is the meaning of this line? It certainly does not denote a life process. Life, according to the genealogical model of relatedness on which this kind of diagram is based, is lived *within* each generation, it does not pass between them. Indeed it is the separation of the life-line from the descent-line that establishes the very concept of the generation as one step in a line of descent from an ancestor, and of history as a succession of such steps, each of which replaces its antecedents (Ingold 2000: 136). So what, if not life, is 'passed down' from A to B, and from B to C?

The answer – still following the genealogical model – must be certain attributes or endowments whose origin, since they are imported into the present lives of recipients, must lie in the already completed past of their predecessors. This much is implied in the conventional idea that lines of descent constitute channels for the *transmission* of personal endowments. In order to be available for transmission, such endowments must be both ready-

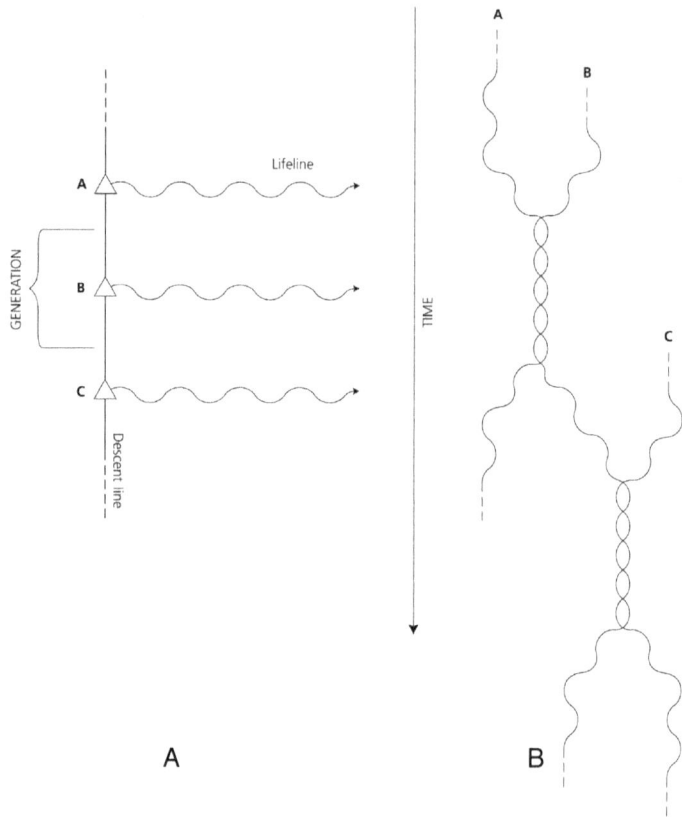

Figure 9.1 (A) The descent-line, life-line and generation, according to the genealogical model of classical social anthropology. Through a denial of the coevalness of persons of successive generations, the descent line is constituted as a channel for the transmission of endowments of memory. (B) The mutually entangled life-lines of coeval persons, according to the relational model. Here, lives are connected over time, not through the transmission of objects of memory, but through the engagement of persons as remembering subjects

made (rather than still under construction) and separable from their previous holders. Moreover, since their possession identifies their holders as descendants of previous generations, they must be recognised as a legacy from the past. That is to say, these endowments must embody *memories* of past lives (or of the activities of which they were comprised), that are nevertheless detached from those lives and objectified either in material items or in such immaterial forms as beliefs, customs and traditions – or what, in a now outmoded anthropological parlance, used to be called 'traits'. In short, what is passed down is *property*.

Now from all the ethnographic evidence presented both in this volume and elsewhere, it would appear that the genealogical view of intergenerational succession, along with the idea of descent as the quasi-hereditary transmission of ready-made endowments of memory, is quite alien to hunters and gatherers. It may even be alien to pastoralists and agriculturalists, but this raises complex issues about the status of land and animals as heritable property that I cannot go into now. At least for hunters and gatherers, in my understanding, lives proceed through history in parallel, as shown schematically in Figure 9.1 (B). People come and go, but do not begin or end. Events such as birth and death punctuate, but do not initiate or terminate life. Through their entanglements with one another, and with nonhuman components of the environment, persons continually bring each other into being. As a Cree man told the ethnographer Colin Scott, in one of the most profound and pithy remarks I have ever encountered in ethnographic literature, life is 'continuous birth' (Scott 1989: 195). We might say, borrowing a useful term from Johannes Fabian, that people are *coeval* with one another (Fabian 1983: 31). They share time. This does not mean, however, that they are together only at the horizon of the present. It means, rather, that every encounter is one moment in the unfolding, *over* time, of a field of relations that encompasses them all.

I believe it is to the mutual entanglement of coeval persons, in relations which combine trust with its inevitable counterpart, suspicion, that we refer when we speak of the immediacy of sharing in hunting and gathering societies. The boundaries of sharing, in this sense, are not set by the boundaries of humanity. Indeed according to what might be called the logic of inclusiveness, there are no boundaries to sharing at all. This logic operates not by setting up persons or things in opposition to one another on the basis of their received, intrinsic attributes (e.g., 'us' versus 'them', human versus nonhuman, animate versus inanimate), but by incorporating every being within a continuous field of relations, and identifying each by its subject-position within the field. Thus beings can meet up, partially coalesce through a sharing of substance or experience, and then split apart again, each taking with them something of the other. In a vivid metaphor, Nurit Bird-David (1994) has described this dynamic in terms of an 'oil-on-water' sociology.

To illustrate what this means in practice, an example may be taken from the work of the native Ojibwa writer Wub-e-ke-niew. He explains that in his language, when you go to collect water from the lake, you don't say that you are going to get water. You say you are going to meet the lake (Wub-e-ke-niew 1995: 218). Both you and the lake are presences in a world that is continually coming into being. So you meet up with the lake, there is an exchange of substance, and you split apart again (see Figure 9.2). The same goes for hunting, where the encounter is with an animal being.

Let me dwell on the hunting encounter for a moment. An animal is intercepted and killed; within a short time it has been distributed and eaten. At first glance this looks like a straightforward case of immediate return. Among most northern hunters, however, hunting, killing and eating are acts that

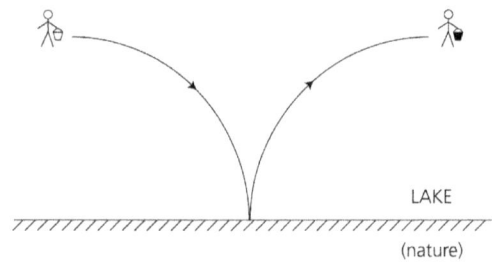

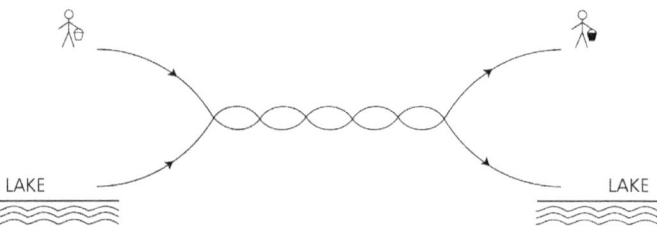

Figure 9.2 (A) 'Getting water' versus (B) 'meeting the lake'

secure the generation ('continuous birth') of the world. Hunting is compared to sexual intercourse, and eating and the disposal of the bones to parturition. By following the proper procedures in these activities, hunters ensure that the animals will come round again in the future. Likewise the animal that came to the hunter today only did so on account of all the work and thought invested in it, and in its kind, in the past. Should we conclude, then, that contrary to first impressions, this is a case of delayed return?

For my part I do not think it is sensible to inquire whether the return is immediate or delayed, or some mixture of the two. The salient point is rather that humans and animals are coevals in the sense I have just outlined. The human and the animal continually bring each other into existence, and each enfolds into its present constitution the life history of its relations with the other (Ingold 2000: 143). Entailed here is a particular way of making the past present in experience. Hunting is an action in the here-and-now that has obvious material consequences for both human and animal. But it is also a practice of remembering, through which the present encounter is connected to previous encounters, sometimes in dreams, sometimes in waking life. In this way the past is actively brought to bear in the very process of carrying life forward, of 'continuous birth'.

Another practice of remembering, with close affinities to hunting, is storytelling. As with the hunting of an animal, through the telling of stories past lives are 'hooked up' to present experience. But the past is not set over against the present, as story to 'real life'. Rather present lives are the continuation of stories from the past. In storytelling as in hunting, people recursively pick up the strands of past lives in the very movement of carrying forward their own. There is no point at which the story ends and life begins. Indeed stories should not end for the same reason that life should not. And precisely because stories in this sense are open-ended rather than closed off, because they merge into life in an active process of remembering rather than being set aside as passive objects of memory, they are *not transmitted*. That is, they are not received ready-made as a legacy from a past that is over and done with, already superseded by subsequent generations. They have an ongoing life of their own.

Indeed there is a certain sense in which stories are not *about* persons. Rather they *are* persons who, in the telling, are not just commemorated but actually *made present*, through the mimetic reenactment of their voices and deeds, to the assembled audience. In his classic account of the ontology of the Ojibwa, hunters and trappers of north-central Canada, A. Irving Hallowell (1960) shows how the narration of myths is a kind of invocation, which brings the characters of whom they tell into the presence of listeners so that the latter will always keep their memory alive. The Ojibwa term for myth is *ätíso'kanak*. This term, Hallowell explains, does not refer – as we might think – to a 'body of narratives'. Rather, it refers to the characters themselves, 'living "persons" of an other-than-human class' (Hallowell 1960: 26–27). Appearing sometimes in human, sometimes in animal form, these persons – otherwise known as 'grandfathers' – have existed from time immemorial. Just as animal persons manifest their presence through the encounter of the hunt, grandfather-persons can make their presence felt in myth-telling. Through myths and stories persons *speak* directly to listeners. As manifestations of persons, stories are not objects of memory but living subjects with whom listeners can engage in acts of remembering. Thus the discovery of their meanings is not a matter of extracting information that has been encrypted in advance, and for which they serve as vehicles. Rather, the meanings of stories emerge from the contexts of people's encounters with them.

This argument has important implications for our understanding of language and speech. In his contribution to this volume, Ivo Strecker shows how people can literally talk themselves into a way of life, while Megan Biesele has stressed the difficulty that people in a hunter-gatherer society have with the idea that anyone can *speak for* anyone else (as the principles of representative democracy require). This is because the *way people speak is the way they are*. People are their stories, their memories. The spoken words through which a person may, in narrative, reenact the events of his of her life, are not detachable. They are not objects that carry the recollection of these events, but belong to the person's very being as it makes its way in the world. Of course persons can – prompted by others' demands – tell of what they know. But this knowledge, likewise, does not exist apart from the knower, as a set of discrete, intellectual products. It is not objectified. As Julie Cruikshank has put it, in her study of narrative and knowledge among native people of the Yukon territory, such knowledge is 'more like a verb than a noun, more process than product' (Cruikshank 1998: 70). It follows that the sharing of knowledge does not disengage people from (intellectual) property. It engages people in a joint process of knowledge creation, once more bringing past experience into the contexts of current lives in the act of carrying those lives forward.

Now just as people talk themselves into a way of life, through the medium of words, in their activities of storytelling, so they weave their own lives into the land, through the medium of tools and equipment, in the activities of hunting and gathering. It is commonplace, in the classical literature on hunting and gathering societies, to read assertions to the effect that in such societies, tools are owned by individuals whereas land is common property. However my feeling, once again, is that concepts of ownership and property are not really appropriate for understanding the kinds of connections that hunters and gatherers have with both land and equipment. Like words, tools facilitate an extension of persons along the lines of their relationships with human and nonhuman others. As the tool augments the powers of the body, one cannot tell where the body ends and the tool begins. Thus the tool is no more an object that is owned than is the body itself. If the body is one of the forms whereby the person can manifest his or her presence in the world (another form, as we have seen, being the story), then the tool is an extension of that presence. Like the body, it is not an object of memory but caught up in a process of remembering. And by the same token, the land is not the opaque surface of materiality implied by its designation as a commons. The idea of land as property, whether common or divided, belongs to a language of occupation. But hunter-gatherers do not occupy the land, they *inhabit* it (on this distinction, see Ingold 2000: 149). The land is no blank slate but a dense and tangled web of trails laid down by its manifold human and nonhuman inhabitants as they grow and move along their respective ways of life. If the land is collective, it is so only in the sense that so many lives commingle there.

To sum up: as people make their way in the world they not only contribute to its coming-into-being (its 'continuous birth') through their encounters with animals, plants, features of the landscape, and so on, but also engage in acts of remembrance that make past persons present in experience. For hunters and gatherers the past is never superseded but is present all around. To repeat, persons – whether human or nonhuman – come and go, but do not begin or end. This leads me to three conclusions.

The first conclusion takes me back to the dichotomy between immediate-return and delayed-return systems of production. It seems to me that much of what has been said about immediate-return systems is framed within the genealogical framework of classical social anthropology, which sets the present generation against the past and the future, and that connects past, present and future through an objectification of memory in the form of property. An immediate-return system, then, is what results if the past and future are taken away, leaving only the 'slice' of the present. With respect, I believe this argument is wrong. Hunter-gatherers are not 'present-oriented', as has so often been claimed (Sahlins 1972: 30). Nor are they oriented to the future, as though their goal were to realise an imagined state of affairs different from that which obtains today. They are rather oriented towards *keeping life going*, that is, to 'continual birth'. The real difference, then, is between systems where memory *is* objectified as property, as it clearly is in societies with elaborate rules of inheritance where property becomes the link between persons of successive generations, and systems where remembering is intrinsic to people's lived engagement – in perception and action – with both human and nonhuman components of the environment. Such engagement, whether it takes the form of activities of procurement (hunting and gathering) or the sharing of proceeds, does not detach people from property. It undercuts the very process of objectification that would convert memory into property in the first place.

My second conclusion concerns the social life of things. Appadurai's (1986) seminal work is referenced by several contributors to this volume, but I feel that his idea of how things come to have social lives is very limited in one respect. For Appadurai, the significance of things lies in the way in which they come to serve as transferable crystallisations or sedimentations of human life histories. Yet again the objectification of memory is presupposed. Strictly speaking, in this approach, things do not have social lives at all; they are but intermediaries in the social life of persons. But for hunters and gatherers, nonhuman components of the environment such as animals, trees, landscape features and so on have lives of their own, which are intertwined with the lives of humans. As co-participants in the lifeworld, human persons do not so much share them as share *with* them. If nonhumans have social lives, it is not because they are caught up in a web of human connections, but because the realm of the social extends across the lifeworld as a whole.

My third and final conclusion has to do with the implications of the argument advanced here for equality and inequality. I have to say that I find the notion of 'egalitarian society' decidedly problematic. This is because I do not see how equality can exist as a *state* of some collectivity. If equality is anything, then it surely has to be *performed*. Or, as Woodburn puts it, equality is 'asserted' (1982: 431). Yet every performance – every assertion – takes place in a particular context, of relations with certain others. How, then, can it extend, in the instant, across an entire collectivity? Equality is not only performed; it is also a *passionate* performance. There may not be property in hunting and gathering societies, but there is most certainly possession. Possession lies in the intimate attachments that people have for one another, and for the land and its manifold other-than-human inhabitants. And these attachments are not devoid of tension. The passion of performance is born of the tension between the possessiveness of love or care and the desire to be a lover or carer oneself. The underside of love and trust is jealousy and suspicion – the suspicion that the person for whom one cares may assert their autonomy by caring for another. Kazuyoshi Sugawara, in his contribution to this volume, asks what it means to possess another person and finds the answer in a contradiction, what he calls 'the dialectic of emotional life'. It is this dialectic, between caring and being cared for, that drives the performance of equality in the conduct of interpersonal relations.

With that, finally, we realise what we always knew: that the people with whom we work and about whom we write are not manifestations of *Homo sociologus*, condemned to the enactment of programmes, scripts or schemata bequeathed by tradition. Nor are they the dispassionate, rational calculators imagined by some recent versions of behavioural ecology. They are rather living, breathing human beings, alternately loving, hating, friendly, quarrelsome, sympathetic and obstinate, depending on the circumstances. We anthropologists, who write about them, are much the same.

References

Appadurai, A. 1986. 'Introduction: Commodities and the Politics of Value'. In: *The Social Life of Things: Commodities in Cultural Perspective*, ed. A. Appadurai. Cambridge: Cambridge University Press, pp. 3–63.

Bird-David, N. 1994. 'Sociality and Immediacy: or, Past and Present Conversations on Bands, *Man* (N.S.), 27: 19–44.

Cruikshank, J. 1998. *The Social Life of Stories: Narrative and Knowledge in the Yukon Territory*. Lincoln, NE: University of Nebraska Press.

Fabian, J. 1983. *Time and the Other*. New York: Columbia University Press.

Hallowell, A.I. 1960. 'Ojibwa Ontology, Behavior and Worldview'. In: *Culture in History: Essays in Honor of Paul Radin*, ed. S. Diamond. New York: Columbia University Press, pp. 19–52.

Ingold, T. 2000. *The Perception of the Environment: Essays on Livelihood, Dwelling and Skill*. London: Routledge.

—— 2001. 'From Complementarity to Obviation: on Dissolving the Boundaries between Social and Biological Anthropology, Archaeology, and Psychology. In: *Cycles of Contingency: Developmental Systems and Evolution*, ed. S. Oyama, P.E. Griffiths and R.D. Gray. Cambridge, Mass.: MIT Press, pp. 255–79.

Lévi-Strauss, C. 1968. *Structural Anthropology*. Harmondsworth: Penguin.

Sahlins, M.D. 1972. *Stone Age Economics*. London: Tavistock.

Schutz, A. 1962. *The Problem of Social Reality* (Collected Papers I, ed. M. Natanson). The Hague: Nijhoff.

Scott, C. 1989. 'Knowledge Construction among Cree Hunters: Metaphors and Literal Understanding', *Journal de la Société des Américanistes*, 75: 193–208.

Woodburn, J. 1982. 'Egalitarian Societies', *Man* (N.S.), 17: 431–51.

Wub-e-ke-niew. 1995. *We Have the Right to Exist*. New York City: Black Thistle Press.

10

To Share or not to Share: Notes about Authority and Anarchy among the Hamar of Southern Ethiopia

Ivo Strecker

Introduction

In his Malinowski Memorial Lecture entitled 'Egalitarian Societies' given on 5 May 1981, James Woodburn criticised Malinowski's view that 'authority is the very essence of social organisation'. His fieldwork among the Hadza as well as the ethnographies of other hunting and gathering societies like the Mbuti Pygmies, the !Kung San, the Pandaran, the Paliyan and the Batok, who all have subsistence economies based on immediate-return practices, had shown him that indeed there are societies with a 'closest approximation to equality' and a lack of 'elaborate instituted hierarchy' (1981: 431–2). Among these hunting and gathering societies 'equalities of power, equalities of wealth and equalities of prestige or rank are not merely sought but are, with certain limited exceptions, genuinely realized'(1981: 432).

The key to this genuine realisation of social equality is the maxim of sharing. What the maxim of sharing does 'is to disengage people from property, from the potentiality in property rights for creating dependency' (1981: 445). In the hunting and gathering way of life the maxim of sharing can be most successfully asserted, but as soon as other elements, such as agriculture and pastoralism, come in, sharing becomes more problematic, the egalitarian ideal less attainable and Malinowski's hydra of authority makes its appearance. The aim of the present paper is to elucidate this problematic of sharing and authority in societies which are neither exclusively based on hunting and gathering, nor on agriculture, nor on pastoralism but combine these three sources of livelihood, often in addition with apiculture.

My analysis is based on texts from *The Hamar of Southern Ethiopia*, Vols I–III (Lydall and Strecker 1979). From 'Baldambe Explains' I take the normative and idealised account of the Hamar ethos of sharing. From 'Conservations in Dambaiti' I draw episodes which reveal the limited adherence to the norms of sharing, and from the 'Work Journal' I select those passages which are best suited to show how I discovered not only the limits of sharing but also the role of hiding in Hamar culture, and how I battled to understand the egalitarian, individualistic and even anarchic character of Hamar social life.

The Ideal of Generosity and Sharing (Notes from 'Baldambe Explains')

In his account of the beginning of Hamar culture, Baldambe addresses the theme of hierarchy and equality and shows how sharing is essential for social life. This is what he says:

> Long ago, in the times of the ancestors, the Hamar had two *bitta*. One was Banki Maro, one was Elto. The first ancestor of Banki Maro came from Ari and settled in Hamar in the mountains. He, the *bitta*, made fire, and seeing this fire the people came …The *bitta* was the first to make fire in Hamar and he said: 'I am the *bitta*, the owner of the land am I, the first to take hold of the land. Now you may become my subjects, may you be my dependents, may you be the ones I command.'
> 'Good, for us you are our *bitta* … (Lydall and Strecker1979b: 2).

Baldambe ennumerates many of the clans who came from various regions in the vicinity of Hamar and asked the *bitta* for land:
   'Take hold of the land! Share out the land!'…
Baldambe now turns from the land to the herds:

> '*Bitta!*'
> '*Woi!*'
> 'We don't have any cattle, only a few clans have cattle, only a few man have some. What shall we do?'
> 'You have no cows?'
> 'We have no cows.'
> 'You have no goats?'
> 'Only one or two men have goats. Most of us are poor.'
> 'If you are poor collect loan cattle and cultivate your fields so you can bring sorghum to those who own cattle. Herding these cows, drink their milk'…
> So then the people began to collect cattle. One man bought cows for goats. The people said to each other: 'The poor should not go down to the waterhole with nothing. The *bitta* told us that those who have cattle should share some of them, calling those to whom they give cattle *bel* (bond-friend).'
> 'Whose cattle are these?'
> 'These are the cattle of so-and-so.'
> 'And yours?'

'I have a cow from a *bel*, an arrow from which I drink.'
A cow from a *bel* is called 'arrow' because one takes a blood-letting arrow to draw blood from the jugular vein of a cow, and mixing four cups of blood with one cup of fresh milk, one feeds the children.' (1979b: 4–5)

Baldambe now turns towards marriage payment:

> When cattle had been collected in this way the elders called upon the *bitta*:
> '*Bitta!*'
> '*Woi!*'
> 'The people are all poor they have no cows, they have no goats. It would be bad if one had to give much to get married. Tell us what to do.'
> 'Do you ask me as the *bitta*?'
> 'We have asked you.'
> 'Eh-eh. My country has mountains only (is dry, poor) …Give twenty-eight goats plus one male goat and one female goat.'
> 'Good. What about the cattle?'
> The *bitta* said:
> 'Both rich and poor should give the same: eighteen head of cattle, plus one "stone cow" and one "cloth bull" which makes twenty altogether".' (1979b: 5–6)

Then Baldambe expresses the ethos of sharing and mutual assistance by evoking the picture of a poor man struggling to prepare for his marriage and obtain a wife:

> 'So the *bitta* told this, and … now he told them to take the *boko* stick [a short ritual staff with a round head].
> 'Take this *boko*, become an *ukuli* [neophyte] and jump over the cattle.'
> 'The boy is poor, he has no cattle, what shall he do?'
> 'He should give gourds to the people and they should fill them with milk for him'.
> So the *ukuli* gave gourds to the local people who filled them for him.
> 'Now he has no girls (sisters, cousins). What shall he do?'
> 'Call the girls of the people to collect the gourds from the cattle camps.'
> They came and he fed them and then they went and brought full gourds to his homestead. Then the boy said:
> 'I have no mother. Who will grind my sorghum?'
> 'Ye! It does not matter whether you have a mother or not. The *bitta* said the women of the people should grind your sorghum.'
> 'The *bitta* said so?'
> 'Yes, he said so.'
> So he called the women of the local people. All the women came and grind-grind-grinding made the beer for him.
> 'I have no father, I have no older brother.'
> 'Call the elders to build a shade.'
> So the elders built a shade.
> 'Eh, now I have jumped over the cattle but I have no wife. What shall I do?'

> 'Ask an elder whom you call "father" to be your marriage-go-between. Tell him to take a staff of *baraza* (grewia mollis) which is a *barjo* tree (tree bringing good fortune), and go to ask for a girl.'
> So the boy did so:
> 'Father!'
> '*Woi*!'
> 'Go and ask for that man's daughter for me.'
> Off he goes and *kurr* [ideophone], he arrives:
> '*Misso* (hunting friend)! I bring you a staff on behalf of a poor man.'
> 'Eh-eh!'
> 'I bring you *bodi* (fat, richness, fertility).'
> 'Why do you bring *bodi*?'
> 'I come on behalf of so-and-so's son. He says he is herding cattle, and after a while, when he has grown up, and has collected cattle for you, he will drive them to you as marriage payment. Give him your daughter. The *bitta* has said it should be so.'
> 'Eh-eh! Did he say so?'
> 'He said so'. (1979b: 8–10)

To share one's wealth and to assist others is an achievement that will be celebrated and recounted at a person's funeral. This is how Baldambe has described what happens:

> 'So all his achievements are enumerated: the beehives he has made, the fields he has prepared, the lions he has killed, the herds he has collected, the children he has begotten, the speeches he has given. All his achievements are recounted … Then comes the stage in the funeral when all the wealth of the dead man is shown. Some people are rich, others have no cattle and some have distributed all their wealth among their bond-friends. Before a rich man dies, he demands: 'The cattle that I have given to people, the cattle that are now dispersed in the bush, the ones I have given to the poor so that they may herd them, so that they may have enough to eat, let them be seen when I have died.' So the cattle are driven to his homestead from … [all over Hamar]. When the bond-friend comes to the homestead he carries with him a cow's horn filled with butter. Arriving at the entrance of the cattle kraal he rubs the foreheads of each of the dead man's sons and then the throats of each of his wives and daughters. After this, he then anoints the throat of each of the women who have come with him. Having anointed the living, they turn to the dead. First the oldest son takes butter from the bond-friend and mixes it with butter from a cow's horn of his own homestead. Four times he rubs the butter on to the forehead of his dead father asking him to herd the cows like he used to do when he was alive. Then the bond-friend mixes his butter with the butter of the dead man's homestead and also rubs the dead man's forehead and calls to him to herd and bless the cattle. Now the oldest son goes and pulls off two branches from a *baraza* tree. He places them in the cow dung so that they are damp and full of cow dung. Then he touches the backs of the cattle that the bond-friend has brought and blessing in this way, he hands them over to the bond-friend. The bond-friend will give some cattle and goats and honey to the dead man's sons.' (1979b: 39–41)

This, then, is how people should respect and care for each other and by doing so to enhance their self-esteem and their name and fame. But everything they collect and share comes ultimately from *barjo*, from luck, good fortune, creation. At the beginning of this account, where Baldambe tells how the *bitta* formulated the first lore of the Hamar, this dependence on *barjo* is expressed as follows:

> Dig fields. When you have done that, here is sorghum. *Barjo* has given us sorghum. Sorghum is man's grass. As cows eat grass so shall man eat sorghum. *Barjo* gave us the meat and milk of cattle and goats long ago, saying:
> 'Drink the milk of cattle and goats and eat their meat. Cattle and goats shall chew leaves from the bushes and cattle shall graze grass. Put fences around your homesteads so that the hyenas, jackals and hunting dogs can not enter. The one who enters is man. You have hands'. Dig fields and when the sorghum is ripe bring some to the cattle owners, your *bel*, bring some to the goat owners, your goat *bel*. Make beehives taking the bark of the *donkala* tree, binding the *arra* grass around it with the *kalle* creeper and smearing the inside with cow dung. Place the beehives well in the forks of trees. The bees will come to you from Ari country ... [Baldambe tells of all the places from where the bees will come]. When the bees have come the honey will ripen. When it is ripe, bring honey to the *bitta* so that he may call forth the *barjo* of your cattle and the *barjo* of your goats and that he may get rid of sickness for you. The elders should come to build my house and erect my cattle gateway. (1979b: 7–8)

Thus *barjo* shares out what is most essential for existence: grass for goats and cattle and 'grass' (in the form of sorghum) for human beings. The bees in turn provide the honey from which honey wine can be made, which then is used to call forth '*barjo*', the source of all well-being.

The Limits of Generosity and Sharing (Notes from 'Conversations in Dambaiti' and 'Work Journal')

The picture which Baldambe has provided of the Hamar sharing their goats and cattle in order to ensure each other's well-being, speaks of a cultural dream and ideal. The dream exists because the reality is all too often quite different. Generosity and sharing have their limits, for the vicissitudes of goat herding lead to many temptations and provide ample opportunities for enriching oneself at the expense of others. The problem begins at home, that is, in the composite herds of a homestead, where it is not always easy to distinguish the different goats and unambiguously identify their owners. Here is a conversation that exemplifies what I mean. It was one early night when women and children were sitting outside, next to the cattle and goat enclosures, relaxing and drinking coffee after a long day of exhausting work in the fields:

> *Anti* [a girl]: Why are the herds so noisy today? They sound as if they have been moving camp.
> *Gino* [Anti's older brother, addressing his younger brother]: Lomoluk, go and see whose kids are making such a noise.

Anti: They have just been milked.
Bargi [her mother]: Most of the kids are drinking from their mothers now, there are only a few goats to milk ...
Gino [to Lomoluk]: Please go over there and find out which kids are calling.
Bargi: The kids which are calling, whose kids may they be? Are they the offspring of the thin goats? Look at them and come back. If they have drunk and are still hungry, they should be driven where there is more grass and a camp should be made for them there.
Lomoluk [from inside the goat enclosure] The kid ...
Bargi [signalling him that she is listening]: Yu!
Lomoluk: It is the kid of the old goat with black spots.
Anti: And the others?
Lomoluk: The others, wait, they are calling down here! [from inside the enclosure like before]. One goat.
Gino (answering Lomoluk): Hm.
Lomoluk: It is one of the yellow goats, ... it is the kid of the yellow blind goat.
Gino: Hm, that kid has become very thin.
Lomoluk [calling]: Mother!
Bargi: Yo!
Lomoluk: The kid that made such noise ...
Bargi: Yes!
Lomoluk: Down there, the freckled goat which we have herded for a long time already, see, it is its kid ...
Bargi: Yes?
Lomoluk: It is the one that makes such noise.
Bargi: So milk the mother and then let the kid drink.
[the conversation now moves on to other topics and Lomoluk returns from the goat enclosure, then Gino picks up the theme of the goats again]
Gino: During the day she can go with the kids, why do you keep the old goat in the enclosure?
Bargi: She goes with the kids.
Gino: Hm.
Aikenda [Gino's father's younger brother's wife]: He doesn't know that we don't keep her in the enclosure.
Anti: The day before yesterday she went up there.
Gino: The girls don't understand anything about goats, they might easily think the old one is small and leave her with the youngest kid in the enclosure throughout the day ...You let the grown-up kids stay together with the very small ones inside the enclosure throughout the day, that's why I asked whether you also left the old one inside.
Anti: Ye, which grown-up kid?
Gino: The kid of the goat with the small black spots.
Anti: Gino, leave such talk, we will let this one graze.
Lomoluk: The kid of the freckled sick goat that cried this morning?
Gino: Yes, the one that made such a noise just now.
Anti: It is my father Baldambe's goat.
Bargi: Ye! Which one is Baldambe's goat?
Anti: Before we used to say it was Baldambe's goat, and then it was said it was Shalombe's goat, Shalombe's.
Bargi (reprimandingly): Ach! You always say 'so-and-so's goat, so-and-so's goat!"

> *Gadi* [Gino's father's younger brother's wife]: When I asked Gino before he said it was Shalombe's goat...
> *Anti*: Ye!
> *Gadi*: And when I asked Gino again he said it was Baldambe's goat.
> *Anti* (laughs): Haha!
> *Gardu* [Gino's classificatory mother]: Your lies, they really are something bad.
> *Bargi*: I have also never heard people beat the names of the owners of a goat so much.
> *Gardu* (addressing Gadi): *Uto*, they have said this about the goat ...
> *Gadi*: Hm.
> *Gardu*: They take just this, just that and say it, saying that Shalombe has bought the goat ...
> *Bargi*: The children just talk like this without thinking.
> *Anti*: Let our grandfather tell you [Shalombe, Anti's classificatory 'grandfather' who has been listening quietly].
> *Bargi*: Whose goat is it then? [to Shalombe] Now Shalombe, why don't you tell us about the goat?
> *Maiza* [Baldambe's sister]: In this homestead I have never heard anyone distinguish between owners of goats like this before.
> *Aikenda*: Ye, isn't it customary to separate the goats from each other and call them by their different owners? Since when does one put goats of different owners together just so?
> *Shalombe*: The goat is the offspring of the goat given by Tsaina's son. It has ears which are cut differently.
> *Bargi*: That was truly said.
> *Shalombe*: How come you all ask about the sick goat? Let this be the concern only of its owner.
> *Aikenda*: Hm. We did not mean this.
> *Gardu*: Yes, right.
> *Bargi*: Hahaha. (Strecker 1979: 121–9)

The need to identify goats correctly and allocate rights and duties accordingly goes, of course, beyond the domain of a single homestead, for it may easily happen that a goat goes astray and is absorbed by another herd. Then it takes much honesty to return the animal to its proper owner. But if honesty prevails, this is much applauded, as in the following example:

> *Baldambe*: Isn't Hamar something good? Look at this goat which once got lost ... Our herding boys said, just so: 'The fox has eaten it.' At that time the sorghum was ripe. 'Gino, look for the goat.' 'I have searched for it at Basho, I have searched for it at Singera, I have searched for it aaall .. over the country.' Recently an age-mate of Lomoluk said: 'Lomoluk.' '*Woi*.' 'Look at this goat, it has the ear-cut of your goats, the goats of Berinas' homestead. Take it, it has already been a long while with us.' Now the goat has grown up ...When it got lost, it was small and thin, now it has become big and fat. See, this is Africa, Hamar.' (Strecker 1979: 37)

The temptation to take from the property of others whenever an opportunity avails itself is an experience which most of the Hamar share. They are keenly aware of the fact that it is all too easy to let other people's animals, especially goats and sheep, run with one's own herds and eventually keep them together with their offspring. This is why they speak of mystical retribution which will follow such dishonest behaviour, as in the following example:

> *Choke* [with a calm, low and quiet voice]: The son of Tini's father, Muga had driven his goats from here to Pali and then again had moved his camp to Korta. At that time many men from Mirsha kept their cattle in the area. Now, aren't we talking about lost goats?
> *Baldambe*: About lost goats.
> *Choke*: He moved from Pali to Korta. When the men of Mirsha had moved away, three thin sheep of theirs were left behind. These three sheep joined his goats. Hadn't the owners of the sheep returned to their own country? So they stayed, stayed, stayed, got healthy. But the owners were not told of this. Didn't Muga have his camp on his own, away from other people? So the sheep lambed, lambed. They did not die and they did not get sick. The sheep lambed. They multiplied, became young castrated sheep, became big, grown-up castrated sheep, became rams. While the sheep multiplied like this, Muga fell sick and could not speak anymore.
> *Aulebais*: Where was that?
> *Choke*: Down at Laetan. Weren't you there yourself when Haila [a diviner] was throwing the sandals? That was when Haila's wife had died down in the fields. He threw the sandals, threw them, threw and watched them:
> '*Kubu*' [reciprocal term of address for someone married into the same lineage as oneself].
> '*Kubu*'.
> 'You have come to death, but you won't die. These sheep, what kind of sheep are they? They come and look at you. Or are these cattle? No, no cattle.'
> He continued throwing the sandals and they kept coming back to the same, coming back, coming back.
> 'What sheep are these?'
> He continued throwing.
> 'First it looked as if the sheep had come on one path to you, but then – I see that you did not drag them by a rope fastened around their necks. It looks as if they have come on two paths -no, on one - not on one, on two.'
> He kept throwing the sandals.
> 'In the bush.'
> He, Haila, was a different man (very special).
> *Aulebais*: *Nyarsh*, he was very sharp.
> *Choke*: This Haila, this Haila, he was a different man.
> *Aulebais*: Wasn't it Haila who pulled me away from death and made me sit up again?
> *Choke*: He threw, threw, threw:
> 'What sheep are these?'
> He asked and listened, but Muga kept silent.
> 'Now if you don't tell me about these sheep, your father's goats and you will not walk this soil for much longer. Why don't you die then? If you talk about these sheep you will not die. What is killing you now are these sheep.'
> *Baldambe*: As his sandals tell the truth he has grown to be disliked by people. They say: 'He always spoils our goats.'
> *Choke*: Yes, that's why people are angry. They ask him to help them survive ...

Baldambe: ... and they hide the stolen goats that are killing them ...
Choke: ... are killing them. So they kill themselves. Haila threw the sandals again:
'Now, what are you doing. Here it is again! It is saying 'take me away from my kraal, let me be slaughtered in the open'.
Baldambe: The sheep.
Choke: A castrated sheep, so fat, fat, fat, fat that it struck anyone who looked at his herd. When you saw his herd from behind you would see this sheep, when you saw the herd from in front you would see it.
Baldambe: Is he an offspring of those lost sheep?
Choke: My father's son, three were lost and they multiplied so much that they became a whole herd.
Maiza: They were like sand.
Choke: Like sand, they multiplied so much. It's they who brought the sickness. Then he began telling the truth:
'When the sheep first came to me they were three. They stayed with my son's goats and no one came asking for them. They stayed with me and they multiplied the most out of all of my goats and sheep. What shall I do?'
'Why don't you separate one of them from the others? Slaughter it out in the open for the people and leave the others with your herd.'
Baldambe: Yes, long ago the master, your father Berinas, told me: 'If any goats that get lost come to you, hand them on and let them run with the herds of someone else.'
Choke: 'Let them graze far away from you.'
Baldambe: 'Far away. If stray animals multiply inside your kraal they will bring sickness.'
Choke: He was right.
Baldambe: They kill the people.
Choke: They kill.
Baldambe: 'Let stray animals be herded by others.' Today people speak differently. They say: 'Leave them, let them multiply and when they have grown old, give them to the people, the scavengers, to eat'.
Choke: To eat.
Baldambe: That's how they steal today. That's what they want.
Choke: See what they want today! Then Muga brought out one castrated sheep and it was slaughtered. The people ate it. They were full and still there was some meat left. Later again at his father's funeral he killed another big sheep ... He got rid of them at funerals, he got rid of them by giving them to those who asked him for animals ...
Baldambe: So now he possesses only those that are truly his own?
Choke: Yes, which are his own, which belong to his head [like the hair which is part of the head].
Baldambe: Don't say that, say: 'those which are his whipping wands' [given to him by his father together with whipping wands].
Choke and Baldambe: (laughing quietly together, delighting in their understanding of the intricacies of Hamar customs)' (Strecker 1979: 40–3).

If generosity and sharing have their limits even in times of plenty, and if people are ever ready to steal each other's goats, this is even more so in times of crisis, when the rains have failed and starvation is imminent. This is the picture which my *misso* (hunting-friend) Banko painted at a time when a severe drought was hitting Hamar and the surrounding regions:

> 'Usually, about the time the Ethiopian police celebrate Easter, the first sorghum ripens and small children 'steal' from it and survive. But look at the fields today. They are empty, a desert! Where can we go to exchange our goats for grain? There is no more grain in Banna, nor in Tsamai, nor in Ari. The doors to Galeba and to Arbore are closed and there is hunger there anyway. We are now slaughtering our goats and those who have none take them by force. Soon we will run out of animals and then we shall kill each other over them: 'why don't you let me have one of your cows?' and we shall take up spears and kill each other. Soon there will be nothing but turmoil'. (Lydall and Strecker 1979a: 102)

Well, luckily Banko's scenario was exaggerated. What we witnessed was no real turmoil but an increase of demands by the poorer members of Hamar society to share the resources of those who were more affluent. Strong confrontations developed, especially between affines who in meagre times always remember first those to whom they have given their daughters and sisters and whom they remind of the fact that they still owe them some marriage payment, as in the following two cases:

> The affine of Dube [baldambe's brother] is at the gateway once again, demanding marriage payment in a provocative manner. Baldambe argues that he should get together with the girl's father to work out what may be due to him. The boy rejects this idea and a violent argument ensues, bringing to light the precarious relationship between affines. Once again the everyday life of Hamar seems to be on the verge of anarchy. The argument is laced with threats. The boy threatens to take what he wants by force. Not today and not here in the homestead but at some future date he will take a cow or two from the herds of the sons of Berinas, he will take them when the herds are out in the bush. Baldambe on the other hand, implies that his family is strong and ruthless and would not mind killing an affine who dares to provoke them. In the end when Wadu [a friend of Baldambe] has severely admonished him, the boy gives in and, intimidated, he sits among the men who settle down to drink their morning coffee. (Lydall and Strecker 1979a: 214–15)

> Yesterday two women of Baldambe's clan Karla arrived at Dambaiti asking Baldambe to help them claim payment for some of their daughters. For the first time I see clan solidarity in a different light. To date the most impressive expression of this solidarity that I have witnessed has been the way in which clan members use the marriage of one of their women to blackmail the family of the husband into giving them goats and cattle. Today, I am seeing this solidarity from a different angle: a woman's classificatory brothers are the main allies of her family should the latter receive no adequate payment for her marriage. Clan members try to keep out of such matters, leaving all the appropriate economic transactions to the families directly involved. But if a woman's family is slow in making the legitimate demands, then the other members of her clan come into the picture. I have the feeling that if members of the woman's clan detect a weakness in the husband's family, they later exploit this weakness to their own advantage, blackmailing the other side into unnecessary payments. In

this way, in-laws can become a real threat. This threat operates dialectically in everyday life: relations between affines are generally good precisely because this relationship is potentially bad. If a potentially bad relationship is turned into a good one, this is considered a true social achievement. Baldambe turned his affines, Hailu and Wadu, into his best friends. This is probably a general feature of social life: friendship and alliance can produce very close relationships when they bridge potentially dangerous gaps such as those between social classes, castes, colourbars ... (1979a: 242)

Next to the affines it is the bond-friends of whose wealth one demands a share in times of need. For example, on the very day when Baldambe refused to give way to the demands of the affine who had come to his gateway, he sent his younger brother Kairambe to collect animals from a bond-friend in order to pay a trader to whom he was indebted. My comment at the time was as follows:

This is yet another example of how the system of bond-friendship is [a form of capital] ... which one lays up against unwelcome surprises. Whenever Baldambe is suddenly in need of 'cash', he starts thinking of his bond-friends. Many of them he has inherited from his father. Calculating which of them he has left in peace for longest and which may have a cow at his disposal, he decides which bond-friend to bother on any specific occasion. Over the course of time, in this system you can receive an infinite number of cattle as a return on an original investment of a single cow' (1979a: 215)

To give one's cattle away as 'loan cattle' (*banne wak*) is not only a useful form of investment, but also a way of hiding them and making one's true wealth invisible. This is how Baldambe told me about it:

As we chew our *muna* (sorghum rolls), I reflect on my attempt to work during the morning. I sigh and tell Baldambe that if I were a proper anthropologist, I would be writing from now on, writing without respite, so that the books would grow fat whilst I myself grew thin. My youth would go into the books and my eyes would darken, I would need glasses, my hair would grow white and with a whisper I would talk to my students. I imitate the speech mannerism of an old professor talking Hamar: '*Nanato, kami wodimate...*' I relate what I would say about Hamar and when I reach the institution of bond-friendship, pointing out that it is in this way that a young man builds up his capital, Baldambe suddenly interrupts my imaginary lecture. 'And by giving his cattle away to his bond-friends, he makes sure that none of his relatives and affines comes and takes them away from him unexpectedly.' I had always thought that this 'hiding' was one of the most important reasons for the institution but I had never heard a Hamar state this clearly. 'Thank you, *misso* Ogotemmeli!' (1979a: 221)

The Distribution of Wealth and Social Influence (Notes from 'Work Journal')

As the drought continued and people kept increasing their demands on each other's wealth, I began to ask them about the way in which they perceived the difference of wealth in Hamar. This is how I described the attempt:

I have developed a graphic scale for measuring wealth. It consists of showing five circles of different sizes. I ask Choke to identify all the individual men of the villages he knows best with one of these circles, the rich with the large circles, the poor with the small circles. My aim is to discover how certain structural features of Hamar society are perceived by the actors. The way that Choke carries out the task shows that he perceives Hamar as rather egalitarian. He enumerates as many poor as rich (Lydall and Strecker 1979a: 235)

As I continued my research into wealth difference in Hamar, I noted down the following observations and reflections:

> Raised voices in Aikenda's house wake me before sunrise. The abbreviations, the pauses, the pace, the quick echoing responses, the varying levels of tone – all these tell me that great speakers have arrived. I can also tell where they come from – only the men of southern Hamar speak so powerfully. So I am not surprised to find Arbala Lomotor (a good friend and inlaw of Baldambe) sitting next to the coffee pot. He, however, does not talk; he leaves the word to an old, grey haired man. The old man, like many of those who I have met from the south, has a strength and confidence and ruthlessness which I attribute to the environment of the wide open spaces of the south and their proximity to hostile neighbours. The south seems to select for strong and rich people. The south offers a regal way of life: large herds, especially herds of goats, periodically exchanged for grain from Banna, Kara, Tsamai. In the south no poor man can survive. That is why the census shows more people the further one moves north. In Hamar terms, 'poor' means lacking herds of cattle and goats. In some ways, wealth and oral competence go together, or more exactly, oral competence and the ownership of herds! A remark of Choke comes to my mind: he said that in the south everybody talks at public meetings. He implies that this is bad, because it prohibits clear decision making, 'Look at Assile, Wungabaino, Mirsha, the men of those places never stop fighting and raiding. Everybody does what he wants, nobody is listened to. Look at Angude and Kadja, those men only allow a small number of selected people to speak, and they stick to the decisions of those speakers. I wonder whether I will ever be able to answer the question concerning the relationship between speaking and wealth and I start thinking about wealth in general: how has the distribution of wealth in Hamar developed over time? It may well have changed considerably during the past generations. The Hamar theory is that wealth used to be concentrated in the hands of only a couple of families just two, or even one generation ago. All the other people used to herd cattle they had been given by the wealthy within a bond-friend relationship. It is said that when the wealthy brought their cattle to the waterhole, no one else would approach. But doesn't the indigenous account always tend to simplify the past? Just as a large number of ancestors are edited out of the account, so too are most wealthy men and all past wealth is said to have been concentrated in the hands of only a few. The Marxist model of progressive concentration of wealth in only a few hands is the exact opposite of the Hamar model … Why do the Hamar see wealth as moving from concentration to dispersion rather than vice versa? Because this is how the wealthy individual's life cycle operates? Because the old people who have the greatest command over wealth always lose their hold when they die? Or does the theory refer to the time when the Hamar were recuperating economically from

Menelik's invasion? At that time warriors such as Berimba accumulated a great deal of wealth in their hands after successful raids on the Borana, Gabare etc ... (1979a: 236-7)

On the relationship between wealth, speaking and the life cycle I had noted a day earlier:

> People may be allowed to speak publicly because their fathers were once wealthy. Could it be that the herds of wealthy fathers provide the sons with a good economic basis for exercising social influence? The son of a rich man is the one who supervises the herds and for this reason, quite frequently initiates actions like moving camp, watering, scouting etc. If his leadership comes to be recognised in this way, he becomes a 'speaker'. But as a 'speaker' he has to be generous, and gradually he is divested of his wealth as he tries to keep his supporters. Lomale, the most important 'speaker' of western Hamar, is the son of a rich father. So is old Bume, who has almost the same prestige as Lomale and who is said to have been rich in cattle and goats in times gone by. Today Choke counts them the poorest of Hamar. (1979a: 235-6)

Reflections about Authority and Anarchy (Notes from 'Work Journal')

From all the examples I have given so far one can see how under varying circumstances both inequality and equality are characteristic features of Hamar culture. The acceptance of authority and the 'premise of inequality', to use Maquet's famous title (1961), lies at the back of the social constitution of Hamar as laid down by the *bitta*, but in everyday life, any outright assumption of authority is rejected and equality is constantly asserted. During fieldwork I was puzzled by these seemingly contradictory strains in Hamar culture, and again and again I came back to the questions of hierarchy and egalitarianism, order and anarchy. Let me provide two examples. The first concerns the nexus between individualised knowledge and individualised social life:

> In the morning we have coffee in Aikenda's house. Baldambe is absent, but there are guests like Choke's friend Wualle Lokarimoi and Kula the 'black'. They say that the position of the stars indicates hard times ahead. While listening to the conversation it strikes me ... how individualized all astronomical knowledge is. Everyone has particular observations to make. Each man puts them forward with much force and mystique, yet no one attempts any systematic account of the various astral phenomena. For me, this reflects the social structure. Knowledge is generally individualized and specific. Hiding and mystique cloud the channels of information so that no unified body of social knowledge can be acquired and maintained. The same individualization seems to affect ritual and almost all levels of social organization. Is 'individualization' the right word? What I mean is free individual choice in the application of general principles. As for example in intermarriage: there are clans but no segmentary structures nor obvious marriage patterns. There are distinctions of

age, but no operational age-set system; there is leadership but no clearly defined office; there are differences in wealth, but these are drastically levelled through the institution of bond-friendship ... I think the census will show in the end that there is a large degree of 'randomness' in the application of general principles. But once this is shown, the 'randomness' will no longer be random but rather a typical feature of individualistic Hamar social organisation in which everyone works towards a maximization of choices in any particular social situation. Because of the strong rejection of authority amongst the Hamar, I have been referring to Hamar society as 'anarchic', but I propose to use the term 'individualization' for the time being" (Lydall and Strecker 1979a: 228–9).

The second example comes from the Hamar cattle camps and is about the acceptance of past and the rejection of present authority:

At night while Bali [Baldambe's younger brother] speaks to us sitting on our cowhides, more and more young men join us and listen with quiet intensity ... An audience materializes almost inaudibly, making the speaker feel that he is saying something they value highly. And then slowly the members of the audience sitting in darkness start to speak themselves. Their speeches are long and are listened to by the assembled company. They constantly invoke the 'old', the 'fathers', the 'older brothers' and refer to the 'precedents' of which I have talked above. There is a confidence and trust in the old and the established which has never seemed to me quite so marked before (although I realize now that it has always been there). I suddenly realize that here may lie one of the keys to understanding Hamar 'conservatism' and (paradoxically?) its 'anarchy'. The cattle camps play a big part in the socialization of the young men. Here, to a large extent, they are free from the strict domination of the elders. Here they have to make their own decisions, and these decisions are made on the basis of precedents, by referring to what 'the great men of the past' would have done in such-and-such a situation. By invoking a precedent the speaker almost becomes the historical person himself, so by invoking historical authority they reject the present authority of others. One might argue that Hamar anarchy is a result of the fact that everybody rejects a living person's decision if it is based on purely individual and contemporary judgement. Outright individual cleverness and power are taboo and no one may openly aspire to them. Instead one must make a precedent of an incident in the historic past which will be acknowledged by others as offering the appropriate answer to a specific problem in the present. (1979a: 249–50)

Conclusion

What I have tried to do in this small homage to James Woodburn is to let the reader accompany me on my journey into what Baldambe used to call the 'thicket' of Hamar social life, and explore themes which always have been close to James Woodburn's heart, themes of sharing, the 'rhetoric of property' – as Carol M. Rose (1994) would call it –, immediate and delayed exchange, authority and, above all, the question of egalitarianism.

At the outset of his lecture on 'Egalitarian Societies' from which I have quoted already in the introduction, James Woodburn stressed that 'although very many societies are in some sense egalitarian, those in which inequalities are at their minimum depend on hunting and gathering for their subsistence ... But there is, of course, no question of the equality being a simple product of the hunting and gathering way of life. Many hunter-gatherers have social systems in which there is very marked inequality of one sort or another, sometimes far more marked than the inequalities in certain simple agricultural or nomadic pastoral societies' (1981: 432). And at the end of his lecture, he returned briefly to these agricultural or pastoral societies, often called in anthropological parlance 'acephalous societies', 'tribes without rulers', 'societies without formal political offices'. Equality between household heads, he argued, are here only a startingpoint, a qualification to compete in a strenuous competition for wealth, power and prestige' (1981: 446).

As the notes which I have presented here have shown, the social life of the Hamar of Southern Ethiopia has a similarly strenuous character. It is torn between hierarchy and anarchy, equality and inequality, individualism and sociality – and the existing tensions are mirrored in the patterns of sharing.

References

Lydall, J.R. and I.A. Strecker 1979a. *The Hamar of Southern Ethiopia. Vol. I: Work Journal.* Hohenschaeftlarn.

Lydall, J.R. and I.A. Strecker 1979b. *The Hamar of Southern Ethiopia. Vol. II: Baldambe Explains.* Hohenschaeftlarn.

Maquet, J.J. 1961. *The Premise of Inequality in Rwanda: a Study of Political Relations in a Central African Kingdom.* London.

Rose, C.M. 1994. *Property and Persuasion: Essays on the History, Theory and Rhetoric of Ownership.* Boulder.

Strecker, I.A. 1979. The Hamar of Southern Ethiopia. Vol. III: Conversations in Dambaiti. Hohenschaeftlarn.

Woodburn, J. 1982. 'Egalitarian Societies', *Man (N.S.)*, 17 (1982): 431–51.

11

'Their own oral histories': Items of Ju/'hoan Belief and Items of Ju/'hoan Property

Megan Biesele

> Some people tell stories one way, some another.
> Perhaps it is because people sometimes separate for
> awhile and still go on telling stories. But all these
> stories about the old times--people use different
> words and names for the same things. There are many
> different ways to talk. Different people just have
> different minds.
> !Unn/obe Morethlwa, 1971

> We never wanted to represent our communities.
> That was a white people's idea in the first place.
> Kxao =Oma, 1994

> African hunter-gatherers of today, or peoples who
> were until recently hunter-gatherers are, for the most part,
> descendants of groups that have a long history of hunting
> and gathering. Their own claims, their own oral histories,
> strongly support such an assumption, and must be treated
> with more respect than the stigmatizing histories allocated to
> them by their farmer neighbours.
> James Woodburn, 'African Hunter-Gatherer Social
Organization', 1988

The oral testimony linking Ju/'hoan San postforagers to their foraging past importantly includes their mythology of the ancient times. Their own oral histories include items of belief treated as semi-restricted property that may be an important form of social control.

We were charged at the Halle conference with contributing to a new model of property relations in the face of current challenges of practice and theory. It was suggested that in so doing we aim at making real progress on some central property issues dealt with in the work of James Woodburn. We were asked to focus on the dynamics existing between property relations and egalitarian social organisation, i.e. we were not merely to reiterate that there are (or were) largely egalitarian societies. We were encouraged to prepare our contributions in such a way that they would facilitate a comparative perspective on the effects of different kinds of property on relationships of equality. In the case of papers such as this one for the 'knowledge as property' section, we were able to deal with (restricted) religious knowledge as well as technical skills.

Introduction

My starting point was the word *restricted* in the circular, as used without nuance to describe religious knowledge as property. In fact, societies exhibit a range of human relations regarding restriction or shared ownership of cultural ideas. They also show a range of attitudes and practices regarding variability in such ideas and the degrees of individuality allowed in expression of them. The idea of *restricted* religious knowledge is far from simple, and for the purposes of this conference I problematised it using Ju/'hoan San examples. I asked colleagues to consider that unrestricted or variably restricted knowledge may as surely be property--enriching each of its possessors although it is shared by all--as is knowledge that is restricted in a cabalistic way.

Other recent anthropological papers and conference sessions (e.g. the session 'Equality: Ideas and Evidence', joint annual meeting of the Canadian Anthropological Society, American Ethnological Society, and Society for Cultural Anthropology, Montreal, 3–6 May, 2001) have also focused on refining notions of equality, framing them so that they represent not a monolithic construct but a range of empirically observed relations. We can look at relative degrees of equality, just as we look at degrees of inequality. We can also realise that in the many areas of life in any society, some are based more on equality and some more on inequality. The specifics of each area of each society at particular historical times must be noted. Thus in the present paper I treat notions of restriction and sharing in religious knowledge by taking a sociolinguistic approach, based on my studies of Ju/'hoan folklore and ideology in the years 1970 to the present.

Taking Woodburn's 1988 paper, 'African Hunter-gatherer Social Organization' as my second starting point, I consider the conference assignment with reference to both knowledge and its expression among Ju/'hoansi. Examples can be drawn from Ju/'hoan ideology as recently expressed in the words of individual storytellers, singers and the like, and from Ju/'hoan social skills as used by individual spokespersons in recent political contexts. I use these examples to explore questions posed by Woodburn about the effects of outside pressures/encapsulation, and the relevance of personality and social style for an understanding of egalitarian and postegalitarian societies. Ultimately I argue that the flexibility and variability of Ju/'hoan communicative culture (embodied not in individual stories, ideas or rhetorical tropes but in the dialogue among them) help us understand the social flexibility and variability which have been so vital to the maintenance of their society. I suggest that together these social habits will serve them well in the future, as the have in the past.

The Paper's Approach

I have long felt that we may learn a great deal about a system like that of the Ju/'hoansi (which now has elements of both immediate and delayed return) from involvement in the politics of current change. In fact, as I believe is demonstrated by the activist involvement of Kalahari colleagues and of people like James Woodburn himself, there are some things about such social systems that can be learnt in no other way. Different indigenous societies have used widely differing social strengths to achieve their aims in dealing with the challenges posed by surrounding peoples. From observing what works for them in changed contexts, we can understand more deeply the social habits they have so long practised to good effect among themselves. Terence Turner's outline of the factors which made Kayapo resistance to the destruction of their Brazilian Amazon environment signally effective includes a flair for the dramatic that was clearly honed in internal contexts. Woodburn describes a kind of insouciant self-sufficiency exhibited by Hadza in their dealings with neighbours, linked to the absence of relationships of dependency in their own society, which stands them in good stead in today's circumstances. He likens this self-sufficiency to the independent spirit Richard Lee admired in the Ju/'hoansi after he learnt the levelling lesson of the Christmas ox (Lee 1969).

I concentrate in this paper not only on Ju/'hoan 'independence' as a useful strength in their dealings with outsiders but on another facet of their society which seems to me equally important. This facet is their insistence on keeping members of their groups 'in the loop' of communication to as great a degree as possible. I argue that this inclusiveness is a piece of social technology that will be as important to their success as 'postforagers' as it was in the foraging context. Along with the powerful consensus decision making with which it goes hand in hand, Ju/'hoan inclusiveness of communication is key to both the solidarity and the flexibility that will be necessary in their future.

The tolerance and effective use by San people of multiple points of view within their groups has received substantial comment in anthropological literature (see Silberbauer 1978; Guenther 1999; Biesele 1993, 1999b). This tolerance is strong, and it extends into areas that anthropology has often seen as tradition-bound--areas such as religious practice and ideology. I discuss in this paper the phenomenon of coexisting varying beliefs in an effort to suggest its very basic nature in Ju/'hoan San social life. In seeming paradox, however, the tolerance coexists with an equally strong insistence on the necessity of precise knowledge and skill in practical areas. Expertise, to remain effective, is subject to the same relentless levelling well known in the San material property arena. I bring in current examples of this levelling to show resistance to challenges to their egalitarian ethos. Again I argue that these persisting social habits have not only served the Ju/'hoansi well but will continue to do so in the conditions--themselves variable--which they now face in southern Africa.

Pervasive tolerance fosters for the Ju/'hoansi useful habits of patience, not only with each other but with the demands of their constantly changing (foraging *and* post-foraging) situations. Tolerance, inclusiveness and the free exchange of information foster both informed consensus and group allegiance. Coming to a premature decision is foolhardy not only in economic/environmental senses but in a social sense. So temporary tolerance for ambiguity is a definite asset for getting along in an isolated, face-to-face, lifelong small-community situation. I argue that it is also an asset in the increasing encapsulation that may characterise some San communities under the pressures of the near future.

Rapidly altering times may prompt apparent changes in egalitarianism in some areas of San values. Contemporary pressures may prompt loss of some of the fluidity which long characterised the way the San handled items of belief and ideology. Yet the flexibility of their approach to tradition bears necessary and meaningful connections to both past and present lifeways. Ju/'hoan San, for instance, have found ideological ways to balance conservatism and autonomous action, including both high tolerance *and* genuine respect for what I (following Theobald 1972) have termed 'sapiential authority'. These mental and social tools should be taken into account in constructing theoretical models such as we sought at the conference.

Background for my Arguments

Tolerance for Multiple Points of View

In her chapter 'The Gods' in *Nyae Nyae !Kung Beliefs and Rites* (1999), Lorna Marshall discussed the Ju/'hoan (!Kung) sociology of religious knowledge. She outlined the kinds of responses offered by individuals to her questions about the puzzling image of =Gao N!a, the creator, and other ambiguous items of belief. Variant beliefs were viewed by the Ju/'hoansi as unproblematic. Their responses to probing questions varied from thoughtful but cautious rumination to the more usual response, 'I don't know.' Not knowing was usually explained as not having been told by parents or other older people. Lorna wrote: 'when my inquiries suggested to the !Kung that I expected them, possibly, to know something that they did not know, they became embarrassed and defensive' (1999: 14). Though they were sorry not to have answers for Lorna, the Ju/'hoans' very practical habit of admitting lack of knowledge, rather than making things up, came to the fore every time. When she asked how =Gao N!a created himself, she could find no myth or lore of explanation. She wrote: 'People simply said they did not know. !U turned on me and asked me if I knew. When I said that I did not, she snapped, "How, then, do you expect me to know?"'(1999: 18).

This anecdote points up the matter-of-fact attitude taken by Ju/'hoansi to the transmission and ownership of religious knowledge, in many ways similar to the open processes of ordinary communication within their groups. One either knows or does not know according to whether or not one has been told something. Though there is deference shown to older people by younger (Biesele 1976, 1993), the Ju/'hoansi seem to be far to the 'unrestricted' side of the range discussed above in regard to ownership of religious knowledge.

I found this lack of restriction to be the case throughout my own fieldwork with the Ju/'hoansi, which began in 1970 and continues now. The 1971 quote from !Unn/obe Morethlwa at the top of this paper ('Different people just have different minds') came when I asked her about the coexistence in Ju/'hoan tradition of many versions of 'the same' folktale. Unfazed by the question, she covered in her answer variability in storytelling aesthetics as completely as variability in plots and storylines. She accompanied her answer with an eloquent shrug.

This shrug was for me the first glimpse of the elaborate and systematic tolerance I came to know in Ju/'hoan society. I eventually saw the extent of a large and pervasive latitude not only for variation in daily behaviour but also for the expressive styles of different individuals. I pondered the relationship between storytelling style and its content or message. If the medium was the message, might personal ostentations in style liberate a tradition from slavish adherence to content, yet somehow preserve that content in its essentials? I began at that time to ask whether 'culture' was perhaps a less monolithic concept than I had thought. I have eventually come to feel that in such a tolerant tradition, individual expressive energies are in fact what combine to *make* culture. The concept of dialogue within a tradition *itself* constituting the tradition began to stir for me.

It is difficult to convey in a short paper the richly individualistic nature of Ju/'hoan oral tradition (however, see Biesele 1993, 1996, 1999a, 1999b). At first in the field I was overwhelmed by this richness and, at times, apparent contradiction. There were as many ways to tell a tale as there were taletellers, and yet I never heard a listener complain, 'You're not telling it right!', except in jest. All the versions told 'the same' story. But how could this be, in what I had been led to believe was a highly 'conservative' culture? How could such diversity exist in a society that prized equality of individuals perhaps beyond all else? I knew the Ju/'hoansi had social technology for getting along with each other that contained many mechanisms for social levelling and the prevention of self-aggrandizement. How could I square this knowledge with the personal flamboyance I was seeing in storytelling?

To answer this question, I had to scrutinise the perspective from which I was gazing. Part of the answer came from the difference between my scribal world and the then-completely-oral one I was trying to understand. Literate people must really struggle to realise that where verbal speech is both norm and model for communication, two messages may be regarded as 'the same' though they are rarely verbatim equivalents. This equivalence of message explains storytellers' insistence that they are faithfully 'repeating' an old story when they are actually telling it in their own words. Each telling thus reflects the performance situation of the moment *and* participates in the timeless authority of tradition. Concentration on specific wording and phraseology per se is a phenomenon of alphabetic literacy that has long distorted scholars' understanding of communication in oral societies.

I began to study the styles of different storytellers, and to ask myself about the social implications of the wildly varying and often flamboyant differences I was hearing. Despite these differences, however, there was always that nugget of social meaning to be found in these 'same-but-different' tales. All versions of a tale would convey the same indirect social lessons, providing a scaffolding of events for graphic portrayal of moral and immoral behaviour, though they varied widely in style, language, and dramatic detail.

It began to seem that among these people of circumspect social behaviour, expanded expressiveness was flourishing in opposite proportion. In the area of material property ownership, the Ju/'hoansi are fierce levellers. Yet verbal agility is not subject to levelling mechanisms in the same way: it seems individuals may push their creativity in speech much further without risk of censure. As George Steiner has commented, 'certain cultures expend on their vocabularies and syntax acquisitive energies and ostentations entirely lacking in their material lives' (1975: 55).

I think that the enthusiasm with which Ju/'hoansi were continuing to develop, in the 1970s and even into the 1990s, their individualistic storytelling tradition must lead us to an understanding of its importance in the larger scheme of their society. Taken as a whole, the stories of the Ju/'hoansi give one a strong feeling for the sense-and-consensus-making value for them of narrated events. These stories tend to fix positive ambience around all aspects of the social and economic enterprises necessary at any given time. They both state and call forth the attitudes towards the economic arrangements by which people have cooperated to make available resources sustain them. Stories thus play a part in engaging and motivating social energies in desirable ways. Stories of the 'old times' are still stories of today.

Besides that, stories and storytellers are makers of sense. Sense must be made of biological and social life, and consensus based on that sense must be reached concerning the rules by which social activity will gain its end, the perpetuation of society. What is more, social agreement or consensus must be reached not once and forever but repeatedly in the lives of each group and generation in order for life to continue. This is true whether the intervening time has been characterised by great change or has been relatively changeless. The process of incorporating new meaning into understanding is fundamentally the same as the process of reiterating old meaning.

Oral traditions thus maintain both continuity and creativity. They are an ever-renewed source of cognitive and imaginative agreement. This agreement has the most intimate connection with the particular sort of cooperation necessary to a specific form of livelihood in a given environment. The storyteller's art both 'makes sense' repeatedly and anew and provides a framework for remembering survival information.

The classicist Eric Havelock (1963) wrote extensively of a similar mnemonic function performed by epic poetry in pre-alphabetic Greece. Surrounded by a relaxed, enjoyable atmosphere, just as in Ju/'hoan storytelling, performances of epic were important in storing, and recalling for the public, the knowledge and values of the society. Oral storage in what Havelock (1978: 30) calls 'enclaves of contrived speech' such as epic was the preliterate analogue of the permanent storage later cultures accomplished in print. But applying such an analogy overlooks the fact that oral communication is astonishingly different from print, and that it is coterminous with very different modes of social agreement. I have come to see that studying an oral tradition as a whole is a fine entry into the meta-message of how a society comes to social agreements: in the Ju/'hoan case, social agreement coalesced around the message of equality implied in the very lenience of their tradition.

Healers, Storytellers and Traditional Values

Along with my study of Ju/'hoan storytelling I investigated the social sharing of out-of-body experiences by the Ju/'hoan healers. I saw the shared phenomenology of healing discourse as an essential enabling feature for altered-state healing. Less-experienced healers were enabled to dare the 'death' of trance because their fear was lessened by the *Wegweiser* older healers' narratives told them they would see along the way. This investigation led me to the conviction that giving each individual a chance to contribute to the store of 'truth' about that other world as plucked from their own experiences might be a most galvanising factor in the dynamism of Ju/'hoan culture.

Healers' dreams, trances and daytime confrontations with the spirits are regarded by the Ju/'hoansi as reliable channels for the transfer of new meaning from the other world into this one. Though dreams may happen at any time, the central religious experiences of Ju/'hoan life are consciously and, as a matter of course, approached through the avenue of trance. The trance dance involves everyone in the society (however, see Guenther, volume 2 of this publication, on recent professionalisation and commoditisation in this area). Those who enter trance and experience the power of the other world directly bring healing and insight to others, and it is shared impartially through the concept of *n/om*, an undifferentiated psychic power which is believed to increase as it is shared.

There is dynamism and creativity embodied, as well, in the concept of *n/om*: the late experienced healer =Oma Djo of /Kae/kae said 'N/om is just the same as long ago, even though it keeps on changing' (quoted in Katz et al. 1997). Healers like =Oma Djo are known as *n/omkxaosi*, meaning 'owners of medicine' or 'owners of supernatural power'. They mediate to the community not only healing power but also information about how things are in the other world and how people in this world would do best to relate to them. Great attention is given to healers' accounts of what they have experienced, and no one's account of a genuinely altered state is belittled.

The rendering of individual kerygmatic accounts of these experiences into culturally shared images is a highly important process in the religious egalitarianism of the Ju/'hoan. It is an interweaving of tradition and creativity said to keep the society itself alive, so that individuals experience their own lives as contributions to shared reality. But how does idiosyncratic experience enter tradition and stay there? Part of the answer lies in the fact that experience itself is, from an early age, already culturally informed. Initiates have certain experiences in trance because they expect to do so, basing their expectations on other accounts they have heard. A high degree of stereotyping is heard in these verbal accounts of travel beyond the ordinary self, yet Ju/'hoansi treat these experiences as unique messages from the beyond, accessible in no other way save through trance. Narratives of the experiences are regarded as valuable documents to be shared as widely as possible, to multiply the public good. These narratives are 'preconstrained' by tradition but also add to it.

The narratives and anecdotes are a kind of language continually discoursing, through dramatic representation, on valued ideas in the structure of Ju/'hoan social relationships and relationships to the other world. Both kerygmatic accounts and tales, far from codifying a single version of dogma, carry on a sort of dialogue among themselves about what is valued and what is believed. Belief is not enshrined somewhere beyond the tales but is rather within the tales themselves, in the intratextual repartee among them and even in apparent contradiction. The truth is in the repertoire and in the involvement of tellers and listeners with all the variants, much more than in immutable facts or principles.

Ju/'hoan verbal and ritual culture, of course, differ from those of other societies, even other orally communicating societies, along many specific axes. However, studying Ju/'hoan oral tradition in depth can sensitise us to its intimate relationship with the social relations it in part enables, and may suggest useful comparative approaches to the traditions of other cultures. I submit that modes of social agreement, such as tolerance of individualism and ambiguity, that are in evidence in Ju/'hoan verbal culture are key to an understanding of a long-term, workable inclusiveness of their society's members in the loop of decision making and consensus. In particular, the unrestricted nature of the flow of religious knowledge among Ju/'hoansi is constitutive, along with other factors, of their egalitarian social relations.

Conclusion: Converging Agendas

The other side of the coin of tolerance may be, contrary to Western assumptions, effective resistance. NGO (nongovernmental organisation) workers closely involved with the Namibian Ju/'hoan bid for self-determination in the 1990s were startled to learn how uncomfortable many Ju/'hoansi were with the notion of 'representing their communities.' We should, however, have known better. 'Speaking for' another, any kind of undertaking 'for' another, is anathema in Ju/'hoan social life today as it has clearly long been. The theme of resistance to Western 'democratic' models has been repeated many times in the years since the 1986 start of the Ju/wa (Ju/'hoan) Farmers Union (JFU), which became the Nyae Nyae Farmers Cooperative (NNFC) and is now, since 1998, the Nyae Nyae Conservancy(NNC). Ju/'hoan leaders both old and young have systematically tried to shed the accretions and assumptions of office automatically placed on them by Western models. They have beggared themselves trying to self-level. They have tried leadership by committee in an effort to dispel the aura of authority which, judging by the bouts of illness and depression many have fought, profoundly disturbs them. In the last analysis their unwillingness to speak for anyone but themselves amounts to a gigantic resistance to an imported and unwelcome form of sociability. They prefer to tell their own oral histories, and to use them in creating their own authentic futures.

One anecdote may aid our understanding. When Kxao Moses =Oma, who spoke the words about representation at the beginning of this paper, had become Manager of the Nyae Nyae Conservancy, he had the opportunity to travel to Copenhagen. He and a Ju/'hoan student teacher, =Oma G/aq'o, attended a conference there on Indigenous Peoples in Africa (1993). Both gave papers that were later printed in the conference proceedings, titled 'Never Drink from the Same Cup', published as IWGIA Document 74. When Kxao returned to Nyae Nyae, he was asked whether he would travel around to the Nyae Nyae villages to tell the story of his trip. He responded that it might take him years to tell this story to the community, because he could only tell a little bit at a time – otherwise people would think he was bragging, and would criticise him, so the learning that could come from the trip would be lost.

This care shows the persistence, in spite of changing values and changing times, of a powerful egalitarian ethic. Kxao is a member of a new generation of San leaders, a person who has had to balance the benefits he receives from his education and his new position with his desire to remain within, and effectively lead within, his own community. 'I would like to point out,' he said in Denmark, 'that despite all the problems (at home) I am not at all interested in leaving Bushmanland: I was born (t)here, and I am prepared to do my share to make things work again' (=Oma 1993: 155).

Personality and social style have close relationships to egalitarian and other values: this truism is made vivid by an examination of verbal culture. The values embraced, as well as the values rejected, by individuals in egalitarian culture will in the long run determine their relationship to a wider world for which such attitudes may be a surprise. The way these values are embodied and communicated in such a society gives profound importance to understanding Havelock's 'enclaves of contrived speech'. In the Ju/'hoan case, the fluid, endlessly varying form of narratives and reports can be seen as a fabulous reflecting mirror of a great theme of their culture--the theme of equality and fairness to each individual, and of the harm that can come from violating that understanding.

Here, however, is the twist on what Westerners may think we understand about 'individuality'. Since Ju/'hoansi allow many degrees of latitude in expressing 'the same' story, the differences among individual raconteurs are experienced by their listeners as *not being in competition with each other*. No matter how flamboyant the storytellers' language and imagery, their lenient storytelling rules find a way of containing what might otherwise emerge as self-aggrandisement. In this context, individualism can be celebrated without becoming divisive. Over the course of years of working with Ju/'hoan stories and political speeches, I came to see that social agreement as mediated orally is a much more complex combination of individual understandings of the world than I had imagined at the outset. In an expressive tradition, engagement of personal expressiveness is inseparable from communal commitment to ideas, beliefs and courses of social action.

In conclusion, I feel it reasonable to agree with Guenther and others that the diverse social formations in the current San repertoire bear close relationship to the theme of the foraging band and its mental habits, which are persistent, and with reason. As cultural historian Morris Berman writes, politics in egalitarian societies 'is in fact about mastery, but not in the coercive sense of the term. What we are witnessing is political genius, even if it has proven to be very fragile'(2000: 61). Opening our minds to an analysis of the communicative culture of San and other foragers and postforagers can reveal promising convergent agendas between more or less egalitarian peoples and the global society of which they are increasingly a part. William Ury (*Getting to Yes*) has argued recently (personal communication) that Ju/'hoan consensus processes may fruitfully be studied by Western organisations for clues to more workable decision making. I in turn argue that, given enough time, the observed 'fragility' of San political stances towards outside pressures could in future circumstances be turned to their advantage. The limiting factor of course is resource depletion over time, but that factor limits every society on the planet. It is the chief reason agendas may in the end *have* to converge.

References

=Oma, Kxao M. 1993. 'Never drink from the same cup'. International Work Group for Indigenous Affairs, Copenhagen, Denmark. Document 74.

Berman, M. 2000. *Wandering God: A Study in Nomadic Spirituality*. Albany, NY: State University of New York Press.

Biesele, M. 1976. 'Aspects of !Kung folklore'. In: *Kalahari Hunter-Gatherers*, ed. R. Lee and I. DeVore. Cambridge, Mass.: Harvard University Press.

—— 1978. 'Sapience and Scarce Resources: Communication Systems of the !Kung and Other Foragers'. Paris: Social Science Information, 17: 6.
—— 1993. *'Women Like Meat': The Folklore and Foraging Ideology of the Kalahari Ju/'hoan*. Bloomington, IN and Johannesburg: Indiana University Press and Witwatersrand University Press.
—— 1996. ' "He stealthily lightened at his brother-in-law" (and thunder echoes in Bushman Oral Tradition a Century Later)'. In: *Voices from the Past: Bleek and Lloyd 1870–1991*. eds, J. Deacon and T. Dowson. Johannesburg: Witwatersrand University Press.
—— 1999a. 'Ju/'hoan Folktales and Storytelling: Context and Variability'. In: *Traditional Storytelling Today*, ed. M.R. MacDonald. London and Chicago: Fitzroy-Dearborn.
—— 1999b. ' "Different people just have different minds": a Personal Attempt to Understand Ju/'hoan Storytelling Aesthetics'. In *Oral Literature and Performance in Southern Africa*, ed. D. Brown. Oxford: James Currey; Cape Town: David Philip; and Columbus, OH: Ohio University Press.
Guenther, M. 1999. *Tricksters and Trancers: Bushman Religion and Society*. Bloomington, IN: Indiana University Press.
Havelock, E. 1963. *Preface to Plato*. Cambridge, Mass.: Harvard University Press.
—— 1978 The Greek Concept of Justice. Cambridge, MA: Harvard University Press.
Katz, R., M. Biesele and V. St. Denis. 1997. *'Healing Makes Our Hearts Happy': Spirituality and Transformation among the Ju/'hoansi of the Kalahari*. Rochester, VT: Inner Traditions International.
Lee, R. 1969. 'Eating Christmas in the Kalahari,' *Natural History* (December), pp. 14–22, 60–63.
Marshall, L. 1999. *Nyae Nyae !Kung Beliefs and Rites*. Cambridge, Mass.: Peabody Museum Press.
Silberbauer, G. 1978. 'Political Process in G/wi Bands'. Paper presented at the First International Conference on Hunting and Gathering Societies, Paris.
Steiner, G. 1975. *After Babel: Aspects of Language and Translation*. Oxford: Oxford University Press.
Theobald, R. 1972. *Habit and Habitat*. Englewood Cliffs, NJ: Prentice-Hall.
Turner, T. 1993. 'The Role of Indigenous Peoples in the Environmental Crisis: the Example of the Kayapo of the Brazilian Amazon', *Perspectives in Biology and Medicine*, 36, 3 (Spring).
Ury, W.L. (AK Roger Fisher). 1981. *Getting to Yes: Negotiating Agreement Without Giving In*. Boston.
—— 1995. In Practice: Conflict Resolution among the Bushmen: Lessons in Dispute Systems Design', *Negotiation Journal*, October, pp. 379–389.
Woodburn, J. 1988. 'African Hunter-gatherer Social Organization: is It Best Understood as a Product of Encapsulation?' In: *Hunters and Gatherers, vol I: History, Evolution, and Social Change*, eds T. Ingold, D. Riches and J. Woodburn. Oxford: Berg.

12

The Property of Sharing: Western Analytical Notions, Nayaka Contexts[1]

Nurit Bird-David

Late evening; already pitch dark. Dogs bark in the distance, announcing the return of the hunters. Children run towards them in excitement, waiting for their arrival at the edge of the hamlet. Indifferent to the commotion, their parents remain at their respective hearths. The hunters lay a dead deer on the ground amidst the huts, and send the children to bring from each hearth a metal pot, a plate, or just a large plantain leaf. The assorted objects are placed around the carcass, next to each other. The children grow excited, and the butchering begins. The meat is cut into small chunks. The children take an active part, here clutching a torch, there a limb to ease the butchering. Chunks of meat slowly pile up: the innards on one side, and the mounds of flesh on the deer's skin. The chunks from both piles are then divided among the various vessels, to the ceaseless, joyous commentary of the children. The young audience keep suggesting and directing the hunters to place this bit here, and that bit there. The hunters tease them, playing hesitant, putting a chunk in this pot ... but no! at the last moment withdrawing it and placing it on another, and so on; all with playful exaggerated gestures. At last the job is done, and the children carry the portions to the respective hearths. The families cook the meat immediately, and eat it, even those who already had their evening meal.

Ethnographers customarily captioned scenes like this specific one from the Nayaka of South India[2] as 'sharing', regarding it, in James Woodburn's words, as

> a much-stressed characteristic of many hunter-gatherer societies. The hunter-gatherers themselves stress it and so do anthropologists. They and we are right to do so. Unquestionably sharing is of central importance in the operation of these societies. (Woodburn 1998: 48)

Sharing is a key notion in 'hunter-gatherer'[3] ethnography, and its interpretation has changed over the past fifty years. The perspective favoured in the 1960s saw here a giving away of meat, which otherwise would be wasted, wrongly premising that these peoples did not know how to preserve meat.[4] The predominant view of the 1970s, in Marshall Sahlins's terms (1972), summed it up as an instance of 'generalized reciprocity', namely, a giving away of meat out of an innate generous disposition or enforced by social norms, expecting generally an unspecified return. Subsequent ethnographic critiques – that generosity is not often stressed in these societies; that frequently shares are not generously offered but are demanded and nagged for; that meat is given to everybody, including those who never or almost never can reciprocate; and meat yields do not balance out, and, even if they did, donation does not establish greater rights over future yields[5] – triggered a shift in the 1980s to another perspective relating 'sharing' to rights over property. Game, in one view (Ingold 1986; Lee 1988), is common property: particular hunters obtain the meat, but each person in the group is entitled to his or her share in it. According to another view (Barnard and Woodburn 1988; Woodburn 1998), game belongs to the hunter through whose labour it has been obtained. But an egalitarian ideology enforces its being shared; all members of the group are entitled to shares not as common owners but as political equals, in a system set out to limit inequalities. Lastly, a 1990s view (see Bird-David 1990; 1992a) took into account perceptions of the environment, suggesting that in the local perception the environment gives food to people, as parents give to children,[6] who therefore share it.

The concept of 'sharing' itself has rarely been reflected on, throughout these waves of interpretations. Exceptionally, Ingold in 1986 distinguished 'sharing in' from 'sharing out', in associating these respectively with reciprocal and distributive transactions, or common access and division.[7] More recently Woodburn cautioned: 'A particular difficulty in dealing with this topic is that our preconceptions badly obstruct our understanding of it' (Woodburn 1998: 61). He warned in particular that 'Certainly, the Hadza or !Kung sharing does not map neatly on to English sharing' (Woodburn 1998: 234, fn 5). Woodburn did not pursue this critical, insightful note, assuming a bias no worse than common and acceptable in anthropology, and directing his effort to developing the proprietary perspective, namely examining local phenomena through the prism of the Western concept of 'property'.

The present paper is an attempt to follow the critical direction Woodburn pointed to, paying attention with Ingold to senses of 'sharing' that we inadvertently read into hunter-gatherers' cultures. First, the paper examines at some length the web of our bourgeois[8] senses in which 'sharing' is grasped, along with, more briefly, several key concepts in our analytical language to which it is tethered, including 'property', 'individual', 'labour' and 'equality'. Turning to the Nayaka ethnography, supported by brief comparative references, the paper then explores Nayaka's own ideational contexts and readings, against the backcloth of narratives we read into their doings from the proprietary perspective. In revisiting what is called the 'sharing of large game animals', I offer an interpretation which complements the proprietary one. This interpretation amends and develops my own work of the 1990s, which studied indigenous structures of meanings, but did not consider nearly enough the peculiarities of our own.

Note that the confrontational positioning of one view 'against' another – that is, 'hunter-gatherers' versus 'Western (or 'our') – is only a heuristic device, applied for a better penetration of what in actuality is a far less dichotomous ontology. Both labels are gross analytical abstractions, inadequate as descriptive representations of a complex changing world, but useful enough as conventional terms (or symbols) in which to talk about it. On the one hand, ideas discussed in relation to 'hunter-gatherers' flourish on the margins of mainstream modernity, under the broad umbrella of what is crudely glossed as 'Western culture' (in ideas of Romanticism, New-Age, Critical Theory, etc.). On the other hand, 'hunter-gatherers' have a manifold view, not reduced to these ideas (which, however, embody core authoritative ways of knowing and acting in the world), which 'hunter-gatherers' try keeping as best they can even when forced to accommodate themselves to changing circumstances.

Our Analytical Language

'Sharing' absorbs a range of concrete actions for each of which Nayaka have their own word, for example, to give (kodu), to receive (e:su), to distribute (ba:gama:du), to beg (eri), and so on. They have no word, to the best of my knowledge, corresponding neatly to 'sharing'. This English word comes from the Old English scearu, meaning 'cutting' or 'division'. Of the several contemporary meanings defined by the Oxford English Dictionary, one is 'the part or portion (of something) which is allotted or belongs to an individual, when a distribution is made among a number'. Or, as a verb, 'to divide (what one has or receives) into portions, and give shares to others as well as oneself'. Another meaning is 'a part taken in (an action, experience, etc.)', or, as a verb, 'to receive, possess, or occupy together with others', 'to perform, enjoy, or suffer in common with others'. A school dictionary sharpens the difference: in the first case, the Collins School Dictionary explains, 'if you share something out, you distribute it equally among a group of people', and in the second, 'if two people share something, they both use it, do it, or have it'.

These two meanings are almost diametrically opposed. The first stresses a division of things between individuals, the second the joining of individuals in common action, experience, or usage. The thing is in focus in the first, the subject in the second. In both cases a plurality is involved, at the very least two persons. But in the first case these 'many' keep separate in dividing the 'one' thing into 'many' parts, one for each of them. In the second, they join in using the same 'one' thing together. They reproduce their separateness in the first case, and affirm and regenerate their closeness in the second.

A sense of division colours the usage of 'sharing' in contemporary economic discourse, diverting attention from the sharers' relations, or rather the lack thereof. This is epitomised clearly, going to the opposite extreme, in selling 'shares' as a commodity in the capitalist market to 'share-holders', who may be complete strangers, even from different countries, otherwise with nothing in common. More striking still is 'time-sharing', as a notion and an institution, referring to synchronised, separate use of the same property (e.g., a holiday apartment) by persons who normally never meet each other; each uses the same property exclusively in a predetermined part of the year. In spiritual and psychological discourse, at the same time, 'sharing' predominantly connotes joining, and furthermore, transcending the modern predicament of life alone as an individual. The sharers of prayers, feelings, secrets and so on enjoy what they construct as a special elated state of togetherness, a Durkheimian sacred sense of society. Both these connotations should be borne in mind when we turn to what we gloss as 'sharing' in hunter-gatherers' cultures. Part of the argument below is that in framing scenes like the specific one above as an economic event, the division of meat receives the analytic highlight, eclipsing from sight the vitality of the joint experience. But the use of 'sharing', notably, still plays implicitly on bourgeois emotional chords, casting 'hunter-gatherers' as a yearned-for 'communitas'.

What is shared equally influences the sense in which the ambivalent[9] 'sharing' is read. A dividable object, like money, apples or clothing – or, for that matter, meat – normally cues reading 'sharing' primarily as a division. 'They share the money', for example, usually means its division among the sharers. A subject, on the other hand, invites reading 'having together'. 'They share a child', for instance, normally connotes not the child's division but the fact that they have the same child.[10] Notably, to share immaterial entities (thoughts, happiness, secrets, fears) is to share these 'with' someone else, while to share an indivisible thing leaves scope for reading 'sharing' either way or both. 'To share a book', say, is to read the same book (not divide the pages); 'to share a room' means, depending on what is emphasised, living together and/or splitting rent and room-space. Part of my argument below is that 'seeing' game as divisible meat, in neglect of hunter-gatherers' regarding it also as a sentient being, skews the reading of what goes on in 'the sharing of the large game animal' scene.

'Sharing' is caught in a web of other bourgeois senses, consistent with and pitted against each other. First is the peculiar Western view of persons as moral individuals, each (in Geertz's oft-quoted words), 'a single entity', 'bounded and integrated, and set contrastingly against other such wholes and against a natural and social background...' (Geertz, cited in Strathern 1988: 57). Such 'individuals', discrete and separate, each alone in the centre of his world, conscious of his individuality, 'share' in the divisive sense of the word. They divide one thing into separate parts, and each takes a separate share. Conversely – reflecting by reversal their everyday sense of separate individuality – such moral individuals experience joint sociality as an exceptional transcendence of their existential aloneness, a kind of 'communitas' (in Turner's sense). Embedded in the argument below is the thesis (explored at length elsewhere[11]) that Nayaka see people as 'given' in the plural, constitutive of and inseparable from multiple relations, while the English 'sharing' premises the modern view of people 'given' in the singular.

'Sharing' is pitted against a dichotomous separation of the world into such individuals: the subjects versus the objects. A sharer/shared relation is commonly 'seen' as a subject/object one. The 'shared' is cast as 'property', the 'sharers' as proprietors with rights over it. The shared, then, is readily denied a subjectivity, and inter-subjective relations with the 'sharer'. By such logic pushed to extremes, even a 'shared child' can be construed as something over which control is fought for, and even concluded in court. To ask a child her wishes is not presumed but negotiated, if at all (on whether, when, and for what). Little wonder that a shared large game-animal is so readily abstracted as a 'property', further banishing from attention its manifold regard by hunter-gatherers also as a volitional sentient being.

'Sharing' in its divisive sense is inextricably associated with 'property', a key modern Western notion, the development of which was associated by nineteenth-century evolutionism with that of modern law, the state and class-society. Of the several meanings defined by the Oxford English Dictionary, 'property' has been employed by anthropologists as 'that which one owns; a possession... (one's) wealth or goods' (OED), reflecting the nineteenth century legal and economic preoccupations. In everyday spoken English 'property' commonly refers to land and buildings in particular. 'Property', notably, has more than one meaning too. Another sense is 'an attribute or a quality belonging to a thing or a person' (OED). If in the first case 'property' is separable and alienable from its holder, in the second case it is nondetachable; it cannot have a separate existence from the thing or person it belongs to.

Anthropologists first approached 'property' as a relation between a particular thing and a particular person (or group), and later as a socially recognised relation between particular persons (or groups) regarding a given thing.[12] But either way, 'property' stands against the modern Western premise that everything, things as well as persons, are 'given' as separate, and from their separate state they 'then' enter into relations. Perceived are 'this' given thing (marked from others) and 'that' given person (marked from others), between which a property-relation 'then' is claimed and recognised. The 'relation', notably, is logical more than concrete,[13] classificatory more than performative. The particular person and the particular thing are 'gathered' in the 'mind'. In actual lived reality, they can be far apart. For example, going to the extreme, one inherits a house from a distant uncle who lived on another continent, or purchases a house for investment abroad. Property rights primarily dwell in a jural sphere; concrete next-ness or with-ness (e.g., living within a house, daily working with a tool) is not a necessary condition, while it can be a sufficient one in circumstances carefully circumscribed by law (such as tied tenancy). Part of the argument below is that a far more performative sense of property applies in the Nayaka case. The Nayaka sense of what we call 'property' is closer to the second than to the first of the meanings mentioned.

The notion of 'work' is closely associated with 'property', from a Western perspective that often universalises it. 'A 'sweat equity', states The Dictionary of Anthropology,

> is a nearly universal folk principle of property. If a jural unit has put work into creating something, the 'ownership' of that something is attached to those who did the work. (Barfield 1997: 379)

Barnard and Woodburn explicitly take this view, using 'labour' for 'work':

> All societies operate implicitly or explicitly on the principle that whatever I, as an individual, obtain from nature or make by myself, using my own labour is residually recognised as in some sense my property, that is, it is mine unless some other explicit principle overrides this basic one and the yield of my labour is alienated from me. (Barnard and Woodburn 1988: 24)

'Labour,' which is a key notion in our analytical language, not less than 'individual', 'nature' and 'property', abstracts and reifies physical endeavour from the broad context of work experience, for example, the sociality of those working. But in nonindustrial societies what we call 'work' is commonly embedded in other facets of life, to the extent that in some cultures there is no separate word for it (Applebaum 1984: 3–8; Applebaum 1997: 497). Coming from the Latin labor, meaning 'toil, exertion, trouble, suffering' (OED), in anthropological usage the term often refers to the 'physical exertion directed to the supply of the material wants of the community' (OED). In this sense, 'labour' connotes a subject producing an object, clearly premising a subject/object dichotomy. It refers to a process resulting in the 'transformation' of one thing into another, commonly things in the environment into something for human use, premising a sort of nature/society divide.

'Labour' secondly also means 'the physiological processes which lead up to birth' (OED). Barnard and Woodburn noted this duality of meaning, reading it as an extension of the idea that work yields rights of property. In their words:

> The same ideology may be mobilized to define rights over people. In English, we call the physiological processes which lead up to birth 'labour,' perhaps partly in order to define a mother's rights over her children. More generally the labour of carrying a child in pregnancy, of giving birth to it, of suckling it and nurturing it after birth, identify the child with its mother and give her rights over it. (Barnard and Woodburn 1988: 24)

More apparent than continuity is the same kind of diametrical opposition, noted above regarding the previous notions. If 'labour' in the first case connotes a subject producing an object, in the second case it connotes a subject producing another (note the twofold use of 'produce'). In the first case, the subject operates on the outside world, heroically transforming his environment for his use. In the second, she brings forth a subject into a relation. Historically, notably, the second sense precedes the first one; Barnard and Woodburn naturalise the modern idea of property, in a typically Western way, by 'seeing' its expression in the mother-child's case. True, 'the labour of carrying a child in pregnancy, of giving birth to it, of suckling it and nurturing it after birth, identify the child with its mother and give her rights over it', but these are not necessarily proprietary rights. This 'labour' constitutes the child primarily as hers – and she at the same time as his – in a social, historical, and emotional sense, rather than in the proprietary, legalistic one. His identity is inextricably linked to hers. He belongs to her – and she to him – owing to a history of joined lives, of being-together, which entangle their identities. Part of my argument is that in this latter sense 'labour' is a term 'good to think with' about the Nayaka sense of property, more than in the sense in which it is commonly used in hunter-gatherer studies.

Lastly, 'egalitarianism' is closely entangled with the previous notions, not least in Woodburn's proprietary perspective, which sees 'egalitarianism' as the overriding explicit principle forcing the hunter to give away the meat which is his. Carefully, Woodburn noted that it derives from 'egality,' which itself

> was introduced into English with its present meaning ... to suggest politically assertive equality of the French variety. Even today 'egalitarianism' carries with it echoes of revolution, of fervor for equality in opposition to elaborate structures of inequality. (Woodburn 1982: 431)

Egalitarianism in this sense is set against a perception of society as constitutive of separate, discrete (moral) individuals, whose lot or situation can be measured, rated and compared. It is to do with an evaluation 'in the mind' of qualities and performances, not with their diversity as such (Beteille 1977). Inequality or its absence is apparent to an essentialising gaze, assessing individuals by a preselected parameter (wealth, power, status, occupation, income). Part of my argument below is that 'sharing' involves a process of levelling, as Woodburn argued, yet moved not by an egalitarian ideology but by the force of kinship ties, by relations more than just comparisons.

The English concept of 'sharing' is ambivalent, and, furthermore, is caught in a web of other Western concepts, foreign to hunter-gatherer cultures. Notwithstanding the contribution of analyses in these terms, there is room for a complementary analysis sensitive to local concepts, inasmuch as can be sensed and conveyed in English, the language in which it is written.[14] Such an analysis, it cannot be stressed enough, purports not to record how Nayaka ethnographically analyse this scene (*they* don't) or to map the landscape of ideas in their mind (*we* can't). The attempt is simply to loosen the Western tether, and bring to bear the indigenous reference points and ontology. I undertake such an analysis in the next section.

Nayaka Contexts

The proprietary perspective reads several propositions into the hunter-gatherers' 'sharing of large game animal' scene, conveniently structuring an examination of the indigenous contexts. Five short assertions are explored below, one by one, drawing primarily on Nayaka ethnography (based on fieldwork in 1978–79 and follow-up visits in 1989 and 2001). Nayaka illustrate the working of a set of structures, which can be seen as variants on themes broadly shared by 'hunter-gatherers', especially those characterised by an 'immediate return system' (Woodburn 1980).

(i) The Game-Animal is in Nature, an Ungarnered Resource

'Nature' ill describes Nayaka senses of their environment; animals in their regard are far more than just a resource. The Nayaka forest (*katu*) is not 'Nature', in the stereotype modern Western senses of the term. Suffice it to bear in mind the very small camp or hamlet,[15] comprising two or three huts, barely marked off from their surroundings, to realise how irrelevant is the modern Western dichotomy 'nature: society', or 'nature: culture' in this case. There are no physical boundaries to separate the settlement off from its surroundings (see Bird-David 1990). Everyday domestic and personal life routinely carries people outside the hamlet, across bourgeois-imagined boundaries. For example: bathing, defecating, bringing water, fetching firewood, enjoying sexual intercourse in privacy, let alone foraging pursuits. Generally, the surroundings are not abstracted as a single unit, or a grand mechanical system, or a store of goods for extraction. They are not perceived as a detached, objective Nature: an opponent to be conquered; a force to be tamed in the service of mankind; a complex physicality to be known by dissecting it into small parts.

An important facet of Nayaka manifold perception of their environment is seeing it rather as an assembly of sentient beings, overriding our subject/object divide (Bird-David 1992a). Knowing the environment is entangled with this view, perfecting a relational epistemology, focused on and rooted in mutual relatedness between knower and known (Bird-David 1999a). This knowing is embedded in a continuous engagement, inseparably utilitarian and spiritual at once. Even though it no longer envelops Nayaka habitats as it did in the 1970s, shrinking rapidly as result of intensified felling in the 1990s, the forest for Nayaka is a parental relation, a home (Bird-David 1990). They regard themselves as people of the forest, and in some cases even its children. They talk and listen to its manifold beings. Their sense of themselves, their history and identity are tied to the forest, as is the case in some other tropical forest groups, for example, Mbuti and Batek (see in Bird-David 1992a). Australian Aborigines and North and South American groups, in a partially similar manner, treat their country and land as sentient beings, providing and needing care (see Ingold 2000).

Animals particularly are regarded intentional beings, as and when engaged with. Nayaka are attentive to their moves and moods. In local views, they are given as food by supernatural beings, or give themselves as food, or even give food. Honey-hunters more than animal-hunters, Nayaka often share fresh game with forest predators, notably wild dogs (*Cuon alpinus*).

Richer examples come from people who identify themselves as 'hunters'. Cree, for example, see the animals they hunt as sexual partners to be wooed and charmed until they 'give in'. Their 'killing' is perceived not just as taking life but inseparably as a merger of man and beast, ensuring the future reproduction of both humans and animals (see, for example, Tanner 1979; see comparative discussion in Bird-David 1993).

(ii) The Hunter Expends Energy and Skill, Hunting the Deer. The Game is the Produce of his Labour

Hunting is a manifold experience to many 'hunter-gatherers', far more than what may be gauged by this one-dimensional economistic perspective on it. True, it involves energy and skill, patience and cunning, even in Nayaka's modest hunting pursuits. But in the local perception these are not abstracted from the broader context of experience. Moving in the forest, Nayaka are consciously attentive to happenings involving and surrounding them: the rustle of dry leaves underfoot, the flapping wings of birds hastily flying off, the crack of bamboo canes striking each other, the bird-like shouts of fellow-hunters disappearing from sight around a corner. Each hunt, and for that matter any other move from place to place in the forest, instigates cumulative interactions and responses. These waves of relatedness the hunters register, and recount when they are back in the hamlet, more than each one's individual-bounded inner sensation of muscle-effort, energy spent, exhaustion, or other bodily signals of toil.

Hunting and gathering constitute no mere 'subsistence pursuits', as framed by the orthodox cultural-ecological analysis, a priori classing these groups, and naming the class in reference to an economic 'foraging mode of subsistence'. A 'total social fact' in Mauss's terms, each trip inside the forest is a social occasion, a religious pursuit, a study, a recreation, an adventure, as well as a means of producing food. Hunts occasion intensive social engagement with both fellow-people and nonhuman[16] neighbours, with whom close relations are regenerated this way. In other groups of 'hunter-gatherers', the Mbuti, for example, 'the moment of killing [is] a moment of intense compassion and reference' (Turnbull 1976 (1965) p.161). 'Between casts of the net, the hunters regroup ... to share tobacco or snacks of fruit and nuts gathered along the way ... to flirt and visit, to play with babies' (Hart 1978: 337). Forced to adopt other occupations, whether working for a casual wage, cultivating land, or notably, in North America, pursuing office careers, people who perceive themselves as 'hunters' return to 'foraging' now and then, in order to 'keep in touch' with the environment (Bird-David 1992b). A striking example is northern American 'hunters' who fly each season from city offices to their traditional hunting territories to participate in the hunt. 'Hunters' (in *this* sense, the category still does apply) care about the activity in and for itself, as much as they care about its produce, as part of a total way of relating with the environment (Bird-David 1992a: 30–31).

The game itself is more than just the 'produce' of the hunters' 'labour'. This is 'real' food, and it inseparably nourishes not only their stomachs but their sense of identity. True, it is tasty to the Nayaka palate, and a special variant on the staple mash of yam, and increasingly rice. But no less important, as any forest food, it is an embodiment of forest-*feeding*, a concrete manifestation of forest-*caring*, a tangible reassurance that the forest is a provisioning home. No meat purchasable in shops, as available, for instance, to some northern 'hunters' living and working in the developed North, can fully substitute for game.

The involvement of Nayaka children in the distribution of meat amplifies the dimension of caring in the 'sharing' of a large game-animal.[17] Caring is associated in Nayaka culture with a parent–child relation, and is talked about in its terms. Requesting the help of animistic beings to heal illnesses, for example, Nayaka approach them as 'big parents', and themselves as 'us, the children' (Bird-David 1999a). Conversely, Nayaka promise to look after the former in return. Children are involved in the sharing of large game animals also in other hunter-gatherer societies, for instance, Batek (Lye Tuck-Po, personal communication), and Inupiat (Barbara Bodernhorn, personal communication). Cree handle the meat itself as a child: the hunters pass the carcass to the women; the carcass is shown great care; none of it is thrown away or wasted; the feast in which the meat is distributed is similar to a feast held after the birth of a baby (Tanner 1979: 153, 163).

(iii) The Game is the Hunter's Property[18]

This legal notion applies in a very limited sense, if at all, to the very small community of close relatives who live together. Generally, Nayaka associate all things with particular persons, commonly noting, for example, who found, or made, or purchased, or gave each thing in their household. Their primary attention, it should be stressed, goes not to who 'produced' it, namely transformed its essence from a thing in nature to a thing of society, or from one thing into something else. Their primary concern lies with *who* brought each thing into their social world, from another network of connections into their own. Things in Nayaka perception, it is possible to say, generally do not exist unattached in-and-for-themselves, just as, say, unattached 'relatives' do not exist. Just as each person joining the community is born to someone, or is from somewhere, so is each thing. Take a knife: in Nayaka ontology there seem to be no pregiven neutral knives, one of which a person makes his own. Just as there are no pregiven free-floating 'brothers', one of whom to make one's own. Each knife has its personal connections, having been given by X, or purchased by Y, or made by Z, and so on. The distinction between 'giving', 'making', 'purchasing', etc., is of secondary importance. The human connection is centrally in focus.

A person–thing association does not exclude the use of a thing by other persons. But just as parental connections are still remembered when one marries and lives 'with' another, so a thing is still associated with the person who 'delivered' it (made it, gave it, picked it up, purchased it, or whatever). User and 'deliverer' often count it respectively as theirs, in the first case mentioning whom they received it from, and in the second whom they gave it to. Interchangeably, *nama* (our) is also a common way of referring to such a thing. This 'property system', if property it can be called, does not entail a zero-sum game situation wherein a knife is either 'mine' or 'yours'. Just as a person can be associated with a plurality of relatives so can a thing be associated with a plurality of persons. Indeed, it is precisely its co-use which brings into focus the users' joint living, highlighting their association and cooperation. For only joined people can use the same knife; co-using it is one of the ways by which their joined living is expressed. A thing which is co-used, it should be stressed, even when deemed nama (ours), is not owned 'collectively' by them. This assertion predicates a new meta-entity, a reified 'group', foreign to Nayaka thinking. Such a thing is simply used-by-X-and-used-by-Y, a concrete situation seen as an inseparable whole, stressing the next-ness of the users.

This 'property system', additionally, is performative more than categorical. Belonging is *born* of concrete use rather than allowing it. It is a fluid state which can alter from moment to moment. Nayaka, for this reason, chose to stress who bought, found or made a thing. *This* aspect is factual, clear-cut, and stable; *whose* a thing is, is not always as easy to say, as it dynamically fluctuates in time. A sense of personal possessions is commonly reported for hunter-gatherers, requiring examining whether it is in a performative or categorical sense, whether stating retrospectively who brought it, or prescribing prospectively who can control its use.

Game is the hunter's 'property' only in this limited sense, epitomising, if anything, this principle. It is associated with the hunter not as the one who laboured to transform this previously ungarnered resource into edible meat, but as the one who brought it. As the meat is co-eaten by everyone in the hamlet, it is connected with them too, reflecting and regenerating their joint life and closeness. They share eating the meat because they are close, and the shared eating regenerates their closeness. In a broader view, the game is still associated with the nonhuman beings who gave it (in the local view), as well as with the hunter who brought it to the hamlet. Its shared eating expresses and regenerates simultaneously a sense of connections with them, too. Eating the meat brings to consciousness a sense of belonging to a trans-species ecological community, comprising both human and nonhuman neighbours.

(iv) The Hunter is forced to give the Meat, which is His, by an Overriding Principle of Egalitarianism

Just as 'generosity' is not explicitly expressed by Nayaka, neither is 'egalitarianism'. As mentioned, 'egalitarianism' predicates a comparison of people, which in turn predicates perceiving them as moral individuals, each by himself. Nayaka do not primarily perceive a hamlet's residents in this way, which is not surprising given that the Nayaka with whom I worked live in very small communities, less than 25 men, women, and children in each of the hamlets studied in 1979, conforming with the hunter-gatherers' 'magic number' (Lee and DeVore 1968). The residents of such a hamlet are closely related; its core is commonly siblings with their spouses and children, who when living together are referred to as *kudumba*. A hamlet's residents refer to themselves as *kudumba*, even if they are not all related in this way. Nayaka 'see' primarily a *kudumba* where, with our Western Modernist attentiveness to 'moral individuals', *we* would 'see' primarily discrete individuals, even here, where in concrete lived-reality people are physically very close to each other, leading their everyday lives *in* constant engagement, often from birth.

Indeed, as clearly evident in the opening scene, *families (not individuals)* receive shares of meat via the children. Each family is apportioned some meat, which it distributes among its members. Visitors who stay in the hamlet usually receive meat from the families they stay with. The involvement of children in the distribution of meat – linked above with caring – also helps to frame it as a familial event. Generally, among hunter-gatherers the meat of large game animals is distributed along kinship links in 'waves of sharing' (as Marshall described it). While eventually everyone receives meat, the recipients receive their shares as not equal citizens but as relatives, through networks of kinship ties. 'Sharing', in this sense, is not as similar to redistributive taxation in Western society as in other senses may appear (Woodburn 1982: 441–2 Barnard and Woodburn 1988: 25).

Levelling is involved, as stressed by Woodburn, but another kind of levelling, not induced by an egalitarian ideology. To pinpoint the difference, let me use an analogy. In the first case, imagine a series of vessels, independent each of the other, into each of which liquid is poured such that each receives an equal share. Only to the extent that they are similar will the vessels be filled to the same level. In the second case, imagine connected vessels: according to the so-called 'law of connected vessels', should liquid be poured into any one of them, it will flow from one to another until it fills them all to the same level. The vessels themselves need not be the same; they can be big and small, wide and narrow, made of this or that material. Without an intentional intervening design, the levelling is attained because they are *connected*. The first image illustrates levelling of Woodburn's 'assertive egalitarianism' kind; the second illustrates another kind, which I would call 'relational levelling'. What is given to one person overflows to the others because people are connected – or rather pick up and primarily regard the fact of their connectedness. Nayaka explicitly express this kind of levelling, which associates giving things not with equality but connections. When relating an instance of giving, for example, a donor would typically say something like 'What can I do, he is my brother', not 'He is my equal'. He would specify the relevant kinship link (sister, nephew, uncle, etc.), or occasionally, a joint domesticity,[19] for instance, 'What can I do, he [the recipient] lives with us'.

Relational levelling reaches its ultimate in the sharing of large game animals, explaining further its great importance to hunter-gatherers. When a Nayaka, say, obtains three knives, two he would give to others. Three Nayaka then would have one knife each; the knives are levelled out, but there remain others without knives, so the knives would continue flowing from those 'with' to those 'without'. In the case of small game, it can be cut small and distributed to everyone. However, there is too little meat to give each an adequate serving. The big game animal is large and divisible, providing enough meat for decent servings to go by 'waves of sharing' to the community, stressing thereby the connectedness of everyone. The sharing of large game has the anti-unequal effect which Woodburn describes, yet not because of an abstract idea about a logical situation of sameness between individuals but because of their connections.

(v) The Game is divided into Shares

The division of meat commands our attention. The butchering is an exotic, even gory sight for bourgeois spectators, used to purchasing precut (if not prepacked) meat in stores. When we describe what happens as 'sharing meat', because the meat is eminently a divisible object to us, we are further inclined to focus on its division rather than its joint eating. This intuitive reading hides from view what Nayaka primarily attend to, namely, *eating* the meat together, for which its butchering and distribution are essential and inseparable preparations. Reflecting this, children are excited by the butchering, while most adults await the eating beside their hearths.[20]

Had the point been distribution of property shares, meat would have been apportioned to *all* members of the group, whether as Ingold's co-owners, or as Woodburn's political equals. The meat instead is given to/eaten by (we had better see here inseparable phases of one fact) to everyone *present* in the hamlet, excluding people away on visits, including visitors from other groups. None is reserved for co-owners or political equals who happen to be away. Most of the meat, furthermore, is eaten immediately. Had its distribution been the point, some recipients might have chosen to keep their servings for later use. In the particular case described above, they ate their servings immediately even though the game had been brought late in the day, after some families already had their evening meal. The inner parts and most of the rest were cooked and consumed immediately. Only very little was preserved for later use, suggesting incidentally that preservation is an option, but immediate consumption is an imposing tradition. A similar situation prevails in other immediate-return hunter-gatherers (e.g., Hadza: see Woodburn 1998).

That the meat is butchered into tiny portions does not necessarily reflect only a concern with equal shares. The fine carving just as much ensures that everyone eats the 'same' one meat, rather than this person eating this part, and that person another part. Special cuts of meat are apportioned to special categories of persons in some hunter-gatherer groups, for example, Hadza initated men, and !Kung hunter's parents-in-law, this way distinguishing them. Nayaka do not make such distinctions; all of them eat all the game, equally.

That the meat is cooked and eaten by each family separately, next to each other, rather than centrally by all of them, does not evince concern only with shares either. This way of giving/eating the meat is more practical, preempting the need to coordinate its cooking and consumption on a larger scale, as in trance celebrations. Equally important, it epitomises a local structure of not a collective but an ad hoc plurality. The community of eaters is not 'one' but 'many', who eat together next to each other, thereby reproducing their relations. Shared eating itself involves, of course, a twofold move: separating meat-parts (to separate pots, separate hands, separate mouths), and orchestrating their eating together. The 'sharing of a large game animal', despite its outward appearance to bourgeois spectators, involves not division into shares, but separation for joint consumption, and the manifestation and regeneration of relations.

Conclusions

Previously interpreted largely through Western notions, the sharing of large game animals is seen from a fresh perspective in this paper, attuned to local perceptions. The paper points to the ambivalence of the contemporary English word 'sharing', arguing that the sharing of large game animals involves shared eating, not just the distribution of meat shares. Shared eating expresses and regenerates a gamut of relations, among people and with the environment. A 'property' from a Western perspective, the game in the indigenous regard is an embodiment of forest-feeding; a concrete manifestation of forest-caring. Its shared eating expresses and regenerates people's sense of their togetherness among themselves and with the environment. Children play an important role in this event, hitherto neglected, symbolically amplifying these properties of gamesharing. The whole event, this paper has argued, demonstrates attributes of hunter-gatherers' social relations: the property of relations more than relations of property.

Notes

1. Special thanks go to Michael Saltman, Joanna Overing and Danny Naveh for insightful comments on this paper. Some of the ideas discussed were first presented at the symposium on Property and Equality, held at the Max Planck Institute for Social Anthropology in Halle (2001), and I thank my fellow participants for stimulating conversations.
2. Fieldwork was carried out during 1978–79. Shorter visits followed in 1989 and 2001. Background can be found in Bird-David (1989, 1994b, 1999b).
3. 'Hunter-gatherers' is a much-debated term, not least because of an earlier literal historical reading, i.e., people who gather and hunt for their living. The phrase is used here not in this descriptive sense but as the conventional term that it has become, referring to an aggregate of diverse groups from different parts of the world, compared by certain ethnographers for over a century.
4. See Woodburn (1998) for a fuller exposition and critique.
5. See Price (1975), Ingold 1986, Bird-David (1990) and Woodburn (1998).

6. This metaphor is largely used by tropical forest 'hunter-gatherers'. Among other hunter-gatherers are found other variants of kinship metaphors (see Bird-David 1993).
7. In Ingold's words, '[the] first, ... a principle of generalized reciprocity or unrestricted access whereby means of subsistence are enjoyed in common, secondly, ... a distributive movement whereby stuff held at the outset by a single person is divided up, so as to be available for use by an aggregate of beneficiaries'.
8. The terminological choice is not easy. Alternative terminological candidates all have their problems. 'Western' is both overgeneralising and ahistoric. 'Euro-American' is a-historic. 'Modern' is neither spatially nor temporally bounded, and does not relate to a particular ethnographically studied population. I use 'modern Western,' referring to the dominant paradigm, at its height in Europe in the nineteenth century, having risen to prominence (yet not suddenly starting) in the seventeenth century, and declining (yet by no means disappearing) in the late twentieth century. 'Bourgeois' serves to emphasise that we largely speak about the middle-class.
9. In Hebrew, for example, there are two separate words for these meanings, lehalek and lehitahlek, although they have the same root, and in common speech are often confounded.
10. The famous tale of King Solomon, who ruled that a baby claimed by two mothers be divided between them, whereupon one relinquished the baby and thereby proved her claim, is an interesting play on this theme.
11. In a book in preparation.
12. 'Property' increasingly refers also to immaterial objects such as name, reputation, knowledge and identity.
13. 'Relation' itself has a double sense, on the one hand to do with kinship and on the other with knowledge and ideas (see Strathern 1995). Strathern dates the emergence of this double sense roughly to the sixteenth and seventeenth centuries, before which, she suggests, a word like affinity would have referred to a relationship by marriage, or an alliance between consociates, and afterwards also to structural resemblance or causal connection [ibid.: 9]. If we understand the kinship 'relation' as logical and classificatory, as Strathern I think does, the sense of 'relation' is double only in pertaining to different domains (kinship and knowledge). But a 'kinship relation' itself has a double sense: a classificatory one and a concrete interactive social one (distinguished as relatedness by Edwards and Strathern (2000). In the first case it is a relation 'in the mind': a relation which gathers 'in the mind' persons who are separate in lived reality. In the second case it has to do with their joined living, namely the ebbs and flows of their social life *with* each other.
14. All ethnographies move somewhere between these two 'ideal type' models, sometimes described as etic and emic.
15. 'Camp' is usually used in 'hunter-gatherer' studies. As for Nayaka, it is not a camp away from the settled home, but home. I prefer using hamlet, emphasising the very small number of huts/homes in each place, between three and five in the hamlets studied.
16. 'Nonhuman' is an awkward and inadequate term in that it distorts the Nayaka nondichotomous view of a diversity of 'persons' living in the world. Alternative terms such as 'other-than-human' or 'super-persons' or 'supernatural beings' or 'spirits' are problematic too, each for a different reason.
17. It also serves to reduce the hunter's prestige and credit.
18. This section sums up an ethnography discussed in a chapter of a book in preparation.
19. This is a problematic term, stressing physical closeness (measurable in metres) rather than the social closeness between those physically close. But for simplicity the term is nonetheless used in this brief paper (a fuller discussion is presented in a book in preparation).
20. An adult other than the hunter butchers and divides the meat among many groups of 'hunter-gatherers'. Commonly, the importance of disengaging the hunter from the hunt, in order to preempt dependencies and a basis of power, has been read into it. Perhaps this also reflects the lesser importance of butchering than hunting on the one hand and eating on the other. To what extent indigenous concern is directed towards the two end-points of the hunting process, more than to its butchering, needs to be comparatively examined.

References

Applebaum, H. 1984. *Work in Non-market and Transitional Societies*. Albany: State University of New York Press.
—— 1997. 'Work'. In: *The Dictionary of Anthropology*, ed. T. Barfield. Oxford: Blackwell.
Barfield, T. (ed.) 1997. *The Dictionary of Anthropology*. Oxford: Blackwell.
Barnard, A. and J. Woodburn 1988. 'Introduction'. In: *Hunters and Gatherers vol 2: Property, Power and Ideology*, eds T. Ingold, D. Riches and J. Woodburn. Oxford: Berg.
Beteille, A. 1977. *Inequality among Men*. Oxford: Basil Blackwell.
Bird-David, N. 1989. 'The people and the Ethnographic Myth: an Introduction to the Study of the Naiken'. In: *Blue Mountains: The Ethnography and Biography of a South Indian Region*, eds P. Hockings. New Delhi, Oxford University Press, pp. 249–81.
—— 1990. 'The Giving Environment: Another Perspective on the Economic System of Gatherer-Hunters', *Current Anthropology* 31, 2: 183–96.
—— 1992. 'Beyond "The Original Affluent Society": a Culturalist Reformulation', *Current Anthropology* 33, 1: 25–47.
—— 1992b. 'Beyond "the Hunting and Gathering Mode of Subsistence": Observations on the Nayaka and Other Modern Hunter-Gatherers', *Man* 27, 1: 19–44.
—— 1993. 'Tribal Metaphorization of Man-Nature Relatedness: a Comparative Analysis'. In: *Anthropological Perspectives on Environmentalism*, ed. K. Milton. London: Routledge.
—— 1994b. 'The Nilgiri Tribal Systems: A View from Below', *Modern Asian Studies* 28, 2: 339–55.
—— 1999a. '"Animism" Revisited: Personhood, Environment, and Relational Epistemology', *Current Anthropology* 40 (Supplement): S67–91.
—— 1999b. 'Research among Nayaka of the Wynaad (South India)'. In: *Cambridge Encyclopedia of Hunters and Gatherers*, eds R. Lee and R. Daly. Cambridge: Cambridge University Press, pp. 257–61.
Edwards, J. and M. Strathern 2000. 'Including Our Own'. In: *Cultures of Relatedness*, ed. J. Carstern. Cambridge: Cambridge University Press.
Hart, J.A. 1978. 'From Subsistence to Market: a Case Study of the Mbuti Net Hunters', *Human Ecology* 6, 3: 325–53.
Ingold, T. 1986. *Evolution and Social Life*. Cambridge: Cambridge University Press.
—— 2000. *The Perception of the Environment: Essays in Livelihood, Dwelling and Skill*. London and New York: Routledge.
Lee, R.B. 1988. 'Reflections on Primitive Communism'. In: *Hunters and Gatherers vol 1: History, Evolution and Social Change*, eds T. Ingold, D. Riches and J. Woodburn. Oxford: Berg.
Lee, R.B. and I. DeVore (eds) 1968. *Man the Hunter*. Chicago: Aldine.
Price, J.A. 1975. 'Sharing: The Integration of Intimate Economics,' *Anthropologica* 17, 1: 3–27.
Sahlins, M. 1972. *Stone Age Economics*. London, Tavistock.
Strathern, M. 1988. *The Gender of the Gift: Problems with Women and Problems with Society in Melansia*. Berkeley: University of California Press.
—— 1995. *The Relation: Issues in Complexity and Scale*. Cambridge: Prickly Pear Pamphlet No. 6.
Tanner, A. 1979. *Bringing Home Animals: Religious Ideology and Mode of Production of the Mistassini Cree Hunters*. London: E. Hurst & Co.
Turnbull, C.M. 1976 (1965). *Wayward Servants: The Two Worlds of the African Pygmies*. Connecticut: Greenwood Press.
Woodburn, J. (ed.) 1980. 'Hunters and Gatherers Today and Reconstruction of the Past'. In: *Soviet and Western Anthropology*, ed. E. Gellner. London: Duckworth.
—— (1982). 'Egalitarian societies', *Man* (N.S.) 17: 431–51.
—— (1998). '"Sharing is not a Form of Exchange": an Analysis of Property-Sharing in Immediate-Return Hunter-Gatherer Societies'. In: *Property Relations: Renewing the Anthropological Tradition*, ed. C.M. Hann. Cambridge: Cambridge University Press, pp. 48–63.

Notes on Contributors

Megan Biesele has taught anthropology at The University of Texas (Austin), Texas A&M University (College Station), and Rice University (Houston). She helped found one of the first U.S. anthropological advocacy organisations, the Kalahari Peoples Fund, in 1973 and currently serves as its Coordinator. For periods during the 1970s, 1980s, and 1990s, Biesele worked with Ju/'hoan San communities in Botswana and Namibia as an advocate and documentarian, and served as director of a nongovernmental organization, the Nyae Nyae Development Foundation of Namibia (NNDFN) during the years spanning Namibia's transition to independence (1987–92). Biesele has served as an elected member of the Committee for Human Rights (CfHR) of the American Anthropological Association. She was the recipient in 2000 of the Lucy Mair Medal for Applied Anthropology from the Royal Anthropological Institute, London. In Texas she has co-founded and serves as president of the Shumla School, a non-profit organization doing comparative research and public education on indigenous arts past and present. Address: 4811-B Shoalwood Ave., Austin, TX. 78756, U.S.A., email: meganbie@io.com

Nurit Bird-David took her B.A. in Economics and Mathematics at Jerusalem University, and her Certificate and Ph.D. in Social Anthropology at Cambridge University. She has been a Research Fellow in New Hall College, a Visiting Research Fellow in the Truman Institute at Jerusalem University, and in the Smuts Institute for Commonwealth Studies in Cambridge. Currently she is a Senior Lecturer and Head of the Social Anthropology Program at the University of Haifa. Address: Department of Sociology and Social Anthropology, University of Haifa, Haifa, 39105 Israel, email: n.bird@soc.haifa.ac.il

Barbara Bodenhorn worked for the Iñupiat Community of the Arctic Slope (the regional tribal government) for three years before beginning her doctorate in social anthropology at Cambridge University. Since then she has balanced ongoing research in the Arctic, under the sponsorship of the IHLC and the AEWC, with teaching and lecturing at Cambridge where she is currently Newton Trust Lecturer in the Department of Social Anthropology. She has taught at Ilisagvik College in Barrow, Alaska and is an affiliated lecturer at the University of Alaska, Fairbanks. Her research interests include '4th world' politics, organisational dynamics, risk and decision-making, kinship, gender and economic anthropology. Addresses: (1) Pembroke College, Cambridge CB2 1RF, England (2) Department of Social Anthropology, Free School Lane, Cambridge CB2 3RF, England, email: bb106@cus.cam.ac.uk

Mitsuo Ichikawa took his M.Sc. and D.Sc. in anthropology at the Laboratory of Human Evolution Studies, Kyoto University, where he has also taught. He has been a researcher with the Center for African Area Studies and the Graduate School of Human and Environmental Studies, Kyoto University. Currently he is professor in anthropology and African area studies at the Graduate School of Asian and African Area Studies, Kyoto University: Address: 46 Yoshida-shimoadachi-cho, Sakyo, Kyoto, 606–8501, email: ichikawa@jambo.africa.kyoto-u.ac.jp

Tim Ingold took his Ph.D. in social anthropology at the University of Cambridge. He taught in the Department of Social Anthropology at the University of Manchester, as Lecturer, Senior Lecturer and Professor, and from 1995 to 1999 as Max Gluckman Professor of Social Anthropology. Currently he is Professor of Social Anthropology at the University of Aberdeen. He is a Fellow of the British Academy and of the Royal Society of Edinburgh. Address: Department of Anthropology, School of Social Science, University of Aberdeen, Aberdeen AB24 3QY, Scotland, UK, email: Tim.Ingold@abdn.ac.uk

Robert Layton gained his B.Sc. and M.Phil. in anthropology at University College London. His D.Phil. (University of Sussex) was based on a study of social change in villages on the Plateau of Levier, eastern France. After completing his D.Phil. he worked for seven years as a research anthropologist, with Aboriginal communities in Australia. He is now Professor of Anthropology at the University of Durham (U.K.) and a member of the department's *Anthropology in Development* and *Evolutionary Anthropology* research groups. His address is: Anthropology Department, University of Durham, 43 Old Elvet, Durham DH1 3HN, email: R.H. Layton@durham.ac.uk

David Riches gained his M.A. degree at Cambridge University and his Ph.D. at the London School of Economics, both in social anthropology. He has lectured at Memorial University of Newfoundland, Queen's University of Belfast, and University of St Andrews, where he is now Senior Lecturer in Social Anthropology. Address: Department of Social Anthropology, University of St Andrews, St Andrews, Fife, Scotland, KY16 9AL, email: djr@st-and.ac.uk

Ivo Strecker studied at the universities of Hamburg and Göttingen where he received his doctorate and habilitation in cultural anthropology. He also spent several years at the London School of Economics where he met Jean Lydall with whom he subsequently went to do fieldwork in Hamar, southern Ethiopia. Since 1984 he has been professor in cultural anthropology at the Johannes Gutenberg University, Mainz (Germany) and visiting professor at Addis Ababa University. Currently he is head of the South Omo Research Centre at Jinka, southern Ethiopia and, together with Stephen Tyler, is acting as chief coordinator of the International Rhetoric Culture Project. Addresses: (1) Institute for Anthropology and African Studies, Forum 6, D-55099 Mainz, Germany; (2) Institute of Ethiopian Studies, P.O. Box 1176, Addis Ababa, Ethiopia, email: (1) istreck@uni-mainz.de; (2) sorc@telecom.net.et

Kazuyoshi Sugawara took his M.Sc. and D.Sc. in primatology at Kyoto University. He studied the social organisation and behaviour of Japanese macaques, and hybrid baboons in Ethiopia. Since 1982 he has continued the research on face-to-face communications and life-history narratives among the Central Kalahari San (Bushmen) in Botswana. He has been a research associate in social ecology at Hokkaido University. Currently he is professor in social anthropology at Kyoto University. Address: Graduate School of Human and Environmental Studies, Kyoto University, Yoshida Nihonmatsu, Sakyo-ku, Kyoto 606–8501 Japan, email: sugawarak-@h02.mbox.media.kyoto-u.ac.jp

Hideaki Terashima received his M.Sc. and D.Sc. in anthropology from Kyoto University. Currently he is professor in anthropology at Kobe Gakuin University. He has also been visiting professor at the Center for African Area Studies (Kyoto University) and National Museum of Ethnology, Osaka, Japan. Address: Faculty of Humanities and Sciences, Kobe Gakuin University, 518 Arise, Ikawadani-cho, Nishi-ku, Kobe-shi, 651–2180, Japan, email: terasima@human.kobegakuin.ac.jp

Robert Tonkinson is Emeritus Professor of Anthropology and Honorary Senior Research Fellow at The University of Western Australia, where he was trained in social anthropology to Master's level. He did his Ph.D. in anthropology at the University of British Columbia, and has taught at the University of Oregon (1967–80), Australian National University (1980–84), University of Heidelberg (1988–89, 2003) and University of Western Australia (1984–2002). He has done a total of seven years' research among Aborigines in the Western Desert of Australia (1963–) and in Vanuatu (1966–). Address: Anthropology and Sociology, The University of Western Australia, 35 Stirling Highway, Crawley, W. Australia 6009, email: Bob.Tonkinson@uwa.edu.au

Thomas Widlok took his M.Sc. and Ph.D. in anthropology at the London School of Economics where he has also taught. He has been a researcher with the Cognitive Anthropology Research Group in Nijmegen, the University of Cologne, the Center for African Area Studies (Kyoto University) and the Max Planck Institute for Social Anthropology in Halle. Currently, he is lecturer in anthropology at the University of Heidelberg and research staff at the Max Planck Institute for Psycholinguistics in Nijmegen. Address: Department of Anthropology, Institut für Ethnologie, Universität Heidelberg, Sandgasse 7, 69117 Heidelberg, Germany, email: Thomas.Widlok@urz.uni-heidelberg.de

Wolde Gossa Tadesse took his M.Sc. and Ph.D. in anthropology at the London School of Economics. He is affiliated to the Max Planck Institute for Social Anthropology where he was a member of a research staff from 2000–2003. Currently he is with the Christensen Fund in California. Address: The Christensenfund, 145 Addison Avenue, Palo Alto, CA 94301, U.S.A., email: wolde@christensenfund.org

James Woodburn carried out his first anthropological field research from 1957 until 1960 among the Hadza hunter-gatherers of Tanzania and wrote up the results for his Ph.D. at the University of Cambridge. He has returned to the same people on numerous occasions up to the present. He taught social anthropology at the London School of Economics from 1965 until 1999. Throughout this period his teaching and research were focused on the comparative analysis of hunter-gatherer social and economic organisation. He was Chairman of the Organising Committee for the Fourth International Conference on Hunting and Gathering Societies in 1986. Although now retired, he remains active in the subject. Address: 140 Cherry Hinton Road, Cambridge CB1 7AJ, England, email: jameswoodburn@talk21.com

Index

A
Aborigines, 32, 35–42, 44n6, 139
Abriès, France, 143
access to assets, 4, 9, 11, 12, 13, 15
accumulation, differential, 77
acephalous societies, 189
Ache, 135, 137
achievement, celebration of, 178, 185
affines, 124, 125, 184–85
agent of force (AgF), 111, 112
agriculture, 175
agro-pastoralism, 108, 115, 119
Ahmaogak, M., 78, 81, 84, 89, 93, 98, 100n17
Aka, 156, 158, 160, 161, 162, 163n1
≠Akhoe, 3, 17
Alaska Eskimo Whaling Commission (AEWC), 89, 100n29
alphabetic literacy, 195
altruism, true, 121
ambiguity, 193, 197
Anangu, 133
anarchy, 184, 187–88
anger, 112, 117, 121, 122, 123, 126
apiculture, 175
Arctic Slope Regional Association (ASRC), 82
Attungana, P., 80, 81
Austin, J., 111
Australia, 12, 13, 16
Australian aboriginal systems, 28
authority, 3, 12, 175, 187–88
autonomy, 33, 77, 79, 91, 92; personal, 3, 4, 5, 6, 13, 15

B
Baka, 65
Bakgalagadi, 108, 115, 119
balance model (for the speech act theory), 127
Baldambe, 176–88
baleen, 78, 88, 90

band, 105, 107
baraza, 178
Bardi, 136
barjo, 178, 179
barriers, social-cultural, 33, 42
Batok, 175
belief, 190–99
Berman, Morris, 199
Biesele, Megan, 10, 15, 190, 192, 194, 217
'big meetings,' 36, 37, 41, 43
billiard ball model (for the speech act theory), 127
Bird-David, Nurit, 1, 6, 7, 8, 10, 79, 91, 93, 201, 217
bitta, 176, 177, 178, 179, 187
Bodenhorn, Barbara, 7, 10, 77, 218
bond-friend, 176, 178, 185, 186, 188
bonobos, 151
Botswana, 108
Bourdieu, P., 90, 91
Brower, H. Sr., 81, 86, 93, 100n15
Burch, E.S., Jr., 80, 93, 99n2, 99n9, 100n13, 100n15, 100n27
bushmen, 9. *See also* San bushmen

C
capital: cultural, 90; social, 91, 92
caring, 210, 212
catastrophe theory, 146
cattle, 176–79, 182, 184–88
cattle camps, 177, 188
Central Kalahari Desert, 106, 108
children, 201, 202, 206, 208, 210, 212, 213, 214
chimpanzees, 131, 151, 152, 156, 157, 158
choice, 83
Choke, 182–83, 186, 187
Christmas ox, 192
claims, 77–82, 84, 85, 90, 92, 93, 99n6, 99n11, 100n19; Native Claims Settlement Act (1971), 81; negotiable, 90; non-negotiable, 77, 79; quit-claims, 86, 92

clans, 176, 184, 187
cognitive anthropology, 108
collectivity, collectivities, 81
commensality, 85, 100n21
commensurability (and incommensurability), 86, 92, 93. *See also* comparability
commodities, 73
communal consensus, 107, 127
communal reason, 123, 126, 127
communal sanctions, 107, 127
communal values, 122
communication, 11, 14, 15, 192, 194, 195, 196, 199
communism, 9
community, 80–82, 84, 88–91, 95, 97, 98
comparable, comparability, 85
conflict, 49, 60–61, 110, 111, 112, 117, 123, 128
confrontation, 184
conjugal linkage (pair), 106, 107, 119, 122, 128n6
consortium, 83, 85, 89
constraints: ecological, 41; social, 49
contribution, 78, 84, 85, 89
conversation analysis, 109; summaries, 113–14, 115, 116, 117–18, 118, 120, 122, 123, 124
cooperation, 13, 77, 85, 86
corporateness, 12
costs: of living, 82; political, 89; sharing, 77–80, 83, 85–87, 90, 92, 93, 99n1, 99n2, 99n11, 100n12, 100n30; start-up, 87; time, 88, 90
creativity, 32–44; denial of, 38–42
crew membership, 83, 84
cross-cousin, 113, 115
cultural determinism, 63, 66–67
cultural model, 108
curing ritual, 109, 128n5

D
Dahrendorf, Ralf, 1, 2, 3, 7
debt, indebtedness, 86, 90, 92
delayed-return system, 59, 130, 131, 138–41, 143, 146
demand sharing, 65, 75n2
Democratic Republic of Congo, 48
dependencies, 3, 4
dependency theory, 67
derivative morphemes, 109
descent, 167, 168, 169
diagnosis, 58, 59, 60
dialectic of emotional life, 125, 126, 127, 128, 174

differential access, 77, 78
differentiation, 78–79
diffusion, 37
direct narration, 112–13, 120
dirt (latent in female body), 110, 111
discourse, 6, 11, 14, 15
discourse analysis, 108, 124, 128n2
discrimination: against hunter-gatherers, 20, 22, 24, 26, 30
disease, 50–53, 55, 56, 58–60. *See also* illness
disengagement, 6
distribution (of wealth and social influence), 185–87
dividuals, 91, 99n11
division of labour, 2, 79, 80, 93
divorce, 109, 113, 117
doctor, 60
domains, 36, 40, 41
dream-spirit rituals, 36–42
dream-spirit travels, 37, 38
dreams, 37, 41, 42, 43n3, 44n5, 196
Dumontian holism, 91
Durkheim, Emile, 2, 18, 25, 79, 93

E
eco-zones, 88, 96
ecology, 13
Efe, 48, 50, 51, 52, 57, 161
egalitarian societies: Australian desert society, 48, 52; possession, equality and gender relations in, 107, 126, 127; space-time, ethnicity and limits on, 62, 63, 64–73, 75; Woodburn on, 1–15
egalitarianism, 107, 193, 197; in Australian desert society, 32, 33, 40; immediate-return strategies, 131, 139, 141; sharing costs, 77, 78, 79, 86, 90, 99n1, 99n2; social bases for, 78, 86
elephant hunting, 49
emotion, 107, 112, 121, 122, 123, 125, 126, 127, 128
emotional life, dialectic of, 125, 126, 127, 128, 174
encapsulation, 63, 64–68
engagement, 6, 7, 13
environment, 202, 206, 208, 209, 214
Enxet (Paraguay), 65
equality: in Australian desert society, 32, 34, 43; autonomy as basis for, 22; direct access provision as basis for, 22; obligation to share as basis for, 22; of opportunity, 14; possession, gender relations and, 107, 125–28; property and, 166, 167, 173, 174, 191, 194, 196,

199; of result, 14; sharing and, 175, 176, 187, 189, 202, 207, 212, 214n1; sharing costs and, 79, 80, 86
esoteric knowledge, 49, 57
Ethiopia, 175–89
ethnic groups, 63, 64, 74
ethnicity, 91
ethnobotany/ethnobotanical, 48, 51, 61
evolutionary ecologists, 158
exertion of force, 111, 119
experience, 49, 58, 59, 60
extramarital relationships, 107, 109, 123

F
face-to-face interaction, 105, 108, 125, 126
feeding (forest-feeding), 210, 214
first distribution, 155, 156, 163n2
flexibility, 192, 193
food: distribution through sharing, 48, 49; preservation of, 159; restriction/taboo on, 50, 51–52; sharing of, 151, 152, 153, 155–57, 157–60. *See also* meat
foraging, 47–61, 190–91, 192, 193, 199
force, exertion of, 111, 119
forest-caring, 210, 214
forests, 208, 209, 210, 214, 215n6
formalisation (of conversational organisation), 124–25
Franche-Comté, 143
'free riders', 144
funerals, 178, 183

G
G/wi, 107
gambling, 65
game-animals, 202–205, 207, 208–209, 209–10, 210–11, 212, 213–14
Game Reserve, Central Kalihari (CKGR), 108
game theory, 134
||Gana, 108–109, 113, 115, 118, 120, 124
=Gao N!a, 193, 194
gathering, 106
gender, 34, 41, 43, 44n4, 105–27
genealogical model, 167, 168
generations, 165, 167, 168–73
generosity, 176–9, 179–85
genitor, 110, 114, 118–19, 121
Gidjingali, 135
gifts (and gifting), 80, 81, 90, 92, 97, 100n24
Glastonbury, 63, 64, 65, 67, 68, 69, 70, 72, 74, 75
global markets, 82, 90
goats, 176–84, 186–87
Goffman, E., 128n1

gom ('agree' in the |Gui language), 114, 119, 122, 123
Greece, 196
Guenther, Mathias, 192, 196, 199
|Gui, 6, 105–28
GYO/Kxo, 114

H
Hadza, 18, 21, 22, 26–29, 30, 66, 135, 138–41, 144, 192
Hai//om, 3
Halle conference, 191
hamadryas baboons, 105–106, 116, 153
Hamar, 14, 175–89
harems, 105
harpooner, 78, 80, 83, 90
Havelock, Eric, 196, 199
healers, 197
healing dance, 60, 61
health, 50–51, 52, 53, 55
herding technique, 105
hiding (stolen goats), 183
hierarchy, 3, 6, 8–14, 35, 41, 43, 77, 93
Hiwi of Venezuela, 137
honesty, 181
horticulturalists, 141
hospitality, 81, 83, 84, 88, 98
host status, 39, 40–41
households, 63–67, 75, 83–86, 100n21
human relationship, 47, 60–61
humans, vs. nonhumans, 165–66, 169, 172, 173
hunter-gatherers, 61, 108, 127, 128, 190, 191; definition of societies of, 30n2; egalitarianism among, 62, 64–68, 70, 75; ethnography of, 2, 3, 5–9, 12, 14, 16; sharing among, 201–205, 207–14, 214n3, 215n6, 215n15, 215n20
hunting, 107, 114, 123, 126; on horseback, 113, 114; hunting-sharing complex, 151, 152, 154, 155–57; property, sharing and, 165, 166, 167, 169, 170, 171; sharing, property and, 201, 202, 209–11, 214n3, 215n17; springhare, 123, 127
hxaro (Kalahari gift exchange), 133, 134, 141

I
Ichikawa, Mitsuo, 10, 13, 151, 218
ideology, 3, 9, 11, 12, 35, 36, 40
illness, 52, 55, 59. *See also* disease
illocutionary act, 127
illocutionary force, 111, 127
Imamura, K., 109, 110, 128n5
immediate return systems: adaptivity in,

130–46
immediate-return systems, 48, 52, 60, 64; absence in Canada and Australia, 20; distinctive characteristics, 20–23; leaders in, 30; as oppositional solidarity, 19–20; past history, 18–19; potential for change, 19, 24; as product of breakdown, 19; religious sharing, 25; resilience, 24, 29; role of religion in change, 24–29; role of secular factors in change, 22–29; societies and, 3, 12
in-laws, threat of, 185
incommensurability, 86, 92, 93
indebtedness, 86, 90, 92
indirect ownership, 152, 153, 160, 163n5
individual: autonomy, 79, 92; as category, 77, 79, 91, 92, 93, 99n11, 100n19; creativity, denial of, 38–42; as form of property, 85, 90, 92, 93, 100n19; independence, 77; as moral person, 79, 80, 93, 99n11
individualism, 176, 187, 188, 189
individuality, 194, 199
inequality, 1–4, 7, 8, 12, 13, 15; in Australian desert society, 32, 33, 34, 41; property and, 166, 173; sharing costs and, 79, 80, 86, 92
inferential structure, 108, 119, 121, 125
influence (social), 185–87
Ingold, Tim, 1, 3, 6, 10, 100n12, 165, 218
inheritance systems, 143–44, 146
initiation ceremonies, 50, 52
innovation, 37, 40, 42
instability, 3
institutions, 152, 161
interdependence, 32, 43, 44n7, 77, 81, 93
intergroup relations, 40, 43
interpersonal relationships, 105, 106, 107, 118
Inuit, 5, 63–75
Inupiat, 65
Ituri, 8, 48–60

J
jealousy, 110, 112, 113, 119, 121, 123, 124, 126
Ju/'hoan, Ju/'hoansi, 15, 121, 190–99

K
Kalahari Desert, 106, 108, 140, 192
Katz, Richard, 197
Kayapo, 192
kerygmatic accounts, 197
kinship, 33, 35, 36, 43
Kippel, Spain, 144

knowledge, 5, 8, 10, 12; categories of, 47, 49–51; environmental, 48; esoteric, 49, 57; of food restrictions, 50; individualised, 187; lack of, 194; necessity for precision in, 193; power and, 40, 43; practice and (in plant world), 51–56; property and, 48–51, 191; of religion, 49–50; religious, 191, 193, 194, 197; and roles of foragers, 50–51; secret, 60; secret-sacred, 33–35, 37–38, 40, 42–43; sharing, 172; of songs, 49–50; storytelling and, 196; of subsistence activities, 49; of supernatural beings, 49–50; unrestricted, 33–36, 38, 41
!Koi!kom, 108
kua ('Bushman' in |Gui language), 115
Kummer, H., 106
!Kung, 21, 25, 26, 121, 131, 133, 135, 137, 139, 141, 175
Kx'oensakene (New Xade), 108, 124
Kx'oko, 109, 110, 111, 117
Kx'ombee, 120

L
labour, 79–81, 89, 93–95, 98, 202, 206, 207, 209–11; returns on (immediate vs. delayed), 165, 166, 167
land, 166, 169, 172, 173
Layton, Robert, 10, 13, 130, 218
leadership, 35, 187, 188; Lévi-Strauss, and obligation, 99n7, 101n31; position of, 90; responsibility and, 99n7, 101n31; Sahlins, and fellowship, 78, 80
Lee, Richard, 192
legitimacy, 107, 112, 117, 119, 121–22, 123, 125, 126
levelling mechanisms, 8, 9, 13, 14, 141, 142, 143
Lévi-Strauss, Claude, 18, 99n7, 101n31
life-history, 170; narratives of, 108, 114, 118
lotteries, 144
love-relationship, 109
lovers, 109, 111, 112, 113

M
magic/magical, 49–52, 60–61
Mardu, 32–42, 43, 44n5
marginal value, 134, 135, 137
marriage, 109, 113, 121, 125, 177, 178, 184, 187
Marshall, Lorna, 193
Marx, Karl, 2, 9
mate-swapping, 114, 115
Mauss, Marcel, 28

Mbendjele, 26
Mbuti, 48, 50, 51, 57, 131, 137, 139, 154–62, 163n1, 163n6, 175
meat, 201, 202, 204, 207, 210, 211–13, 214, 215n20; sharing of, 130, 133–38, 143, 144. *See also* food
medical: care, 50, 51, 52, 56–61; plants, 53–56, 56–61; systems, 54, 58–61; treatment, 48, 52–61
medicine, 48–61; symbolic, 49, 50, 56, 58, 60
memory, 165, 166, 167, 168, 169, 171, 172, 173
metaphor, 105, 106, 110, 121
metonymy, 110
mixing blood (marriage ceremony among the |Gui), 110, 111, 113, 122
mnemonic function, 196
money, 82, 83, 88, 92
mutual aid, 142, 143, 144
mutualism, 122–23

N
Nakagawa, H., 128n3
Nalukataq, 84, 95, 97, 98
Nama, 5, 9, 10
Namibia, 3
Native Claims Settlement Act (1971), 81
natural phenomena, 58, 60
Nayaka, 8, 201–15
Neakok, Raymond, 81, 85, 86, 93, 100n17
negotiation, 114, 126, 127, 128
neo-Darwinian theory, 144–45
New Agers, 5, 62–75
'new religious movements,' 69
ningik, 77, 83, 85, 90. See also shares and sharing
niqipiaq (real, hunted food), 85, 97
nomadism, 131
North Slope, 78, 79, 81, 82, 86, 88, 90, 91, 92, 100n25

O
objectifcation, 165, 167, 172, 173
obligations, 3, 4, 7, 9, 14, 79, 90, 99n7, 100n30. *See also* responsibility
oil (and revenue from), 81, 82, 88, 90
Ojibwa, 169, 171
=Oma Djo, 197
=Oma G/aq'o, 198
=Oma Kxao Moses, 190, 198
one-male unit, 105, 106
oral history, 190–99
oral tradition, 194–97
organisation, social, 190, 191

ownership, 2, 6, 8, 9, 10, 13, 126, 151–63; in Australian desert society, 33, 39, 42, 44n7, 44n8; of boat, as condition of captaincy, 87; claims to shares on basis of, 78, 83, 85; constraints on, 80; definition of, 152, 156, 161, 163n1; harpoons, 78, 83; Ingold and, 100n12; rights of, 78, 80; sharing costs and, 78, 80, 83, 85, 87, 92, 100n12, 100n30; Williams, on rights and obligations, 100n30

P
pair-gestalt inhibition, 106, 116
Paliyan, 175
Pandaran, 175
Parsons, T., 2
passivity, 42, 44n6
past, and present, 166, 167, 168, 170, 171, 172
pastoralism, 175, 189
pater, 115, 121
paternity, 117–19, 121
patients, 54, 55, 58, 60, 61
peasants, 130, 141, 142
Pellaport, France, 144
performance (of roles), 50
person: human and nonhuman, 92; Mauss, 79; as moral category, 79, 80; *persona*, connected to role, 79, 80; relational, 167, 171, 172, 173
personal names, 108, 111–12, 119
personal pronouns, 128n8
Peterson, Nick, 86, 93
piatchiaq (giving without expectation of return), 86
Pintipu, 43n2
Plains Indians, 139
plant medicine/medicinal plant, 53–56, 56–61
political power, 3, 12
polyandry, 114, 125
polygamy, 111
polygyny, 125
position: inherited, 100n26; of leadership, 90; political, 88, 91; responsibilities of, 90; social, 77, 78, 79, 80, 87, 91, 92
possession, 105–106, 107, 118, 119–25, 152, 153–55
post-foraging, 190, 192, 193, 199
potlatch, 141
poverty ('the poor'), 176, 177, 178, 186
power, 78, 82, 85, 90, 91, 92; collective, 34, 42; individual, 32, 33, 34, 35; knowledge and, 40, 43; nature of,

35–36; political, 34, 41; spiritual, 33, 38–39, 40, 42, 43
power relations, 34
practice, knowledge and (of plant world), 51–56
precedent, 188
primary care, 59, 60
primates, 13, 151, 152, 153, 157, 158, 159, 160
primatology, 105
property: as asset, attribute, 202, 204, 205, 206, 210–11, 213, 214, 215n12; Burch, and, 100n13; claims, 79, 85; collective, 7–10; common, 79, 85; communal, 7, 8, 9; definition of, 90, 99n6; disengagement from, 33; equality and, 166, 167, 173, 174, 191, 194, 196, 199; Firth on, 99n6, 99n7; heritable, 169, 173; Humphrey and, 80; hunting, sharing and, 165, 166, 167, 169, 170, 171, 201, 202, 209–11, 214n3, 215n17; individual as form of, 85, 90, 92, 93, 100n19; inequality and, 166, 173; intellectual, 4, 12, 32, 33, 34, 38–42, 172; Ju/'hoan, 190–91, 193, 195; knowledge and, 48–51, 191; land as, 172; material and nonmaterial, 91, 92; memory and, 173; personal, 7–10, 79, 80, 85, 90, 91, 93; private, 1, 2, 7, 8, 9, 80, 90; process and, 166; responsibilities and, 78, 79, 86–87, 90, 93, 99n3, 99n6; rights, 86–87, 93; sharing costs, 78, 79, 85, 90, 93, 99n11; taxes, 82; time, memory and, 165, 168, 172, 173; types of, 5, 8, 10
property objects, 5–7
property regimes, 4, 8, 9, 14
property relations, 4, 5, 6, 7, 8, 11, 12, 13, 14
property rights, 4, 9, 12, 15, 18, 23, 26, 28
protest religion, 25–26
pygmy groups, 24, 26, 27, 49, 60, 65, 71, 72. *See also* Aka; Mbuti

Q
quadruple relationship, 114, 122, 123, 125, 127

R
reciprocal altruism, 138, 145
reciprocity, 33, 85, 86, 90, 92
recognition, 78, 91
regulation, 89
relational levelling, 212
religious knowledge, 191, 193, 194, 197

relocation programme, 108, 124
remarriage, 109
remote control of ownership, 152, 153–55, 160–61
representation, 197, 198
reproduction, social, 33, 40
reproductive success, 137, 144, 145
resources: access to, 77, 78, 81, 82–86; accumulated, 87; animal, 86; base, 82; circulation of, 79, 85, 87, 92; claims to, 80, 93; common, 78, 84, 85, 86; distribution of, 91, 92; material, nonmaterial, 77, 78, 90, 99n6; monetary, 78, 81, 87; richness of, 80; time, 88; whaling, nonwhaling, 80, 89, 90, 94
responsibility: collective, 83, 91; gendered, 96; leadership and, 99n7, 101n31; as part of property, 78, 79, 90, 93, 99n3, 99n6; practical, 80, 81, 83, 87, 89, 90, 94, 95, 99n7; ritual and, 83–84, 86–87
restricted (and unrestricted) religious knowledge, 191, 194, 197
retribution, mystical, 182
return: delayed, 77, 86; immediate, 77, 85, 86
revelation, 37, 41–42
revenue: baleen, 78, 88, 90; global markets, 82, 90; oil, 81, 82, 88, 90; wages, 82, 87
rhetoric, 11, 14
Riches, David, 3, 5, 10, 62, 219
rights: as earned, 78, 84, 85, 87, 88, 90, 91, 92; as entitlement, 78, 83; as expectation, 86, 99n3; as part of responsibility, 78, 79, 86, 90, 93, 99n6; performance, 39; transmission, 39
risk, 132, 133, 136, 139, 142, 143
ritual: in Australian desert society, 32, 33, 34, 36–38, 39, 40, 42, 43, 44n4, 44n8; in |Gui discourse, 105, 109, 110, 115, 128n5; as mode of production, 40; as social/political capital, 33, 39
ritualisation, 8, 10, 11–13, 14, 15
rivals, 106, 107, 110, 111, 114, 116, 119, 123, 126
Rousseau, J.J., 1, 2, 5

S
Sahlins, Marshall, 78, 80
St Felix, Italy, 143
Ste Foy, France, 143, 144
San bushmen, 3, 10, 15, 108–109, 137, 140, 190–93, 198, 199
sanctions, 6, 107, 113, 119, 127
Santa Maria del Monte, Spain, 143, 144

sapiential authority, 193
Schapera, I., 9
science/scientific, 47, 56–57
scribal world, 195
second distribution, 155, 162
secrecy, 33, 34, 37, 38, 39
secret knowledge, 60
seduction, 113
self-aggrandisement, 195, 199
self-regulation, 42
Setswana, 116, 118, 120, 124, 128n2
sexual relationship, 107, 109, 110, 111, 117, 119–25, 127
sexuality, 109, 117, 123, 125, 126, 128, 137
shaman, 58, 60
shame, 42
shared schema, 107, 108, 126
shares: differential access to, 83, 84; distribution of, 81, 83, 84, 85, 86, 92; earned, 78, 84, 85, 88, 90, 91; entitlement to, 77, 80, 83; named, 90
sharing, 5, 6, 7, 8, 9, 10, 11, 12, 13–14, 15; of arrows, 160; central importance to hunter-gatherers, 201–202, 207–208, 210, 212–13; concept of, 202, 203, 204, 205, 207; costs, 77–80, 83, 85–87, 90, 92, 93, 99n1, 99n2, 99n11, 100n12, 100n30; demand sharing, 65, 75n2; as division, 202, 204, 213; in egalitarian societies, 19, 21–23, 25–26, 29, 62–66, 70, 73, 74–75; equality and, 86, 91, 92, 93, 175, 176, 187, 189, 202, 207, 212, 214n1; and expectation of return, 86; food, 48, 49, 151, 152, 153, 155–57; hunter-gatherers and, 201–205, 207–14, 214n3, 215n6, 215n15, 215n20; hunting, property and, 165, 166, 167, 169, 170, 171, 201, 202, 209–11, 214n3, 215n17; hunting-sharing complex, 151, 152, 154, 155–57; ideal of, 175, 176–79, 188, 189; individual autonomy and, 92; insurance function of, 158; as joining (kinship aspect), 212–13, 214; knowledge, 172; levelling function of, 207; limits of, 179–85; meat, 130, 133–38, 143, 144; property and, 165, 166, 169, 172, 173; religious sharing in immediate-return systems, 25; sharing networks, 85, 86, 100n24; significance of, 82, 92; time, 169
sharing system, 123
sharing way of life, 155, 159, 162
sheep, 182, 183
sieku (marriage among the |Gui), 109–12, 117, 119, 121–26

Silberbauer, G., 107, 108, 192
similarity index, 57
skills, 49, 50, 51
social boundary defence, 132, 140
social organisation, 190, 191
sociality, 5, 6, 63, 68, 69–73, 74, 75
society, 2, 3, 4, 5, 6, 7, 8, 9, 12, 13, 14, 15
songlines, 34, 37, 38
sorcery/sorcerer, 50, 51, 52, 60
sororate marriage, 121
South American Indians, 125
space-time, 62–75
speakers, 186, 187, 188
specialists, 49, 50, 51, 58, 59, 60
speech, 171; acts (and theory), 111, 127; 'ground', 113; negative, 111
spirit-intermediaries, 37, 38, 42, 43
spokesman, 178, 185, 188
springhares, 123, 127
status, stature, 78, 79, 91
stealing, 183, 184
Steiner, George, 195
storage, 138, 139, 159
stories, 171, 190, 192, 194, 195, 198, 199
storytellers, 192, 194, 195, 196–97, 199
storytelling, 171, 172
Strecker, Ivo, 10, 14, 175, 219
subject-object relations, 6, 13
subsistence, 78, 82, 83, 85
Sugawara, Kazuyoshi, 6, 10, 105, 219
supernatural being/agent, 47, 49, 59–60
symbolic medicine, 49, 50, 56, 58, 60

T
Tadesse, Wolde Gossa, 5, 220
Tanaka, J., 108, 109, 123, 127, 128n3
technology, 80, 89, 92, 95, 131, 139, 140, 141
teknonymy, 115, 119, 120
temptation, 179, 181
Terashima, Hideaki, 8, 10, 47, 219
territoriality, 131, 132, 140, 141, 146
Theobald, Robert, 193
things, social life of, 173
time, 165, 166, 167, 168; 'Old Man Time', 166; real, 167; sharing, 169, 204
time immemorial, 171
time-sharing, 204
'tit-for-tat' strategy, 136, 145
Tiwi, Northern Australia, 137, 140
tolerance, 192–94, 197, 198
Tonkinson, Robert, 10, 12, 13, 32, 220
tools, 152, 153–54, 155, 158, 160–61, 162, 163n5, 172
Törbel, Switzerland, 143, 144
Torres Straits, 136

totemism, 139
trade, 77, 90, 100n13
trance, 196, 197
transformative processes, 39, 42, 43
trespass, 107, 117, 122, 125
Tret, Italy, 143
triadic relationship, 111, 112, 114, 117, 122, 123, 126, 128n6
triangle of desire, 106, 111
true altruism, 121
Turner, Terence, 192

U

!U, 194
ukuli (neophyte), 177
!Unn/obe Morethlwa, 190, 194
Uluru, 132, 133
umialik, 77, 78, 80, 84, 87, 88, 90, 100n14. (*See also* whaling captain)
umiaq, 84, 87, 94. *See also* ownership, boat; *umialik*
uncertainty, 132, 142, 145
Ury, William, 199

V

variability, 191, 192, 193, 194
violence, 111, 112, 119

W

wages, 82, 87
wealth, 175, 178, 185–87, 188, 189; differential accumulation of, 77, 90; durable, 78; meritocracy and, 79; power and, 92
Weber, 25
Wegweiser, 196
well-being, 179
Western Desert, 32–33, 34, 35, 37, 38, 39, 40, 41, 43, 43n2, 43n3, 133, 134
whaling, 65
whaling captain couple, 77–81, 83, 87, 91, 94, 96–98, 100n14
whaling captain (*umialik*), 77–84, 86–9, 90, 91, 94–98, 100n14, 100n26
whaling captain wife, 77, 80, 81, 82, 83, 84, 90, 94, 95, 97, 100n14, 100n26
whaling crew, 78, 81, 83, 84, 85, 87, 89, 94, 95, 97, 98, 100n20
Widlok, Thomas, 1, 220
witchcraft *see* sorcery
Woodburn, James, 3, 4, 5, 6, 8, 10, 12, 13, 18, 77, 79, 85, 86, 92, 93, 99n1, 99n7, 107, 175, 188, 189, 190, 191, 192, 220
work, concept of, 206

X

Xade, 108, 109, 113, 114, 122, 124

Y

Yolngu, 140

Z

zaaku (love-relationship among the |Gui), 109–26, 128n6

www.ingramcontent.com/pod-product-compliance
Lightning Source LLC
Chambersburg PA
CBHW071231080526
44587CB00013BA/1567